Worth Your Weight

Worth Your Weight

What you *can* do about a weight problem

Barbara Altman Bruno, Ph.D.

Rutledge Books, Inc.

Bethel, CT

Worth Your Weight is dedicated to ending people's suffering about weight.

Rutledge Books, Inc.
8 F.J. Clarke Circle, Bethel, CT 06801

Manufactured in the United States of America

Cataloging in Publication Data
Bruno, Barbara Altman
Worth your weight / Barbara Altman Bruno.
p. cm.
ISBN 1-887750-32-0
1. Reducing diets. 2. Weight loss--
Psychological aspects. 3. Body image.
I. Title.

613.25--dc20 96-69979

ACKNOWLEDGEMENTS

Writing and producing a book is a very big job! *Worth Your Weight* would never have come to existence were it not for a tremendous amount of support. Many people contributed to this project and deserve heartfelt thanks. My husband Joe, and Pinstripe Presentations, provided faith in my abilities; tender, loving care; the space and freedom to write; and tremendous computer expertise. Iris VanderPutten convinced me that I had something important to say to others and inspired this book. Rebecca Daniels and Miriam Berg helped me organize my thoughts, so that others could make sense of them; Miriam helped to make the book gentler and more accurate, and Willendorf Press helped me to produce the final copy. Francie Vecchi contributed her artistic talent to make the cover alive. NAAFA, the National Association to Advance Fat Acceptance, and AHELP, the Association for the Health Enrichment of Large People, provided tons of information and support, as did their leaders, Sally Smith and Dr. Joe McVoy, and their members. Dr. Warren Berland and our therapists' supervision group (Barbara Spector, Barbara Campbell, and Donna Madnick) kept me focused on psychotherapy as humane service. Experts such as Drs. Bob Shaw, David Garner, Paul Ernsberger, Moe Lerner, Susan Wooley, Margaret MacKenzie, and Esther Rothblum (and her readers), kept me informed and educated. Dr. Bruce Delman, Chief of Library Services at the FDR Veterans Hospital in Montrose, New York, provided literature searches. The late Virginia Satir showed me what it is to be a great therapist and educator. Bob Schwartz of *Diets Don't Work* convinced me that my suspicions made sense and encouraged me to move forward against dieting. My clients and students, over the years, taught me most of what I know about healing and educating. My friends and family loved and nurtured me the best they could, even when that meant putting me on diets or hassling me about my weight. If it weren't for them, I probably would have chosen a different career.

TABLE OF CONTENTS

Introduction
OPEN QUESTIONS

THE DILEMMA

Americans have developed bizarre behaviors around weight, eating, and food in the late twentieth-century. Girls' and women's body images are so distorted, that disliking one's looks has been called a "normative discontent" (a form of dissatisfaction that has become the rule rather than the exception). Many people feel and express guilt, rather than pleasure, when they eat. Eating disorder treatment centers are beginning to see preschool children who think they are too fat and must restrict the food they eat.

Americans' fear of fat—in food or on one's body—results in a wide range of strange and sometimes disturbing behaviors.

• In Los Angeles, where appearance is everything, anyone who wants to be taken seriously eats only vegetables, fruits, and grains—sans fat—in public.

• Some fat children are killing themselves rather than endure socially accepted ostracism in school.

• While some people want the results of exercise without doing the work, others exercise feverishly, trying to fend off the triple demons of aging, death, and fatness.

• Dissatisfied with how they compare to media images of exceptionally thin, young models, and fearing looking older or "too fat," thousands of adults and adolescents have sought plastic and gastric surgery.

• Desperate to end the socially acceptable prejudice against their bodies, many fat people have undergone gastric or intestinal bypass surgery. If survived at all (thousands of people have died from it), such surgery is likely to lead to lifelong pain, anemia and other medical complications, and—in more than half the survivors—weight regain.

• Currently touted as medically acceptable antiobesity treatments are medications—with dangerous side effects—which lead to a small weight loss, followed by weight regain as soon as the medications are stopped. The results of long-term ingestion of the medications are unknown, yet drug companies are lobbying to get them approved for lifelong use.

Entering into this situation, is a growing recognition of the failure of diets. Several large diet companies were chastised by the federal government for false and misleading advertising. New York City's Consumer Advocate created regulations which require diet establishments to post a notice about the negative effects of rapid weight loss, the need for permanent lifestyle changes, and the consumer's right to question the diet establishment about risks, success rates, hidden costs, and other details of their programs. A class action suit was filed against a prominent diet company after many of its clients developed gall bladder problems. Very-low-calorie-diets (VLCD's) took a public beating, when a television star quickly and publicly lost and regained about 70 pounds on such a diet. Diet companies are selling diets, but calling them something else. Some call this deception "diet doublespeak."

We are in the strange position of having created a problem (the demonization of fatness), without having created a viable solution. We have created a multi-billion dollar industry, marketing its services to people desperate not to be fat. With a little research, people have been discovering that none of the solutions work.

Worth Your Weight is offered as a way to heal from this insanity. It presumes that people have (1) intelligence and (2) bodies that function adequately. It is designed to take you out of the weight-related struggle into which you have been placed, by virtue of living in late-20th-century North America. It offers you a way to clear out the hype and misinformation, and use your problems with weight, eating, or food as the means to having the life you really want. It requires a little time, thought, and curiosity, and your willingness to find what is true and useful for you, individually.

THE INQUIRY

I invite you to join me in an inquiry, a series of questions which will probably improve the quality of your life. While this book deals primarily with weight, eating, and food, I have found that questions related to these topics generally apply to all aspects of our lives. People who come to me, initially with concerns about their weight or eating habits, usually find their lives improving as they explore the questions and answers that are most relevant at the moment. Starting with a question like, **"What fits now?"** often leads not only to different actions and selections concerning food, but to new vocational choices, changes in relationships, or different ways of expressing withheld feelings.

There are certain questions which are basic to our lives, which probably cannot and should not be answered right away. One such question is **"What do I want to be when I grow up?"** Answering it too early could result in a life that fits like a too-tight shoe, which you tried on in the morning—before your feet expanded to their full size.

If we were lucky as children, we were urged to keep these basic questions open for a long time, while we tried out many different possibilities. We were given the opportunity to find the combination of qualities which fit us well or even perfectly, with the right amount of room to grow or change. Answering these questions may have taken a few years or many decades. The questions may have been open for a while, then closed for a while, then reopened.

"What do I want to be when I grow up?" was probably answered initially as Mommy, Daddy, ballet dancer, or firefighter. If you had a particularly good or awful teacher, that put teaching on or off the list. Certain occupations, or certain people in certain occupations, probably intrigued you. You played doctor or nurse, soldier or cook, perhaps all in one afternoon. When you went to a movie or watched television, someone you admired—like Superman—became your role model. Your parents may have had certain plans and dreams for your future; you may have felt happy or uncomfortable about those plans and dreams. As your aptitudes revealed themselves, your teachers may have steered you toward or away from certain fields. You may have had after-school and summer jobs which helped you decide what you wanted to do with your work life. How you did in school may have ruled out some possibilities, such as careers involving science, reading, or physical coordination. You considered, or your parents did, how much you could progress in a certain career, and how much you could earn from it, and perhaps where you should live to do best in a certain field.

Perhaps you spent most of your early years deciding *against* certain occupations, while nothing in particular seemed to fit. If you were very wise, or someone guiding you was, you kept checking into possible occupations to find what felt best to you. Perhaps you discovered that, at age 16, you no longer cherished the mental image of yourself as a firefighter, doctor, or teacher. When you looked around at your classmates, some seemed to know exactly where they were headed, while most were unsure, tried out various possibilities, took whatever job they could find, or entered college as liberal arts students. Some probably went into the family business. Some found mentors. You may have taken a thousand and one aptitude tests, dropped out of school, entered the armed services, traveled, vegetated, hoped for a rich relative to leave you a hefty bequest. Or you may have made a beeline through school and gone directly to your right livelihood. Whatever you did, and however you lived, you were fitting pieces into the puzzle: "What do I want to be when I grow up?"

Many people ask themselves that question throughout their lives. Some lock themselves into a certain direction, perhaps out of financial necessity. At some time, around middle age, they may re-examine whether they are happy doing what they are doing. Others try a variety of jobs or academic programs, but nothing seems right. Some seem to have resigned themselves to being whatever they are. For them, the question is closed. Others are fulfilled and thrilled to be whatever they are, and the question is also closed.

Those who live with the question open, may get sick and tired of not feeling settled, and wish they could find something right or at least acceptable. At other times, living with the question open may feel like being in the midst of a great adventure.

It has felt both ways to me. I am blessed with several abilities. I sometimes felt like it was a curse, to be so able, because it made it harder to choose a career. In college, I majored in art, then English. After graduation, I moved across the country and became first a waitress, then an office worker, a volunteer teacher, and a Red Cross Friendly Visitor. I took my first psychology course *after* I finished college, went to graduate school in social work, and—after several jobs—burned out and started riding horses and studying animal, then primate, behavior. I finally realized that humans were still my favorite primates.

When I returned to working with people, I was very careful about which people I wanted to work with and in which setting. I had learned from my experiences, especially the negative ones, to accept what felt right at the time. I went to two more graduate schools, the last of which was a perfect fit, and got my doctorate. For several years, I have enjoyed being a therapist (except for the occasions when I've wanted to resign and live on the moon). More recently, I've added educator and writer to how I see myself.

Asking ourselves these basic open questions—many of which are in bold typeface in this book—is one of the most valuable ways to improve the quality of our lives. The inquiry allows us to continue growing and learning, to interact with life so that we are enriched and, hopefully, fulfilled. Along with the question we have already explored, some others which are loaded with potential are: **"Who will I marry?" "What is possible?" "What feels right, now?" "What do I want?"** And, a particular favorite of mine, **"What is delicious?"**

For people who belong to an unpopular group, asking one of the most basic open questions, **"Who am I?"** can be very painful. For a fat person in our society— as for a homosexual in "straight" society, or a black person in white society—it is not uncommon to consider oneself faulty because of one's difference, and try to become whatever is popular. Fat people have gone on countless diets. They have had their jaws wired, stomachs stapled, thighs liposuctioned, and intestines bypassed. Homosexuals have dated and married. Black people have bleached their skin and straightened their hair.

People who don't fit others' preconceptions of how they should be, must come up with original answers to the question, "Who am I?" The media, and most of the people in our lives, remind us continually if we don't fit into culturally accepted norms. If we want to establish our own standards of worth, it takes work. We can be anything we want, as long as we're willing to follow our dreams and have those dreams be more important than anything else.

I
GIVEN THE CIRCUMSTANCES, HOW DO YOU WANT YOUR LIFE TO BE?

You probably feel that you have a weight problem. The problem may be those stubborn last few pounds, or several hundred. Welcome to the USA at the end of the 20th century! Part of being a resident here includes having received a powerful cultural message about fatness being unacceptable. Calling someone "fat" is such an insult that many people can barely bring themselves to whisper the word, while a sure way to compliment someone is to remark that she/he seems to have lost weight. In this book, however, we reclaim the word "fat" and change it back from its use as a derogatory term, to its original use as a descriptive adjective. "Fat" in this book may have more to do with how you feel about yourself than how you look to anyone else. It may be a feeling about one pound or several hundred. Regardless of your actual size, if you feel "too fat," this book is for you.

If you find that using the "f " word—whether alone or in relation to yourself—is upsetting, then you have been programmed with this cultural bias. Do you flinch when someone refers to you by the color of your hair or your eyes? Is it a problem for you to have your height described? What about your ethnic group?

Probably, you find yourself much more upset about the word "fat," especially in its relationship to how you think of yourself, than you are by any of the other descriptors mentioned above, or that you can think of. In our culture, size and weight are linked with morality. Being "overweight" is considered akin to having been Communist in the 1950s—you are presumed to be anti-American (actually, the prejudice extends amply into other Western cultures).

A well used tool in psychotherapy involves progressively desensitizing people who are afraid of something. They are trained to first relax, and then to gradually face what they fear. Along the way, they often rate their level of fear. You can test your progress in desensitizing yourself to the negative cultural programming around fat.

1------2------3------4------5------6------7------8------9-----10
Not at all　Somewhat　Upset　Extremely　Totally

1) On a scale of one to 10, with one equalling "not at all" and 10 equalling "totally," how upset are you at reading the word "fat"?

2) How upset are you at linking the word "fat" with yourself? You can write down these two numbers in the margin or on a separate piece of paper.

At the end of the book, the difference between your score and a score of one for each question indicates the level of upset you are still left with. That is the degree to which you have more peacemaking to do. Make abundant use of the resources in the Appendix to facilitate this peacemaking. (NOTE: Making peace with fat will not make you fat, unless fat is your natural size, you have been unnaturally suppressing it, and you allow yourself to blossom into your natural body. Accepting yourself will not injure your health, or detract from your beauty. Quite the contrary.)

Other chapters will raise other questions which you can use to explore and alter your concerns about eating or weighing too much.

WEIGHT PROBLEMS, EATING PROBLEMS

A weight problem is something weight-related that seems to interfere with your having the life you want; an eating problem is something eating-related. Fat people don't necessarily have eating problems or eating disorders. Thin people are not necessarily free of eating or weight problems. One of the first things I learned, when I started specializing in weight problems, is that you can't tell who has a weight problem by what they look like. I have worked with women weighing under 100 pounds whose weight problems are much bigger than some 400-pound women's.

We Americans live in a culture with a weight problem. For most of the 20th century, we have considered fatness to be aesthetically unattractive and, increasingly in recent years, unhealthy. We have ignored evidence to the contrary, which cites lower incidences of certain diseases, and lower death rates from certain diseases, among fat people. In its 1985 Consensus Development Conference on the Health Implications of Obesity, the National Institutes of Health disregarded evidence from long-term studies of millions of people in several countries, which indicated that the longest-lived people were heavier than average. People seeking medical care are usually weighed (either on the scale or by estimate) and, if over the various Metropolitan Life insurance tables, admonished to lose weight—regardless of the medical condition for which they sought help. Women's magazines have, for decades, featured the latest diets (regardless of their absurdity or unhealthfulness), along with occasional before-and-after pictures and stories about fat women who became slim. Newspapers and magazines, radio and television, have been saturated with stories and advertisements praising thinness and demeaning fatness.

These cultural messages, which were encapsulated in the Duchess of Windsor's (attributed) statement that one can never be too rich or too thin, have powerfully affected people of all ages and sizes. Most Americans consider themselves too fat, regardless of their weight. Many people, when they feel bad or unacceptable, translate those feelings into a statement to themselves, which is, "I'm too fat."

We have experienced an epidemic of eating disorders, like bulimia and anorexia, which can be fatal. Studies of schoolchildren have shown large numbers of nine-year-olds, and nearly all 17-year-old girls, dieting (regardless of their weight) and using various unhealthy practices, like swallowing multiple fiber pills or vomiting, to control their weight. Eating disorder therapists report youngsters as young as four years old exhibiting eating disorders. Some toddlers from prosperous families have been found to be undersized, their ambitious parents having underfed them for fear of having chubby children. Other equally ambitious parents-to-be, fearing both the weight gain of pregnancy and a fat baby, have borne underweight infants. A survey of parents, cited in *Newsweek* magazine in 1989, suggested that 11 percent of the parents would abort a child predisposed to obesity.

The dieting industry, which is estimated to be worth more than $33 billion a year, lives off the (fear of) fat of the land. The failure rate of diets is more than 90%, yet for decades people have tried to diet their way to slimness. When they—almost inevitably—have regained the weight, dieters have blamed themselves for deficient willpower and gone on still more diets. I suspect that one major reason why Americans are growing increasingly corpulent, despite eating fewer calories than in midcentury, is that we have dieted so much (see Chapter 2 for more about this dilemma).

While there may be little you can do to permanently reduce your weight, there is plenty you can do to eliminate your weight and/or eating *problem* and have a wonderful life. Using your weight or eating problem to get the life you want is what this book is about. Some chapters are geared toward people who eat too much; some are geared toward people who are quite fat; some are for people who think they are too fat; some are for all of us. Feel free to choose and use what works for you, individually. This book is very much about identifying and respecting your individual wants and needs, within the context of a culture that equates size with worth.

BEING FAT IN A FAT-PHOBIC CULTURE

All of us face different circumstances. Some are wealthy, some impoverished; some are born into loving families, others raised in institutions. Some are gifted with talent or looks; some feast and many starve; some have faced more adversity in their first ten years than others face in fifty.

Carlos and Jaime were two brothers I met when I was a social worker in foster-care group homes. Both were raised in one of New York City's worst ghettos, by an alcoholic mother who abused her children. They had no father. Carlos was a year or two older than his brother. He was on the gymnastics team at his school. He had a girlfriend, a wide circle of friends, and he got good grades. Jaime, on the other hand, was named, at age eleven, in a paternity suit. He took drugs. He was always in trouble—at school, at the group home, and with the police. He had difficulty getting along with everyone, even his gymnastics coach, who was trying to get him a scholarship. I have often wondered how two such boys, reared under similar circumstances, could be so different—one seemingly the victim of his circumstances, and the other seemingly a victor.

Very fat people in our culture often live in another sort of ghetto. They are socially isolated during school and may not get to date at all. They are less readily accepted into college and are often turned down for decent jobs. People who would no more insult a crippled person than a homeless person might think nothing of jeering at a fat person, or even removing groceries from her cart at the supermarket. Doctors and other medical personnel may refuse to treat a fat person unless they first lose fifty pounds. A woman in Michigan was actually shot by her father for being too fat! As documented in a study by Dr. Steven Gortmaker of the Harvard School of Public Health, fat women in our culture earn less money than thinner women, and if they marry, they usually marry less affluent people—and often in desperation, rather than in love. I have spoken to several fat people who, not surprisingly, had developed agoraphobia—that is, they so feared going out in public that they were virtually housebound. Some were extremely depressed, never got out of their nightgowns, and had given up all hope of getting a good job, or even a date. But not every fat person in our culture becomes a victim of cultural prejudice. Others rise to the top of their profession, have dozens of friends, go out dancing, have a rich and varied social life, raise loving families, and so on. When you get to know them, their weight is no more significant than their hair color.

What is it that allows some people to win, despite very difficult circumstances? What I have observed is that people who succeed have defined themselves for themselves. They have decided how they want their lives to be, regardless of how other people, or even society in general, might predict their lives will turn out.

My friend Maryann is an example. She weighs nearly 300 pounds and has always been fat. She was very popular in high school, almost always had a lover, and is now happily married; has been a nurse, opera singer, medical care coordinator for a hospital, and is now setting productivity records in a corporate position. She sews, embroiders, paints, does calligraphy, and is an excellent dancer. She never has enough time in her day to do everything she has taken on, which includes lots of social engagements.

When I asked her what she thought made the difference between her life and those of so many fat people, she replied that (1) she had been raised in a family where she was told she could do anything she wanted if she just did the work, and (2) she did the work. She is one of the hardest working people I know. When she left her last job for a better offer, I asked her if her former employer was hiring three people to replace her. She said they were finding that they needed at least two!

It wasn't easy for Maryann to get where she was. She told me about having been tops in her nursing school class, and then getting hired by a prestigious metropolitan hospital. The evening before she was to report for the first day of work, the supervisor called her and explained that the staff thought Maryann "just wouldn't fit in"—literally and figuratively—at the new job. While Maryann did not take legal action against this discrimination, another fat nurse with a similar story, Sharon Russell, took her case to the Supreme Court.

Sharon Russell was accepted to Salve Regina College in

Rhode Island in 1982. After earning good grades in her first two years of college, she entered their nursing program. Her instructor told her she would not be able to find a uniform to fit her and would "never get around a bed." Russell said she was used as a "human guinea pig" in class, to show students how to make a bed with a fat person or how to give a shot to a fat person. In December 1984, faculty members offered Sharon a choice: sign a contract to lose two pounds a week or face dismissal. She signed the contract because she was determined to be a nurse. She had already lost 31 pounds before signing the agreement; she regained six pounds subsequently and Salve Regina told her she could not attend her senior year.

At that point, Russell sued Salve Regina and five faculty members for handicap discrimination, emotional distress, invasion of privacy, and breach of contract. A judge allowed only the breach of contract allegation. A federal jury and an appeals court upheld the judgment, which ordered Salve Regina to pay about $44,000 in damages.

Salve Regina appealed to the Supreme Court, but Russell ultimately won the lawsuit. All victims of discrimination find there is a great deal of hard work and pain involved in winning respect and equal treatment from those who are biased against them. Sharon's family took out a second mortgage on their house, and NAAFA (the National Association to Advance Fat Acceptance) helped to raise funds toward her legal battles.

Bonnie Cook—who had worked as an attendant in a Rhode Island home for the mentally disabled before taking a leave of absence— was refused rehiring because she was considered too fat, despite an exemplary performance record. Like Russell, she was unwilling to accept this discrimination, and fought in court for her job. In 1993, the First Circuit of the U.S. Court of Appeals declared her as "perceived disabled," and therefore protected from job discrimination under the Americans with Disabilities Act. She was awarded $100,000, the next available job, and seniority retroactive to 1988, when she had been refused re-employment.

FITTING IN OR FINDING WHAT FITS

Some people spend their lives locked in a struggle to fit into whatever is defined as popular. Beautiful women, and even teenage girls, may spend much of their lives and money running to the plastic surgeon's office for breast implants or reductions, facelifts, tummy tucks, etc. Women have had their ribs removed in order to have smaller waists. Chinese women, trying to have small feet, had theirs bound until they were crippled.

Cultural agreements about beauty or health change with the times and the place. In times or cultures where food is scarce, fleshiness is looked upon as attractive and a sign of prosperity. Our immigrant grandparents viewed chubby children as healthy. Lillian Russell, considered a great beauty in the late nineteenth century, weighed about 200 pounds. I have a poster in my office for a product called "Fat-ten-U Food," sold a century ago, in which the before and after pictures are exactly the reverse of what we would see today.

Today, fat, and even plump, people are often viewed as: unhealthy, neurotic, or worse; fearful of close relationships and sex; doomed to an early death; caught between a male-dominated power hierarchy and feminism; weak-willed, self-indulgent, depressed, undisciplined, low-class, ugly, undesirable, bad, and wrong. Children shun and tease fat children. Until the clothing industry recently discovered that women larger than size 14 exist, and have money to spend on attractive clothing, large-size clothing consisted of muumuus and black, brown, navy blue, or gray "bullet-proof polyester."

After the first two decades of the twentieth century, a woman who was plump or fat found herself out of fashion. If she defined herself as a fat (i.e., bad and unattractive) person, she spent the rest of her life on a diet or in surgery—or both—trying to fit the culturally agreed-upon definition of who she was and what she must do to rectify that.

Maryann, Sharon Russell, and Bonnie Cook are exceptions. These outstanding women define themselves as fat, but *not* as bad and unattractive. If they agreed with the cultural definition of what it means to be fat, they would still be living miserable existences. Maryann and Sharon realized that they were bigger than the cultural definition of who they must be; Bonnie used the cultural perception to her advantage. Sharon was determined to be a nurse and was willing to fight for that right before the Supreme Court. Bonnie was determined to be reinstated in a job in which she was more than competent. Maryann was determined to live a full life, and was willing to work very long and hard to get the job she wanted, the man she wanted, and the friends, pastimes, and fun she wanted.

Another exceptional woman I know, Debra West, is a stunning, statuesque blonde. She wears gorgeous outfits, immaculate makeup, jewelry of her own design, and makes a living coaching people on their appearance. Debra weighs 250 pounds. When I met Debra, I was struck by her size and her presentation of herself. When she told me what she did for a living, I was incredulous. How could a fat woman presume to tell others how to look? Why didn't she get herself in shape first? Who would possibly pay for her advice on appearance, for heaven's sake? Fortunately, Debra did not limit her definition of herself to my narrow preconceptions and, also fortunately, I have since raised my own consciousness about size.

ANYTHING CAN BE AN OPPORTUNITY

Circumstances do not determine the quality of your life; you do. You bring value to your life. As Victor Frankl said, "Man is ultimately self-determining. Man does not simply exist, but always decides what his existence will be, what he will become in the next moment."[1]

Sydney Rittenberg—an American who has lived since 1945 in China, with a Chinese wife and children—was imprisoned in solitary confinement during the Cultural Revolution. Ten years later, he was released in good health and good spirits, without any bitterness. How did he do it?

According to the *Christian Science Monitior*, 4/1/80 [2], Rittenberg had to get back to fundamentals. What made life worth living? Wife, children, friends, books, music, food? All these he loved. But what really counted, he decided, was the sense of having made some contribution, however small, to human progress and happiness. Even enclosed within four walls, Rittenberg realized he could make his contribution. It was the quality of contribution, not its scale, that mattered.

Rittenberg had his own definition of freedom: "the ability to develop a rational course of action based on facts and aimed at human happiness." It followed then that his sense of personal freedom depended on himself, not on his jailers. Rittenberg talked to his guards about his boyhood in Charleston, South Carolina, about methods of treating hiccups, about life in the United States. "I'm making a contribution," he kept telling himself. "I'm making a contribution." He also decided to keep his cell spotlessly clean. Whatever scraps of rags he had, he used to scrub and scrub until he could literally eat off the floor. When the keepers came around with their mops, he could truthfully tell them that there was no work for them to do. He could see that his actions, as well as his speech, had an effect on his guards. Even in prison, one human being could communicate effectively with another.

Which is not to say that Rittenberg had an easy time of it. He awoke each day with the crushing realization that he was still in prison. Every morning, for ten years, he had to recontextualize his situation: "I'm not passive. I'm learning something, doing something. I'm going to live on, I'm not going to die." As he disciplined his thinking, he found that his prison experience was "not a subtraction from life, but an addition; not a black hole, but part of my ongoing education." [with gratitude to Bob Shaw, MD, for this version]

HOW DO YOU WANT YOUR LIFE TO BE?

If you are or feel fat in a fat-hating society, how do you want your life to be? If you are well, ill, poor, rich, single, married, divorced or widowed, young, old, imprisoned, unemployed or at the top of your profession—**how do you want your life to be?**

I want mine to be happy, full of life, joy, service, healing, learning, and love. What I find truly thrilling is that I am in charge of these qualities, even though I have only minor control over some of the circumstances. I am not in control over a boulder landing on my head while I drive on the highway, or age, or infirmity taking my loved ones away. But I have complete freedom to bring meaning to whatever the circumstances are, and so do you.

When my husband was first diagnosed with cancer, our future looked bleak indeed. He was lying, gaunt and bleeding, in a hospital bed, the smells and sounds of illness all around. Our experience, along with grief and fear, was of immense love. We experienced almost everyone who came as bringing love and healing. I thanked those few whom I felt drained energy and sent them home, still grateful for their positive intentions. My husband and I measured our time together in small bits, grateful for minutes we could be together, not thinking about years. Along with the pain, I felt a window open in my life which enlarged my experience of living way beyond my prior snug existence. I felt emotionally available to people, like some of the homeless beggars on the New York City streets, who had previously frightened me. The lessons I learned from that time have contributed to my husband and me having a wonderful relationship today.

Many people are grateful for the positive changes in their lives which grew out of terrible circumstances. Many others have been given all the advantages—good looks, financial stability, education—and still live miserable existences. When I lived in California, I was surprised to learn that the incidence of alcoholism and suicide was extremely high among residents of Marin County, California, even though it is one of the most affluent and beautiful areas in the United States. In *Healthy Pleasures*,[3] Ornstein and Sobel say that the lottery winners they questioned were almost no happier a year after winning than before they won. Winners found considerably less pleasure in daily life activities (such as gardening, their relationships, etc.) than non-winners. Ornstein and Sobel attribute this to people's tendency to compare their present happiness with "what has gone before and what is yet to come with a flexible mental yardstick."

People who expect outer circumstances (money, house, car, jewelry, etc.) to determine their happiness, are setting themselves up for despair when they get the outer trappings and still don't feel happy. Happiness is not available from things. However, by *choosing* to have a happy life you can then find ways to center on the positive events, the small and large pleasures, the blessings and reliefs which occur every day. If your past has been unhappy, whether from size discrimination or other factors, all the more happiness can be available to you by comparing how much better off you are now! The first step to having a happier life is to choose one. The next step is to *find specfic ways to bring more happiness into your life*. The choice is completely yours!

Maryann did not have a choice about the form her body took. She was genetically programmed to be fat. But she could eat and exercise to promote her health. She could dress and style her hair to be most flattering, develop her considerable skills and intellect to further her career, and choose as friends people who accorded her respect, as she accorded it to herself. A smart woman, she got actively involved in NAAFA, where she was more likely to meet men attracted to large women. Through NAAFA she could be both an advocate and a spokesperson for size acceptance. She used fatness as an opportunity to learn about being strong. Another woman I know, Helen, used fatness to learn about being sexy at any size. She has no shortage of dates and lovers; she is gorgeous, in her own style, and aware of her power.

What opportunity is life presenting you with now? You may or may not have the body you thought would bring you happiness and the right relationship. While you may have as little ability to adjust your weight, healthfully, as to adjust your height or age, you can have a happy life and great relationships. You can be productive and make a contribution to the world. You can be self-expressive.

Jim and Eileen have been happily married now for several years. They live in a white clapboard house in the country. Jim is working on his college degree in psychology. Eileen is a nurse. Jim spends a lot of time working and playing on his computer, while Eileen keeps up with their social life. My husband and I went to a Fourth of July party at their home, complete with red, white, and blue decorations, children and adults of all ages, dogs and puppies, hot dogs and beer, music and firecrackers. A good time was had by all.

Jim is a disabled veteran, a quadriplegic. He can move only his head. He steers his wheelchair by puffing on a straw-like device and works his computer via a light shining from a headband he wears. He met Eileen after he was disabled. They are very much in love. They have not let his body circumstances determine the quality of their lives.

This book is about you, your weight, eating, and food. Mostly it is about your life. There are things that you can and cannot do about your weight, eating, and food. There is plenty you can do about your life. The choices are yours. How do you want your life to be?

1. Frankl, Viktor, *Man's Search for Meaning*. New York: Pocket Books, 1963, p. 206.
2. Oka, Takashi, "Survival in China Jail: One American's Saga" in *The Christian Science Monitor,* 4/1/80. Reprinted by permission from *The Christian Science Monitor* ©1980. The Christian Science Publishing Society. All rights reserved.
3. Ornstein, Robert, Ph.D., and Sobel, David, M.D. *Healthy Pleasures*. Addison-Wesley Publishing Company, Inc, 1989.

II
IS FATNESS YOUR FAULT?

BELIEVING IS SEEING

In the children's story, "The Emperor's New Clothes," what people believe is what they see. The emperor's tailors persuade him that they have made him glorious, sumptuous new clothes, when in fact they have not. The emperor is deluded into believing that these invisible garments do indeed exist, and manages to influence all but one of his subjects into "seeing" these garments. One little child, however, cannot be deluded. To everyone's chagrin, he announces that the emperor is unclothed. Suddenly, everyone else realizes (or admits) that he speaks the truth, and what has been right in front of their eyes becomes visible and agreed on by all.

During most of the 20th century, the prevailing beliefs about weight have been that weight is within our control, that people are fat because they eat too much food, and that carrying above-average weight is lethal. These beliefs have colored scientific research. Physicians have shared these beliefs, and treated patients accordingly.

"Can you help me?" pleads the woman on the phone. "I've been trying to find a doctor to give me a checkup without automatically lecturing me that I have to lose 100 pounds. I haven't been able to find one on my own, and I have a condition that needs medical attention." I get several calls like that each year. Sometimes the request is for a "fat-friendly" lawyer to help fight job discrimination, or a psychotherapist who won't attribute every concern to the patient's weight.

In our fat-hating culture, we have been so convinced that any body that is fat got that way because its owner eats too much—demonstrating moral weakness and unacceptable self-indulgence—that we have ignored the evidence, which disputes this conviction. We have made certain body sizes and shapes wrong, and believed that people can and SHOULD fix them! Morality has spilled into our language of eating: How many times have you heard people—perhaps even yourself—describing themselves as "good" or "bad," because of the food they ate or managed not to eat? And how often have you heard people refer to "good" and "bad" food, not meaning whether or not it is spoiled, but whether or not it is considered "fattening" or out-of-bounds for a particular diet? Because of these assumptions, we have alternately blamed, shamed, and ridiculed people with fat bodies, or applauded them for dieting and thereby "finally taking care of themselves." Walter Hudson, deemed "the world's fattest man," came to public attention when he weighed well over a thousand pounds, couldn't get out of his house, and was "saved" by Dick Gregory's Bahamian Diet, which helped him reduce his weight by several hundred pounds. His progress was followed and cheered on national television, and he became a supporter, by telephone and by example, to many other fat people. He also developed a line of inexpensive clothing for super-sized (very fat) people. He died of a heart attack on Christmas Eve, 1991, having regained nearly all the lost weight. He was used by the media as an example of excess and the medical dangers of obesity. No thought was given to the very real possibility that his death was caused by the diet.

WEIGHT CYCLING

Ironically, it appears that losing and regaining weight seems to shorten lives more readily than maintaining a stable, high weight.[1] In *Rethinking Obesity: An Alternative View of Its Health Implications* [2], authors Paul Ernsberger and Paul Haskew mention the Siege of Leningrad, when people were cut off from their food supply for two years. Hospital admissions for hypertension-related illness went down during the siege, but then soared to 50% of all hospital admissions once food supplies were restored. Say the authors:

> Another study more directly demonstrated that loss-regain cycles shorten life. Nearly 200 fat men were placed on total fasts, some for more than two months, the rest from three to eight weeks. After release from the hospital the men regained the weight they had lost, often with a few extra pounds. As they regained, 80 percent developed diabetes; one-half of these cases were severe. Fully 25 percent died, mainly of heart disease. Their death rate during the follow-up was up to 13 times higher than equally heavy men in large-scale studies of the general population in Norway and Denmark...Incredibly, the deaths of these crash dieters have been widely cited as proof that obesity is highly dangerous and as justification for dangerous surgical treatments. Commenting on this tendency to 'blame the victim,' Herman and Polivy note, 'It is ironic that most such deaths are blamed on the victims' overweight rather than the true culprit, radical attempts to lose weight.' The astronomical death rate of crash dieters who regain their lost weight suggests that the hazards associated with fatness may be mainly related to rapid loss and regain of weight, not to obesity itself.

Their conclusions were repeated, in *The New England Journal of Medicine* in 1991[3], by other weight researchers who studied thousands of people over decades. One of the researchers, Dr. George Blackburn of Harvard Medical School, said, "We've made a monumental mistake telling everyone to be a replica of a Vogue model. The national obsession with weight loss using techniques that lead to weight cycling needs to be abandoned."[4]

The weight cycling debate has raged on since then. It is difficult to sort out truth from falsehood, because many of the people demonizing obesity, and advocating a return to weight cycling, derive their income from dieting-related programs. It is impossible to consider them impartial, particularly since they continue to advocate dieting despite its clear, outrageously high failure rate. There is also debate about what weight offers the greatest longevity and least chance of illness; however, since there is no effective "cure" for obesity, there is little beyond what this book offers that many people can do to permanently alter their weight.

HOW MUCH DO FAT PEOPLE EAT?

When I first heard of Walter Hudson, I remember him describing what he used to eat before the Bahamian Diet. It was enough food for a group of people: dozens of eggs, loaves of bread, bottles of soda. At the time, I too thought that all very fat people ate vast quantities of food, as Hudson had, and were therefore physically and mentally unhealthy. Hudson confirmed my suspicions.

I was astonished to learn that study after study has shown that, *as a group, fat people eat NO MORE than thin people,* and often less.[5] Drs. Susan Wooley and David Garner cite "the tremendous body of research employing a great variety of methodologies that has failed to yield any meaningful or replicable differences in the caloric intake or eating patterns of the obese compared to the nonobese."[6] "Regardless of these factors," they continue, "the myth of overeating by the obese is sustained for the casual observer by selective attention. Each time that a fat person is observed to have a 'healthy appetite' or an affinity for sweets or other high calorie foods, a stereotypic leap into causality is made. The same behaviors in a thin person attract little or no attention."[7] Like many other people, I accepted that people naturally come in all heights (unless they were malnourished or took various hormones). Somehow, however, people were all supposed to be naturally slim—not thin, necessarily, but certainly not fat.

Dieters become "'compulsive overeaters" in response to food deprivation. "'Compulsive overeating' is another term that has been used to denote binge-eating. It implies that the binge-eating has a psychological cause (i.e., compulsion); however, there is little evidence to support this notion for most fat people who binge-eat."[8] Since fat people in our culture are ostracized into dieting, they become placed at risk for binge-eating. However, one's weight is not necessarily an indication of one's eating habits. Anorexics and bulimics—whose weight tends to be below average or average—have eating habits many would consider bizarre, such as regularly vomiting after eating.

ARE FAT PEOPLE PSYCHOLOGICALLY DIFFERENT?

A popular assumption is that fat people eat more than thin people, and do so for psychological reasons. This assumption stems from both selective attention and from psychoanalytic theories, propounded during the 1950s, that fat people are not only weak-willed, but psychologically disturbed. In fact, in 1957, psychiatrist Harold and psychologist Helen Singer Kaplan said, "Almost all conceivable psychological impulses and conflicts have been accused of causing overeating, and many symbolic meanings have been assigned to food." [9] When I was in graduate school in the early 1970s, I was taught that fat people had sexual hangups and that they were stuck in an early phase of development, and thus ate more for psychological reasons. However, in a review of 164 studies on obesity, psychologist Judith Rodin, Ph.D., formerly of Yale University, concludes:

> Many of the factors thought to be of etiologic [causal] significance—field dependence [dependence on others rather than self], lack of impulse control, inability to delay gratification, or a maladaptive eating style—have not been supported by experimental evidence. Other factors once thought to be of importance as causes of obesity, depression and dysphoria [feeling "low"], for example, appear, instead, to be consequences of being obese and may serve to maintain and intensify weight-related problems. Dieting behavior in response to weight concerns appears, perversely, to be implicated in increasing overweight and adiposity.[10]

So, fat people don't eat differently than thin people, in general. Their psychological makeup does not differ from thin people's in making them eat more. They don't overeat because they are depressed, and therefore get fat; they are fat and/or fail at dieting, and get depressed about that. Do you know anyone who has been depressed about being too fat? So many girls and women feel too fat, that disliking their bodies has been labeled by Rodin a "normative discontent"—in other words, disliking their bodies is how most women normally feel. There is evidence that this body dislike is spreading to females in other Western cultures,[11] and civil rights groups for fat people are emerging and uniting in Europe.

Most Americans feel too fat. There are many reasons for feeling that way. Turn on the television, open a magazine or a newspaper, and we are bombarded with images of slender, pretty, young women, who seemingly "have it all"—happiness, prosperity, a fulfilling love life, glowing good health. They are the "after" picture, where the "before" is fat, surprisingly older looking, unhappy, and presumably poor and unhealthy. Advertisements for all sorts of delectable foods, promising complete fulfillment, alternate with those for diet programs, promising complete fulfillment and quick, painless (except in the wallet), permanent transformation via slenderness. Physicians and their patients feel obligated to honor height and weight tables, wrongly considering them guidelines to optimal physical health.

HEIGHT AND WEIGHT TABLES

I first felt tortured by the height and weight tables, put forth by Metropolitan Life Insurance, when I was a girl. The tables recommended certain weights for certain heights, divided by small-, medium-, and large-frame categories. Even if I claimed to have a large frame, I never approached the recommended weights for my height. Usually, I was the right weight for a large-framed man at least half a foot taller than I. I never dreamed that there might be anything wrong with the tables; I assumed that the fault lay with me.

Actually, those tables were based on a skewed population—one not representative of the wide range of American bodies. This population consisted primarily of Anglo-Saxons who had purchased life insurance policies between 1925 and 1934, when buying life insurance was not the norm. Anglo-Saxons tend to be taller and leaner than other racial and national groups. Also, at least 20% of those applicants self-reported their weights and heights. In 1959, the Society of Actuaries found that applicants consistently *underestimated* their weights. Furthermore, applicants were weighed when they initially bought their policies, and never again unless they bought a new policy or reapplied to change their risk category. Since humans normally gain weight as they age, normal changes were not accounted for, and people were expected to maintain the weight of 25-year-olds.

In addition, Louis Dublin—the Metropolitan Life Insurance biologist whose research backed the height and weight tables—confused correlation with cause. In other words, although "overweight" is correlated with diabetes, there is no proof that overweight *causes* diabetes. While reducing weight helps relieve symptoms of diabetes, it does not prevent its occurrence. As Roberta Pollack Seid, Ph.D., explains in her historical review of women and their bodies, *Never Too Thin*, "Dublin might also have found that people who lived in white houses had higher rates of premature mortality, but such an association would have no meaning."[12]

Finally, the tables were based not on average weights—even average weights of Anglo-Saxon insurance buyers in their twenties—but on *ideal* weights, below average for their heights. Seid says, "These tables were based on the presumptions that there were weights that correlated with better health and longer life, that everyone ought to stay at these weights, and that what was average and so, normal, was not healthy."[13] Suddenly, average weight people were deemed overweight, and America had an epidemic of corpulence! Physicians joined in the unease. Says Seid, "The medical profession, and the nation as a whole, embraced the antifat campaign because they were responding to contemporary moral and social values and specific historical circumstances. At the root of the condemnation of fatness and overeating was concern about the effects of America's growing prosperity and technology."[14] Seid adds that Dublin justified "his dictum that people reduce on the basis of pre-existing cultural preferences [for the long, lean bodies of aristocrats], not on the basis of health."[15]

There have been many long-term studies of thousands of subjects, seeking information about weight and mortality. According to Garner and Wooley, who reviewed 300 studies and articles relating to obesity treatment:

> There are few studies in the medical literature that indicate that mortality risk is actually reduced by weight loss, and

> there are some that suggest that weight loss increases the risk of death. In an American Cancer Society prospective survey of over one million people, individuals indicating that they had lost weight in the past five years were more likely to die from cardiovascular disease than those whose weight was stable...[I]n a study of mortality risks among 16,936 Harvard alumni, Paffenbarger et. al, (1986) not only found that the highest mortality occurred in those with the lowest body mass index (below 32), but also that those who had gained weight since college had a significantly lower mortality risk compared to those who had minimal weight gain since college.[16]

According to *Obesity & Health*, preliminary findings of the National Institutes of Health panel on Voluntary Weight Loss and Control "show weight loss in the general population is associated with increased risk of death."[17] Says Ernsberger, "There are no controlled trials showing reduced mortality with weight loss—mainly because there are no treatments with long-term success." [18] Ernsberger states that, based on the Norway study of 1.8 million people, the estimated difference in longevity for a 25-year-old at the "ideal weight" on the charts and one at the highest weight is five years. The thinner person, he estimates, will average 79 years and the fattest, 74 years. He adds that much of the five years that are lost could be from hazardous treatments, such as crash diets, pills, and surgery, and the ill effects of weight cycling.[19] While it is true that Americans are getting fatter, we have not seen a concomitant rise in heart disease. In fact, the number of deaths from heart disease has been declining continuously.

In 1983, Metropolitan Life issued new height/weight charts based on updated actuarial data. The weights correlating with best longevity were now 10 to 15 pounds heavier than in the 1959 tables. Says Seid, "More than 16 million Americans—whose weights had not budged an ounce—suddenly discovered that they were no longer unhealthily fat."[20] And, in 1990, the US departments of Agriculture and of Health and Human Services finally released a height/weight chart that allows for higher weights for people over age 35, regardless of their gender. Currently, with the American population getting fatter, the height/weight charts are in dispute again, with some advocating a return to the 1959 levels.

WEIGHT CONTROL

Why are so many people trying to get thinner? Certainly, many people think they will live longer and healthier lives if they are thin enough. Most people think they will look more attractive when they are thinner. Many others have linked morality to weight. If one assumes that fat people are gluttons, then fat people are assumed to be sinners. Seid mentions a national fear during the mid-20th century that Americans were getting "soft," as increasing numbers of us gained access to abundant food and labor-saving devices, and that we would lose our edge in the Cold War. Now, she says, "People want to look fit for the same reason they have obeyed other fashion rules: They need to see that gleam of approval and respect in the eyes of those who behold them. Today, this need is especially pressing. We have little inner self-confidence because of the breakdown both of social institutions that once provided approval and security and of other values with which we judge ourselves—such as the church, family, and community."[21] She refers to Americans' quest for the "perfect" body as our new religion. Dr. Barbara Ehrenreich, author of many books and articles including *Fear of Falling: The Inner Life of the Middle Class,* considers dieting to be a way that we cope with an unparalleled emphasis on self-indulgence and materialism, along with growing anxiety about the future and about what we want.

We live in the "postmodern era," where there seems to be no solid ground. People can no longer be assured of a rising standard of living, a permanent job, a permanent marriage. People uproot themselves in search of better lives, tearing apart what family ties did exist. Those who dare run for political office are assured of public exposure of past mistakes. In some areas, children are shot randomly in the streets, in their schools, through a window. Sex is increasingly deadly. Medical care is a luxury. Political ideologies shift and fall before our eyes. The very impermanence and hazards of modern life are brought to us relentlessly through the media, especially television (which is a powerful hypnotic trance-inducer).

Disciplining our bodies gives us something to hold onto.

Working hard to improve one's station in life is part of the American Dream, even if the economy no longer supports this dream. The media present images of slim, young, muscled bodies as something we can all aspire to, regardless of our income, marital status, or even age. Capitalism and the media have led us to believe that any and all problems can and should be immediately fixed or suppressed by buying some product or service. We'd like to believe that the gnawing fear and spiritual hunger spawned by the loss of faith in anything long-term, can be fixed by a good workout and low-fat, high-fiber food. If we work hard enough, we can all turn into the "after" picture: the slim, strong, smiling young adult who is presumably completely happy and fulfilled. We are sold—relentlessly—on an illusion of control. This illusion of control extends to a peculiarly American trait: the fantasy that death is optional. We are so afraid of aging and dying, that we pursue all the latest health-food and exercise fads—often to absurd extremes. Many of us are so consumed with how we do not want to die, that we fail to consider how we want our lives to be lived.

In addition, many feminists believe that our cultural obsession with weight is part of an antifeminist movement: whenever women start to get power in men's traditional domains (basically, outside of child-rearing at home or in other menial, low-paying work), a thin female body type becomes popular. Feminists believe that women stop being threatening when they struggle more with themselves—trying to be thin—than with the men who have traditionally held powerful, higher-paying jobs. Writers such as Kim Chernin, Susie Orbach, and Naomi Wolf offer some powerful arguments to support this view.[22] Says Wolf:

> Researchers J. Polivy and C.P. Herman found that 'prolonged and periodic caloric restriction' resulted in a distinctive personality whose traits are 'passivity, anxiety, and emotionality.' *It is those traits, and not thinness for its own sake, that the dominant culture wants to create in the private sense of self of recently liberated women in order to cancel out the dangers of their liberation.*[23] [Emphasis original]

While Wolf is talking about controlling women's weight as a means of controlling women's power, most people associate weight with control in another way. Most people assume that our weight is within our control, and that diets are the way to "control" our weight, such that we can be slim and therefore, healthy and attractive. These assumptions follow from the notion that fat people all overeat. For years, weight control was expressed as a formula: it takes 3,500 calories to make a pound, therefore, take in fewer calories and/or burn up more, and you'll lose one pound for each 3,500-calorie deficit. People were commonly put on 1,000-calorie-a-day diets; for extra-quick weight loss—for an upcoming wedding or reunion, for example—you would eat even fewer calories. Weight control meant calorie control plus "self control," (or "willpower") which is what you used in order to keep your calorie intake low.

What happened, though, is that people didn't lose weight according to the formula. Some people seemed to lose vast quantities of weight on the same caloric intake at which others lost nothing. We heard about "plateaus," those frustrating weeks or months when, regardless of how we scrimped on calories, our bodies lost no weight. Even if we were strict about the calories, our doctors accused us of lying about the portions we ate. Even worse, demonic possession sometimes seemed to take over a dieter, leading her to midnight binges while the rest of the household was asleep. After bingeing, the former dieter felt guilty, ashamed, and desperate; blamed herself for yet another failure, and eventually embarked on yet another diet. People who could not tolerate another 1,000-calorie-a-day menu sought other diets which recommended that they eat only a few foods, or foods in specific combinations, or certain foods at certain times of day or on certain days, or no carbohydrates, or no fats, etc. Diet books, claiming to be new and different, appeared weekly on bestseller lists, and every women's magazine featured at least one new diet per issue.

We got fatter and more desperate, and developed "eating disorders." Some women starved themselves to death. Others forced themselves to vomit after eating, eventually getting addicted to vomiting. Most people dreaded Mondays, New Year's Day, bathing-suit season, and reunions, and being "on a diet" became the social norm. Eating became a struggle between "willpower and won't-power," and women were either dieting or bingeing. Psychologically-oriented people attributed weight-control problems to unconscious, buried conflicts, unresolved developmental issues, past traumas, and fixations. Dieting was morally superior to not dieting. Weighing more was linked to binge-eating, which was then managed by a Twelve-Step program which asserted that admitting loss of control and powerlessness over food was the prerequisite to mental, moral, and physical healing.

DIETS

If one assumes that fat people overeat, then the natural "solution" to obesity is to restrict caloric intake (i.e., to diet). In fact, this has been the model of obesity and its treatment for most of the twentieth century. Over the decades, all kinds of absurdities have been propounded for weight loss: eggs-and-grapefruit; everything but carbohydrates; everything but fats; everything but proteins. The same diet authorities have even published diet books promoting diets exactly opposite each other in composition![24]

Typically, dieters start new diets swearing that this time they will succeed, at long last. They have been told that all they need, in order to succeed, is a quality called "willpower." With great determination, they follow the diet religiously for anywhere from an hour to more than a year. At some point, their willpower disappears, and they gobble up all kinds of foods not allowed on the diet. They decide that they either lack willpower or need to use more, perhaps by assigning someone to watch them and prevent them from overeating. New dieters often find it easy to lose weight on their first diet, and may be surprised at other dieters' complaints of difficulty losing weight. However, most dieters find it harder and harder to lose weight—either they reach a "plateau" when, regardless of how little they eat, their weight remains the same, or they end the diet and, at some later point, start another one. Most people's diets end when the dieter binges. Psychologically, the failed dieter blames herself for her lack of willpower, or other moral failings, which she assumes caused her to fail at dieting. She assumes that the diet works—after all, she and others first lost weight on it—but that *she* is at fault. She feels guilty and ashamed of herself, and often then overeats in an attempt to feel better. At some point, when she can psychologically prepare herself for the next round of diet deprivation, she begins another diet. This cycle is enormously profitable for the diet industry: a repeat clientele which blames itself for failure. It is estimated that Americans will spend $77 billion on diet-related services and products by the year 2000.

Ironically, it appears that dieting is not only ineffective, but damaging. Garner and Wooley's review of hundreds of dietary and behavioral treatments for obesity concludes that, "It is only the rate of weight regain, not the fact of weight regain, that appears open to debate."[25] The figure most often given as an estimate of the diet failure rate is 95%, although failure rates of 90-98% have been cited. Garner and Wooley's comments about VLCD's (very-low-calorie-diets of 300-500 calories per day) include: "Although the rate and magnitude of weight loss have been the basis for recommending the VLCD, its most remarkable feature is the speed of weight regain following treatment."[26]

Dieters also may end up with more fat in their bodies, and particularly in their abdomens. People with specifically abdominal fat accumulations are at higher risk for atherosclerosis, and women with abdominal fat have an increased risk of developing cancer of the breast and of the endometrium. Dr. Kelly Brownell concurs with Jane Brody, health writer at *The New York Times*, who says that, "while lost weight consists of both fat and muscle tissue, what is regained is nearly always all fat. Since fat tissue uses fewer calories to sustain itself than muscle uses, this change in body composition makes it harder to lose weight again on the same low-calorie diet."[27] People who fast in order to lose weight may burn up protein instead of fat, which may produce permanent muscle damage to the heart. Indeed, in 1991 the *New England Journal of Medicine* reported a long-term study of several thousand people which indicated that those whose weight cycled (fell and rose) risked an increased rate of heart disease, death from heart disease, or any other cause. Another study, reported in *The New York Times*, found that people who lost and regained more than 25 pounds had a higher risk of dying prematurely than those who smoke cigarettes. A study published in *The New York Times* in 1990 found that "when obese people lost weight, they started overproducing an enzyme that makes it easier to get fat again. The enzyme helps plump up fat cells that were deflated by dieting, allowing fat to be stored once again in body tissues. The effect of these high enzyme levels is to make weight gain far easier for the formerly obese than it is for people who were never fat to begin with...And the fatter the person was to begin with, the more of the fat-regaining enzyme they produced once they were thin."[28] The enzyme, lipoprotein lipase, was increased because a gene inside fat cells was activated. Lipoprotein lipase may be responsible for the increased cravings for fat and sweet foods which develop in people whose caloric intake has been restricted.

GENETICS

The increasing sophistication of genetic research has so far indicated two things about obesity: it is a very complicated condition, and it has genetic components. In December 1994, with much fanfare, the so-called "obesity (Ob) gene" was located. This gene was responsible for the body's ability to recognize satiety, and speculation was that fat people had a mutated version of this gene.[29] A genetic engineering company, Amgen, paid 20 million dollars to develop research on this gene. In the spring of 1995, researchers discovered no differences in the Ob gene between fat and thin people.[30] *Science News* [31] reported on another gene, the CPE (carboxypoptidase E) gene, which seems to render biologically inactive proteins active. A mutation in this gene may fail to convert proinsulin to insulin in laboratory mice. Whether differences in laboratory mice translate to similar differences in humans remains to be seen. Such differences do not similarly translate to humans in the case of a protein called leptin, which changes the weight and body-fat composition of laboratory rodents but not humans. Undoubtedly, new genes affecting body size and metabolism will be discovered during and after publication of this book. More will be announced, with much fanfare, only to be found shortly thereafter to be fallible or insufficient to "cure" fatness. Americans, eager for a quick fix, will seize on anything that hints at a quick and easy way to get thinner. Others will use such eagerness to make outrageous claims and quick money off of people desperate to change their bodies rather than tackle societal (and medical) prejudice.

SETPOINTS

In *The Dieter's Dilemma*, authors William Bennett, MD, and Joel Gurin posit the existence of a "setpoint," probably a combination of physiological elements designed to maintain a particular range of body fat or weight for each body, similar to a thermostat which regulates room temperature. Citing numerous research studies (including studies of underfed young men and overfed twins), they argue that the body vigorously defends its setpoint. People can approach the lower end of their setpoint range by exercising or by using substances such as tobacco or amphetamines. Restrict food intake enough, as dieting does, and the metabolism slows down; overfeed the body enough, and the metabolism increases, so that body weight and fat levels are held more or less constant. It appears that our bodies intend for us to maintain certain setpoint weights, regardless of the current mania for thinness, and fight our attempts to change their weights with more vigor than all but a few people can muster. That the body defends its natural weight range keeps getting rediscovered; noted obesity researchers Drs. Jules Hirsch and Rudy Leibel of Rockefeller University reconfirmed this situation again in 1995.[32] If the fashion was to be extremely fat, most people would find themselves unable to sustain the measures necessary to exceed their setpoints.

Few people have enough willpower to get and remain as slim as they think they should be. We all have priorities which we honor, and what some people call willpower may simply be a matter of priorities. Perhaps eons of evolution are stronger than an individual's "willpower" to go hungry. Perhaps people whose setpoints are closer to the ideal might find it easier to reach and maintain that weight. Perhaps people who are more dependent on the societal rewards for looking "right" have enough at stake to do anything and everything necessary to look that way. While Hitler and anorexia sufferers have demonstrated that extreme enough measures can make anyone thin, most people cannot sustain these extremes long enough to permanently maintain fashionably low weights. Some people, however, feel safer being directed and contained via a detailed, prescribed diet—particularly if they had felt out of control.

Perhaps one function of setpoints is to ensure successful reproduction. If a woman's weight/body fat level is low enough, she will lose her ability to reproduce. This amenorrhea is adaptive: the underfed/underfat body cannot nourish both itself and a fetus. In the Australian outback, many Aboriginal women get married in their early teens. Food is so scarce that it might take years for a woman to sustain enough body weight to bear a child, and so attempts to impregnate her have to start when she is very young. It is fortunate that our bodies are not slaves to our ultra-thin fashion ideal, or nobody would be left to read this book!

EATING DISORDERS

Dieting precipitates eating disorders. Geneen Roth claims that, "for every diet there is an equal and opposite binge." Most people with bulimia and anorexia nervosa, the most deadly of the eating disorders (about 10-15% of anorexics are estimated to die from their illness), start by dieting and then keep going, either vomiting after eating/bingeing, abusing laxatives and diuretics, or starving themselves to death. The number of people with eating disorders has mushroomed in recent years. There are probably millions of people in America today who are much fatter than when they first dieted, and who have become binge-eaters as a result of the physical and psychological strains imposed by dieting.

Physically, when people restrict the amount of calories (fuel) they take in, the body reacts as if to a famine. The remote outposts of the body—hands and feet—lose warmth, which is conserved for the vital organs and, in general, people become much more sensitive to cold. The metabolism, responsible for the rate at which fuel is burned, slows down. People tend to be more tired, weak, depressed, and apathetic, and their sexual interest can wane or disappear. These adaptations to famine were designed to enable our ancestors to survive regular food shortages. While some of us are fortunate to have problems of too much food, excess food is a very recent development in our genetic history, and our bodies have been programmed for survival over the eons of time we've existed. Many people develop cravings for food higher in fat and sweetness, possibly in connection with the lipoprotein lipase released from fat cells.

Psychologically, diets set up the equivalent of telling a person not to think of an elephant, or of a hot fudge sundae. Chances are, they picture an elephant or a hot fudge sundae, perhaps with a red slash bar and circle superimposed over it. In order to think "not-something," we call up whatever the "something" is. Likewise with "forbidden" foods: they become increasingly prominent in our imaginations. When you think about it, this is an extremely adaptive—if seemingly perverse—adjustment. Becoming increasingly obsessed with food is useful when it is scarce. We are driven to seek it. But many diets set up a similar obsessive situation by asking us not to include certain foods. My cousin, who recently developed diabetes, has become totally fascinated with cakes and sweet desserts. He didn't particularly care about them before they became off-limits. When people talk about "trigger foods," which set off uncontrollable cravings, they are probably referring to these forbidden foods.

Linguistically, "on a diet" implies that at some point we will be *off* a diet. It's very hard for people on a diet not to imagine and long for the point at which they no longer have to be deprived. Many people experience diets like jail sentences. When the diet ends, they break out of jail in a binge that can continue for days, weeks, or longer.

Through all of our dieting rules, many people have lost all confidence in their ability to determine how and what to eat. They may feel safer being directed and contained via a detailed, prescribed diet—particularly if they had felt out of control.

SURGERY

Among the myriad attempts to make fat people into thin ones have been surgical procedures such as jaw wiring or stomach stapling. These procedures aim to limit the amount of food a person can ingest, by various means. As we have already seen, fat people as a group eat no more than thin people. Why would surgery, meant to limit what they ingest, work for those fat people who do not overeat? What happens is that the patient becomes chronically malnourished (if she survives the surgery and its complications), developing various forms of anemia and often muscle wastage, kidney and urinary tract damage, liver disease, gallstones, and hair loss. Common results of stomach stapling are severe pain, vomiting, nausea, and chronic diarrhea (which can cause potassium loss which, in turn, can lead to heart attacks). In his Report on Weight Loss Surgery, Dr. Ernsberger says:

> If death rates of staple patients are compared to 'morbidly' obese women from the world's largest study of mortality, which examined 1.8 million Norwegians, gastric weight-loss operations appear to cause a ten-fold increase in death rate....On top of severe complications and side-effects, stomach stapling may simply not work. Dr. Joel Freeman, chief of general surgery at the University of Ottawa, reviewed 6,000 cases and found that over 50% of patients failed to lose even 15% of their starting weight, or lost that much and then regained it within two years. A controlled study showed that 75% of surviving patients failed to lose weight or regained at two years of follow-up.[33]

NAAFA, whose membership would comprise the primary consumers of weight-loss surgery, has taken a vehement stand against it. If it works at all, it injures or kills many people. Some doctors will even perform weight-loss surgery on women who are as little as 50 pounds over their chart weight. In these and many other cases, it is a surgical "solution"—which many consider to be barbaric—to a social problem: ostracism of fat people.

Unfortunately, physicians are subject to both financial pressures and societal prejudices. Some may consider that they are helping people by giving them altered bodies. Others may be unscrupulous. In Naomi Wolf's opinion,

> Modern cosmetic surgeons have a direct financial interest in a social role for women that requires them to feel ugly...If you tell someone she has cancer, you cannot create in her the disease and its agony. But tell a woman persuasively enough that she is ugly, you do create the "disease," and its agony is real. If you wrap up your advertisement, alongside an article promoting

surgery, in a context that makes women feel ugly, and leads us to believe that other women are competing in this way, then you have paid for promoting a disease that you alone can cure.[34]

WEIGHT LOSS, MEDICINE, SCIENCE, AND THE EMPEROR'S NEW CLOTHES

Evidence about the unworkability of diets has been like the emperor's new clothes. For decades, we put people on diets. They almost never stayed at low weights, but we refused to accept the evidence before our eyes. Instead, we blamed the weight regain on weak willpower and other supposed faults of dieters. It has only been in the last decade of the twentieth century that some people have started to notice that diets themselves fail, and contribute to health problems.

One of the problems with most of the studies which purportedly demonstrate that being fat makes people sick, is that the subjects of the studies have almost always been people who have dieted extensively. If we could find enough fat Americans who have not dieted, we would undoubtedly find that fat people can be quite healthy. In fact, I have spoken with numerous fat people who were told by their doctors that they seemed perfectly healthy (i.e., their blood pressure, blood sugar, and blood lipid levels were all within healthy norms, they had enough energy and were free of diseases), *but* they were fat and therefore should lose weight. Saying "You're healthy *but* you're fat" is like saying, "the floor is down there BUT the ceiling's up there." Negative antifat attitudes by doctors have resulted in many people avoiding preventive medical care, because they fear they will be attacked for their weight, regardless of their presenting problem.[35] Once more medical professionals get enlightened about the possibility of people being both fat *and* healthy, they will start to recognize more fat and healthy patients. Their selective attention will open up to new possibilities. Those medical professionals whose incomes are not dependent on living off the fat-phobia of the land, will be able to truly support their patients of all sizes. Those medical professionals, however, whose incomes depend on fat-phobia, will resist any threat to their wallets. Unfortunately, nearly all of the members of the

National Task Force on the Prevention and Treatment of Obesity (eight out of nine people) had clear financial conflicts of interest.[36] This Task Force reported, in 1994, that weight cycling concerns were "not sufficiently compelling" to dissuade fat people from trying to lose weight. But, since nearly all of these obesity experts had a vested interest in keeping people dieting, their conclusion is dubious.

Furthermore, Cornell University sociologist Jeffery Sobal refers to a phenomenon which he calls "the medicalization of obesity." He delineates how some medical specialists make various claims in order to include "obesity" as a medical condition which is within their turf. In addition, a majority of medical professionals continue to take a moral stance on obesity, treating fatness as badness. On the other hand, human rights groups, such as NAAFA—along with this author and many others in the size acceptance movement—are reclaiming fatness as a natural variation in body size.

We must vote with our wallets, and with the quality of our lives. Those people who profit from socially-approved looks, or from catering to those wanting socially approved looks, will resist any changes. But we don't have to fatten the wallets of cosmetic and bariatric surgeons in order to be acceptable. All-rightness comes from self-acceptance. Good health is not a function of body size, but of heredity, habits, and thoughts about oneself. Liking ourselves and accepting ourselves is good for our health. Even if you have hated your looks up until this moment, you can start now to find one thing, and then another and another, that you can accept and value about yourself and your looks.

There is a civil rights battle to be won. People who are not a popular size (95% of us are heavier than the models we have emulated) can and should advocate for our right to exist, as we are. As we accept ourselves, we can allow ourselves to choose full lives. As we live full lives, others will see that people can live fully in all types of bodies, and that weight has nothing to do with fulfillment. Beauty radiates from within. If we allow ourselves to shine in the bodies and faces we have—and if we demand that vendors of goods and services treat and portray us well in all our variety of sizes, ages, and colors—we will change how money is made. If we change how money is made in this culture, we will change the culture.

1. What do you think your weight means about your health?
2. If higher body weight were considered healthy and attractive, how might your life have been different?

1. *Obesity and Health*; Vol. 6, No. 4, July/August 1992, pp. 64-74.
2. *Journal of Obesity and Weight Regulation*, Vol. 9, No. 2, Summer 1987, p. 39-40 (95-96).
3. 6/27/91.
4. *The New York Times,* 6/27/91; "Fanatic Dieters May Shed Years Along With Pounds" by Jane Brody.©1991 by the New York Times Co.Reprinted by permission.
5. Atrens, Dale, Ph.D. *Don't Diet*. William Morrow and Company, Inc., 1988, p. 41; Garner, David, Ph.D. and Garfinkle, Paul, MD. *Handbook of Psychotherapy for Anorexia Nervosa and Bulimia*. Guilford Publications, Inc., 1985, pp. 521, 534; Rothblum, Esther, Ph.D. "Women and Weight: Fad and Fiction," in *The Journal of Psychology,* Vol. 124, No. 1, pp. 9-12.
6. Garner, David, Ph.D. and Wooley, Susan, Ph.D. "Confronting the Failure of Behavioral and Dietary Treatments for Obesity," in *Clinical Psychology Review*, Vol. 11, 1991, p. 748.
7. Ibid.
8. Garner, David, Ph.D. and Bruno, Barbara Altman, Ph.D. "Do You Have an Eating Disorder?" NAAFA publication, 1993.
9. Bennett, William, MD, and Gurin, Joel. *The Dieter's Dilemma*. Basic Books, Inc., Publishers, 1982, p. 29.
10. *Medical Clinics of North America,* Vol. 73, No. 1, 1/89, pp. 47-66.
11. Wilkinson, et.al., "An insight into the personal and cultural significance of weight and shape in large Samoan women," in *International Journal of Obesity and Related Metabolic Disorders,* 18:9, 9/94, pp. 602-6; Tienboon, P., et.al., "Adolescents' perception of body weight and parents' weight for height status," in *Journal of Adolescent Health*, 15:3, 5/94, pp. 263-8; Neumark-Sztainer, et.al., "Weight concerns and dieting behaviors among high school girls in Israel," in *Journal of Adolescent Health*, 16:1, 1/95, pp. 53-9.
12. Seid, Roberta Pollack, Ph.D. *Never Too Thin: Why Women Are at War with Their Bodies*. Prentice Hall Press, 1989, p. 119.
13. Ibid., p. 117.
14. Ibid., p. 128.
15. Ibid., p. 131.
16. Garner and Wooley, op.cit., p. 754.

17. *Obesity & Health*, Vol. 6, No. 4, July/August 1992, p. 64.
18. Personal correspondence, 11/95.
19. Personal correspondence, 11/95.
20. Seid, op.cit., p. 282.
21. Ibid., p. 256.
22. Chernin, Kim. *The Obsession: Reflections on the Tyranny of Slenderness*. New York: Harper & Row, Publishers, 1981; Orbach, Susie. *Fat is a Feminist Issue,* Vols. I (1979) and II. New York:Berkley Books, 1982; Wolf, Naomi, *The Beauty Myth.* New York: Anchor/Doubleday, 1992.
23. Wolf, ibid, pp. 187-8.
24. Goldberg, Larry. *Goldberg's Diet Catalog*. New York: Collier Books, 1977, p. 13.
25. Garner and Wooley, op.cit., p. 740.
26. Ibid.
27. *The New York Times,* 3/18/87; Jane Brody, "Personal Health".©1987, The New York Times Co. Reprinted by permission.
28. *The New York Times,* 4/12/90: "One Reason It's Hard to Keep Off Lost Weight" by Gina Kolata. ©1990, The New York Times Co. Reprinted by permission.
29. *The New York Times*, 12/1/94.
30. *Newsweek,* 6/12/95.
31. *Science News*, 6/3/95.
32. *New England Journal of Medicine,* 332: 621-8, as reported in *Healthy Weight Journal,* May/June 1995.
33. *Report on Weight-Loss Surgery,* Paul Ernsberger, Ph.D. for NAAFA, Inc., p. 8.
34. Wolf, Naomi, op. cit., pp. 233-4.
35. A revealing study by C. Adams, N. Smith, D. Wilbur, and K. Grady in Women Health, 20:2, 1993, pp. 45-57, examined the difference in the frequency of pelvic screening examinations between fat and non-fat women. Their subjects were nearly 300 women and more than 1,300 physicians. As subjects' weight rose, negative opinions about their appearance and reluctance to get pelvic examinations increased, while the likelihood of having annual pelvic examinations decreased. The authors concluded that "if physicians are more reluctant to perform pelvic exami-

nations on obese and reluctant women and obese women are more reluctant to be examined, there may be a critical delay in detecting adenocarcinomas of the female genital tract." This may explain the higher risk in fat women of endometrial and ovarian cancers.

A study of 100 physicians and an unspecified number of lay peo ple, performed by DYG, Inc., for the TV Food Network in February 1995, concluded that "There is an information 'disconnect' that is extraordinary. Doctors and the public are well read on treatments, recent research and the increasing prevalence of obesity in the United States. Yet they largely reject what they have read and been told by experts regarding heredity, and other biological bases for obesity which lie outside the individual's control."

36. From the 1995 annual meeting of AHELP, the Association for the Health Enrichment of Large People.

III
HOW IS THIS SERVING ME?

(If you think you usually eat too much or are over your natural weight, read this chapter.)

One of the abilities that most impresses me about people is how they can put to use what comes their way. Two of the best therapists I ever knew of had illnesses in their youth, and because of the illnesses, developed exceptional skills to compensate for them. One of these therapists, Milton Erickson, was paralyzed by polio. While he could not move, he could observe. In minute detail, he observed his youngest sister, who was just learning to walk. "I learned to stand up by watching baby sister learn to stand up: use two hands for a base, uncross your legs, use the knees for a wide base, and then put more pressure on one arm and hand to get up. Sway back and forth to get balance. Practice knee bends and keep balance. Move head after the body balances. Move hand and shoulder after the body balances. Put one foot in front of the other with balance. Fall. Try again."[1] Erickson's keen and precise observations not only enabled him to walk again, they were to ground his absolute mastery of healing and hypnotherapy.

If we have been dealing with a problem long enough, we have found ways for it to serve us—even if it is a terrible problem. While being fat is usually biologically determined, if we have been fat for a while, we have managed to use it to our advantage some of the time.

If we overeat (again, some fat people overeat and some do not—as do some thin people), we probably started overeating as an adaptation or a solution to a problem. Very likely, the problem was one of caloric scarcity. Either this behavior (or any other unwanted behavior) is still helping us, or we have stopped paying attention to whether or not we are still getting value from it. It is far more useful to find out what the behavior has done for us, so that we can consider other alternatives for ourselves, than to try to "get rid of it." Tom, a chiropractor, wanted to lose some extra weight and stop eating "bad" food, like sweets and fried foods. All of his training and reading told him that he would be healthier if he just shaped up and ate "right." He kept trying to muscle himself into good habits, by lecturing to himself. Then, when he was tired, it seemed as if he became possessed by a cookie monster: he ate all sorts of forbidden foods and then felt bad, weak, and a bit crazy. As long as he kept trying to talk himself into giving up the undesired behavior, it stayed around.

As we worked together, I urged Tom to give voice to the part of him that wanted those sweets, even though he considered that part not valid. What happened is that he realized he needed to take care of himself when he was tired, or wanted a reward for a job well done, or just because it reminded him that he was special. We created new ways for him to take care of these needs. He didn't have to excise part of who he was, but became a richer person, owning both the professional, rational parts of himself and also the tender, needy parts. His life became more balanced, just like he wanted his patients to be.

We may have just gotten into a habit of overeating, whether or not it still serves a purpose. For some people, both overeating and being fat have been purposeful. Finding out how we have been served by overeating, and/or being fat from overeating, shows what we need to take care of. If we can find other ways to take care of ourselves, we can choose whether or not to make room for overeating and overeating-based fatness to leave. (NOTE: Fatness based purely on our biological inheritance is not likely to disappear, except by extreme measures or wasting disease.)

Some overeating/fatness may be past-based and some future-based. *Reasons* are past-based. That is, something in one's history led one to choose something at one time. Whether or not the original reason still exists, a person might repeat a behavior, either because it still works, it has become a habit, or it once worked and she has not re-examined it lately. For example, often as children, we were rewarded for undergoing an ordeal—such as a visit to the doctor—by being given a lollipop. As adults, we may find ourselves burrowed in a cookie box when we know we should be computing our income taxes. Or we may have had an awful day and want nothing more than rice pudding. Our bodies may not crave these sweets, but the long-ago connection between ordeal, reward, and sweet may still be operating.

Often, mothers of young children, or people who both work full-time and go to school, or other similarly overburdened people, find they cannot resist eating "goodies" at night. If they were to ask themselves what they were eating for, and they really took the time to uncover their answers, they might connect that they wanted a reward or a treat. If they recalled the conditions leading up to the craving for a sweet, they might note that the day had been hard. While they might not remember the childhood rewards, just connecting that they wanted something to literally and figurately sweeten their experience that day would be sufficient. If not physically hungry for the sweet, they could invent other possible rewards, such as a nap, a good movie or book, a manicure, etc. In fact, they could even simply appreciate themselves for having had a hard day and gotten through it, and that could be sufficient. If they did not take the few moments of conscious reflection, however, they would be likely to keep eating sweets, trying via the food to get to the feeling which they crave, often failing.

We may overeat in an attempt to recapture a certain feeling. The feeling may be as simple as the burst of deliciousness in the first few bites of food one is hungry for, or it may be a longing for the kind of security felt as a child, when our parents were in the house peacefully cooking or doing household chores, and we were safe, warm, and fed. Or, in contrast, if we were raised in an abusive household, we may have learned that people and their bodies are to be abused. While the abuse may have been via beating, sex, alcohol, or drugs, we may have adapted food as the abusive method. Even when it hurts, people tend to choose what is familiar. A familiar pain can ground us when the unfamiliar feels out of control. Pain can feel safe.

Ellen sought my help for binge eating, which had plagued her since her teens. Her mother developed a brain aneurism when Ellen was an adolescent, and her behavior became erratic and explosive. Ellen would hide in her room and eat. As an adult, Ellen worked full-time, went to school, and lived in a house full of in-laws, many of whom spoke a different language. Ellen's favorite place and time to binge was in her car, between commitments. After a lot of exploration, she realized that bingeing gave her a feeling of safety and security which helped balance the tumult of her days. While she did outstanding work at her supervisory job, she had an insubordinate employee who at any moment might try to take over some of Ellen's work—and even her office—without Ellen's permission. At night Ellen studied toward her professional degree. An A student, she had to contend with the antifat bias of her fellow students and instructors. [Particularly in health-related professions, such as medicine or nutrition, fat people have been persecuted as representing ill health—whether or not they themselves are healthy, and whether or not they are capable professionals.] At home, she never had any time or space to herself.

For Ellen, bingeing was a soothing, repetitive behavior. In addition, her car was her only private, quiet space. She began to work on some of the conditions which "drove her to binge": she and her boss clearly delineated the insubordinate employee's work duties and limits, and she forbade the employee to take over her office when she was not there. She started investigating NAAFA to learn about fat and health, and to network with other fat health professionals for support and solutions to the bigotry she faced. She talked with her husband about their taking some weekend trips away from his family, and he told one of the people living in their home to find another place of residence. While Ellen did not eliminate bingeing, she began to have several binge-free days and even weekends, for the first time in decades.

CRAVING

People may overeat because, physiologically, their bodies are craving calories or other nutrients. Dieting, especially very severe dieting, produces irresistible needs for calories. Our bodies *need* more food! We develop cravings for extra-fatty, extra-sweet foods in response to this need. Try as we might, with all our strength, we cannot defeat our biologically determined impetus to survive. (And thank goodness—or we wouldn't be here!) It is only our antifat cultural insanity that places a moral condemnation on a biological necessity. When I was in graduate school, we thought people became schizophrenic in response to two mutually exclusive demands they had to meet. Then we found out there were biological reasons why some people were schizophrenic. With regard to overeating, there are both biological reasons for why we do it, and crazy-making, mutually exclusive demands we have tried to meet: starve, but do not do what is physically necessary to survive; do not expect to have a life unless we can be thin enough; use a fat-producing method as the means to be thin enough; blame ourselves for our failure to get thin. Who's crazy here?

SCARCITY

Another reason why some people overeat is because they experienced food scarcity when they were young. Either there literally was not enough food to eat (or enough butter, or sugar, or whatever), or there were many people in the household and one had to eat quickly to get one's share. Frances was raised during the Depression. Rich foods like butter were scarce when she was a child. Now, 60 years later, she could not bear to eat bread unless it was thickly coated with butter. If she went out to a restaurant, she could not leave food on the plate (although legitimizing "doggie bags" for the leftovers allowed her not to have to "waste" the extra food). Even though our work convinced her of the value of eating only what she was specifically hungry for, she could not let food in her refrigerator go to waste, regardless of whether or not it appealed to her. The pain of throwing away food, after facing hunger in her childhood, was greater than the pain of being a fat adult.

I was raised by another survivor of the Depression. What eventually enabled me to free myself from concerns about letting food go to waste was (1) realizing that I could choose between food going to waste or to (my) waist, and (2) Tupperware. I have food containers that hold anywhere from two ounces to a half-gallon of food. I also have a freezer that is packed with morsels. I can defrost last week's two-bites-of-sandwich or the leftover turkey dinner from Thanksgiving, and enjoy it when I am hungry, rather than dutifully swallowing it into my satiated body.

When I was a child, there was plenty of food, but I was singled out from my brothers and put on a diet when I was in grade school. They could have second portions of whatever they wanted, and they could have goodies for dessert. Well-meaning as they were, my parents were still the Food Police. I could not have bread or potatoes or sweets—especially sweets. When I was a newlywed, my husband commented on the vast quantities of soda I drank. I realized that I was still reacting to the one-glass-per-week rule I had been raised with. While I rarely drink soda anymore, I can still find myself heading for sweets in response to deprivation, or if in some way I feel like the Food Police—whoever they may be now—are lurking. I gave up dieting in 1974, so my only current experience of food deprivation comes with the one-day fast I observe for religious reasons. I usually eat until I can hardly breathe in anticipation of that fast.

Dieters usually binge in response to the food deprivation they have already undergone, or in anticipation of the next famine. I'd better eat it before I can't. Feast or famine. Those are the choices. Our bodies do not distinguish between a famine which occurs in nature or one that we subjected ourselves to in the name of beauty. Human survival has depended over the eons on our being able to feast and store extra calories to tide us through the next famine, and just because fashion changed in the 20th century does not mean our bodies will respond any differently now.

Scarcity is one of the main reasons why diets create eating problems. How many times have you gobbled down lots of rich foods the night before the next diet? While there may be physiological reasons behind this kind of eating, there are often strong psychological responses to deprivation. When we feel deprived, or fear we will be, we can get obsessed with counteracting the anticipated scarcity. In their successful antidiet program, Overcoming Overeating's founders Jane Hirschmann and Carol Munter urge people to stock their homes with abundant supplies of goodies. When we know we have "enough," whatever that amount is, we tend to relax. If this is true for you, you probably need to give yourself lots of reassurance that there is plenty of food. Letting yourself eat what you are hungry for, when you are hungry, helps to provide this reassurance. Carrying with you some "security food" will help. Hirschmann and Munter call this security food a "food bag."

OTHER REASONS

Sometimes the foods we choose to overeat can uncover for us the reasons for eating them. Ritual foods might include pasta on Sundays, after church, in my husband's family; red beans and rice in New Orleans on Mondays; Christmas cookies or fish for Lent. Healing foods might be chicken soup (for almost anything, in a Jewish household), tea with honey and lemon for colds, whiskey for chills, steak for fortifying, chocolate for heartbreak or premenstrual syndrome. Fresh-baked bread may recall our grandmother's kitchen, hotdogs the Fourth of July or outings to the ballpark with Dad. We may be eating for healing, for connection with someone or a feeling from our past. If the eating does not bring us the healing or the connection, we might still keep eating, trying for the feeling.

People also overeat in response to rules which they learned from parents or writers, nutritionists, doctors, and others. While this aspect of overeating is explored more fully elsewhere, common rules that govern overeating include: "The four/five basic food groups," "The clean plate club," "It's time," "Breakfast is the most important meal of the day," "You can't have dessert until you've eaten your vegetables/meat," "Because it's free/paid for already," "Because they made it for me," "This is your only/last chance to have it," and "It's good for you." While the rules come usually from a person's past, they may eat for purposes of promoting health or maintaining warm relationships. Many people's parents, in attempts to raise healthy children, required them to eat the "healthy" food before they were permitted the "reward" food—i.e., meat and vegetables before dessert. Nobody wanted to raise a "cookie monster" with scurvy and rickets, and parents feared that, left to their own choices, children would always opt for sweets rather than carrots (actually, a classic study demonstrated that children chose a well-rounded diet, on their own, during a few weeks' time). Adults raised under this rule may go to a restaurant yearning for the apple pie with cinnamon ice cream, but decide that they must first nourish themselves with chicken and salad before they could "earn" dessert. Or they may imagine the waiter refusing to serve them dessert first, or their dinner companions rolling their eyes in horror at their nutritional wantonness.

Purposes for overeating, or being overweight, are future-based—that is, one wants to accomplish something by way of the behavior. Purposes for overeating could include the healing foods and attempts to medicate our bodies and/or psyches. While Ellen's reasons for bingeing were past-based, her purpose was to be soothed. People often act as if "more is better"—that is, if something is good, or good for you, more of it must be better for you. That is many people's reasoning behind megadoses of vitamins, and part of the driving force behind repeated bingeing.

People also overeat (that is, eat when their bodies are not hungry) when they want to avoid doing something else. For some, eating equals nourishing their bodies, which makes it a legitimate use of time, whereas they may feel that reading a magazine or watching a bit of television is not legitimate. Some people use eating as a transitional activity between tasks. Others use eating to "ground" themselves—that is, to calm anxiety, focus their thoughts, distract them from something upsetting.

Overeating is often used as an oasis in the midst of upset. "When all else fails, eat!" When my husband was seriously ill, and spent a great deal of time hospitalized, I was faced with fears about his future and mine, medical bills, running our home, fixing the cars, the possibility of widowhood, side effects of his chemotherapy medication, getting him to the hospital in a snowstorm and/or traffic jam, etc., etc. Furthermore, not having him around upset my normal daily rhythms of eating and sleeping. Thank goodness for chocolate! The rich, creamy, sweet/bitter, intense bursts of flavor took prominence in my awareness and gave me respite from my fears, and after I ate enough chocolate, I could finally fall asleep. Chocolate literally sweetened my life.

Often people describe a sort of vicious cycle of overeating. Whether it is because the scale or a magazine article tells them they weigh more than they think they should, or their favorite skirt is suddenly too tight, or a mirror or a rude stranger or relative/friend/co-worker insults them, or their doctor insists that they are killing themselves with fatness, they feel pain. The most soothing activity they can think of to assuage the pain is to eat, and they do. Then they feel ashamed and guilty for adding to the very problem which brought them pain in the first place. To assuage the pain, they eat...

People who binge are frequently seeking to numb themselves. If one does not vomit up a food overdose, eating a vast quantity can leave one sleepy, in pain, and barely able to move. Recovering alcoholics and drug addicts sometimes describe using food in the same ways they had previously used other substances, to run away from pain. The pain in one's stomach from too much food can distract one from psychic pain; the oblivion of the eating and/or the sleepiness is what is ultimately sought. Unlike drugs, food is legal and needs no prescription; unlike alcohol, there is no minimum age and one need not and cannot go "on the wagon" from it. As in alcohol and drug abuse, the original anxiety that may have prompted reaching for a substance to quell it, does not disappear when it is avoided, but seems to loom ever larger with each avoidance. Many people who have experienced intense grief have the fearful fantasy that once they start to cry, they will never stop, and will ultimately dissolve into a puddle on the floor. The grief seems overwhelming, all-consuming. When they let themselves cry, however, the tears flow and eventually stop. The person feels both the relief that the crying brought, and perhaps an astonished relief that she survived. The same is true for anxiety: if we can just sit with it for a time, remembering to breathe, it passes. If we fend it off, via substance abuse, it stays and seems even more potentially overwhelming.

Ilene was a recovering alcoholic, sober for several years after a booze-and sex-filled young adulthood. Enormously determined, energetic, and courageous, she had survived a traumatic youth and was now well on her way to being the first-ever college graduate in her family. Binge-eating still troubled her. I suggested that she once allow herself to stop, breathe, and feel her feelings before bingeing. She was terrified! It took her many months before she was willing to try this approach.

One evening, feeling rotten, she chose not to binge but instead to walk to a tranquil spot, breathe, and allow herself just to feel. She cried for several minutes. She felt angry that she had been doing all the "right" things—staying sober and faithful, working hard, doing her homework, eating healthy foods, exercising—and yet still felt bad. Soon the feelings passed and she went home. Her bingeing subsequently diminished, along with her fear. (Just as we are led to believe that being thin will make our lives perfect, we are misled to believe that if we do all the right things, life will never hurt and we will never die. Life sometimes hurts, and we all die. Sorry.)

In my office I have a greeting card. On the front is a bear with one paw in a cookie jar and the other holding a cookie to his mouth. The caption reads, "Everyone knows that food is no substitute for love...with the possible exception of the chocolate chip cookie." People often overeat because they are lonely. They come home to an empty house, with nobody to talk to. More than anything, they want a hug, or someone warm in their bed at night. But they have no lover or no friend close by, no children or estranged children, no pet. They may have just ended a relationship and are not ready for another one. They may be accustomed to being the giver and supporter, and never even consider that they deserve to ask someone for something they want. For whatever reasons, they cannot readily get the intimacy and warmth they crave. Some of the adolescent girls I used to work with got pregnant in attempts to fill this same emptiness. Craving love, some people reach into a cupboard, stop at a store, and take in something that seems like it could fill the empty space. Geneen Roth calls it "Feeding the Hungry Heart" in her book of the same name. And whether it helps a little bit or not, for lack of what we really want, we often eat even more. Maybe the next bite will fill me up...

Another void that people may use overeating to fill involves their low self-esteem. We are bombarded constantly by messages that we are unacceptable and undesirable if we do not conform to a certain weight/size. Since it is likely that we will fail to reach that size, we can not only become obsessed with the weight/food struggle, but we can forget that we are more than just a weight/size/walking eating problem. As Nancy so poignantly said, "Eating is the one thing in my life that I'm really good at."

COMMUNICATION

Many of our everyday phrases capture the connection between communication and eating. They include being fed up with something, stuffing down feelings, being unable to stomach something intolerable and unable to swallow something unbelievable. Other phrases connect communication and heaviness: getting a load off one's chest or a weight off one's mind.

People often stuff something edible in their mouths rather than express something they feel unable or unwilling to express. Perhaps their boss "chewed them out" or their relative made a "biting comment." Perhaps they have not learned how to assert themselves. Especially for people who feel guilty about weighing more than is socially acceptable, assertiveness can be quite difficult. Women in our culture are socialized not to express anger, and may be uncomfortable experiencing and expressing it. If we don't want to stuff down superfluous food along with our emotions, we can learn to communicate more effectively. I am grateful to Bob Schwartz, of *Diets Don't Work*, for his input in the following model, which you can use to assist you in unburdening yourself of weighty communications.

1. List those communications you have not delivered. Choose one to work with first.

2. Figure out your intention in delivering the communication. If your intention is to prove to the other person that she is an idiot/wrong/bad, you are not yet ready to communicate. That kind of intention will likely lead to more trouble. If, however, your intention is to unburden yourself, clear the air, clean up your relationship with the other person without making her wrong, then you're ready for Step 3.

3. Tell the other person that you'd like a few minutes of her time. Ask if she is available now. If not, ask her when she will be available.

4. Breathe. When we get nervous, we tend to take shallow breaths. Our heart may be racing, our palms clammy. We have tapped into an ages-old "fight-or-flight" response, which once helped us to

survive saber-toothed tigers and other threats. Taking a deep, slow breath counteracts this response, physiologically. (If you ever feel nervous or panicky, deep breathing can calm you and relax you quickly.)

5. Set the scene. Tell the other person how you'd like her to listen: for example, to let you say your communication without interrupting you, after which you will allow her to respond without interrupting her. Or request that she look you in the eyes, or whatever.

6. Breathe again.

7. Let the other person know that communicating this is hard for you, and describe your fears about what would happen if you said what you are about to say. For example, "I've been afraid to tell you this until now because I thought you might hate me, and I didn't want you to."

8. Deliver your communication. Use "I messages." In other words, rather than saying something like, "You make me feel guilty" (implying that you're the passive victim of the other person's badness), turn the message around to include yourself as an active agent. Be specific about what the other person does or did. For example, "When you told me to get out of your house last Tuesday, I felt guilty and angry and embarrassed." Or, "When you tell me I have such a pretty face, I wonder what you think of the rest of me." "When you gossipped about me behind my back, I felt betrayed by you and now I don't trust you anymore." Instead of saying something like, "You stink and I hate you, and I'm right and you're wrong," stick to the facts, Ma'am. What happened, when it happened, your reaction to what happened. No blanket statements about how right you are and how wrong she is.

9. Breathe. Let the other person know she can respond now.

10. Listen to what she has to communicate back to you. Keep breathing, and make her right—in other words, listen for *her* point of view. Being able to receive her communication will help it defuse, just as her being able to hear your communication will help it defuse for you.

11. Keep communicating back and forth until you both feel complete. Thank her for her willingness to clear up your relationship. (You are likely to feel much better about her and yourself as a result of this exercise.)

Many of us have been socialized to be agreeable, whether because we are women, because we have tried to be likable despite our weight, because a parent trained us not to talk back, or whatever. We may have lost our independent voice over such a seemingly simple act as saying yes or no. There are many ways to say yes or no. In my NAAFA workshops, we often practice some. We can simply say "yes" to something agreeable. Or "Yes, thank you," "Yes, I'd like that," "Yes indeed," etc. If something doesn't feel right to us—whether it is a second helping, sex, or spending time with a person or activity—we may have difficulty refusing it. It is perfectly within our rights to refuse something that doesn't fit for us! We can simply say, "No, thank you," "No, thanks, it doesn't fit for me right now," "No way!," "No; I'm not comfortable with this," etc. We may have learned, growing up, that we have no right to say no. Perhaps we were sexually abused as children, and learned that our bodies were not ours to command. Now, however, we can re-own ourselves. Learning what feels right or wrong to us, and then being able to assert that through yeses and no's, can turn our lives around. In some of my workshops, we make signs with crayons and paper. We write, in big, colorful letters, "no" on one side and "yes" on the other. We practice situations when we would like extra help in speaking for ourselves, and use the signs to emphasize our words and feelings.

Some communications seem even more difficult to unload. Perhaps the recipient is unwilling to communicate with you, or is unavailable (moved, dead, mentally incompetent). You can still unburden your festering messages. In fact, there may be some communications for which *you* would be the recipient. You can work with these situations, too. Judy Wardell of *Thin Within* calls "forgivenesses," which you are about to learn, the Master Eraser. Forgiveness does not mean necessarily that you condone what/who you are forgiving. It just allows you to *let go* of something that has been burdening you and which may have been prompting you to overeat. It frees you. It is worth it.

1. Make three lists. One will be "Regrets"—something that you didn't do, and wish you had, or did do and wish you hadn't. One will be "Resentments"—usually involving someone else. One will be

"Withholds"—in other words, those words or actions which you withheld, rather than performing. You might have withheld telling someone that you loved them, or that they had a big stain on the back of their clothes. You might have withheld giving money to a beggar, or picking up litter on the street, or hugging an elder. These lists can be difficult for people. Notice if you have a sudden urge to eat or smoke or leave the room. If you do, you have just signalled yourself that the items on these lists are still burdening you.

2. Choose one item from each list that is "hot"—that most upsets you.

3. Write the following statement, filling in the blanks."I, ___,forgive ___for____. Your name fills in the first blank. If you are releasing a regret, you will probably be writing "myself" in the second blank. Or some other name will go there. Fill in the third blank with whatever the item is. So you might write, "I, Barbara, forgive myself for writing slowly." Keep writing the statement, over and over again, until you feel lighter. You may feel heavier for a while as you do this. Keep going. Write the forgiveness over and over until you feel the item lightening or releasing.

One of my clients, a social worker, loved forgivenesses so much that she started doing them every night before she went to sleep. What I like about them is that (1) they work, and (2) you can do them all by yourself.

A final note about communication: It is not necessary to express every feeling. Knowing which statements to stuff is an important survival skill.

OBSESSION

Many people are obsessed with their weight/eating problems. Dieting and deprivation can put food uppermost in anybody's mind: if the body is undernourished, it keeps signalling us to get food. A landmark study of food deprivation[2] showed that one of the natural responses to food deprivation was an obsession with food. Some diets recommend carefully measured portions, which can also contribute to increased focus on food. Furthermore, our minds don't picture "not-somethings." As already mentioned, telling a person *not* to picture an elephant brings up the picture of an elephant. If a diet told you not to eat sweets or fatty foods, you would be likely to imagine sweets and high-fat foods.

An obsession with any substance abuse problem, or with any other problem, can also be purposeful. Nancy was caught in a squeeze between marital and financial problems. She had handled tension and frustration by overeating, and then, when she went on a very-low-calorie diet, shopped instead. She reached her credit limits. When she came to see me, we worked first on other ways for her to handle tension and frustration, and she began exercising. But regardless of what her weight was, it was always uppermost in her mind. Would she fit into a favorite suit for a special occasion? When would she be thin enough for her husband? How could she follow a diet while traveling on business? She was a very powerful, smart woman who was at the top of her profession, but there was little she thought about besides eating and her weight. I suggested that the obsession was functional: it helped screen her from upsets which felt out of control. We have been sold the illusion that we can totally control our weight. There is much in life which is out of control. If we focus on controlling our weight or eating, we can foster the illusion that everything will be in control once our weight is at the right number. We can also deal with a very familiar problem. If we were to remove weight/eating as our focus, worse problems might impinge on us. Most people prefer familiar problems—no matter how terrible—to new ones.

BEING HEAVY

People are heavy for various reasons and purposes. There are more than 50 known contributors to obesity. To assume that all fat people overeat is both incorrect and inaccurate. In one study of twin males, the pairs were confined to a college dormitory for 100 days, given a diet with 1,000 extra calories per day, and told not to exercise. Weight gain varied from 9.5 to 30 pounds. Each twin gained about as much as his other twin, while the variation between pairs was three times as great. Furthermore, identical twins tended to gain weight in identical places on their bodies. In another twin study, pairs of identical twins who had been raised in different families were just as similar as pairs raised together. Albert Stunkard, a physician at the University of Pennsylvania and author of one of the reports, said, "The early family rearing environment apparently had no effect at all" on adult weight.[3]

In addition to genes, however, people are raised with different attitudes about food and weight. There are few occasions, in most Jewish or Italian families, that are not marked with food. In other cultures, food may be much less important than drink or dancing.[4] The connection between eating and celebration, and eating and grieving, can be made through these ritual meals. Many children of first-generation immigrants have been considered healthy if they were plump. Their parents could afford to feed them well.

SEXUAL PROTECTION

Many psychologically-minded people buy into a stereotype that any fat person, especially female, has been sexually abused or is otherwise seeking sexual immunity via fatness. For some people, there is a link between body size and sex. For many others, however, they simply are fat because of genetics and/or their history of dieting.

People can use extra fatness as sexual protection, either from themselves or from others. If one's boundaries have been violated by sexual abuse/incest, one may have learned to overeat, since overeating can be a form of relief from abuse. It can also be a learned behavior. A child who has grown up in an abusive home (abuse may have been sexual, verbal, or physical, or via alcohol or drugs) may have learned that her body exists to be abused. If she then overeats, and gets fatter, she may feel protected from the outside world of sexual advances, or the inside world of sexual urges or psychic pain. She may feel that weight is controllable, whereas the abuse may not have been.

In *Weight, Sex & Marriage,*[5] authors Stuart and Jacobson suggest several other possibilities. "Having little trust in her own ability to handle sexual attention, a woman may see weight gain as the easiest way to avoid being propositioned in the first place. She can also call on self-consciousness about weight to give her the strength to refuse propositions, and thereby keep her marriage stable." (p. 53) Or, she may gain weight to avoid marital sex. "Weight gain usually serves a double purpose: it diminishes a husband's sexual interest, and it inhibits a woman's own sexual desire." (p. 56)

Weight gain can protect a marriage in other ways. Bob discovered that his weight gain coincided with his wife's total absorption in their newborn twins and toddler. As the twins became toddlers themselves, and the parents could resume their sex lives, his weight diminished. Overeating and weight gain were his way of taking care of himself while his wife was unavailable.

Extra fat can protect a person who is seeking a partner. She may feel that she is truly liked and appreciated for herself if someone chooses her fat. If she were thin, she may fear, she could not be sure of an admirer's real motives. Ironically, many Fat Admirers (a NAAFA term for people who prefer fat partners) may desire a partner who gets fat.

POWER

If weight is a struggle area between family members, a member may use extra weight to express unwillingness to give in to the other's demands or requests. Also, if one member becomes the Food Police for the other, the policed member may rebel against the other by overeating when she is unwatched. Parents who police their children's eating and weight can create children who binge-eat and/or secretly eat to maintain enough weight to defy them. Or the child may simply be driven to sneak food in order to have enough sustenance. Children may use eating struggles to deal with many other family issues, such as a new stepparent or sibling, or during separation struggles which are part of the child's development toward independence.

Weight struggles between family members can mask underlying issues such as power struggles or—in the case of one of my clients—the husband's problems maintaining an erection. As long as he could blame his wife's weight for their sexual problems, he did not have to face his own impotence.

Extra weight can be an expression of an attempt to have more power, strength, or presence in the world, particularly for a small man or a woman in business. Women have commented that they feel they are not taken seriously when they are slim, but are treated as sexual objects. When they are heavier, men listen to their ideas. As Bob Schwartz says in *Diets Don't Work*, "If you're getting more attention for being overweight than you did for being thin, the chances are that you will continue to be overweight. This holds true whether the attention is from yourself or from others."[6] (p. 113) At one point in my career, I had to commute through New York's Grand Central Station late at night. A lot of scary people lurked there. I felt that my extra weight gave me a measure of strength and protection which I subsequently missed when I lost weight. Even though I could probably run faster, I felt more vulnerable.

IDENTITY, ROLES

Extra weight can be part of how one has come to identify oneself. For me, weight was part of my strength, and I am a strong woman. My mother was fat as a girl, and both of my grandmothers were heavy. People may fear that if they lose weight, they will lose loved ones as well, whether it is friends with whom they commiserate about weight, or their spouse, or even an unconscious identification with a beloved forebear. My father died when I was 13; he was fat, and as I have come to appreciate my body, I cherish my round, bodily connection with him. Many people fear that if they got thin, they would become shallow, uncaring social butterflies. They would stop being themselves.

As Susie Orbach and Kim Chernin have detailed in *Fat Is A Feminist Issue* and *The Obsession: Reflections on the Tyranny of Slenderness*, respectively, the changing roles and opportunities for women in the latter part of the 20th century can be involved in women's weight problems. Says Orbach:

> The roots of compulsive eating in women stem from women's position in society—she feeds everyone else, but her needs are personally illegitimate. Food, therefore, can become a way to try to give to herself. Her fatness can become a way to express a protest at the definitions of her social role. Fatness, as an unspo-

ken communication, can imply bigness, strength, motherliness, solidity; it can embrace any problem. (p. 25)

Is the stigma that attaches to large or fat women not just another subtle way to divide one woman from another, thus promoting a false and individual solution to what should be at root a social concern—namely, the position of women in our society? Perhaps we can understand the impetus and energy behind the thinness campaign inflicted on so many women as a (possibly unconscious) skewed reaction to women's desires to be regarded seriously and take up more space. (p. 30)

EXPECTATIONS

Expectations can play a large part in people's purposes for carrying extra weight. As we have seen, some people feel their extra weight shields them from others' sexual expectations. (On the other hand, some people consider people's extra weight as demonstrative of their large sensual appetites, a turn-on.) For anyone who has tried to lose weight, in fact has announced that she will never again get fat, and then (re)gained the weight, the fear of letting others down again could be a purpose for keeping the weight on. Or she might fear that people would expect much more of her if she were thin.

HONOR

We are honorable beings. If we describe ourselves as chocoholics or compulsive overeaters, we tend to "script" ourselves into acting consistently with these self-descriptions. Would people still know and like us if we were different? Who would we BE if we were different from the usual? While many people find Overeaters Anonymous to be just what they need, I did not. I neither believed nor wanted to affirm that I was a compulsive overeater, since I knew that most of the time I ate just fine. If we are "built just like our mother/Aunt Tillie," we may hold onto that resemblance through our weight, whether or not it is a natural weight for us.

We may also discover that we have both "fat voices" and "thin voices" in our heads. The thin voice may tell us that we are not hungry for something, and the fat voice may say, "Eat this, you may never get another piece of candy again." At any moment, we can choose which voice to honor.

HOW IS THIS SERVING ME?

If we have taken advantage of our situation, we have put it to good use in our lives. Perhaps the good use is no longer necessary, but we may be still clinging to old habits. Perhaps we no longer want to overeat or be fatter than our natural weight. If you find yourself obsessing about your weight, ask yourself how that obsession has been serving you. If you feel that you are naturally thinner than your present body is, ask yourself how being heavier has been serving you. If you know you are not hungry, and still reach for food, ask yourself what you want the food to do for you. **"How is this serving me?"** is a power question.

We may find that our reasons and purposes for carrying extra fat are too valuable to discard. Despite internal or cultural pressures to conform to a thinner body size, we need to respect what works for us.

We have our own wisdom, conscious or unconscious, about what we need. If we choose to tap into it—by allowing the puzzling behaviors to be, and assuming they were useful at some point—we can uncover that wisdom and take care of ourselves optimally. Practically any behavior or condition can be useful. Rather than trying to rid ourselves of something we developed, we can keep it in our repertoire for emergencies. And invent something new and more fitting for the present.

1. Do you think you are over your natural weight, or are regularly overeating?
2. How have you used either extra weight or extra eating to serve you in your life?

1. Erickson, Milton, MD, *Healing in Hypnosis*. New York: Irvington Publishers, Inc., co-published with Horizon/New Horizon Press Publishers, 1983, pp. 13-14.
2. Keys, Ancel. *The Biology of Human Starvation*. Minneapolis, University of Minnesota Press, 1950.
3. *New England Journal of Medicine,* 5/24/90.
4. McGoldrick, Monica, Pearce, John, and Giordano, Joseph, *Ethnicity and Family Therapy*. New York: The Guilford Press, 1982, p. 10.
5. Stuart, Richard and Jacobson, Barbara, *Weight, Sex & Marriage*. New York: W.W. Norton & Company, 1987.
6. Schwartz, Bob, *Diets Don't Work!* Houston, Texas: Breakthru Publishing, 1982, p. 113.

IV
ARE YOU HUNGRY? THIRSTY?

(If you think you eat too much, read this chapter.)

Toby had spent much of her life bingeing and then purging the food she ate. As with many bulimics, what had started as a means to controlling her weight became the central focus and problem controlling her life. She spent so much of her time struggling with food, and with her concerns about being crazy and out of control, that she had no confidence in her body or her natural abilities. She was certain that if she just let herself eat, she would balloon up to an immense weight. Because she was so fearful about food and hunger, I aimed her in a slightly different direction.

"Do you have to go to the bathroom now?" I asked.

"No," she replied.

"How do you know?"

Toby and I began to explore how she knew whether she had to urinate: In a particular part of her body, her lower abdomen, she would get feelings of pressure, which meant her bladder was filling. If she did not empty it, the feelings would get more insistent, gradually occupying and finally dominating her consciousness. As she responded to the feelings, by emptying her bladder, she would feel relief and the pressure would disappear. With a lot of effort, she could stop urinating before she had emptied her bladder. But what was most natural and easiest was to empty it.

"How do you know when you are finished going to the bathroom?" She knew she was finished when both the pressure and the urine were gone. At that point, her awareness shifted to whatever was next in her day.

There are some things we know so well, it is startling to examine them. We usually take them for granted. We know when we need to go to the bathroom, and when we are done. We know when we are tired, thirsty, hot, or cold. We are born knowing when we are hungry and when our hunger is satisfied.[1] Despite the havoc that dieting and our cultural dissatisfaction with our natural bodies have wrought, our natural state—our home base—is to know about nourishing ourselves.

When we listen to our bodies, we notice all sorts of signals. Some of them may have become confusing. People who have dieted have learned to suppress some signals to the point that they may have forgotten ever receiving them. The good news is that they are there when we attend to them. Hunger, for most people, is accompanied by a feeling of hollowness or emptiness in the stomach area. Not in the abdomen. Sometimes people feel, and hear, "growling" from their stomachs. Growling does not always signal hunger; it may signal that your stomach is processing food. If your stomach growls *and* you feel emptiness or hollowness in your stomach, chances are you are hungry. Another sign of hunger signals is that they come and go. People usually feel hungry for a while, then are not aware of hunger, and then in a little while—if they have not eaten—the hunger signals come back more insistently.

Some people say they feel lightheaded or have headaches when they get hungry. Their blood sugar levels may be low.

Some people think they are hungry when they feel something in their mouths or throats. Chances are, they are feeling thirsty, and misinterpreting the signals. If you are not sure, take a drink of water and see if the mouth/throat signals diminish or disappear. If not, it may be that you have a sore throat.

Many people describe feeling hunger in their heads. When they check in with their stomachs, their stomachs are not empty. This "mind hunger" or "mouth hunger" could more accurately be described as a psychological readiness for food. If you were not hungry before you smelled the aromas from the bakery—or saw something that looked good on TV, in a picture, in the refrigerator, or in front of another eater—

then suddenly feeling "hungry," under these conditions, really means you want to eat to satisfy a different part of you. Perhaps you are "hungry" for excitement, reward, variety, or affection, or perhaps your concerns about survival are connected with making sure you get some of the food—anytime, anywhere. I once heard that chickens will eat until they are no longer hungry, unless they then see other chickens eating. If they are full and they see other chickens eating, they eat some more. This anecdote crosses my mind whenever I see people eating together, especially if one has already claimed to be full and continues eating. We are social creatures whose actions are affected by those around us.

You can watch our body wisdom in action, if you watch small children or babies eat. When they are hungry, they can signal us for food by crying. They show us their excitement by reaching for the food and readily taking it in. When they have eaten enough, they signal us that they are full by turning their heads away from the food or spitting it out.

Youngsters can be trained to ignore their own body signals if their parents are anxious enough. In *How To Get Your Kid To Eat...But Not Too Much*, Ellyn Satter says,

> If you feed (or try to feed) a child less or more than he really wants, it can produce the opposite of what you want. Children who are overfed become revolted by food and prone to undereat when they get a chance. They also become skillful at manipulating their parents to do what they want them to do by refusing to eat.
>
> On the other hand, children who are underfed become preoccupied with food and prone to overeat when they get the chance. The more parents try to restrict children's eating the more pressure children put on eating. They feel like they have to put up a struggle to get food.
>
> In the struggle with their parents about eating, children learn that there is something the matter with their bodies, and with them. Since their desires are so often in conflict with what their parents seem willing to give to them, eventually they become embarrassed at their needs. Later, when they grow up, children enter into the struggle with themselves. They feel a great deal

of conflict between what they want and what they think they should want. And they continue to be ashamed of their desires.[2]

EATING LESSONS

Some people, having learned enough about dieting's ill effects, will be ready and willing to simply abandon dieting forevermore, letting their eating normalize gradually. For those of you who can do that, you don't need to read the rest of this chapter. For those of you who feel afraid of your own appetites, or are afraid that you will eat until you burst, keep reading.

Fortunately for us, our bodies continue to give us signals, even if we have spent decades ignoring them. We can rehabilitate our natural ability regarding eating by setting up conditions which respect and enhance the signals. I arrange "eating lessons" for most of my clients and students, for this purpose. First, we clarify which body signals indicate physical hunger, rather than thirst, appetite, gas, and so on. As we noted in the previous chapter, people tend to feel appetite in their heads, minds, or mouths—whether or not their stomachs are empty, they have the desire to eat. People tend to feel thirst in their mouths and throats, usually as feelings of dryness, fuzziness, heat. Abdominal pain may be related to gas. Some people even interpret a burning sensation near their throats (heartburn, probably) as hunger. Then I ask my clients/students to make sure that they arrive for the eating lesson prepared: hungry and with the food and drink (not alcohol: alcohol is an anesthetic) they want to eat. Then we discover what our hunger levels are before we start eating.

BRUNO HUNGER SCALE

+3 Too stuffed to breathe

+2

+1

—————————- —————- Zero——————————————

-1

-2

-3 I could eat shoes

(Copyright 1985, 1989, Barbara Altman Bruno, Ph.D.)

Usually people know what it feels like to be absolutely stuffed (plus three on the scale). When I think of being this full, I remember a time when, as a girl on vacation with my family, we ate in a restaurant in a resort town. I had my dinner and then ordered dessert: the biggest piece of chocolate cake I had ever seen. Since this was my chance to eat dessert without getting hassled, I ate the whole thing. I was so full that I couldn't even take a deep breath. I could only take shallow breaths, and hope I wasn't going to burst! When you think of being this full, is it a comfortable feeling? None of my clients or students has thought so.

On the opposite end of the scale, minus three, people are so hungry that they are contemplating eating anything smaller than themselves. This is beyond famished. There's little else you can think of besides your empty stomach, and how much you would like to eat...anything! Like plus three, this is a painful state of being and one I do not recommend. Not only is it painful, but people who are this hungry will eat anything they can get, very quickly, so that when their bodies finally register the food intake, they have probably eaten too much.

I recommend not allowing yourself to get to either extreme, if at all possible. We don't need any more painful experiences in our lives, particularly ones we can avoid.

If, when you check in with your stomach, you are feeling hungry/empty/hollow, perhaps with intermittent rumbling, you are hungry. If you are a little hungry, you are probably at about minus one. If you are ready for a whole meal, you are probably at about minus two. When you are at either of these hunger levels, or between them, it is a good idea to let yourself eat what you are hungry for.

Should you eat until the food is gone? It depends on whether your hunger is satisfied. The goal is to eat (or drink) the next most delicious mouthful, savoring it fully while attending to the signals from your stomach. When your hunger disappears, it is time to stop eating—for now. As soon as you get hungry again, you can eat whatever you are hungry for, until your hunger is satisfied. When you are thirsty, you can drink what you are thirsty for, until your thirst disappears. And so on.

When you get accustomed to waiting until you are hungry to eat, being hungry becomes something exciting. It signals your opportunity to give yourself exactly what you want, as much as you physically want. It's sort of a titillating sensation, akin to expecting good sex when you're horny, or looking forward to something exciting. Many people enjoy feeling somewhat hungry.

Other people are scared. Somewhere in their past, they associated feeling hungry with badness or death, and they have been controlled by this fear such that they may not have experienced hunger in decades. Having enough food is a profound security issue. If you are scared to get hungry, make sure you keep food near you at all times. You can keep fruit or crackers in your handbag, your pocket, your car, or your desk, and make sure there's food in the refrigerator. This approach is not about deprivation, by any means! Actually, it's about abundance and security. Allowing yourself to get hungry is an act of faith and an assumption of security: you have faith that your needs will be provided for.

Some people, checking their hunger levels, find that they are neither stuffed nor hungry. They are full; they are getting no signals of hunger. If you are at this level, wait until you get to the point when you can identify hunger sensations. If you came to me for an eating lesson, and you were already not hungry, there are a couple of things we could do. We could check your thirst level. If you are not hungry, but you are thirsty, notice what it feels like to anticipate satisfying your thirst. Pour yourself some cool water and see what you can discover about its properties. Does it have any tint? Any odor? Any flavor? What does your mouth feel like as you drink? What does your throat feel like? Sip water, slowly, discovering whatever you can, until your thirst disappears. Where does your attention go when your thirst is satisfied?

If you are neither hungry nor thirsty, what is it like for you not to be permitted to eat now? What memories, feelings, thoughts, associations come up? Do you feel deprived? If so, deprived of what? If you feel deprived of the food you had planned to eat, remember that you can have it as soon as you are hungry for it. If you still feel deprived, find out what you feel deprived about. Some possibilities: excitement, reward. When you find out what you feel deprived of, you have a clue about how to take care of yourself. If, for example, you feel deprived of excitement, what else could you do that would be exciting, that is do-able soon, and that doesn't involve putting food into an already fed body?

For those who discover that they are not hungry, they can observe what their bodies feel like when they're not hungry, and what comes up for them as they sit in a room where other people may be eating and they are not. They can arrange their own eating lesson, at a time when they are hungry, and can create the other required conditions. The other conditions include: no interruptions or distractions (such as talking on the phone, watching television, arguing, reading); setting the table so that it looks special (for example, with nice dishes and flowers); allowing enough time for the lesson (I usually estimate $1\frac{1}{2}$ hours total, but $\frac{1}{2}$ hour may be enough once people have clarified their hunger and thirst levels), and having the food and drink they are hungry and thirsty for. I like to play soft, soothing background music.

For those who are hungry, we pretend we are discovering the properties of our food for the very first time. We never before saw a tomato or a piece of bread; we don't know what is hot or cold, sweet or salty, hard or soft, rough or smooth. We don't know how something feels, smells, or sounds as we chew it. The object of this part of the eating lesson is to discover as much as possible about the food and drink, both before and during tasting it. Before we take a first bite or sip, we determine what would be the most appealing first thing to put in our mouths, using our senses of sight, smell, and touch. We notice what the item might remind us of. We notice its texture and density, with our fingers. We describe these properties.

Then we take a mouthful. We chew and notice the texture, temperature, density, and sound. We roll the food around our mouths, noticing the different flavors in differents parts of the mouth. We notice how the food feels as we swallow, what we taste after we have swallowed, and what happens to our hunger level after each mouthful. Eating in silence, putting the utensil or the hand down after taking each bite or sip, and paying exquisite attention, we eat or drink the next most appealing mouthful. When our hunger and thirst disappear (are satisfied), we stop consuming. We notice what our bodies feel like when our hunger and thirst are satisfied; we notice our posture, recollections, thoughts, feelings. We notice what is left on the plate, and how we feel about the amount we ate and the food we left over. We take a moment to appreciate the food for having become our nourishment. We take home the leftovers, or experiment with throwing away food (a particular challenge for some people).

Most people I work with are astonished at the amount of food it takes to satisfy them (usually much less than they had expected), and delighted with the sensuous pleasure of eating and drinking in this way. Many tell me they never knew food could taste this delicious! Occasionally, a person has difficulty determining if her hunger has been satisfied. She eats everything she brought, and still can't tell. She may not have really been physically hungry to start with, so I suggest that she create an opportunity another time when she can allow herself *not* to eat long enough to really feel hunger. If she is anxious about not eating, I remind her that she can eat exactly what she is hungry for, as soon as she is hungry.

It is pretty easy to discover when we are satisfied if we start out hungry. If we start out not hungry—and this happens fairly often among my clients and students—then it takes a lot more food before our bodies start registering signals of discomfort or pain. If you aren't sure whether you are still hungry or not, have the next most delicious mouthful of food or drink, savor it, and check back in with your body sensations. Continue to do this until your body registers something. If your body registers discomfort, then allow yourself to get hungry before you next eat. Part of the beauty of this method is that eventually, everyone uses up the fuel they had eaten, and gets hungry again. So there are continual opportunities to learn.

If you are surprised at how little food it takes to satisfy your hunger, think about how much you have been overeating up until now. When you realize how much you have been feeding your body, it's a wonder you don't weigh double what you weigh! Perhaps your body is not as faulty and fat-producing as you feared!

I think that the rehabilitation process often warrants many eating lessons, and I recommend to my clients and students that they arrange to have as many meals as possible alone, peacefully, as they can. The aim is to become very clear and respectful of body signals of hunger and satiety—to be "present" with the food and the body.

I frequently hear from people (once they have relearned these body signals) who notice that they sometimes continue to eat after their stomachs have signalled satiety. Any of several possibilities may be occurring: they may be trying to eat and do another activity at the same time, like driving their car or watching television. They may find the food so delicious, or otherwise special, that they don't want to stop eating it (although food never tastes as good on a full stomach as on an empty one). Perhaps they don't feel they can save the leftovers, and choose not to "waste" them. They may be upset about something and decide that eating, and even overeating, is soothing. They may be reacting to their body signals as just another version of rules left over from dieting days, and want to rebel against any restrictions on their eating. They may have unresolved concerns about getting thinner. They may feel they have to be polite or pleasing to the cook, and have not yet perfected how to say "no." They may be obeying eating rules which no longer serve them. Sometimes, even people who usually stop eating when satiety signals, overeat. Just not usually.

EATING RULES

We have been raised and socialized with all sorts of rules about eating. Some of the rules are useful for hunger-related eating or healthful eating and some are useless. Among the rules which I consider useless for hunger-related eating are:

Clean your plate.
No dessert until you eat the main course.
Eat three square meals a day (or six small meals, or whatever).
A square meal consists of meat, starch, vegetables (or whatever).
Eat because children are starving in (choose the country).
Breakfast is the most important meal of the day.
Never eat after 8 P.M.
Meals must consist of foods from the four food groups (or whatever variation).
It's impolite to refuse food.
Chocolate (or whatever) is always delicious.
Never let food go to waste.
Whatever you eat secretly isn't fattening.

Sugar, salt, fat, and red meat are bad foods. Organic carrots are good food.
It's lunchtime/dinnertime/time for breakfast.
Fat is bad; lowfat is better; fat-free is best.

While some of these rules may offer useful guidelines, I consider only the following to be useful rules regarding hunger-related eating:

Only eat when your body is hungry.
Only eat delicious food.
Pay attention to the food and your body when you eat.
Stop eating when your body is no longer hungry.

What doesn't work about the useless rules is that they don't take into consideration that people like to eat all different sorts of foods, and can be more or less hungry at all different times of the day. Any rule which urges you to eat when you are not hungry, or to eat food you are not hungry for, whether for thriftiness or courtesy, urges you to violate your own body.

If you are just beginning to relearn hunger-related eating, it is more important that you learn to listen to your hunger signals than to any other food guidelines. If you are already listening to your body—and eating what it wants when it wants; *and* in the amounts it wants; and you want to carry less fat on your body—I recommend seeking a somewhat lower-fat version of what you are hungry for (for example, frozen non-fat or lowfat yogurt instead of ice cream, or white-meat chicken instead of dark-meat), or a less-fat version (like using a teaspoon of margarine instead of two tablespoons of it). It is essential that you keep your body and soul satisfied. Some people who drastically cut their fat intake find themselves craving and eating other high-fat and/or high-calorie foods, and the diet/binge syndrome re-emerges. Furthermore, some people will have fat bodies even if they eat very little fat.

In my experience, when we listen to our bodies and give them the food they want, they tend to ask us for food currently recommended as healthful, such as whole grains, fruits, vegetables, and water. From time to time, they may ask us for red meats, foods high in fats and sugar, etc. Generally, our bodies do not ask us to eat the same thing day after day, although we may go through periods when we crave certain foods for a while.

WHAT IS DELICIOUS?

Probably my favorite homework assignment to my clients and students is that they only eat delicious food. This is quite different from the sacrifices they are accustomed to making for a diet! Usually, people have firm notions of what would be delicious: food they have labeled as "fattening." However, I urge you, and them, to go out and actually *discover* what are the components of deliciousness.

When people are really attentive, they discover two aspects of deliciousness: timeliness and variety. What is delicious on an empty stomach tends to be far less delicious on a full one. What is delicious eaten at noon, or on a hot day, may no longer be delicious at midnight, or on a cold day. So deliciousness depends on hunger and timing. You can try an experiment. Try giving yourself the same food to eat day after day. Find out for how long the food appeals to you. Every Thanksgiving I have an opportunity to do this experiment. On Thanksgiving Day and the day after, I realize all over again how delicious turkey is. By the sixth day of eating variations of turkey leftovers, I find I really crave fish, or beef, or pasta. The last thing I want to see is another piece of turkey! So deliciousness is not inherent in the turkey, but rather, in my hunger for it. If you are being honest with yourself, and day after day the same food is really delicious to you, by all means enjoy it. However, if one of my clients or students claims that something eaten every day for several weeks in a row is delicious, I begin to suspect that she has been feeding her "head hunger"—she has been responding more to making up for past deprivations than to what her body is actually telling her, confusing a concept of deliciousness with the experience of it. If you are not sure whether it is your head or your body which is signalling you, notice what you are experiencing. Does the "delicious" food taste as good as you thought it was going to taste? Better? Or worse? Have you equated the particular food with satisfaction, regardless of whether or not it really satisfies you *now*? Discovering deliciousness requires both the faith that there are more delicious items out there in the universe, just waiting for you to find them, and the trust that you are capable of finding them. It also assumes that you are worth having deliciousness in your life. Assume you are worth it.

"What is delicious?" is a power question, whether you are asking about food, companionship, solitude, or any other aspect of living. One of my clients got so excited by the idea of being allowed and encouraged to seek deliciousness, that he decided to apply the question to the rest of his life. Spending a Sunday with his wife's relatives, he decided, was not delicious. Rounding up his family to drive to the other side of the county, to see a particularly brilliant sunset on the water, was delicious one particular day. He started weeding out those people and experiences in his life which were not delicious to him, and filling his time increasingly with deliciousness. His entire life got better, he changed his career, he lost weight, and he walked around smiling a lot. One caution: having a delicious relationship usually involves some measure of compromise for both people. I recommend discovering how delicious you can have any relationship be for ALL the people in that relationship. I invite you to make finding deliciousness one of your life's priorities.

HUMMERS AND BECKONERS

In *The Psychologist's Eat-Anything Diet*—the earliest book I have seen which recommends this approach to eating—authors Dr. Leonard and Lillian Pearson make a distinction between two categories of food: "hummers" and "beckoners."

> Foods that "hum" to you are those that you really crave and love quite regardless of immediate availability. Foods that "beckon" to you are those that you had not been craving. It is a food that's available now. "It looks good," "it will taste fine," it starts to appeal to you, to invite you. When a certain food hums to you, you yearn for it. When a food beckons, it calls out to you. They are two distinct, quite different events.
>
> The image of humming derives from its similarity to a tune that you can't get out of your head. Foods that hum can almost be heard

inside your head. It's as if a message is coming up from inner depths, directing you toward a particular food, persisting until you respond.

Beckoning foods aren't on your mind. Quite often, even the idea of eating isn't on your mind—until you look in that bakery window, get a whiff from that candy kitchen, or notice delicious-looking food being served at the next table.

It is important, at the outset, to distinguish between these two situations. Not that there is anything wrong with eating food that beckons to you. But if you don't follow your craving, if you don't eat the food that hums and eat a beckoning food *instead*, you will not feel satisfied. You may still feel hungry.[3]

Hummers are inherently satisfying. Beckoners are not. Hummers are delicious in your experience. Beckoners may be delicious in concept, but they are not delicious in experience. When you eat a hummer, no matter how "fattening" its ingredients, it is not fattening: your body called for it. When you eat a beckoner, no matter how "nonfattening" its ingredients, it is likely to be fattening. People frequently overeat foods which are not satisfying to them, trying to get the feeling of satisfaction. When you eat a hummer, you are likely to know the point at which you are satisfied. When you eat a beckoner, you may only feel full or stuffed.

Perhaps as a result of what some call "the diet mentality"—ways we tend to think when we are following diets—many people seem to equate their own worth with the foods they eat. For example, if they eat carrots and celery, they are good; if they eat brownies, they are bad. This way of speaking about our eating is confusing and sometimes damaging. People who crave hot fudge sundaes, and have them, and at the same time tell themselves they are bad for eating such bad food, lose much of the food's enjoyment while they are berating themselves and feeling guilty. If they lose the enjoyment, they are likely to overeat, searching for it. If they overeat, they feel bad about themselves. Since many people use food to help themselves feel better, they might then overeat in order to assuage the bad feelings.

So by equating the food with self-worth, we can actually end up fatter and feeling worse, when all we were trying to do was to enjoy ourselves!

Allowing ourselves to eat exactly what we are hungry for—at whatever time of day we are hungry, and in whatever amounts and combinations we are hungry for—requires a fundamental faith. The faith required is the faith that *our bodies actually know what is good for them*. The diet mentality generally assumes that we are willful, wayward, self-destructive, and silly about food. If left to our own devices, we would surely do something stupid. I believe that people will "act into" your expectations: if you expect people to demonstrate their inability, they are more likely to act in unable ways; if you expect people to demonstrate their ability, they are more likely to act ably. (The most effective psychotherapy approaches follow similar assumptions.) Since the diet mentality assumes we are unable regarding food, it is fortunate for us that there exist some wise, benevolent guardians of our health and wellbeing: whoever the particular diet expert is for each particular diet program. One problem with this setup is that, in general, prescriptions for what is good for us change every few years, often directly reversing the prior prescriptions. When I was young, the diet experts said that dieters were supposed to eat foods like steak and salad. Carbohydrates like pasta, potatoes, and bread were considered the most fattening foods. Some time after that came a reducing diet which recommended only high-fat and high-protein foods, and discouraged foods like fruits and breads. Several years later came a diet recommending tons of fruit and little else. Currently, nutritional advice recommends whole grains, beans, fruits, and vegetables, with little bits of fat and meat/fish/poultry/dairy. What will it be in ten years? Listening to your body is more likely to provide you with personalized, up-to-the-minute advice about what your individual body needs.

We may try to fit ourselves into notions of rightness, like telling ourselves we want carrots when we really want brownies. Again, this is a reversion to the moralism of the diet mentality, which labels certain foods as "good" or "legal," and others as "bad" or "illegal." There is currently a fitness mentality which also equates certain foods with moral qualities. If we remove morality from food choices, we can be worthwhile people regardless of what foods we eat. Think about it: do you know anyone worthwhile who eats "fattening" food? Do you know anyone unsavory who eats "nonfattening" food? If we are hungry for a particular food, that hunger says nothing about our value as human beings. If we confuse food choices with worthiness, however, we are more likely to lie to ourselves about what is really satisfying. If we lie to ourselves about what is satisfying, we are more likely to overeat or overindulge in other substances, because—ultimately—we are seeking to satisfy ourselves. For example, if we want a brownie and eat a carrot instead, we can never have enough carrots to satisfy our hunger for the brownie. Many people in this situation eat the carrots during the daytime and the brownie—anyway—at night (when their resistance is likely to be lower).

In addition to attributing morality to food, or to their intake of certain foods, people often attribute other abstract qualities to food. Many people have particular "comfort foods"—foods they associate with their childhood years, for example. Lizzie's grandmother baked every Friday, and since her grandmother was a comforting figure to her, she associated fresh-baked bread with comfort and security. My husband's family always had pasta for Sunday lunch. For him, a proper Sunday requires pasta, or else he feels a bit less settled, less satisfied. Chocolate is a favorite comfort food of mine (apparently there are biochemical reasons for so many people's fondness for chocolate. Chocolate contains phenylethylamine, which decreases depression and anxiety, leaving us feeling better).

There may be certain foods you associate with celebrations (for me, champagne and caviar celebrate New Year's Eve). There are ritual foods associated with certain holidays. Some Catholics associate fish with Lent. My nephews celebrate their birthdays with baked ziti.

People often may associate certain foods with healing. Chicken soup is my favorite panacea of that sort. Others may think of applesauce, or orange juice.

Some people have asked about the relationship of cravings to food sensitivities or allergies, assuming that we crave the foods we are sensitive or allergic to. That has never made sense to me. My friend Toni is sensitive to wheat. When she eats products made with wheat, she develops a terrible headache. I am sensitive to avocadoes. When I eat avocadoes, I get terrible stomach cramps. My husband is allergic to shellfish. When he eats shellfish, he breaks out in a terrible rash. And so on. People who are sensitive or allergic to foods, as far as I can tell, generally avoid eating them because they do not want to pay the consequences.

I have begun to suspect, however, that people may overeat certain foods because their lives are out of balance in some way. Perhaps they ate a particular food in order to comfort themselves, and then got into the habit of eating that food day after day. They stopped being specific about their needs and applied a formula (such as, "chocolate heals all wounds"). Certainly, after people first stop dieting and begin hunger-related eating, many overeat the foods they had not permitted themselves while dieting. When Geneen Roth, founder of the "Breaking Free from Compulsive Eating" workshop, first stopped dieting, she spent a few weeks eating raw and baked chocolate-chip-cookie dough.

I believe that the proper organ to advise us about our nutritional needs is the stomach, not the brain. The brain can offer suggestions. So if we crave protein, the brain can let us know which choices constitute proteins; which choices fit our time and money budgets; what the current nutritional guidelines recommend. The stomach can let us know whether we are hungry, for what, and how much. These data—whether we are hungry, for what, and how much—are the foundational data for hunger-related eating. If you are not hungry, do not eat. If you are not hungry for what is in front of you, try to find what you *are* hungry for. If you have to settle for a substitute, make a deal with your body to give it what it wants as soon as you can possibly get that food; then honor the deal.

When I first started to trust my body's hunger signals, I took vitamin supplements just in case my body was faulty. (It isn't.) Now, after several years, I can notice that I might crave certain foods for a few days; I prefer some different foods depending on the season and the weather, my menstrual cycle, or what my body has been doing lately (sitting a lot or moving a lot).

HOW IT IS

While most people with whom I've spoken are aware of the eating rules they've been obeying, few are aware of what Bob Schwartz called "personal laws" and I call "the unexplored how-it-is." What I mean by this is that most of us believe the world and ourselves to be a certain way, such that there is much we don't question. Unless something big shakes us up, such as a serious calamity, we take certain things for granted. We assume we will wake up tomorrow, having air to breathe, food, clothing, and shelter. We assume our jobs, our bodies, our friends and family, our homes and cars will all exist, more or less like the way they are now, or like our plans for them.

We assume we are certain ways: serious or frivolous, crazy or sane, masculine or feminine, French Canadian, Afro-American, athletic or sedentary, just like our mothers (or not at all like them!), chocoholics, salespeople, fat. It often seems to me that we are honorable; we try to be consistent with how we have defined ourselves, and often go to great lengths to convince ourselves and others of this consistency. We speak ourselves into being consistent: In nearly every conversation I have with a client or student, I hear her saying, "I always XYZ" or "I never ABC," and thinking that her characteristics are written in stone. For example, I used to consider myself a chocoholic. I never let an opportunity for choosing sweets pass by without choosing the most chocolatey morsel I could find. I considered any confection without chocolate to be second-class, at best. Sampling various types of chocolate was a favorite pastime, as was collecting chocolate-related recipes. When it came to choosing an ice cream flavor, the only choices were between the different versions of chocolate. My mother and brother were also chocoholics, so it ran in the family. People giving me gifts usually felt confident that chocolate was the way to my heart. I got T-shirts: "If there's no chocolate in Heaven I'm not going," and mugs about administering hot chocolate in case I got ill. I raided the gift shop at the Hershey chocolate factory and still use a chocolate-colored portfolio that says "Hershey's," while magnets looking like Hershey's kisses hold items on my refrigerator door.

After I learned about hunger-related eating, I discovered I could choose vanilla ice cream, or strawberries for dessert. But first I had to let go of my identity as a chocoholic. I was concerned that people wouldn't know who I was anymore! I had to venture out into an entirely new part of the world, the non-chocolate part. It was risky—after all, I'd spent all of my adult life and most of my childhood perfecting my chocolate sensibilities. What if I tried something non-chocolate and it was really awful? What would I do when the dessert menu showed up? Would my mother and brother still love me as much, even if I no longer chose chocolate? Letting go of how I had defined myself was threatening, even if there was liberation just ahead.

I was well aware of, and proud of, my chocolateness. When I started listening to my body, I had to break my law about my being a chocoholic, but at least I was aware that I had made up the law! There are many laws which people observe without even knowing that they are doing so, and without even knowing what the laws are. For example, in our culture for most of this century, there has been a law called "fat-and-ugly." People who have looked at their own or other people's fat bodies have seen bodies which have been fat-and-ugly. Because they were unaware, they could not even consider other possibilities, such as "thin-and-ugly" or "fat-and-beautiful." Thanks to the former Duchess of Windsor, another law came into being: "thin-and-rich." Other laws we have abided have included:

fat and jolly
fat and unhealthy
fat and lazy
fat and lonely
thin and sexy
thin and pretty
thin and healthy
thin and happy

and even,

I must be serious

I'm just like my mother/father/Aunt Tillie
I'm the opposite of my mother/father/Aunt Tillie
I love baseball/cats/New Zealand/Mozart
I hate physics/dogs/Las Vegas/rap music
I never do anything right
I'm too old/young for that
All good men are already taken
Accidents come in threes
I don't dance.

If we're not careful, the world confirms that it conforms to these laws, these unexamined how-it-isms. If we believe that we cannot be fat and healthy (which we have been told ad nauseam), we give up on doing things which healthy people do, such as eating healthfully, exercising, getting adequate rest, and getting medical checkups. Eventually, our health does suffer. If we think we cannot be happy unless we are thin, we are left with a life choice of perpetual weight-loss attempts or misery. In either case, our assumption that these "laws" are statements of fact keeps us from finding out that they are not. In other words, we see what we believe.

But ask yourself: have you ever known anyone thin and unhealthy, unhappy, or lonely? Have you ever known anyone fat and sexy, industrious, attractive? Have you ever done something right, liked a particular dog or hated a particular cat, or been a little like your mother/father/Aunt Tillie and also a little different? Have you ever wished you could be different from the ways you've been? Or been astonished when someone in your life up and did something "out of character?"

There are no laws requiring fat people to have any particular character traits, although so many people have made fatness bad that many fat people automatically feel ashamed and guilty because they are fat. If you went to a non-Western culture, you would find notions about fatness and thinness to be radically different from how they are in North America. If you transported yourself to a different century, you would also find vast differences.

There are no laws requiring you to be consistent with your history. Even if you have been depressed every day for the last forty years, you could have a happy day, afternoon, future. Even if you don't remember the last time you were hungry, you could get hungry before you eat your next meal. Even if you have considered yourself to have two left feet, you could learn to do a jig. Even if your parents abused you, you can be a gentle and nurturing parent. Even if you are an accountant, you can bounce a check. Even if you are in mourning, you can laugh heartily at a good joke. Even if you are fat, you can be happy, healthy, sexy, athletic, graceful, and a picky eater. Even if you are a chocoholic, you can choose vanilla.

Once you know that you have been obeying laws, you can unearth what they are. It is probably helpful to work with a therapist or a friend who understands the premise, someone outside of your own head who has a different perspective from yours. For anything you think must be a certain way, ask yourself if you know any exceptions. If you come up with an exception, demote the law to—perhaps—"in-general" status, or even "sometimes" status.

Virginia Satir, my favorite therapist and teacher, used to teach that you can change your rules about such things as "musts" and "alwayses." For example, rather than sticking with a law such as "I *must* always be polite," you could examine if there might be an instance when it would be more useful not to be polite. (My mother tells a joke about a pregnant woman who did not deliver her twins after nine, 10, 25 months. Finally, when she died, still pregnant at age 95, scientists and doctors did an autopsy. Much to their surprise, in her womb they found two tiny old men, each gesturing toward the birth canal and saying to the other, "After you, sir." "No, after you, sir.") When you find an occasion when it might be useful not to be polite, you can change your rule to "I *can* always be polite," to "I can *sometimes* be polite."

You can deliver yourself. What you can eat, or not eat, is up to you. Who you are, and can be, is up to you. You are the one who makes the laws about the quality of your life. That's how it is.

1. Can you recognize when your body is hungry? Satisfied?
2. Would you be willing to be committed to deliciousness in food and in your life?

1. Recent genetic research has indicated that a very small percentage of fat people may lack a gene which signals satiety. These very few people may be unable to detect when their bodies have had enough food.
2. Satter, Ellyn, *How to Get Your Kid to Eat...But Not Too Much*. Palo Alto, California: Bull Publishing Company, 1987, pp. 42-3.
3. Pearson, Leonard, Ph.D., and Lillian, MSW, *The Psychologist's Eat-Anything Diet*. New York: Popular Library, 1973, p. 13.

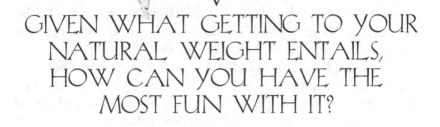

V
GIVEN WHAT GETTING TO YOUR NATURAL WEIGHT ENTAILS, HOW CAN YOU HAVE THE MOST FUN WITH IT?

(If you think you are above your natural weight, and you want to do something about it, read this chapter.)

This book does not in any way advocate your finding ways of achieving an unnaturally low weight for your body. People who succeed at doing that have to constantly act in eating-disordered ways. They have to make struggling with weight the center of their lives. *Worth Your Weight* is about having the quality of your life be the center of your life. While our dominant culture advocates thinness at any cost—and food obsessions, damaged health, and eating disorders are usually the cost—this book can enable you to get to, and live well with, your natural weight. Your natural weight is probably a weight range, rather than one particular number. By modifying your behavior in healthy ways, if you so choose, you can move toward the lower end of your natural weight range. You may already be there. However, if you know that you have been consistently eating more than your body wants, and/or you have been living a very sedentary lifestyle, then you can probably let go of some of the weight you are carrying. *If* you want to. And if it does not diminish the quality of your life. If any or all of the information in this chapter feels to you just like another diet, or feels like criticism against you—or seems like yet another invalidation of yourself and your body imposed from outside—do not read any further. This chapter is not for you.

Fat people (and thin people who think they are too fat) have spent too much of their lives listening to so-called authorities telling them what is wrong with their bodies and how to get better. Many people in the size acceptance movement run the other way when they detect anything at all resembling dieting instructions. That's a healthy step in self- and size- acceptance. Some fat people and some recovering dieters, however, do overeat consistently (eat more than their bodies want). This chapter is for those of you who suspect you might fit that description *and* want to adjust your eating to fit your body.

Once people declare an end to dieting, and relearn their body signals regarding eating, they are usually faced with a new dilemma. Given that their bodies are satisfied with less food than their minds want, how can they be satisfied with less food? There are lots of ways. One is just to allow yourself to eat whatever you want—and let your weight do whatever it does—until finally your mental hunger is satisfied, after which you won't need to eat as much. If you had been underfeeding yourself prior to giving up dieting, your body would probably have to return to its natural weight before it would stop signalling you to take in lots of calories. This process could take a long time. For some people, finally being free to eat and enjoy as much as they want of anything, without any restrictions, is exactly what they want. If the thought of one more prescription about how and/or what to eat makes you upset, then just let go of all prescriptions, and allow yourself to eat anything, in any amount, that doesn't make you sick. Some people, however, find complete freedom with food to be terrifying. If you don't feel safe being totally free in the world of food, my clients and students and I have come up with the following suggestions:

DO PLAY WITH YOUR FOOD

"Don't play with your food!" is one of the statements we hear from our parents (or from our own mouths), as we learn or teach the social graces. As we learn to be "polite company," we learn that food is not a sculpting medium or a toy. But food is both nourishment and a great source of comfort and pleasure. Kids know that. They seek fun and are usually more in touch with their body signals than adults, and they do play with their food. Peas stick well to mashed potatoes, and you can make rivers with gravy. Jellied foods shimmer and wobble. Some cereals are noisier than others. You can slurp spaghetti, and meatballs can roll pretty far. Learn from your kids! If they are no longer hungry and have not yet been fully socialized regarding food, they probably invent all sorts of ways to push excess food around the plate, rather than having to put it into their mouths.

Pretending you have just arrived from another galaxy, and are discovering the properties of "earth food" for the first time, is a great way to begin games of discovery. If you didn't know what that shiny round, red object was, how might you discover its qualities? Sight, smell, temperature, texture, density. The sounds the food makes in your mouth. How it responds to different tools (knife, fork, spoon, fingers). How well it combines with other earth foods.

Pretending you are a master chef, assigned to create the most exquisite arrangement of food on a plate, is another favorite game of mine. Since I love to eat at restaurants, I also enjoy creating beautiful arrangements at my table: flowers, table linens, china and glassware. What ambience can you create for your meals? What is the most "delicious" music to accompany the particular meal you are about to have? How else could you create a SATISFYING experience for yourself out of the meal, particularly if you aren't going to eat tons of food? Rather than assuming that more food is better, how could the right amount of food be better?

In addition to spicing up meals with beautiful table settings, you can enjoy inviting good friends over. There's nothing like stimulating conversation and lots of laughter to fill up one's spirit! So much of our overeating is an attempt to fill ourselves up with satisfaction, and so often we forget that satisfaction doesn't only come from a full plate or a full belly.

For some people, satisfaction at mealtimes comes more with having peace and quiet than with having other conversation. The point is, find what would most balance the rest of your life in ways that are satisfying, and apply what you can to your mealtimes.

Many people find their food is more satisfying when they can acknowledge its spiritual component. Saying grace before meals is a wonderful way to get back in touch with how fortunate we are to be faced with problems of abundance! My favorite grace before meals is silent, holding hands with the other diners at the table and taking a moment for our spirits. We can also appreciate the food for having given its life to sustain us.

For many people, food is a terribly serious issue. Certainly it's become that in our culture. We have become grim about eating. Now that we have connected the traditional, high-fat American diet with increased incidence of certain diseases, food has become our magic potion against death. We have lost sight of how to live, focusing instead on which diseases to avoid, in our desperate denial of our own mortality. We have treated substances such as fat, red meat, sugar, and white flour as if they were lethal poisons. There are even "politically correct" ways to eat. An article in *The New York Times* (3/94) said that many Hollywood personalities and moguls eat a vegan vegetarian menu in public in order to make the best business deals, but prefer red meat and fried foods when they eat in private.

People whose parents were raised during the Depression, or who have suffered from food scarcity for other reasons, find it enormously difficult to let food go "to waste." They cannot seem in good conscience to leave food on their plate, even if their body is full. We have a choice. We do not have to be human garbage disposals, but can store or redistribute leftovers. Some people have well-fed dogs who relish the table scraps. Not having a dog, I do have the best-fed squirrels and birds of all the backyards in my neighborhood. We also have a pretty well-stocked compost pile for our garden. I collect all sorts of food tidbits, which are often just the snack I want later on. I have a freezer full of tidbits of food. My mother, who makes better soup than anyone else I've ever met, uses her leftovers to make richer soups. Many people use leftovers as the basis for their lunchboxes the next day. While buying the largest size of an item is often most economical, it may not pay if you discover you can't finish the item before it spoils. If you're changing your eating habits, you probably will be changing other habits (such as food storage and shopping) in response.

Some of my clients have started "fun funds" with the money they save by not buying food when they're not hungry. We often get into comforting rituals at work—a morning Danish, bagel, or donut with coffee, or even getting lunch—which are habitual, but not necessarily appropriate at that particular time on that particular day. If you're worried that you'll be hungry later, and that's why you overeat now, buy or bring food to keep with you that you can eat when you really are hungry. If you eat to restore your energy, or to take a break, take a walk instead. Walking is also a wonderful way to alleviate stress. So is taking a few deep breaths.

SCALING DOWN

One game which a lot of people with weight problems have played is, "...and what do I weigh now?" People check their body weight by the scale. Some weigh themselves once a day, like my mother. "I gained two pounds," is my mother's way of saying "Good morning." During my lifetime, I figure she has gained at least 30,000 pounds. For some reason, my mother never announced weight lost! But for many other people, weight lost is announced out loud while weight gained is a secret shame.

Weighing yourself every day can make you crazy. If you're a menstruating female, you can gain 10 pounds or more premenstrually. If you don't gain and lose menstrual weight, you can still gain and lose "water weight" via exercise, the weather, eating salty foods, or having various health conditions other than excess weight. Furthermore, I used to find out whether my scale weighed less when I stood on one leg or the other, whether I stepped on it and jiggled it first, or where in the house the scale was.

Some of my clients have weighed themselves before and after urinating or defecating, exercising, or cutting their hair. If you have "weighed in" at the doctor's office or a weight-loss program, you may have discovered that different clothing affects what you weigh. Anorexics may play the game in reverse, putting weights inside their pockets to fool caretakers into thinking they have stopped losing weight or are gaining weight.

Most weight-loss programs, by depriving dieters of food and/or promising quick weight loss, encourage scale games. One of my major incentives for sticking to a diet was to rush to the scale each day to see how much weight I had lost by undereating the previous day. One problem with that strategy is that whenever you don't lose weight you get discouraged. Many a diet has been lost to weight loss "plateaus," sometimes very long periods of time when the body does not drop weight, regardless of how little the dieter eats.

My major objection to scales, besides their inaccuracy, is that they take authority away from us. How many of us have had our day made or broken by the number on the scale that morning? A lower number made my day, and vice versa. Diets taught me that I was untrustworthy around food; scales taught me that I could not gauge my weight without a machine. I may have felt svelte, but the scale said otherwise. I may have felt like a blimp, but the scale said otherwise.

If you feel that you absolutely need some way to measure your size, I recommend using a particular item of clothing. It will get tighter if you swell and looser if you shrink. Just remember, you can also swell or shrink by retaining or releasing fluids from your body.

I strongly recommend getting rid of your scale! If that is too risky for you to try, then put it somewhere where it will take considerable effort to retrieve it. Like in someone else's house.

GOLD STARS

In *Keeping It Off: Winning at Weight Loss*, authors Robert Colvin and Susan Olson noted that people who successfully maintained weight loss used certain strategies in common, such as celebrating their successes. Success for you shouldn't be measured in pounds. It can—and should—include getting through a day or even an hour when you stick to your goals, keep your word, honor your body, find your way out of something that heretofore may have trapped you (such as a half-eaten candy bar, a gorgeous and prepaid buffet table, or a stressful phone call). They refer to such events as "small wins." I am a big fan of celebrating small wins. They add spice to our lives. They are the markers of our day-to-day, hour-to-hour existence. They let us know quickly when we are on track.

Many people think that they will do better by beating or shaming themselves into action. In my experience, those tactics lead to *in*action and a focus on failure. Often, when we are trying to lose weight, we think only of the big wins: when people notice our slimmer body, when we fit into a smaller size or when the number on the scale goes down. Then, when we get discouraged or thwarted (particularly bingeing or regaining weight after a diet), we may forget we ever had any success. While almost everyone fails at dieting, we think our failure means we fail entirely, all over our lives. We slink away in shame. Small wins are encouraging and energizing. Just as "Fun Funds" reward people for moving in their desired directions, so do small wins. Remember when you were a kid, and your teacher gave you a gold star for your having done an extra good homework assignment? You probably felt proud as punch, you probably showed your gold star to your parents, and you probably were eager to try for another gold star as soon as possible. Chances are, your hobbies and (hopefully) your work involve doing as many of the things you enjoy and succeed at as possible. People like to succeed. While many people like challenges, they also like to overcome them.

If you have ever trained a young child or animal, you have probably learned that there's a place for "no!" in training, and there's a place for reward. When you praise someone for a job well done, whether the job is using the potty or the newspaper, putting away a toy, or making the Dean's list, that someone is likely to glow with pride, feel more capable and powerful, and consider the experience worthwhile. As they say, "You can catch more flies with honey than with vinegar."

Like everyone else, you improve with well-earned praise and acknowledgement of your accomplishments. And the more you can recognize and reward your successes, no matter how small, the more likely you are to have more success in your life.

So I recommend to many clients that they get themselves a package of gold stars, and paste them on their calendars when they have achieved something they aimed for. Then, when they have earned whatever number of gold stars merits a prize, they give themselves a prize. (We often draw up reward lists, to create the prizes.)

SMALL APPRECIATIONS

Terry had grown up in a home where she was belittled. She ran away from home while still a teenager and, 10 years later, had finished school, supported herself financially, fallen in love and married a good man, and was now expecting her first baby. She had managed to create a happy, productive life despite the odds against her. Yet she was still highly critical of herself. Whatever she did was too little. She was never thin enough or pretty enough, smart enough or successful enough. I finally asked her to appreciate herself for something every day. While she had carried out all her other assignments thoroughly and completely, this was a really hard one for her. Some days, like when she wallpapered the dining room or planted 300 flower bulbs, she could note her achievement with satisfaction. I reminded her that all of us have days when just getting out of bed is a major achievement. If all she could do one day was feed and walk the dog, that was worthy of appreciation. In fact, I suggested, she should note achievements which made her giggle.

She created small appreciations. First, it was just one a day, like preparing dinner after work. While it was difficult for her, at first, to reconcile appreciating herself for small accomplishments, I was delighted to see her progressing. From an internal perspective which was usually critical, she began to view herself more and more positively. Her whole life brightened! We all can use small appreciations. Especially on the hard days.

SMALL PROMISES, SMALL STEPS

People who have dieted generally have experienced themselves as unreliable around food, eating, and weight. Chances are, they have vowed on many a Monday morning or New Year's Day never to overeat, or eat fattening stuff, or gain weight, again. Then, by Tuesday or Wednesday or January 10 they have broken those vows. People might be enormously trustworthy in the other areas of their lives; however, very few can fight biology enough to resist necessary calories. So they half expect, and fully dread, breaking down and overeating at some point. That is why some people avoid eating anywhere but at home when they diet, so they will not be unduly tempted. That is also why some people try to shame themselves into sticking to a diet.

Following the principle behind gold stars—that success builds success—we work on people getting a winning track record. That entails them making small promises about eating or food. (I don't recommend making promises about weight, since so much about weight is not in our control.) If they want to give up constant overeating, for example, they might agree initially not to overeat one meal or snack between our appointments. If they succeed at keeping the promise, then they can make a slightly bigger agreement next time. The best promises to make are do-able, difficult enough to require some effort, and easy enough that they can be kept without turning the promisor's life upside down. I never let someone promise to "Never overeat again," or something else so extreme. One lapse of awareness and that sort of promise is likely to be broken, the promisor is likely to feel terrible and more unable around eating/food than ever. Besides, everyone overeats at times. I also don't like people to promise to do something they have managed to achieve relatively easily. I believe they stop being so aware of their actions when they don't have to stretch a little.

When people make promises with me, there are two things I check before I accept the promise. The first is, does the promise seem to me to be one that they can keep? The answer to this depends on their track record so far, and on whatever my internal "wisdom" knows. I believe we all have ways of knowing what is true for us, some inner voice or feeling. If someone isn't making an appropriate decision, or if something else is off kilter, I can usually tell. So can other people: when my students or group members make agreements, everyone else in the group checks their own internal wisdom about the agreement and the promisor, and we adjust the agreement until it feels to everyone like the appropriate agreement for that promisor to make at that time.

Felicia had a history of excesses. A former drug abuser, she had gotten herself deeply into and out of debt several times in her life. She had just broken up with her boyfriend, and had not yet found someone new, so she was spending a lot of evenings home alone in front of the television. Until we started working together, she had no idea what it felt like to be hungry before she ate. While she had progressed to the point, where she could now be aware of the difference between being hungry and not being hungry, she had been unable to stop eating after her hunger was satisfied. Small steps were definitely called for. She agreed not to overeat one time during the next week. Also, since she felt "out of shape," and since the concept of exercise seemed to her too much like the diet-and-exercise prescriptions which she wanted no part of, we found a way she could move her body (dancing) which appealed to her. She agreed to dance for five minutes once during the week.

The other thing I check, before agreeing to someone's promise, is whether they are committed enough to keeping it. I tell people who make agreements with me that if they don't keep the agreement, I will cut off their right foot. Fortunately, for all of us, I have no collection of feet stashed in a closet—people understand that their agreement must be one they take seriously, and if it's too big an agreement, we make it a manageable size.

There are at least two parties to an agreement: the promisor and the person(s) promised. I consider all parties to be agreeing to the agreement. In other words, if Felicia had agreed never again to overeat, and my internal wisdom sensed that that was way too big an agreement, I would be setting her up for failure by accepting that agreement. I would be setting up a covenant likely to be broken. If she then broke the agreement, she would feel like a failure and probably would be less eager to come in for her next session (thinking she would be hopping out the door!—but also, feeling that she had let us both down). And I would feel bad, since I don't like breaking agreements. Breaking agreements, in general, is harmful to our self-esteem. Being fat in our culture, or having been a dieter, can be damaging enough to our self-esteem already; we don't need any more damage.

As we make and keep small promises, we develop a new track record, a new personal history regarding ourselves and food/eating. We develop a record of reliability. We begin to learn that we can be trustworthy around eating and food. From small wins come big ones.

And from small steps come big ones. If you explore someone or something to whom you are committed, you will probably find that there was a time in your life before you were committed to that person or thing. Chances are, you didn't go from uncommitted to committed overnight, but in a series of steps. You took a step, noticed how it fit for you and, if it fit enough, took another one. Eventually the person or thing became essential; you were committed. While you may not yet be committed to body-determined eating, you can develop a commitment by taking small steps. Every time you make a promise and keep it, you are taking another step toward commitment. Every time you check in with your hunger, before you eat something, you are taking another step. Every time you choose to eat exactly what you are hungry for, or not to eat what you are not hungry for, you are taking another step. Every time you listen to your body respectfully, every time you feed emotional hunger with what it hungers for, rather than food, every time you acknowledge an unexpressed statement rather than stuffing it down, you are taking more steps. Take a step. Then give yourself a gold star.

SUPPORT BUDDIES

"I know I'm overeating," Jane said, "but I just can't seem to make myself stop. I decide that tomorrow I'm going to eat only what I'm hungry for, and then tomorrow comes and I eat from morning till evening." Many people find they simply cannot make themselves stop overeating all by themselves. If you feel like Jane, I recommend you get yourself a support buddy.

A support buddy can be a close friend of yours, a sponsor from a 12-step program like Overeaters Anonymous, perhaps a relative, perhaps someone you don't know too well but who may also be interested in handling a problem such as overeating. The purpose of having, and being, a support buddy is to get bigger than your obstacles, not physically bigger, but able to ride out the times when it seems so hard to do what you rationally want to do. For some reason, we often seem to let ourselves down when we would never dream of letting down someone else.

A support buddy could be someone you call when you are about to reach for food you're not hungry for, so that you can talk about what you really are hungry for. It's a person who can understand something about what you are struggling with, and who has agreed to support you. The support can be as simple as being there—whether for emergency calls, for prearranged times when you will call each other to talk about your small steps and keeping your small promises, to take a walk with, to celebrate a small or large win with. The support buddy, ideally, remembers and reminds you when you forget, that you are bigger than whatever seems about to send you into the refrigerator. She or he knows you are fundamentally capable, sane, rational, and a valuable human being—even when you feel you belong under a rock. She or he keeps you in touch with your aims, even when it's hard for you to remember them yourself. A support buddy is someone outside of yourself. Sometimes a client tells me just knowing they will check in with me makes all the difference in their compliance with their goals.

You do not have to be a professional psychotherapist to be a good support buddy. Delta was upset; she felt she was not being supportive enough because she did not know "the right thing to say" to her buddy. Delta, however, was the mother of two grown children and a competent receptionist in an office. She knew plenty about how to support and help other people, and she especially knew how to listen. She didn't know that the best therapy comes from someone who can be in touch with her own humanity while receiving the communications of another person—in other words, someone who listens well to you and hears what you have to say, and accepts you. If you're still concerned about what you should say, you can (1) ask your support buddy if you correctly understand her, and repeat what you gathered from her communication (including if you notice that she might seem happy, sad, angry, or whatever she might be feeling but not stating), and (2) ask what she wants from you now by way of support.

JOURNALS

You may not know anyone who could be a support buddy to you. You can use a journal to be your own best friend and portable therapist. Frequently, people remain stuck in a problem until they can somehow get it out of the orbit inside their own heads, where it may have been spinning around for a long time. Talking to someone else is a wonderful way to do this. Writing down what you are thinking, feeling, concerned about, remembering—getting it out of your head and onto paper can free you to move on. For example (from my own journal many years ago):

> 1/3: I weighed myself this afternoon. I was furious! I worked hard this week and I only lost 2 pounds! I realized that I interpreted the news as "not good enough," which is how I usually receive input of any sort. My reaction to the news was to have a tantrum and eat in rebellion. What would that do? I'm the one who chose to follow the rules. Eating myself sick doesn't add anything useful. Who am I rebelling against? I think it's against my notion that things are supposed to be fair.
>
> Never mind that my self esteem has been way up this week—I still feel cheated out of all the overeating I didn't do.

Using a journal can also remind us of our progress. We may get stuck in old ways of thinking about what is happening. When I used to diet, a binge meant that I had failed at the diet and might as well give up. After studying "contextual therapy" with Dr. Bob Shaw of the Family Institute of Berkeley, however, I learned that we are the interpreters of our experiences and, therefore, we have power over the meaning we make of the events in our lives. Using this enormously powerful tool made a huge difference in how I interpreted my own movement, and the journal helped me to concretize the difference:

> 10/6: Last night I felt fat. I made that significant for awhile: feeling fat must mean that I've failed. Then it occurred to me that I could be a thin person feeling fat.
>
> 10/16: Last night I was very discouraged. My belly seemed to be sticking out a mile, I felt like I'd gained back the weight and was barely better off than when I started. I thought, "I

really have felt like I've been going full steam ahead, but instead I'm just fat and stuck. Another monumental failure. I guess I'll just have to be satisfied being fat." Then I realized that all the above is what it looks like for me to be going full steam ahead!

2/5: The other day, talking with my current buddy Ruth, I was upset. I was eating too much and for the "wrong reasons." I had a problem, which meant I had to handle it, find a solution, manage it. I was in bad shape. Not only that, but she felt shut out: I wasn't letting her support me in solving my problem. I was a bad person, too.

Yesterday I realized that I could decide nothing was going wrong; I am a thin person who had been overeating, and so what? Boom! My problem disappeared. My eating has been more conscious and I've been back in touch with my power.

It's so easy to create a problem. Nothing wrong with doing that if you want to spend your energy handling the problem. But I find it empowering to redefine what is happening as "nothing going wrong." Then I don't have to do anything before I can move on.

Journals can also remind us that we have been through something and survived it. At first, every time I felt fat I thought it meant I was failing. After a few instances like those documented above, I learned that feeling fat was a transitory feeling, like other feelings; it was no more significant than any other feelings, and I would feel different in the near future. And, for many people, "feeling fat" is their way of saying to themselves that they don't feel good; it really has nothing to do with their body size.

One of my clients keeps a journal just of how she is doing in keeping her eating and exercise agreements. You don't have to be Shakespeare. You can buy yourself a notebook, make up whatever rules will be helpful to you (like writing every day, or keeping track of agreements, or writing out conversations with yourself, and so on), and start writing. A journal can be invaluable. And it's free. If you want further guidance about how you can use a journal, see *The New Diary* by Tristine Rainer.[1]

THE PEANUT GALLERY

When I was a child, there was a very popular children's television program called "Howdy Doody." The show was performed in front of a live audience made up of youngsters. Those who were in the audience were referred to as "the peanut gallery."

Most people I know have some version of a peanut gallery, which they carry around in their heads. This peanut gallery may consist of children from our past or, more likely, voices of adults from our past. We may have taken some of the critical messages we heard earlier in our lives, and hear those messages now, without associating them to anyone in particular from our history.

The peanut gallery makes comments about us—our performance, our looks, our worthiness. It is sort of like one or several judges making pronouncements. While I rarely hear any comments these days, I remember when I hardly spent a waking moment without this commentary running somewhere in the back of my mind, sometimes controlling my actions and always, always judging me.

Peanut galleries can run our lives. When I was debating whether or not I wanted to marry Joe, I noticed lots of comments from my peanut gallery. The gist of the comments was: Is he a good enough catch? The peanut gallery was so loud that I could hardly think! In a moment of desperation, I asked myself who was in my peanut gallery. I was surprised to discover it contained people from high school and even someone from my college sorority whom I had particularly disliked! When I realized who had been running my love life, and realized that I didn't care about their approval, the commentary stopped.

When I was fatter, I heard lots of comments from the peanut gallery about the size of my rear end, how much food I was eating or shouldn't be eating, what I looked like vs. what I should look like, etc. I imagined waitresses judging what I had eaten in their restaurant, people in the back of the train judging my girth, salespeople judging the clothes I tried on. My head was crowded!

If you are carrying around extra weight in the form of a peanut gallery, there is a lot you can do to silence it. First, notice who is making judgments. Notice what the judgments are. Decide if anyone making the comments still matters to you. If not, just recognize what the comments are and who is making them. Don't consider them significant; they're vestigial, like your appendix: they've been hanging around, doing no good.

If the commentators are still important to you, notice whether their comments are current or from the distant past. If from the distant past, are they relevant any more? If not, just notice them.

In fact, whether or not the comments and commentators are important to you in your present life, you can just recognize who they are and what they are saying, and then just "thank them for sharing." In other words, just notice that a part of your mind is offering a running commentary. Don't attach any significance to it, don't respond to it, just notice it and go on with your day.

If you would like to have a peanut gallery which cheers you on, applauds you, gives you messages about your magnificence—then you can create it. The tool that works wonders is called affirmations. Affirmations are positive messages which you can use to reprogram your mind. By positive messages, I don't necessarily mean "Yay, team!"—although that is a great message. I mean assertions, rather than negations. For example, rather than affirming that you don't overeat, you never let chocolate pass your lips, or you're *not-anything,* affirmations assert what you are and do. So rather than not overeating, you eat appropriately for your body. Rather than never eating chocolate, you love vegetables.

Useful affirmations might include, "I love eating exactly what my body wants," "I enjoy feeling good with exercise," or "I love and support my body." You don't have to believe these affirmations yet. In fact, you can notice how your position starts to shift regarding the affirmations if you try the following exercise:

Write an affirmation about how you would like to be or what you would like to do, and phrase it in the present tense. If you would someday like to exercise, for example, write, "I, ______________ (fill in your first name), like to exercise." Then, after that sentence, write what your mind responds. Chances are, the response will be something like, "Baloney! I hate exercise!" Then, write your affirmation again, and then your mind's response to the affirmation that time. Keep writing until your mind keeps coming up with something like, "Okay" or "Yes." That lets you know you have begun reprogramming yourself in positive ways.

You can do affirmations about anything. You can write, "I enjoy being wealthy," "I feel nurtured by my relationships," "I love the work I do," and so forth. Eventually these positive statements form a new reality about yourself. And as you move into the positions created by these affirmations, your world becomes more and more in synch with them.

You don't have to just write affirmations over and over again, although that is an effective way to do them. You can tape record yourself saying affirmations to yourself, and play them back any time—while you're out walking or at the gym, before you go to sleep at night, in the car on the way to work. The subliminal tapes you can buy are full of affirmations. Although current thinking is that subliminals don't work, hearing the affirmations out loud does, so if you don't want to make tapes, buy those that have positive, audible statements that you find supportive to your goals.

You can also take the time (preferably about 20 minutes upon first arising in the morning and 20 minutes just before going to sleep) to imagine yourself already being, doing, and having whatever you want. You could imagine yourself in your most attractive and healthiest natural body, moving freely and gracefully, dressed beautifully, alone or with anyone you want, in whatever setting(s) you desire. In fact, the more fully you can imagine the sights, sounds, feelings, smells, and tastes, the more effective the visualizations are likely to be. You can do visualizations as a "time out" in a stressful day. Daydreams are a form of visualization; you can program them to support yourself.

You can make collages with a picture of yourself, in any setting you imagine. Then, look often at the pictures. I once went to a handicrafts group where we all made cows from felt fabric, then pasted alphabet noodles on them to spell, "Holy cow, are you eating again?" which we could stick on our refrigerators with magnets. Sometimes people put pictures of pigs, hippos, or very fat people on their refrigerators to remind themselves not to overeat. I find that not only offensive, but ineffective. It is far more effective to put positive images and even affirmative notes all over your home, to remind yourself of who you really are.

A friend of mine, who owned a printing shop, made packages of affirmation cards which one could buy. I keep one on my desk: "All problems are opportunities for me to be creative, and I am ingeniously creative." I have heard of people writing affirmations on little slips of paper and placing them in their shoes, and affirming that every step they take brings them closer to their desired goals. Sometimes on airplanes I imagine that every mile I am traveling brings me closer to fulfilling my goals, whatever they may be at the time. When I was working toward my doctorate, I could see in my mind's eye and hear in my mind's ear, "doctor" attached to my name. Writing this chapter, I want this book so much I can practically taste it! I imagine it in bookstores, being bought and cherished by lots of people. I imagine autographing copies and discussing its contents on TV talk shows and—especially—making a difference in people's lives. Getting through school, or writing a book, involves a great deal of work and a lot of occasions when you have to choose work over going to the movies or a ballgame. Visualizing yourself with the desired goal can keep you going, keep you making the millions of choices involved in moving toward what you want. If I hear anything from my own peanut gallery, it tends to be cheering me on. I created it that way, and so can you.

YOUR FAN CLUB

You can create a cheering peanut gallery, *and* you don't have to do it all alone. In fact, whenever possible, I recommend you create a fan club for yourself. When I was training to be a psychotherapist, I discovered that analytically oriented psychotherapy tended to give me headaches. I worried about what was wrong with me, and felt generally hopeless and helpless. Luckily, I was living in Northern California where anything was possible, newer was generally better, and Freudian analysis was generally not valued. I found myself gravitating toward teachers with a different attitude: that people are functional and health-oriented; that psychotherapy does not necessarily have to be a slow, arduous process; and that we are capable of much more than we give ourselves credit for. Increasingly, I put myself in situations where the prevailing attitude was "Can do." I chose teachers who most embodied that. I went to hear speakers whose message was positive. I chose books to read that had a positive tone. I chose to be around friends who reflected what I most liked in myself, and whom I admired and enjoyed. I avoided—as much as possible—people who seemed to sap my energy, or who experienced the world as constantly victimizing them.

If you have ever listened to people who have succeeded despite grim odds, you have probably heard them talk about believing in themselves or in the possibility of their aims. People who were paralyzed in an accident refused to believe they would never walk again, and eventually walked. People rose from great poverty to become financially successful. When I was in graduate school, we thought Down's Syndrome children probably needed to be institutionalized for life. Then I read a little book that had actually been written by a boy with Down's Syndrome. Recently, a long-running, popular television show starred a young man with Down's Syndrome.

You can be, do, or have almost anything if you do the work. While genetics has pretty much determined your coloring, height, and weight (and therefore, the work involved in radically changing your weight might include starvation, exercising eight hours a day, or dangerous surgery—none of which I advocate), you CAN be, do, and have those qualities you want in your life like happiness, fulfillment, love, and satisfaction. Find people who embody the qualities you want. Surround yourself with those who remind you that you can have the life you want. Rid yourself of as much negativity as you can. Check your internal wisdom: if you are feeling that there are possibilities, that you have some degree of power, and that you like yourself, then chances are you are around influences which belong in your fan club. That doesn't mean you won't or shouldn't feel pain or fear. It just means there's more available to you in your life than just pain or fear. As Sondra Ray says, "The only diet there is is dieting from negative thinking. It is a diet of forgiveness and love!" [2]

MEETING YOUR NEEDS, TOO

Often I see people who are overwhelmed with their tasks in life. Working unbelievably long hours, they find it difficult to take five minutes for themselves. These people tend to be "working mothers." That is a funny phrase. Have you ever met a nonworking mother? Whether or not they hold a job outside the home, they are focused on all the big and little jobs that need to be done to keep a family going. Working mothers are at risk for overeating, because they need energy and they need something in their lives that doesn't make even more demands on them. Leftovers from the table, cookies and other goodies seem to help fortify them. And suddenly, they notice their clothes no longer fit.

I tell mothers that they, too, need time out. If you have unfulfilled needs, you are likely to use something to substitute for those needs, whether it is food, sex, shopping, or some other sedative. What can you do to give yourself a breather? Do a babysitting exchange with another mother? Go on strike? Pay a babysitter? One student of mine, a mother of five, said she had noticed that she always sacrificed everything for her kids. Their needs were getting met; hers weren't. Then she decided to make herself as much of a priority as her kids. It was as if there were now six kids. Money got divided accordingly. So did some of the work. So did some of the vacation time. Everyone got taken care of. I've seen aprons that say, "If Momma ain't happy, ain't nobody happy." When you take care of yourself, not only is home a happier place to be, but your kids learn more about how a grownup takes care of herself.

Being in a service profession, I have to remember my own advice. One night I finally had an evening off, and I spent it with my best friend Iris. I was feeling guilty because I had not contacted a cousin in three days who was about to undergo open heart surgery. Iris reminded me that I, too, needed a breather. Then I realized why I had not called the cousin. In addition to my regular work week, and the large amount of volunteer work I do with NAAFA, I had been running around trying to get an elderly relative into a nursing home; I had just participated in a fund-raiser for the cancer society; I had been calming down my parents regarding the nursing home situation; and I had been trying to reach dear friends who lived in my old neighborhood, in California, which was currently being devastated by a huge fire. No wonder! Even though part of me told myself I really ought to be a saint, I knew that if I didn't refill my own well it would run dry. Time off is legitimate. Time off is *necessary*. It is not a luxury, but a basic part of what is required in order to do what you have to do. Even for saints, social workers, and mothers. Even for you.

1. Would you be willing to have fun finding your natural weight?
2. Would you be willing to accept yourself at whatever your natural weight?

1. Rainer, Tristine, *The New Diary*. Los Angeles: J.P. Tarcher, Inc., 1978.
2. Ray, Sondra, *The Only Diet There Is*. Berkeley: Celestial Arts, 1981, p. 32.

VI
LIFE IS A BALANCING ART

(This chapter is for those who think they overeat too often and want to stop it.)

Each of us has integrity: we know when we need something, when we are out of balance, or when something is wrong. We signal ourselves about these imbalances in many ways. One is by having physical symptoms.

Sonia, in her early 40s and unmarried, successful in her career, developed intense itching on various parts of her body. Doctors found nothing physically wrong with her. Whereas some people might have tried salves, antihistamines, etc. to try to suppress the itching, Sonia and I decided to consult with her itching body parts. We called up in front of her, in her mind's eye, one of the itching body parts—her back. After introducing herself to this part, and vice versa, Sonia asked it what it was trying to let her know now about her life. The reply she got didn't make much sense to her, but I urged her to just accept the communication. The itching in her back, which had plagued her for weeks, disappeared. Several nights later, when another body part itched, she again consulted with it, accepted the information it offered, and the itching disappeared from that body part as well. She subsequently realized that the itching was connected with her moving forward with plans for her life.

In our culture, advertising has trained us that if something itches or hurts we must take medication to get rid of the discomfort, to numb it. If we get a cold, an upset stomach or a headache, there is a myriad of formulas we can purchase to quell the symptoms. We have been taught to suppress whatever is bothering us.

Ironically, I have found that many symptoms disappear when we do the opposite and respond to them with curiosity. A question like, "What are you trying to let me know now?" can bring miraculous results. Years ago I learned that "the only way out is through." Rather than avoiding an uncomfortable situation, we can use it to get vital information. By giving attention to ourselves we can clear up problems that plague us. Avoiding or resisting a problem—on the other hand—can compound it, making it much bigger and longer lasting than if we faced it.

Eating when our bodies are not hungry can be a signal to ourselves that we need something. What we need may be emotional or physical. We are out of balance. Typically, most people berate themselves for this "bizarre behavior" and decide to go on yet another diet, to control themselves so they will no longer overeat. Instead of learning the source of the imbalance and correcting it, they try to suppress the symptom.

Sally, a mother of three, found herself eating many more Christmas cookies than her body actually hungered for. When we explored this signal, we discovered that Sally was working so hard, helping her family to have the best possible Christmas season, that she was exhausted and had no time for herself. Since she is a very busy woman, we agreed that she would take five minutes per day just for herself. The children could watch television, the laundry could wait, her husband would fend for himself. She could sit and daydream, lock herself in the bathroom, read a magazine, watch television—it didn't matter. What mattered was giving herself this brief oasis of solitude and freedom.

The next time we met, she was much happier and more relaxed, and had stopped overeating the cookies. Her family was perfectly okay without her for those few minutes, and she was planning Saturday mornings to herself because this free time felt so right and good to her. In fact, it was entirely satisfying, whereas no amount of cookies had satisfied her.

If you are recovering from the starvation response to too few calories (if you were on a very strict diet, or a fast, for example), you will probably feel insatiable until your body weight has returned to what is natural for you. If you continue to find that no amount of food satisfies you, you are not hungry for food. Laura, a teacher in her 30s, suddenly found herself eating nonstop. It didn't matter what she ate—there were no so-called "trigger foods"—just that she ate until whatever food there was in the house was gone. There were many situations taking place in her life simultaneously. She had lost enough weight so that she felt attractive to men. She was in a new relationship after many years alone. Although this new man treated her badly, she hadn't told him how angry she was with his treatment of her. She felt she had to settle for anyone who was interested in her. Meanwhile, the anniversary of her mother's death was drawing near, summoning up sad and angry feelings she thought were gone.

After weeks of this desperate overeating, which would be followed each morning after by self-recrimination and vows to go back to cottage cheese, she came to see me. I suggested that the self-recrimination was keeping her from focusing on the many emotionally-charged situations in her life. Her overeating was a signal for her to pay attention to them.

Many of my clients who live alone have told me that they start eating dinner and don't stop eating until they fall asleep. I believe that, for some of them, overeating is a way to fill in empty spaces. It serves as a companion, as comfort, as a way to spend the evening which does not involve working. Some people have noticed that they typically binge on Friday nights, when they are making a weekend transition from work to home. One married woman, in her 70s, realized that her frozen yogurt mini-binges helped to drown out the incessant news broadcasts which her husband insisted on watching every evening in her company. As she became more assertive about spending her evenings in ways that pleased her, her overeating diminished.

Sometimes our overeating is an attempt to rebalance ourselves after having undereaten or dieted strenuously. Psychological rebalancing after deprivation usually entails bingeing on exactly the foods which were forbidden or denied during the deprivation. Overeating can also be a response to physiological needs. In a famous experiment, wherein subjects were underfed for several months and then refed[1], those subjects found themselves insatiably hungry, regardless of how much they ate, until their bodies returned to their pre-experiment weights. Many studies have found that people who have yo-yo dieted extensively have increased their cravings for fatty and sweet foods. There are also correlations between premenstrual food cravings and body chemistry imbalances. Similarly, people who are sensitive to varying amounts of sunlight may crave more sweets during the winter months. People may also crave more fatty foods in the winter, to tide them through the darkness and cold. Many other imbalances can also manifest themselves in our urges to put more food into our bodies than would satisfy our hunger.

Alcoholics Anonymous cautions its members to be especially careful if they get hungry, angry, lonely, or tired (HALT). People who are out of balance in any of those areas are more likely to drink. Dora, a recovering alcoholic, had long and eagerly anticipated going on a midwinter vacation to the South. When she got to the airport, she learned that the flight would be delayed for several hours. Instead of basking under a palm tree, she found herself fuming in the airport waiting area, longing for a drink for the first time in quite a while. That craving signalled to her that she was out of balance. She did a quick inventory of her emotional and physical well-being and realized she was both angry at the delay and tired from a restless pre-trip night. Choosing not to drink, she acknowledged her anger and frustration at the airline delay, then grabbed a nap before the next outbound flight.

If you have chosen not to overeat, you have a wonderful opportunity available to you. You can use your urges to eat as signals from you to yourself that there is something you want and need. Then, like Dora, you can take inventory. Are you hungry? If your body is hungry, by all means eat what you are hungry for. If your body is not hungry, are you angry? If you are, you can recognize who or what angered you and figure out what the appropriate response would be. Are you lonely? Sonia began to recognize a pattern of overeating on Friday nights when she was faced with a long, lonely weekend. Recognizing that her overeating was an attempt to fill her hunger for companionship, she got herself a pet kitten and arranged some social gatherings for Friday nights. Had she just yelled at herself for being a miserable, out-of-control overeater and gone on another diet to prevent herself from overeating, she would have missed her own signal. She would have ended up being even more out of balance—lonely and trying to beat herself into submission.

When you ignore your own signals, or consider yourself bad for overeating, you are acting like a mother who ignores the child tugging on her skirt. If you ignore a child who is seeking your attention, the child will usually repeat the request for attention, often louder and more insistently. If you belittle yourself for overeating, it is like beating the child who seeks your attention. The child learns that she is undeserving of having her needs filled, or that the world is not a safe place to be vulnerable, or that the particular need she has is wrong. Hence, the beginning of a deeper, more serious and lasting problem, instead of a simple problem and solution. When you give the child what she needs, however, she will usually quiet and calm down.

I discovered something about balance when my husband and I, newly married, began planning our vacations. I had moved across the country and was trying to reestablish my professional career, which was faltering. I wanted to vacation near or in cities where I could walk, shop, go to museums, take tours, see shows. At the time, my husband was working hard at his job, while simultaneously studying for a graduate degree and leading a national professional organization. He wanted to lie on the beach. We worked out a compromise. Today I find myself in the same position he was in. The vacation I long for now is one with peace, quiet, rest, and no telephones.

Fantasizing about your ideal vacation can also cue you in on what would create balance in your life. If you could choose your ideal vacation now, would it be restful and quiet, stimulating and active, filled with new people and places, or familiar? Chances are, the vacation you would choose now is one that would fill in the empty places, balancing out the tipped scale.

Often a client will say something like, "The other night I wanted to eat. I checked and my body wasn't hungry, so I asked myself what I wanted the food to handle, and I realized I was bored." The client may then conclude that overeating *always* means she is bored. Every time she overeats, she responds in a way appropriate to handling boredom. However, her overeating may be signalling other things. At times she may be lonely, other times angry, etc. Deciding that overeating always signals one thing—and responding accordingly—is as inappropriate as a mother who diapers her child every time it cries, regardless of what it is crying about.

DOING THE WORK

Letting go of overeating takes time, attention, and commitment. It takes the commitment to check whether you are hungry for food, or for something else entirely, without first giving in to the urge to eat. It then takes the commitment to handle, appropriately, whatever you have used food to handle, even if it requires work. People sometimes feel it's too hard to do the work, so they go back on a diet. It takes commitment and work to change a habit, whether by changing what you eat (by dieting), or how and when you eat (as I am suggesting). If you are not willing to do the work, do not expect your body to get slimmer. Millions of dollars have been spent on diet frauds, by people who want to go to sleep fat and wake up thin.

If you are willing to do the work, here it is:

Whenever you want to eat, check if your *body* is hungry. If it is not, ask yourself what you want the food to do for you. Then do whatever that is. Rest if you are tired. Choose an activity if you are bored. Call a friend if you are lonely... Notice what food(s) you choose when you are lonely, bored, angry, and so on. I discovered that if I choose food to chomp on, like celery or popcorn, I may be angry about something. Ellen found she chose chocolate pudding when she needed soothing and security.

Life requires us constantly to find our balance. One day we may wake up tired and grouchy, and need a lot of peace and quiet. Another day, or series of days, may be routine and quiet, and we find we need stimulation. When my husband was ill, it seemed like living was akin to surfing on rough seas: a chemotherapy-related fever and frantic rush to the hospital, a new diagnosis, a change in treatment with its attendant threats and promises. Staying afloat was a matter of absorbing the most recent event and finding out how to balance it. Often, chocolate and silly comedies helped, but not always.

IS LESS BETTER?

Dieting is an enormous challenge to our balance. For a few people, dieting *does* balance them: it enables them to regain control after a period of overeating; or it enables them to eat in ways that better serve their bodies, like a hypoglycemic person reducing her sugar intake. For many people, however, dieting tilts them toward going without—dessert, sweets, potato chips. Dieters who want to lose extra weight as fast as possible (so they don't have to be deprived for long) believe that the less they eat, the better they'll do. Fewer calories consumed means more fat burned, or so they think.

Until recently, one could always find another version of this "less is better" philosophy. Lose ten pounds-in-a-week-/five-in-a-weekend-type diets generally restrict calories to under 1,000/day and sometimes under 500. Or they restrict dieters to very few foods, like eggs and grapefruit. Fortunately, research has shown that this approach backfires, and it has become harder to find these diets. After several banner years, the spectacular failure rate of VLCDs (very-low-calorie-diets) is helping to reduce the sale of many liquid formula diets.

Still, despite evidence that eating too little slows the metabolism, prompting the body to use all means possible to defend against starvation, many people still try to employ the less-is-better approach. In fact, our culture seems to take this approach to valuing people's weight: less is better. Anorexics take this to an extreme. Inversely equating weight with worth and control, they can never be thin enough, to the point where some of them starve themselves to death.

People almost invariably binge-eat as a result of dieting deprivation. They have been physically and psychologically deprived. In a rush to balance the deprivation, they adopt a "more-is-better" approach to the foods they previously avoided. If one piece of pie would be delicious, then three would be even more delicious. People often operate on the same principle regarding money, as did Leona Helmsley.

BETTER IS BETTER

In fact, neither less nor more is better. Better is better. Find out what you most want *now*, and as often as possible let yourself have exactly that. If your body is hungry and wants an orange, have one. If it is delicious, enjoy its deliciousness. Don't assume a second orange will be equally as delicious; it probably won't be. Also, don't assume that an orange which is delicious today will taste delicious tomorrow. Pay attention to your experience and find out what fits! Don't make a rule that something which is delicious to you today, like a brownie, will always be delicious. Discover for yourself. It takes a little extra attention to discover rather than to follow a rule, even if you made the rule. But it's worth it.

INTERPRETING OUR EXPERIENCE

I learn a lot from vacations. My husband and I were describing our vacation to somebody when I suddenly realized that we had experienced two entirely different vacations. We had been together most of the time, had gone to the same places, eaten at the same restaurants, stayed in the same hotel rooms, met the same people. Yet his version of how we spent our time on our vacation was almost entirely different from mine. He had been much more aware of the automobiles, and I of the fashions, for example. I realized then that, while certain circumstances might be agreed on (like whether or not it was raining), each individual's experience of those circumstances is unique to that individual.

Not only that, but the same individual can interpret the same circumstances differently, depending on other variables. For example, let's imagine it's raining outside. To one person it's "pouring"; to another, it's watering thirsty plants and animals; to a third, it's a replay of Noah's flood. My interpretation of a forecast of snow varies depending on whether Joe and I are planning to be home together, whether we have enough food in the house, and how long it's been since I've been out. If we're both home and safe with no commitments on Saturday, a Friday night snowstorm is marvelous—romantic and cozy. If I have to drive somewhere the next day, or if Joe has a long ride in the snow to get home, then the storm is a threat to my well-being and peace of mind, an unwanted intrusion. A snowstorm just before I plan to leave on a tropical vacation can bring me great distress, while to Joe it adds to the challenge he enjoys. Same weather, different interpretations.

A major shift in my relationship to my weight took place once I interpreted it differently. Since childhood, my being "overweight" had been the bane of my existence. I was constantly either being deprived of food, anticipating the next deprivation, or reacting to the last one. Besides schoolwork or professional reading, the other reading matter that occupied most of my attention was related to the latest diets, before and after stories, and so forth. I tried to find attractive clothing (not always so easy) that I thought would best disguise the unwanted pounds. My friends and I constantly discussed the latest diets and our results with them. In the forefront of my stream of consciousness were my self-critical comments about my fat-and-ugly body and my lack of willpower. They were accompanied by my latest speculations about why I so obstinately refused to get slim, when it was seemingly the most important goal of my life.

Then, one day, I realized that weight was my favorite problem. It had occupied most of my mental energy throughout most of my life. Where I existed, so did my weight problem. I ate with it, dressed and undressed with it. It went to bed with me and my lovers. It lurked ever-present in the doctor's office and in my family's conversations with me. It attended my courses and workshops. I made elaborate plans for its demise and my life thereafter. Love me, love my weight problem. It was part of my identity, my constant companion. While I had other problems, they were usually transient. My weight problem was never gone for more than a few hours.

When I realized it was my *favorite* problem, I began to feel a little fondness for it. After all, it helped to locate and anchor me in the swirl which was the universe. I had spent more time, money, and energy on it than any other aspect of my existence. If it was my favorite problem, that meant I had a choice about which problems to favor and which to give less energy to. If I wanted, I could search for another favorite problem, such as what to do when I won the lottery.

It even occurred to me that I could keep it a favorite problem in my life without being its victim. I didn't have to get rid of it if I didn't want to. I could use it as the focus of my work, and even get paid for messing around with it, without having it ruin my life.

A great deal of people's suffering about weight comes from interpretations they and/or our culture have made about weight, especially: (1) that carrying extra weight is necessarily harmful to health and longevity, and (2) that we can always reduce our weight by not overeating. The impact of these two interpretations (both of which are discussed at length elsewhere in this book) has profound implications for those who believe them.

People who want to be healthy and consider themselves, or are considered, too fat, usually try to lose weight. Through most of this century, we have tried to do so by dieting, which almost always results in weight regained and often supplemented. The regainers, thinking they are to blame, then assume they have a death wish or some equally dark, morbid, underlying badness or wrongness—which means to them that they are actually more unhealthy than they had thought! At that point, many people give up trying to be healthy, immobilized by fear and shame. Or they go to a doctor who also interprets being fat as deadly and entirely controllable, and who chides them for not losing weight. Then they stop seeking preventive medical care. Ignorance and prejudice thus damage their health.

REINTERPRETING ASPECTS OF YOUR LIFE

Here are a couple of exercises which may help you to reinterpret aspects of your life:

Imagine that your weight means that you are helplessly, hopelessly headed for an unhealthy life and an early death. How do you feel about yourself? What will you do for fun? For relaxation? How will you eat? What is it like to get up in the morning? How do you feel about getting medical and psychotherapeutic care?

Now, take a couple of deep breaths and stretch out your limbs. Imagine that your weight means that you will live a long, healthy life.

There is plenty available to you, within your control, that you can continue to do to get even healthier. How do you feel about yourself now? What will you do for fun? For relaxation? What will you eat? What is it like to get up in the morning? How do you feel about getting medical or psychotherapeutic care?

Chances are, your emotional response to the first exercise, or interpretation, will be quite different from the second. You will probably feel discouraged, hopeless, helpless, enervated with the first interpretation. Conversely, with the second interpretation, you will probably feel pleased, curious, energetic, and eager to find abundant resources for yourself. The difference in your feeling of wellbeing and power is entirely due to your interpretation. Which do you prefer?

IS THERE A RIGHT INTERPRETATION?

People often want to know which is the *right* interpretation of circumstances. There are several variables to consider, two of which are most important:

(1) *The agreement factor*. If you are taking an examination in school, there is likely to be a "right" answer for each question. This answer is likely to be based on agreement. Most people would agree that 2 + 2 = 4, and if you were taking a math test, that would be the right answer.

Society is based on a number of agreements. Marriage vows are agreements. The Ten Commandments are a set of agreements. A lease is a set of agreements. The Bill of Rights is a set of agreements. If you commit murder or adultery, you are breaking agreements. Depending on the society you live in, you could be put in jail, granted a divorce, or executed for breaking these agreements.

Some agreements change over time. During Prohibition in the United States, it was agreed that liquor was illegal. For the past several decades, however, we have agreed that liquor is legal. Gone are the stills, speakeasies, and bootleggers. A century ago, most people in our culture agreed that a curvaceous female body was beautiful. One hundred years later, most people in our culture agree that leanness is beautiful.

(2) *The individual factor*. Every person in the world is an individual. Even identical twins are individuals. There is *nobody* else in the entire world who has exactly your genetic heritage, your set of learning experiences, your ways of seeing, hearing, tasting, smelling, and feeling the world. Nobody else knows precisely what it is like to live inside your skin and your mind. You are the one and only you in the whole world. Nobody else but you really knows what you need and want, aspire to and wish for, although others have their interpretations of who you are. Nobody else but you goes at your rate of speed down the path of your life.

Nobody else determines your worth. While the current North American agreement is that a fair-skinned, long-legged, full-breasted, 18- to 25-year-old woman is worth more than a dark-skinned, squat, 70-year-old woman, you do not have to succumb to the agreements. You have complete control over how you interpret your worth. And as you interpret, so shall people respond to you.

If you consider yourself a worthwhile person, with a lot to offer, you will most likely treat yourself as such. You will care for your body as if it is worthwhile. You will dress yourself as if you are worthwhile. You will associate with people who recognize you as worthwhile, and spend your time as if it were valuable. Listen to Francesca: "I'm 50, fat, and beautiful. I love my daughters, I love sex, I love men, and most assuredly, I love myself." Men, in turn, love Francesca, who built up her self-worth partly by putting herself where she felt happiest—among friends, people who admired her, situations in which she could best experience her competence.

Many people think that if they were really worthwhile they would be thin, or at least not overeating. Worth, weight, and how much you eat are not necessarily related. Many worthy people overeat, especially if they are recovering from dieting. Everyone overeats sometimes. I believe that many overeaters overeat to help them be "good" people—i.e. support and nurture others, be nice, not get angry, not demand too much. I believe sublimation of destructive impulses is an important social skill.

Being thin is not necessarily an indication of self-worth. Ask any anorexic. How many seemingly worthy people can you think of, who have the agreed-upon "right" physical characteristics, and are not in touch with their worth?

We actually can use any circumstances to forward us, depending on the interpretations we use (see Chapter VII). We are in charge of our interpretations, the stories we tell ourselves about the meaning of the circumstances.

You can use all the evidence that has held you back—your eating, your weight, your finances, your relationships or lack of them—to forward you. Whatever you thought your limitations were can actually serve you. While this is an invaluable tool for weight release, it has enormous implications for your entire life. "**How can I interpret this to forward me?**" is a very powerful question.

1. What about yourself have you used to prove that you are unworthy?
2. How could you reinterpret these very same items to experience that you are worthy?
3. What would balance your life?

1. Keys, Ancel, op. cit.

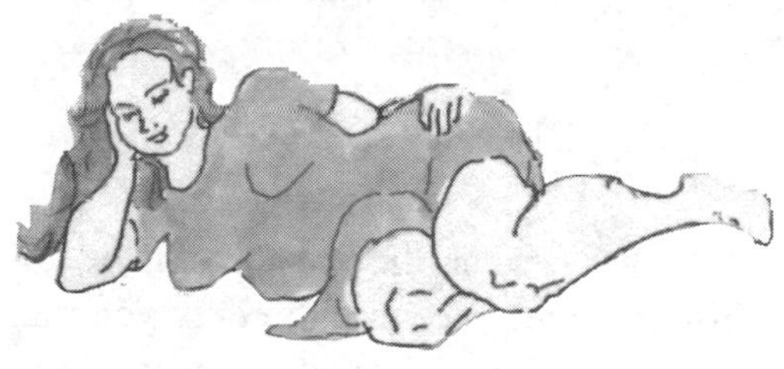

VII
WHAT IS HAPPENING, AND HOW CAN YOU USE IT BEST?

(If you know you frequently overeat, and don't want to, read this chapter.)

Many an aspiring weight reducer has experienced the end of her reducing regime following a binge, a plateau, or flagging enthusiasm. Certainly anyone who has tried to lose weight for a class reunion or other special event, has experienced the binge following the event. And then there are the times when we may have felt possessed by the Eating Monster, and cleaned out the refrigerator, the leftover Halloween candy, and a half gallon of ice cream in one blind binge.

The scenario usually goes like this: The person who just overate tells herself something like, "That's it. It's hopeless. I'm a fat slob who is doomed to be fat forever. I just can't control myself. I must hate myself. I definitely need a shrink. I'll probably eat and eat forever, and die when I burst from too much fatness." Then they gobble up all the food they denied themselves while they were losing weight.

This is the throw-out-the-baby-with-the-bathwater approach. There is no forgiveness in it. The thinking behind it is something like, "black OR white"—one is either doing everything to lose weight or one can do nothing. While much about our weight is genetically predetermined and biologically regulated, to the extent that we can and want to affect our weight, it is important to use what is happening to forward us. So, first and foremost, we have to make room for who and how we are.

YOU ARE AN ORIGINAL

As Virginia Satir wrote in her book, *Self Esteem*, "In all the world there is no one else like me." You are the only you that exists. Even if you are one of a set of identical quadruplets, you are the only one born when you were born, the only one held, fed, and diapered when you were held, fed, and diapered. You are the only one who has put together your exact thoughts, feelings, and history, your exact position in your family, in your generation, in the world. Nobody else has exactly your talents, your likes and dislikes, and your memories and dreams. Nobody else knows exactly what you want and need, so nobody else can have exactly the same priorities as you have for your life. Since you are the only you in the whole world, the rate of progress you make through the path of your life can hardly be determined by anyone else. How would anyone else know how fast you ought to be going? And how would anyone else know whether what you're doing now means you're advancing or not? After all, they haven't lived inside your life, even if they live inside your house! You could be hurtling along at your version of top speed. If last night you ate a million calories, SO WHAT?

Big deal. That has nothing to do with today, or with your future. For whatever reasons and purposes, you ate a lot yesterday. That predicts NOTHING about your success. It also has nothing to do with how fast you should be progressing. Unless you deem it an irrevocable failure, which is what the baby-with-the-bathwater approach does.

INTERPRETING TO WIN

We are entirely in charge of our interpretations of events, even if we cannot control the events themselves. Whether a binge comes from the kind of caloric or other nutritional deprivation that diets often entail, or from psychological needs, it has no necessary connection to our value or our success—unless we say it does. You can see for yourself if you try the following exercise:

1. Think of something in your life that you succeeded at. It could be a relationship, a project, something connected with work or school, etc. Now think of a glitch or obstacle you met with while you were involved with this something. How did you interpret the glitch? What did you tell yourself it meant? Did it mean total failure? Was it a temporary condition? How did you use it?

2. Think of something in your life that you failed at. Now think of a glitch or obstacle you met with while you were involved with this something. How did you interpret the glitch? What did you tell yourself it meant? Did it mean total failure? Was it a temporary condition? How did you use it?

Chances are, you interpreted an obstacle en route to success as just that: an obstacle *en route to success*. You included the obstacle in your path to success. You decided you would not let it throw you, or at least not for very long. You outlasted it. You found ways to deal with it, to use it, to learn from it, to get bigger and stronger because of it. Just as when Joe was sick and I decided that whatever happened would enhance our relationship—we would go through everything together—whatever happened *did* enhance our relationship. I remember being in a workshop once, when the leader asked a parent how he interpreted his teenage daughter's actions toward him: did they mean the teenager didn't love him? Even though the parent would sometimes have liked to send the teenager to the moon, he knew she loved him even when she acted hatefully, and he viewed all of her actions as coming from love. What do you think might have happened if the parent had thought himself unloved?

You can tell yourself anything at all about the meaning of events. If you interpret them as indicating your eventual success on a project, you are pointing yourself in the direction of eventual success. For example, you can interpret a binge as something to learn from on your path to your natural body. When you do that, you open yourself to learn from the binge and apply the learning to your goal of returning to the body you were born to have. However, if you interpret a binge as total failure, you are likely to feel depressed, crazy, hopeless, and helpless. Reinterpreting the meaning of an event in my own weight-loss journey transformed it from an obstacle to something minor, and I felt an immediate boost in energy as a result of interpreting to win:

> Last night I was discouraged. My belly seemed to be sticking out a mile, I felt like I'd gained back the weight and was barely better off than when I started. I thought, 'I really have felt like I've been going full steam ahead, but instead I'm just fat and stuck. Another monumental failure. I guess I'll just have to be satisfied being fat.' Then I realized that all the above *is* what it looks like for me to be going full steam ahead!

How do you change something around, interpret it to win? First, consider anything as instructive, as something to learn from. How could you do something differently next time? What would you want to do again? What can you find that is useful about what happened? Asking yourself, **"What can I learn from this that will forward me?"** is a power question.

The other thing I find to be totally invaluable, is to *include anything that occurs as the next step in achieving your goals*. It may sound absolutely crazy to you to consider gaining 50 pounds as the next step in your having your natural body, but try it out. What if gaining 50 pounds meant you were hopelessly, helplessly doomed to fatness? I bet you'd feel like crawling under the bed and not coming out for a few years. But if gaining 50 pounds were just your next step in your natural progression toward your natural body, then it might seem like a setback, but it would be something you could learn from, something you could apply. Think about it: if you hadn't tried and failed so many times to get a body you could live with, would you be reading this book now? What would you have missed out on?

You might be wondering if your interpretation is the "right" one, or the truth. The answer to this dilemma goes back to realizing that you are unique. Even if 10 million people binged and then remained hopelessly, helplessly fat—no one can predict what will happen for you. Except you! There is no "right" assessment of the situation. You may notice that when you binge you feel excited before bingeing, great during the binge, and bloated and self-hating afterward. The significance of having those feelings, however, is open to your interpretation. I recommend you choose any way to interpret those feelings which leaves you feeling more powerful and aiming toward the outcome you ultimately desire.

In 1984 I got laid off from a job I had loved. I worked in the counseling center of a university. I liked my co-workers, I loved my clients, and I couldn't really imagine anything better. However, the director converted my position and several others to graduate psychology internships. I left the job not knowing what I would do next, knowing only that I wanted a doctorate, I wanted to end people's suffering about weight, and I wanted only to do work that interested me and that I enjoyed. Sitting at home the first few days, I just decided that whatever happened from that point would lead to my getting a doctorate, ending people's suffering about weight, and earning my living doing what I love. Then I did whatever was next in my day. It might have been washing the dishes or going to the bathroom, reading the paper or making a phone call. What I did didn't matter so much. What I would have it lead to, did matter. In the next few weeks I got involved as a participant in Bob Schwartz's "Diets Don't Work" program, which led to all sorts of personal and professional growth, along with my losing a significant amount of weight without dieting. I also realized, during that period, that the postgraduate academic program I had been involved in was not delicious to me. I got headaches from the classes and from what they were teaching. So I set about finding a doctoral program that was delicious. Since then, I have gotten my doctorate, ended perhaps thousands of people's suffering about weight, and am earning my living doing what I have wanted to do ever since I can remember.

A few years ago, the news on TV and in the papers was all about an outstanding athlete named "Magic" Johnson. Johnson, an extraordinary basketball player and a terrific person, had just revealed that he had contracted the HIV virus, responsible for AIDS. Johnson ended his team basketball career in his prime, and declared that he would dedicate his life to helping others prevent AIDS. He could certainly have crawled into a hole, or into a bar, and spent the rest of his life feeling sorry for himself and furious about the untimely end of his career. What he did instead was to interpret the medical situation as meaning that he is to go on to the next part of his life. He intends it to be happy and to be useful to others. AIDS hotlines around the country were besieged with calls from people who had previously thought themselves invincible, who then learned how to protect themselves from exposure to AIDS. They finally realized that if Magic Johnson could become HIV positive, so could they. Johnson started saving lives as soon as he made his announcement. The difference in people's reception of Johnson, when he returned to professional basketball in 1996, indicates how much progress society made in AIDS awareness—due partly to his efforts.

It doesn't matter what the circumstances are. You decide what they will mean. You might as well have them mean something positive. It's completely up to you. Interpret to win. And then do whatever is next in your day.

BREAKDOWNS

Bob Shaw used to say that, after a breakdown, we should interpret, or declare, the opportunity for a breakthrough. In other words, while we may have interpreted some events to mean that things were going very wrong, we could reinterpret them to mean that success could be just around the corner. This is not to say that we will always get exactly the *things* that we want, like a red Porsche or a million dollars. But we can always get the *qualities* we want, like freedom or security. If, for example, you've just had your hundredth fight with your mate, who beat you up again, you may not get that mate to become nonviolent. But you can use that fight as the next step in having a happy relationship with a partner who cherishes you, and whom you may or may not have met yet. If, however, you just interpreted the fight as meaning that you will never have a cherishing mate, that is likely to become the truth. The breakdown in your relationship with the violent mate can be exactly what you need to decide never again to be in an abusive relationship. You can both get counseling, or you can move out, get an order of protection, take care of whatever in you led you to a violent mate, and then weed out future bullies, so that your life can become filled with people who cherish you. In that case, that hundredth fight would have provided the opportunity for your breakthrough into new kinds of relationships.

In his autobiography, Lee Iacocca discussed getting fired from Ford Motor Company:

> They say that the bigger you are, the harder you fall. Well, I fell a great distance that week. I instantly identified with every person I had ever fired.
>
> When I moved to Chrysler a few months later, I had to lay off hundreds of executives in order to keep the company alive. I tried my best to do it with some degree of sensitivity. For the first time in my life, I learned how terrible it felt to be let go.[1]

Iacocca, a consummate automobile company executive, instantly used the breakdown—getting fired—to open up new ways of being a better executive, by being more sensitive to his employees.

Breakdowns only occur after you aim. In other words, if you don't have a direction, you are not likely to think anything is going wrong. You could be like Oscar Madison of "The Odd Couple," a person who doesn't notice or doesn't care about filth and mess in his house. It's not until after you decide you want a clean house that you are likely to notice the mess. In fact, the mess is likely to be *exactly* the next thing you notice after deciding to live in a clean house. Noticing all the dirt may seem enormously discouraging—in fact, worse than you ever thought it could be. Does the mess mean that you can't live in a clean house? Only if you say so. If you declare the mess means the opportunity for a breakthrough (a clean house), then the next thing you do can be the first bit of cleaning.

Frequently, after my clients and students relearn how to eat in accord with their body hunger, they become distressed to see how much they are overeating. Before they learned hunger signals, however, they might have thought they were eating just fine. So, even though things look worse to them than before, they are eating more appropriately than ever, and/or they are learning what it feels like to overeat or not to overeat.

Progress often doesn't fit our pictures of how we thought it was supposed to look. However, if we define whatever is happening as indicating progress toward our goal, that's exactly what we have created.

MOTIVATION

Sylvia's request, in a recent group, was the source of some reflection for me. The request was one I'd heard before, often expressed as someone's wistful fantasy. "I'd like you to motivate me not to overeat." They don't want to stop overeating; they *want to want* to stop. Typically, Weight Release clients and students start with a great deal of enthusiasm: "You mean I can really eat ANYTHING?!" After a while, the enthusiasm may wane, they're overeating much more of the time—and wishing that something could make them stop overeating—as when they first "started the program." Since they felt so enthusiastic once, they return to the site of the enthusiasm, trying to recapture the magic.

More than once, I've believed I could motivate them sufficiently for them to behave differently. However, I don't know how to do that. I think their wish comes partly from a history of trying and failing at diets. Frequently, we undertake a new project with enthusiasm and high energy. We think the impetus comes from the new project, out there, since the energy and enthusiasm coincided with its beginning. "That diet was great; I lost seven pounds the first week!" The new becomes familiar, something else more important or different enters, we binge, we give up. Eventually we try something else that's new, bringing to it new enthusiasm, high energy, or desperation.

To me, motivation involves prioritizing. What is most important to you? What needs to happen for that to come about? Are you honestly willing to do what it takes to bring about what you say you want? Can you make what you want more important than what you've been used to? New experiences are often uncomfortable at first. What degree of discomfort will you live with, in order to bring about what you say you want? For example, are you willing to get hungry? To eat all by yourself, concentrating on the food and on your body, until it becomes second nature again to only eat for your body's hunger?

We are not too busy for our priorities. We somehow manage to "find the time" for what is most important for us. We may not want to acknowledge just what our priorities have been, however. In the northeastern United States, the generally acceptable priorities for middle-class people have been (1) earning a "good" living, which might include getting a certain kind of education, and (2) everything else. During the 1980s, a "good" living would have meant purchasing (via credit, usually) the flashiest home, car, and gadgets money could buy. Whereas the "best and the brightest" of the college students might have become teachers or social workers in the 1960s, in the 1980s they got MBAs and worked in finance. Those who had different aims felt pressured to conform, to choose the highest paying work regardless of what they really liked. Someone who would have been a gifted teacher became instead a stockbroker. Someone who didn't want to work on Wall Street felt out of place.

In our culture, it has not been acceptable to choose a large body size, regardless of the natural size of one's body. If one chooses not to starve herself, or not to exercise for several hours a day in order to conform to fashion, she is looked upon with contempt or, most benevolently, curiosity. I believe that when people find out—as they do when they work with me—that they can have all the qualities of the life they always wanted, regardless of their body size, they stop prioritizing slenderizing activities. If you, however, want to do "whatever it takes" to have a slimmer body, you can have it—possibly at an extremely high cost. You just have to want it enough to do the work, and to make it a priority.

PRIORITIZING

When I worked at the university counseling center, I taught classes in time management. Most of the students had full-time jobs and fit classes around their jobs. Many had family responsibilities, also. In order to get all of that done, they had to know about prioritizing. You can try this exercise, which we use in my classes, to clarify your priorities and find out how to fit them in your life.

1. List what is important to you. It may be your job, your schooling, your family, your friends, having fun and leisure activities, being physically fit, going to church or temple. It may be your upcoming

wedding, solitude, being healthy, playing with your children, eating, having a clean house, doing your hobby, or other items entirely. The list can be as long as you like.

2. Once you've completed the list, go back over it and put an "A" next to any item which is absolutely essential.

3. Now go over the list again and put a "B" next to any item which is important, but not life-or-death.

4. And now, put a "C" next to any item which you'd like, but is less important than an A or B item.

5. Finally, go through the "A" items and number them in order of importance—the most important being A1, and so on. Then number your "B" items, and then the "C" ones.

6. This is vital: make sure that you do whatever you need to do to accomplish your "A" list, and especially your A1 and A2 items. I recommend arranging your schedule such that you do your "A" items first in your day, before anything can interfere. If, after doing your "A" items, you still have time, start in on your "B" list. And if you still have time and energy, begin on your "C" list.

If getting slimmer is of top priority to you, put it on your "A" list, and don't let anything stop you from whatever you need to do that day that will forward you in having a slimmer body. If it's just something you'd like, however, it belongs on the "C" list. It may be that it's really been a "C" list item up till now. If you only want to get slimmer in order to have something from your "A" list, like the right mate, for example, then right-mate-meeting activities belong on the "A" list, rather than get-slimmer activities.

Prioritizing means that you will choose exercise over, say, a half hour or hour of TV or even of sleep. It means that you will choose to take the time to set up conditions conducive to paying attention to your body signals, like peaceful, quiet mealtimes. It means that you will choose something other than what you've chosen up till now. It will be something that gets taken care of, regardless of circumstances—like brushing your teeth or bathing or getting dressed.

THIS IS YOUR LIFE

Nobody else is in charge of your priorities. This, now, is your life.

It is *YOUR* life. Nobody else's. You can make choices at any moment, regardless of everything you've done up till now. If having a slimmer body is important enough, you can *choose, over and over and over and over and over*, to honor that priority.

If you keep not choosing to make it a priority, you've chosen others instead. There is NOTHING WRONG with a different choice; just recognize your priorities, and don't lie to yourself. How do you recognize your priorities? What is in your life now? If it's a fatter body and a mind full of wishes for a slimmer one, then THAT combination, up till now, has been your priority. Your priorities up till now may not have been leading you toward the life you want. If that's the case, either change your priorities or change your goals. If what you want is to eat anything that your mind says looks appealing, you're not likely to have as slim a body as if you only eat for your stomach hunger. If what you want is to eat anything you want at any time, not exercise, and have a slim, healthy body, then what you want is the equivalent of wanting to swim and not get wet—what Bob Shaw refers to as an "existential dilemma." It's like wanting to have a monogamous mate and play the field, wanting to have children and not have to take care of them, wanting to be a doctor and not study or work hard. Which do you want more? Choose one.

It's fine to want what you want. Own it. Since you're the only you in the entire world, it's only natural that some of what you want may be different from what anyone else wants. You can decide that your preferences are valid and, in fact, that you are a valid human being (and therefore, what you want, who you are, how you look, how you live, etc., are all valid). Just notice if your choices are bringing you what you really want.

WHAT DO YOU REALLY WANT?

When I first started practicing psychotherapy, I used to hear experienced therapists say that what the client said she or he wanted was almost always different from what she or he really wanted. While that puzzled me, I now understand some of what they meant. People often think they ought to want certain things, even if they don't (like wanting to want to eat less); or they want mutually exclusive situations (like wanting to swim and not get wet); or they want something but have decided they have to move toward that in an orderly, step-wise fashion (like wanting to be in charge of a business and thinking they must first work their way up, step by step, through the ranks); or they want an abstraction, and think that having something in particular will get them the abstraction (like wanting to be thin so that they can be happy).

WANTING TO WANT

We have been brainwashed, propagandized, and sold a bill of goods that says thin is better and fat is immoral/bad. We have been trained to view thin, young women and thin, wealthier, and somewhat older men as the most desirable. We have also been socialized to work hard at wealth, slimness, and looking young. Any actions or preferences which point in a different direction from these socially approved paths tend to bring us trouble.

Tracie, a slender, pixie-ish, working mother, came to see me about her daughter, Colleen. Colleen, 12 years old, was built just like her tall, big-boned, heavy-set father. Tracie's mother, whom Tracie resembled, also lived with them, and constantly badgered her daughter to get Colleen slim. Both of them monitored Colleen's every mouthful. Colleen was developing an eating disorder—binge-eating— in response to her home environment. She had begun eating "fattening" foods in secret and to excess. While she wanted to please her mother and grandmother by restricting her eating (she wanted to want to eat less), what she truly wanted was just to be left alone. She didn't want her family, teachers, or classmates to hassle her about food. Although she was a good student, she was failing at making the socially acceptable "choice" to get thin. Fortunately, the damage was not irreparable. After I educated Tracie and Colleen about hunger-related eating, Tracie got herself and her mother out of the Food Police patrol. She began allowing Colleen to choose the foods she really wanted. She was astonished to see Colleen once again eating oranges and leaving unwanted food on her plate. In addition, she and her mother had to learn to accept that Colleen's body type was not petite like theirs.

Invariably, many of my incoming students and clients tell me they want to "get motivated" to stop overeating, restrict what they eat, and thereby get slim. However, they really don't want to change anything about their eating. They know that they are eating past the point where their bodies are satisfied; they just don't want to stop. They know that eating lower-fat foods would allow them to eat more, but they don't want to give up ice cream for ice milk, or potato chips for pretzels. Puritannical cultural messages to the contrary, there is *nothing wrong* with wanting to eat what you want to eat—provided you are willing to accept the consequences (for example, contentment about food, along with a body that is fatter than your natural size, if you always overeat).

When you "want to want" something, your power is absent. You are choosing one thing and refusing to acknowledge that choice. You feel bad about yourself (but not as bad as you fear you'd feel if you actually "gave up" and told everybody to accept you in the body you're in). You feel caught between the socially acceptable requirement and the desires you really have.

If you're in this situation, it's helpful to remember that you are unique. Nobody else can know exactly what is right for you, in all your fullness (your history, your learnings, your troubles and your remedies for coping with those troubles). While your choice may not look right for the rest of society, what you eat and what you weigh is personal—"nobody's business but your own."

"I WANT TO SWIM AND NOT GET WET"

Many people want to continue to do exactly what they've been doing with regard to food, but they want a different outcome. While it's certainly true that many people eat healthfully, exercise faithfully, and are still fatter than our culture has deemed acceptable, many others overeat constantly and get no exercise. They know what is necessary in order to stop overeating; they know that there are all sorts of ways to exercise which can feel good, supposedly. But they "can't find the time" or they "keep forgetting" to make changes. They prefer to dream about how good things will be when they're finally slim, while they continually overeat.

It's certainly understandable that many people who have spent huge amounts of energy, time, and money trying unsuccessfully to diet themselves to slimness would be "burned out" on dieting. I think that's a healthy progression from the diet seesaw. But if you still hold onto the dream of slimness, while you know you're eating more than your body wants, what you're wanting is virtually impossible. You want to do the equivalent of swimming without getting wet. As my friend Iris says, "You can't have your fanny in two places at the same time." While my favorite choice tends to be "both," sometimes you can't have both. When I met Joe, I was visiting on the East Coast temporarily. I had a home, friends, and professional contacts in California, and I loved living in the Bay Area. However, I also came to love Joe. For two years, I tried to choose both: we scrounged as much time and money as possible to visit, phone, write, and even exchange messages by Ham radio. We managed to spend most special occasions together and pined for each other when we were apart. Yet I wouldn't give up my California life, nor he his New York one. Finally, as our relationship was on the brink of disappearing, I decided to move back east. I could no longer choose both. While I have missed California ever since, I know I made the most wonderful choice for us both.

There is great power in choosing. Once you acknowledge what is most important to you, you can consolidate your energies. Those people who give up dieting, while they might not be as slim as they had desired, generally end up feeling happier, more at peace with themselves, more accepting of their bodies, less ashamed, less compelled to please others, less willing to postpone their lives, more tolerant of conflict, and more in control.[2] Many people stop *gaining* weight once they give up dieting. When you don't have to disown part of yourself, you can use all of yourself to further what you really want.

WHAT PEOPLE REALLY WANT

I believe that what most people really want is to be happy, to be loved and to love, to be healthy and productive, to express themselves, to make a contribution to the world. What people often say, though, is that they want to be thin; they want to be stress-free; they want to be into or out of a relationship; they want more money, they want to understand why they do whatever they deem self-destructive; they want to feel better, and they think they have to X, Y, and Z in order to feel that way.

"I want behavior modification to make me over."
"I want to learn why I reach for food."
"I want to learn how to overcome my weight problem so I can feel normal."
"I just want to be thin because I feel if I lose weight, the rest of my life will just fall into place."

When people ask me for "behavior modification," I usually wonder what they're talking about. In the request above, it appears that the person thinks behavior modification is something that can be done on her, like a facelift, to change what is there. Perhaps they have learned the term, "behavior modification," and think it's a form of magic spell. Or if they learn whatever it is, they will then stop overeating. That's behind the second request, to "learn why I reach for food."

Often people are under the misconception that if they can learn why they do something, they will no longer do it. As you saw in Chapter III, we have reasons and purposes for overeating and for being overweight. But knowing why you do or did something does not prevent you from doing it again. Choosing not to do it again, being committed to taking care of whatever "doing it" took care of, but in a different way—these are what enable us not to repeat something. Finding out what works to move you in your desired direction will move you there; focusing on why you couldn't get there will not.

Bob Schwartz noticed that scientists were always studying fat people to find out how to get them thin. So he started studying "naturally thin" people who had normal, healthy relationships with food, in order to find out how to have a normal, healthy relationship with food. If you want to have a happy life, start interviewing people who have happy lives, read about people who have had happy lives—find out what is important and useful to them in having happy lives.

The third request, "I want to learn how to overcome my weight problem so I can feel normal," is another kind of poignant puzzle. It presupposes several things: that one can "overcome" a "weight problem"; that doing so will bring about feeling normal; and that there is a "normal" feeling. As you have read in this book, it is extremely difficult to change one's biologically regulated weight. "Overcoming" one's natural weight requires either dedicated and persistent undereating or dedicated and persistent overeating. As we have also discussed, our culture has a weight problem—in other words, culturally, almost everyone is considered or considers herself fatter than they should be, and those who are "too fat" are judged bad, wrong, slovenly, immoral, weak, and unhealthy. Certainly we can begin to tackle our cultural weight problem, through such means as education, advocacy for the rights of people of all sizes, dispelling myths about weight, health, and diets, and so on. This book and this writer are aiming to do just that. But that isn't the most direct route for that person to "feel normal." First of all, what is "normal?" Do normal people always feel like they fit in? Are normal people happy? What, specifically, does that person consider desirable about normalcy? Once we know that, we can aim for what she really wants.

"If I lose weight the rest of my life will just fall into place." The $33-billion-a-year diet industry wants us to believe exactly this: losing weight will bring us heaven-on-earth. We will be happy, healthy, beautiful, beloved, young, rich, and popular if we can just get rid of our ugly fat. But think about it: do you know anyone who is thin and also old, poor, unloved, unhappy, ugly, or unpopular? Or fat and also happy, healthy, beautiful, beloved, young, rich, or popular? Even though the evidence is right before our eyes, we have been propagandized into thinking that thinness is the means to the life we always wanted. The enormous damage this does to both those who cannot get thin—or those who get thin and find out they are still unfulfilled—is only offset by the wealth collected by the diet promoters, which is why we keep seeing this nonsense plastered all over the television, magazines, newspapers, and radio programs. Capitalism breeds hype. Surround us with enough suggestions, and we begin to believe the ads, which sell products and diet programs. You don't first have to lose weight to have your life "fall into place." You don't first have to *anything*.

What would it look like for your life to be "in place"? How would you feel? What would people say about you? What would it be like to wake up in the morning with your life in place? If you think you would no longer have stresses, guess again. If you think you would no longer have to deal with bills, traffic, aches and pains, sorrow and loss, guess again. What if the way your life is now, is the way it looks when it's working?

When Joe was really ill, all I wanted was for us to have our cozy life again. Even though I learned and grew in ways inconceivable to me during happier times, I was willing to give that all up for the bliss of our happy life together. Then he got well, and eventually I was able to sleep through the night again, and make plans for next weekend, and concentrate on my work, etc. And I realized that I am living in my version of heaven on earth, and guess what? I still have to go to the dentist, and sometimes I wish Joe were in China instead of in the next room, and my back hurts, and the roof needs to be fixed at an exorbitant cost. After I lost 40 pounds, my knee still cracked going down stairs, and I was still 37 years old—not 17, as I was in my fantasies.

People think that if they can just get the right combination of external circumstances, they will have what they always wanted. Elizabeth Taylor's second career was to search for the right husband. Leona Helmsley never had enough money. Chances are you have found out that there is not enough chocolate, or beer, or whatever substance in the whole world to bring you happiness, relief, and fulfillment. Ironically, the Duchess of Windsor was right: you can never be too rich or too thin. Wealth and slenderness do not bring what we really want. They only offer wealth and slenderness. All you need to do in order to find that out is to either get thin or rich, or study enough thin or rich people. The good news is, we can have what we really want. If we want happiness, or security, or love, or health, or fulfillment—whatever abstract qualities we think we need to get via material things or people—we can get those qualities. Not by getting the things or people. But *by bringing those qualities to our daily experience*. How do you do this? By living with certain open questions.

Try this: Ask yourself what you really want for yourself from your life. If you come up with any particular items involving things or people (such as a rich husband, a house in the country, a size-six body, ten million dollars, a clean bill of health, etc.), then ask yourself what you would want from having those things or people in your life. Keep working on your items until your list narrows down to abstractions such as fulfillment, happiness, freedom, and so on. Those abstractions are what you really want. I promise you. If you have been trying to get them through getting the particular items, you have been taking the long route and may not get them at all.

Now, for each abstraction on your list, open a question to live with in your daily life. For example, if you wanted ten million dollars so that you could feel secure and also be free to spend your time in the most fulfilling ways, then your questions would be, "How can I bring security to my life today?" "How can I spend my time in the most fulfilling ways, today, given what I have to do today?" Don't assume that you first have to get rid of anything about your daily life. Include it. So, actually, the full question would be, "Given what I have to do and who is in my life today, how can I bring security to my life today?" or "Given what I have to do and who is in my life today, how can I spend my time in the most fulfilling ways?" By asking these sorts of questions, you can start to eliminate what you don't have to do and who you don't have to be with. And you can be living with the experiences of security and fulfillment. Mother Teresa is a wealthy woman. Magic Johnson is a healthy man. Victor Frankl, the Holocaust survivor, was a free man. Never mind their external circumstances. They didn't.

The quality of your life has nothing to do with your body size or shape, the size of your wallet, or virtually any other external circumstances. The quality of your life is up to you. What do you really want for yourself?

1. Is changing your body size your top priority? If so, toward what goals? How else could you reach those goals?
2. If weight loss is important, how willing are you to make major changes in your life, and to work at weight loss as a top priority project?

1. Iacocca, Lee, with Novak, William. *Iacocca*. Toronto, New York, London: Bantam Books, 1986, p. 136.
2. See "Is Giving Up on Dieting Giving Up on Yourself?" by Debby Burgard, Ph.D., in *Radiance*, Fall 1991.

VIII
TO RECOGNIZE YOU ARE ON TRACK, RECOGNIZE WHO YOU ARE

How many times have you awakened feeling fine, only to weigh yourself and have the number on the scale, higher than you'd hoped, ruin your day? (Or, occasionally, have an unexpectedly lower number make your day?) Nearly everyone I've talked with about weight problems has had this experience. We give the number on the scale the power to determine our lives, as if the sum on the scale is the sum of our lives. Some people seem to feel that they're measured by their clothing size. Granted that our culture currently values smaller sizes, how is it that, along with diminishing their weight and their clothing size, so many people narrow their self-definition to a particular number? Is that all we are? While advertising has led us to define ourselves by our outward appearance (and equated our salvation with our buying particular products or services), we are much, much greater than that.

One indication of mental health, strength, and adaptability is the number of different roles by which one can define oneself. How many ways can you define yourself? For one, you are a reader if you're reading this now. You are a daughter or son, and perhaps a parent, sibling, or spouse. You may be occupied as a student, or employed. You may be a driver or a pedestrian, a Republican or Democrat, a charity volunteer, athlete, artist, cook, musician, tinker, tailor, soldier, spy. You are a theist, agnostic, or atheist. You are probably a friend. You are someone who learns, and you are a survivor. As we saw in Chapter VI, you are also, and most powerfully, the interpreter of your experiences.

You may not have any idea of your inherent worth. One way that people narrow their self-definitions is through having been abused. Perhaps you were raised in an abusive home. You may have absorbed a message that people and their bodies exist in order to be abused. You may have assumed the abuse meant something bad about who you are, rather than that you were just young and living there. You may have done terrible or desperate things to others, or to yourself, in order to survive—or just because you haven't known any other way.

Regardless of what you or others did, you are worth cleaning up the messes you may have made. Perhaps because alcoholics tend to make considerable messes during their drinking careers, Alcoholics Anonymous devotes much of its program to assisting its members in cleaning up their lives. Other "Twelve-Step" programs—generally, those with "anonymous" in the title—follow similar guidelines. The guidelines involve making a "searching and fearless moral inventory" of oneself, making a list of all persons one has harmed, and making direct amends to them whenever possible, unless doing so would harm them or others. This may seem overwhelming; however, the Twelve-Step programs recommend relying on God's help. As the song "Amazing Grace" reminds us, God's grace has saved many a "wretch." If you don't believe in God, assume that Nature has put you on earth for a purpose. I assume that a million years of evolution indicate the usefulness of every living thing. You weren't put here by accident. You *can* feel and be worthwhile. If you do the work required to connect with your worth, you will be rewarded more than you can imagine; more, even, than if you were a permanent size six who could eat everything she wanted.

JUDGMENTS

Nearly everyone makes judgments constantly. Some of them are useful for our survival—for example, judging whether someone looks threatening; judging what to wear or how slowly to drive when the weather outside is frightful; judging whether it's time to see a doctor or go to the hospital. Some judgments are vestigial, like those from our peanut gallery (see Chapter V). Like the peanut gallery, many of our judgments are messages from the outside world which we have internalized. "I'm too fat" is one such judgment. What is meant by "too fat" has changed considerably during this century. In some societies, there is no such thing as too fat; fatter is judged to be better. However, phrases such as "too much" and "not enough" are judgment-related phrases.

People are accustomed to responding to their judgments, often without questioning them. This is a useful strategy when one must think and act quickly, as in a survival situation. With regard to eating and weight problems, however, it is more useful to do something a bit different:

1. Notice that you have been judging.

2. Notice what the judgments say.

3. If a judgment has immediate survival value (for example: "Do not eat any of that chicken; it is spoiled."), heed it quickly.

4. If the judgment(s) do not have immediate survival value (for example, "You look like a blimp."), thank your judgments for "sharing" with you, and just go on with your day.

If a judgment keeps coming up, it can provide an opportunity for healing. For example, if you keep telling yourself, "I'm fat and ugly," you can:

1. Notice whose voice(s) are saying that statement to you. Is it yourself? Your mother or father? Other relatives or friends? Television, magazines, movies? Doctors? Books? Diet programs? Remember, diet programs and advertisements have a financial interest in your being discontented with yourself. Unfortunately, so do

some doctors—even those with impressive titles who may be on weight-related governmental committees. Other people may have self-interest, such as wanting to make sure you will feel too bad about yourself to leave them (the situation in some marriages, for example). And most will be products of our culture, with its gigantic weight problem.

2. Notice that the judgment has linked two descriptions that may not have anything to do with each other. Fat does not equal ugly unless you agree that it does.

3. Remember that you are an *original*. You look like the one and only you. Judgments often pit you against some standard which, if you took the time to think about it, has nothing to do with you. You may be too fat to be Miss America, but just right as a mom with a cuddly body. Or "ugly" by *Playboy* bunny standards, but the person with the most beautiful eyes, voice, or soul of anyone around. Many FA's (NAAFA's term for people who prefer fat partners) have commented that they find *Playboy* bunnies and Miss America contestants totally unappealing, preferring someone with much larger dimensions. I have heard dark-skinned people comment that blondes look pale, weak, and sickly. Beauty standards keep changing, and differ from one country to the next and one era to the next. Remember that Lillian Russell, a great beauty 100 years ago, weighed 200-plus pounds. The point is, you are incomparable since you are unique.

4. If you are fat, then judging yourself as fat means you are describing one of your physical characteristics. You may also be short or tall, flat-footed, brown-eyed, or conservatively dressed. If judging yourself as fat makes you cringe, you are a product of our culture—but you can recover. Keep this book handy.

5. You may be using Weightspeak. You may, for example, be feeling depressed or angry about something, but translating that into "I'm fat and ugly." My friend Iris is a beautiful woman, and has been ever since I first met her in college. When we got together one night, she said, "I'm too old, too fat, I have wrinkles, my body is scarred, I have

witchy hair, and no clothes." She continued on with several more judgments, and told me she'd spent the afternoon dumping on herself. What was actually going on was some self-doubt connected with her having begun to date an extremely appealing man (who, by the way, was enormously attracted to her). Everybody has bad days. You don't have to take them (or most judgments) seriously. And sometimes, it's easier just to go to bed early and wake up to a new day.

JUDGING BINGEING

Along with making judgments about your weight, you may have made judgments about bingeing. Typically, dieters yield to a binge, often late at night when their defenses are weakened. They follow the binge with truckloads of recriminations: "I must be crazy. I spent the last three weeks starving so that I would be thin for the reunion/wedding/party, and blew everything last night," "What's wrong with me? I can't even do a simple thing like control my appetite. I'm disgustingly weak," "I must really need a shrink. There I go, sabotaging myself again. Why don't I want to be thin?"

Just as people sometimes overpsychologize fatness, they also overpsychologize bingeing. Bingeing, first and foremost, is a biological response, a *survival mechanism*, designed to keep us from starving to death. Calorie-reducing diets are interpreted by the body as starvation, which is why becoming obsessed with food or certain foods occurs in response to dieting. In a well-known experiment on the effects of human starvation[1], which was done on healthy conscientious objectors to World War II, Ancel Keys found that the people who had undergone a six-month reduced-calorie diet were insatiable, following the diet, until they returned to their natural body weights.

Bingeing is also a psychobiological response to deprivation. Geneen Roth says, "Bingeing, as a 'last stand against deprivation' is the voice of a self that will not tolerate, not for another minute, the denial of all that *it* thinks is necessary and that *you* think is indulgent."[2] Likening being on a diet to being in jail, Leonard and Lillian Pearson describe bingeing this way: "[W]hen you have the feeling that tomorrow the jailers will be back in power, maybe forever after, the binge becomes a necessity for emotional survival. No human being can live with so bleak a prospect as never again being allowed to do (or eat) what he wants. In this way the binging does have psychological value—it is an assertion of basic rights and a rejection of enslavement."[3]

Like many obsessions and compulsions, repetitive bingeing serves as a screen between the binger and anxiety. For example, we may be unhappy; we translate that into feeling unhappy because we are not thin enough, which we would be if only we could stop bingeing. We may get anxious because someone we love just got hit by a car or a serious disease; we may "eat over it"—overeat or binge to feel better—and then yell at ourselves for having overeaten. If we focus on our bingeing problem, regret the last instances of it, vow never to repeat it, feel guilty about other failed attempts to resist it, fantasize about and plan the next binge, etc., we can distract ourselves from other pressing problems, and start to imagine that all our problems will be solved once we are binge-free. Of course, since bingeing is frequently a response to anxiety, we will soon be ready to binge again, since life does not come anxiety-free. Yet, like weight-loss fantasies, binge-freedom fantasies give us an illusion of control, an illusion that the only thing we have not *yet* controlled, our eating or weight, will soon be solved. An illusion that life will be perfect, if only this problem is handled.

As Roth points out, bingeing is also what she calls a "plunge into oblivion." It is a way to get out of oneself for a brief period of time, a respite from daily cares. For the time when one is eating—and also if one follows bingeing by sleeping—one is in an altered state of consciousness. Roth and I recommend that each person "plunge into oblivion" each day. Everyone needs time off. And if we don't give it to ourselves one way, we will give it to ourselves some other way. I have heard from many people that they overeat to take time off because just dallying is not legitimate, but nourishing oneself with food (regardless of how much!) is a valid reason for not rushing to the next activity. Over the years, my students, clients, and I have come up with the following list of favorite oblivions. I recommend them to you in case you cannot think of any that don't involve food. If you have others, I would appreciate your sending them to me (care of the publisher) to add to the list.

FAVORITE OBLIVIONS

Driving	Going to a museum	Puzzles
Slow dancing	Bathing by candlelight	Reading
Working out	Sunbathing	Swimming
Walking	Daydreaming	Sleeping
Good sex	Keying in on the computer	Music
Shopping	Watching running water	Cleaning
Window shopping	Sewing	Crying
Flowers	Art	Television
Movies	Magazines	Books
Stargazing	Watching a sunset	Pets

and "leaning on the washing machine, watching the clothes spin in the dryer."

You may look at the list, say "That's nice," and continue on with your day. Caution: If bingeing is a problem for you, it's important that you grant yourself oblivion time. There is a part of you which keeps score. It's possible, and indeed necessary at times, to delay gratification. But if you do not give yourself goodies in the form of free time and TLC, you will find yourself at the bottom of a king-size bag of cookies, emerging guiltily from another plunge into oblivion.

You may have noticed that bingeing is not just a bad, self-destructive, insane activity conducted by someone demented. However, if all you had done was to binge and then judge bingeing and yourself negatively, you would not have gotten what bingeing offers: the richness available to you to better balance your life. In fact, you would probably be at least twice as miserable, which would probably lead you more quickly to the next binge. Be willing to give yourself the benefit of the doubt. Assume that bingeing has been a way you have tried to take care of yourself. Then find out how *else* to take care of yourself around whatever needs the bingeing was trying to handle. If bingeing has become a ritual or a habit, create new rituals and new habits. For example, my sister-in-law makes herself a big pot of tea to get through rough times. I have a fabulous pair of sheepskin-lined, rubber-soled slippers that seem to caress my feet and say, "There, there." I love kicking off my shoes and easing my feet into those slippers; to me, they signify that I can now get comfortable.

For some people who regularly and desperately binge, psychotherapy and possibly medication can resolve the imbalances which led to the bingeing. Listen to yourself with love and compassion, and act accordingly.

THE BENEFIT OF THE DOUBT

You probably don't give yourself enough mercy. Most people with weight problems, and/or fat people, have spent too long feeling bad, wrong, and guilty for eating the way they do and having the bodies they have. Many have been berated, insulted, or worse. Remember, you are an original. You have tried to do the best you could, given how you thought you and the world were. For example, if you had known 15 diets ago that diets fail, chances are you would be thinner and richer now than you are. But you didn't know, and going on and off 15 diets was doing the best you could.

If there is something you have really been wanting (let's call it Point B), but it seems like you can't manage to get there no matter how hard you try, perhaps what you have been doing is ineffectual, given what you want. Or perhaps it needs more time. It does not necessarily indicate that you are self-destructive or have "unconscious resistances" to getting to Point B. I think sometimes that people or therapists make up reasons why they (or their psychotherapy clients) must secretly hate or defeat themselves (e.g., "unconscious resistance" or "blocks"), because they don't know how to explain why they're not yet at Point B. That's like assuming every fat person is mentally ill. It's what happens when you try to fit an original into a mold. Many people still assume fat people are not thin because they are mentally ill—never mind heredity or the failure of diets. *Some* people, *sometimes*, are even more afraid of getting what they want than they are eager for fulfillment, and *some* people *sometimes* don't know *how* to get what they want. Not everyone. Be truthful with yourself, and think positively. And, perhaps, find yourself a good therapist to help you get what you want.

Here is a power question for you to consider: **What if this were exactly how you and your life were supposed to look right now, if you were doing the best you could?** Your path in life is different from every other person's in the whole world. Consider that your life looks the way it does *while* you are going as fast as you possibly can toward where you have been wanting to go.

You are a rainbow of qualities and abilities. Which abilities and qualities become evident depends on what is evoked in you. You have probably noticed that you like yourself much more around certain people than around others. Different people evoke different aspects of ourselves. Advertisers often evoke our insecurities, so that they can sell us products and services. Around the best therapists, what is evoked in people is their ability to heal, learn, and grow. Other people evoke the worst in us.

When I work with people, I aim toward the best in them. I look for their strength, ingenuity, intelligence, creativity, adaptability, lovability. I assume that there are good, solid, survival-based reasons behind people's (sometimes astonishing) actions and thoughts, and what happens in class or in therapy is that those strengths and reasons come up. Then people have the opportunity and the strength to make corrections, and the freedom to act in new ways.

When I first started doing therapy, I was pathology-oriented. I stayed away from choosing anyone as my own therapist who was "analytically oriented," because I didn't want someone to tell me that even more was wrong with me and my subconscious mind than I'd suspected. Yet the work I did on other people was pathology-oriented. I had learned how to diagnose various forms of mental illness by putting together symptoms. I would ask myself the equivalent of "What's wrong with this picture?" Then I would find all the wrong things and come up with the proper label. Then therapy consisted in fixing as many wrong things as possible, according to what the label prescribed. Knowing what I know now, I am surprised that people got better—or that they even stayed in therapy.

What I learned since then—which, thankfully, increasing numbers of "solution-oriented" therapists like me have been learning—is that we should aim toward what's working, not what's broken. When you can see bingeing as an attempt to remedy anxiety that might otherwise feel unbearable, you can recognize bingeing's positive intentions. And then seek what would best fit those intentions, now.

WHAT FITS NOW?

Just as trying to fit yourself into a mold does not work because you are an original, so, too, other people's solutions many not fit for you. Being a member of society means that we are given guidelines about how to be part of society—for example, stop at red lights, do not kill or harm anybody except in self defense, get married, raise children, have a job, pay taxes, and be thin. We are led to believe that having the right size body, the right income level, a spouse and 2.2 children and a house will make us happy, and most of us spend our lives trying to get these things in order to get happy and fulfilled. But not everybody can or should be thin, or married, or a parent. Conformity does not produce satisfaction for everybody, or every body. Because you are an original, you are the primary authority on what you need. You may think you need what "everyone else" has. But you might find that getting whatever it is does not bring you what you hoped for.

If you were invited to a party, what would you wear? Unless you wanted to shock people, you would not wear a tuxedo to a football tailgate party or a bathing suit to a black-tie affair. You would look in your closet and assess what would be appropriate to the situation and your goals. If you wanted to get people's attention, you might wear unusual clothing; if you wanted to "fit in," you would probably dress similarly to how you would expect others to dress. If you did not have what was appropriate to the situation and your goals, you would go outside your house to find something that fit, or you would create a new ensemble.

Other people's solutions may not satisfy you; you may also outgrow your own, earlier solutions. Nell always thought she wanted a corporate career. She majored in business in college, and then worked in several corporate jobs. Then the big recession hit, and corporations started laying off thousands of employees. Corporate careers were no longer assured. Furthermore, her work did not satisfy her. Her secret dream had always been to work in broadcasting. It took a lot of courage to venture out from what had been secure, and start all over as a volunteer in a local radio station. But Nell started making new friends, found she was more interesting to people she met, and began fitting her life to the person she had become. Many people go through a "midlife crisis" when they reexamine what they had always thought they should be and do, and emerge with different marital and occupational status. This midlife crisis is the equivalent of finding out that their life no longer fits; the best way to handle it is to find out what fits *now*. At any moment in your life, you can ask yourself the power question, **"What fits now?"**

ALL OF YOU

In my experience, much of what gets people into trouble is their being ashamed or otherwise unwilling to acknowledge and own parts of themselves they find unacceptable. Certain parts are acceptable, socially approved, politically correct. Certain parts are not. Everyone has socially unapproved aspects. I am generally a polite, thoughtful person, but sometimes I am totally selfish, greedy, and mean-spirited. And I cuss like a sailor behind the wheel of a car.

Virginia Satir taught me about all of me. She had devised a technique called a "parts party." At the beginning of a parts party, the "host" (the patient or person being worked with) lists 6-10 people, preferably public figures past and present, who attract or repel her. What they represent to the host is also mentioned. Volunteers then role-play each of these people, with guidance from the therapist. In the parts parties I have seen, typical public figures have included Hitler, Buddha, Jesus, Einstein, Marilyn Monroe. The different parts/role players then meet and interact, then try to dominate the party, and then learn how to interact so that each can be integrated and of most benefit to the host. I learned how even aspects of a person which seem repugnant have value in certain situations. While anger, for example, may alienate some people from you, it also can mobilize you to act on your behalf. Dishonesty may not win you a clear conscience, but it may allow you to spare yourself or someone else from embarrassment. Embarrassment may feel crummy, but it also can allow others to identify with and sympathize with you. Power question: **If everything had some kind of value, how could you best use *anything* that came up in your life?**

I recommend spending a day adopting the point of view that everything that occurs in your life can offer you something of value. Then going about your day seeking the value in each experience. What you are likely to find is that you have an unusually large amount of valuable experiences during that day. I don't mean to suggest that things won't hurt or bother you, just that regardless of what happens, it will be useful to you.

Some years ago I started studying a phenomenon I noticed in therapy. It seemed that there were some people whose lives changed greatly, and for the better, when we worked together. Other people seemed to spend a lot of time in therapy and without anything improving, even when I tried my best stuff with them. I wondered why. Was my approach so drastically different from client to client? Was there anything similar about those who got the most value? It began to appear to me that those who got the most value shared some similar attitudes, namely:

1. They assumed that they would get value from each session (and indeed, from whatever occurred in their lives);

2. They assumed that their lives would change for the better, as a result of our efforts;

3. They assumed that they would and could learn from anything that happened.

I started coaching my new students to adopt these attitudes. Many of them had life-changing experiences (for example, an alcoholic stopped drinking; other people became free for the first and final time from food- and weight-related problems which had run their lives; still others found out that they, too, could laugh and dance and have friends). While it's impossible to know what would have happened had they not been so coached, I believe that changing your attitude can totally change your life. You can try similar experiments: seek out the people you know who seem to thrive in their lives and ask them what they believe about life and possibilities. Also, seek out those who seem generally unhappy and unfulfilled, and ask them what they believe about life and possibilities. Are there any common beliefs among the winners? Among the losers? If so, try adopting the winners' beliefs.

My great-aunt Vera, age 92, was born in a Russian village a few months after a pogrom (an organized massacre against Jewish people) decimated the village. Her husband and only child were killed during a bombing raid in World War II. She met her second husband and future stepson (the only Holocaust survivors in their family) as they were escaping from a Siberian prison camp. Now a Medicaid patient in a nursing home, she has made new friends; contributed to others (she spoon-fed one disabled woman at every meal); opened up a whole new arena for self-expression (she spends every morning in the crafts room, weaving fabric out of colorful yarn and making pillows and baskets); and she revels in abundance (she gets an allowance of $20 a month, plus chits that she wins in Bingo games). When I visit her, she begs me to allow her to treat me to lunch. Her worldly goods fit into five drawers and a small closet. She has never had much money in her life, and she has had a great deal of pain, but she has always been rich.

WHAT ARE YOU WILLING TO PAY FOR WHAT YOU SAY YOU WANT?

Psychiatrist Bob Shaw once mentioned that the patients he saw came to him in search of abstractions such as happiness or fulfillment. As we saw in Chapter VII, many people want certain things because they think those things will make them happy or fulfilled—whether the things are objects, people, or positions. Sometimes the things are what we have been told or taught to want (a slim body, a high income, a college education, a home and family). Sometimes they are what someone whom we emulate has or does (the boss's car; our best friend's career). Moving from eating and food to the rest of your life, asking yourself "What fits now?" and "What is delicious?" are the best ways to find out what you really want.

Asking yourself these questions may bring you in conflict with what you always thought you wanted, though. I always thought I wanted to marry a doctor like my father. Joe wasn't a doctor. At a crucial point in our relationship, I had to decide whether the top item on my "wish list" was more important than Joe. I'm glad I chose Joe; I've since noticed that most doctors are married to their professions at least as much as they are married to their spouses, while I like the attention Joe gives to me and our relationship. Wanting to be a doctor's wife fit my youthful ambitions, but not those of my adulthood.

Our choices have costs and benefits. Were I to have married a doctor, I would have had certain status, and most likely a better income, a nicer house, car, and clothes. I also would probably have spent most of my time supporting his career, rather than mine; I would have had more time to myself instead of with my husband. If I wanted a size-six figure, I would be spending my time exercising almost all day long, and would have to watch like a hawk everything I ate. I would probably have a closet full of exquisite, small clothes, and probably a career focused on exercise. I might or might not feel good about my body. Would the benefits be worth the costs?

What would it cost you to have the body size you always thought you wanted? What would you get if you had it? I think that if my career were in modeling, television, or movies, the size of my body would be more important, and I would be willing to "pay" more. When I was at my slimmest adult weight, I had to ask myself what meant the most to me. I could continue spending three hours a day exercising, which was fun, or I could put more of that time into my therapy career—or, for that matter, into different hobbies or work. I chose what was most fulfilling—lessening people's suffering about weight.

I frequently see clients or students who say they want to be thinner. Much less frequently, I see clients and students who actually do the work necessary to get those bodies. It's very simple to shift how and what you eat to what your body calls for; it's pretty difficult to change habits. It usually requires hard work, dedication, attention, commitment. And if your body wants you to be a size 20, and you want it to be a size six, you will have to make size-six your career. Is it worth it to you? Will paying for your size-six body with almost all of your time and energy provide you with the rewards you want?

If you were a size eight whose high-paying modeling career

required a size-six body, it might not cost you so much, and the benefits might be worth your investment. But if you've been seeking a smaller body size because you thought that would make your life whole, you're probably on the wrong track. The way to make your life whole is to find out what abstractions (for example, love, health, happiness) the whole life consists of—for you, not anybody else, and then bringing those abstractions to your experience. And checking all the time for deliciousness and timeliness.

If you find that it costs you too much to pursue a thin-enough body, then make peace with having a heavier body. Remind yourself that you're an original, and go about living your life authentically, in the body *you* have, with the choices *you* have chosen. Make room for you to be yourself and to have your body. Evaluate the costs and benefits, and make peace with your choices.

WHAT DO YOU WANT YOUR LIFE TO BE FILLED WITH?

We have been given the gift of time on earth. The time is limited. How do you want to spend the time of your life? I want to spend as little of it as possible in self-recrimination, blame, guilt, hatred, envy, inadequacy. Those are not usually delicious ways for me to spend my time. Delicious ways for me to spend my time are with people I love and like and admire, doing fulfilling work, supporting my physical and mental health, and having as much fun as I possibly can. As I have shifted more and more of my life into "wants" from "shoulds," I have had less tolerance for aspects that don't fit. I almost never wear clothes that hurt, eat nondelicious food, spend time with nondelicious people. I have become very choosy and I like it that way. God or fate, at any moment, could take away my health, my husband, my home. But I will have had a life of abundant riches to remember. For some part of my life, it will have been complete. I never married the doctor, or had the children I had always expected to have. I never was a size six or lived by the sea. But I have had everything I have really wanted.

Beyond food, water, air, and shelter (human needs), what people really want are the abstractions. If you think about it enough, they are available to you regardless of your circumstances. Given that your time on earth is limited, perhaps much more than you think, **what do you want your life to be filled with?** Given your responsibilities, if you had permission to have the most possible peace, fun, and fulfillment, how could you arrange for those? Since you are an original, I invite you to find your own, unique answers.

1. What are the abstractions you want for yourself?
2. What are you willing to pay for what you say you want?

1. Keys, A., op. cit.
2. Roth, Geneen, *Breaking Free From Compulsive Eating*. Indianapolis/New York: The Bobbs-Merrill Co., Inc., 1984, p. 69.
3. Pearson and Pearson, op.cit., p. 24.

IX
EVEN YOU ARE OKAY

(If you want to feel worth your weight at any weight, read this chapter.)

"I've been so depressed that I've barely gotten anything done this week," said Nancy despairingly. "I need a good kick to get myself going." While Nancy was certainly not unique in her thinking, she was taking the long route to where she wanted to go. Many people think that "a good kick in the pants" will move them faster toward their goals. Indeed, certain people might benefit from such treatment—people who are not telling the truth to themselves or others, such as active addicts or pathological liars. However, most people with weight or eating problems tend to go overboard on self-criticism, and adding more will not get them what they want. Hirschmann and Munter consider binge-eating a "soothing disorder." If someone overeats to be soothed, and then yells at herself, she just adds to a vicious cycle. Generally, someone who has a problem about eating or weight has been agreeing with others in our fat-phobic culture, and treating herself too harshly already. And as we have seen, people using Weightspeak may declare themselves too fat—regardless of their weight—when they feel undeserving and bad.

FEELING NOT OK

Very, very few people consider themselves good enough, whatever that is, and deserving of a great life. Because of our cultural negativity about weight, many people assume they are unworthy because they are "too fat," regardless of their size. There is a phenomenon called "internalized oppression," in which people belonging to a stigmatized group start believing that they deserve the stigma, and blame themselves for being rejected. This is evident with fat people, children of abusive parents, or abused spouses, among other groups. However, people who do not belong to a stigmatized group may also feel that they are just not worthy enough people. Some people feel that luck, fate, or God is really against them, and they cannot possibly have the life they want. Others feel so guilty about real or imagined harm they have perpetrated, that they don't feel they deserve happiness or success; while those raised in homes where parental talk or actions were harsh or abusive, like Nancy, assume the abuse meant that they were unworthy. However, *feeling unworthy is a function of having been a helpless infant. Period.* People *start out* by feeling unworthy, and then find reasons to explain why they feel that way! Says psychiatrist Thomas Harris in *I'm OK—You're OK:*

> Since the little person has no vocabulary during the most critical of his early experiences, most of his reactions are *feelings*. We must keep in mind his situation in these early years. He is small, he is dependent, he is inept, he is clumsy, he has no words with which to construct meanings...A sour look turned in his direction can only produce feelings that add to his reservoir of negative data about himself. *It's my fault. Again. Always is. Ever will be. World without end.*
>
> During this time of helplessness there are an infinite number of total and uncompromising demands on the child. On the one hand, he has the urges (genetic recordings) to empty his bowels ad lib., to explore, to know, to crush and to bang, to express feelings, and to experience all of the pleasant sensations associated with movement and discovery. On the other hand, there is the constant demand from the environment, essentially the parents, that he give up these basic satisfactions for the reward of parental approval. This approval,

> which can disappear as fast as it appears, is an unfathomable mystery to the child, who has not yet made any certain connection between cause and effect....
>
> It is the *situation of childhood* and *not* the intention of parents which produces the problem...When the children of "good" parents carry the NOT OK burden, one can begin to appreciate the load carried by children whose parents are guilty of gross neglect, abuse, and cruelty.[1]

MASKS

People handle feeling not OK with differing coping styles. Many fat people or people with weight problems think that they have to be agreeable or jolly, regardless of their inner feelings. They are living in a way that apologizes for their existence, for their taking up too much space or not conforming to a cultural dictate about appearance. Many other people seek the trappings of success in an attempt to feel okay or fool other people into thinking they are more worthwhile than they secretly believe they are. I know people at the top of their professions, with very high incomes, fancy houses and cars and clothes—and sometimes a long succession of lovers or spouses—who feel empty inside. On top of that, they feel desperate because they have achieved what society told them meant success, and *still* feel bad. I think that is why Marin County, California, had such a high suicide rate (as described in Chapter I). Huge numbers of people settle for unsatisfying relationships, occupations, and daily experiences, because they assume they are not worth having what they really want, for whatever reasons. Other huge numbers of people drug themselves in various ways, including with food, in order to numb this internal pain. Still others mistreat and harm themselves, and the people around them, again as an expression of how bad they feel inside.

Many people develop a mask for themselves. This mask is what they present to the external world, to cover up the crummy person they believe lurks underneath. People assume that they are the crummy person underneath the mask. *Underneath* the crummy person inside, however, is a being so magnificent that the mask couldn't even approach it, no matter how well put-together the mask. Imagine being better than you can imagine! I realize now that those healers who have most powerfully affected my life and learning are those who somehow have interacted with that most magnificent being. Some might refer to that being as God in every person, or spirit, or love, or grace, or the "still, small voice." Whatever you call it, it is real good news, because if you seek it, it is available. It is the part of you that is bigger than your worries, plans, and history. It is bigger than your mask. It is the part of people that takes over when they are being heroic, and it has nothing to do with egotism.

ACTING AS IF

One technique we therapists sometimes prescribe is "acting as if." In other words, if you wanted to be a dancer, you could act as if you were one, even if you weren't. You might then practice for several hours a day, eat and sleep in ways that supported your dancing, study dance, and so on. Bob Schwartz's "Diets Don't Work" program basically followed that direction: Schwartz studied "naturally thin" people who could eat anything they wanted without worrying about their weight; found out what they had in common, and then started teaching other people to act in similar ways, such as eating only when they were hungry and not eating what they did not want. He started teaching people to act as if they were "naturally thin." Many then became "naturally thin," regardless of their history.

If you are one of the millions of people who are not yet in touch with their own worth, you can nevertheless act as if you were a worthy person. How might a worthy person think and feel about how she spent her time? With whom might she want to spend her time? How would a worthwhile person dress? Eat? Do you know anybody, or have you heard of anybody, who seems to feel worthwhile? If you know anyone who treats herself as worthwhile, interview her. Find out what she thinks and feels about herself, her time, her life and the people in it.

An excellent way to uncover someone whose self-worth is in good shape, is to notice how you feel around different people. You are more likely to feel worthwhile around someone else who feels worthwhile. You may feel more whole, more fully yourself, more able, more forgiving.

People who have status symbols are not necessarily those who feel worthwhile. In fact, they are often people trying—and failing—to feel better, by making their outsides conform to cultural dictates. Speaking of supermodel Kim Alexis (5'10" tall, 138 pounds; married to a hockey star and mother of two sons; host of a television show on parenting), supermodel Carol Alt said, "I've known Kim for 13 years. She has been on every cover there is. She's one of the most beautiful women in the world, and I've never seen anyone with lower self-esteem."[2] By contrast, some of the people I have met with the healthiest self-esteem do not look the way society would imagine. Take Maryann (Chapter I), who was talented, popular, and well respected. Or my friend Tara. Tara works very hard and plays hard. She enjoys a good laugh, a good man, a good time, a job well done. She is committed and compassionate. Part of her work involves innumerable media interviews, which she handles as eloquently and efficiently as she handles the rest of her life. She travels frequently as part of her work, despite the problems that fat people often have to face with transportation sized to smaller people. She is and has several very close friends, and a large social circle. I have always seen her in stylish, colorful, neat clothing with perfectly matched earrings, and carefully styled hair and makeup. She is an extraordinary asset to her employer, whose mission she believes in wholeheartedly. She recently embarked on a well-deserved extended vacation to the South Pacific, in search of new adventures. Her life is as full, round, and rich as her body.

If she can have a life like that, despite being a fat woman in our fat-hating culture, so can you. Keep reading.

BECOMING WORTHWHILE

If you wanted to get in touch with your self-worth, the first thing you would do is to assume you were worthwhile. Many people will have a "Yes, but..." reaction to this assumption. Recognize that the "Yes, but..." reaction comes from the part of you that feels not-worthwhile. Thank that part for sharing, and assume you are worthwhile anyway.

One tool you can use to get more in touch with your worth is to use an affirmation, such as "I am worth it," until your mind replies, "Yup."

Another vital one is to clean up whatever damage you may have done to other people. See Chapter VIII for suggestions on how to do so.

A third, which we will discuss later, is to make a contribution to the world, in whatever way would be most delicious to you.

If you have thought that being too fat meant that you were not worthwhile, remember that that particular bit of nonsense is only a time-limited, location-limited agreement in the part of the world and the part of time that you have been in. Since it is only an agreement, and not a fact, you can make a different agreement. Start with yourself. Agree with yourself that you are worthwhile, at exactly the size you are. Period. And then treat yourself in worthwhile ways, such as those we are about to cover.

WORTHWHILE WAYS

An excellent place for anybody who is fat, or troubled by connecting low self-esteem with too-high weight, is NAAFA (the National Association to Advance Fat Acceptance). Regardless of your weight, if you have hangups about it, you will get an amazing education through NAAFA. Because the primary membership of NAAFA consists of fat people—who have faced intense persecution and have desperately tried not to be fat—NAAFA uncovered many of the myths about weight long before nearly anyone else was aware of them. In fact, Lew Louderback, a fat man married to a fat woman, wrote an article[3] containing the following facts in 1967, prompting Bill Fabrey to create NAAFA in 1969:

- Sexual responsiveness in women is positively and significantly correlated with a general positive attitude toward food and eating.
- Among survivors of heart attacks, fat people live longer than thin ones.
- Fat people have a lower risk of tuberculosis.
- Fat people have a lower suicide rate.
- There are "thin fat people" who suffer physically and emotionally from having dieted to below their natural body weight.
- Eating normally, without dieting, allowed Louderback and his wife to relax, feel physically better, and normalize and stabilize their eating and weight.

- Forced changes in weight are not only likely to be temporary, but also to cause physical and emotional damage.
- Dieting seems to unleash destructive emotional forces.
- The five-year cure rate for obesity is virtually zero.
- It has now become so "in" to be thin that fat people's civil rights are repeatedly and openly violated.
- Fat people are discriminated against in jobs and in education.
- The persecution of fat people is not for health reasons, but aesthetics.

More than 25 years later, the National Institutes of Health and *The New York Times* finally "discovered" many of these same items.

It is important that you *educate yourself* about weight and food, to counteract the myths and prejudice which abound about both. In addition to this book, a number of other good publications are listed in Appendix A. NAAFA also offers an excellent book service to its members, including some volumes which are out of print elsewhere.

You are also likely to get other kinds of education from NAAFA. I did not know that men and women existed who preferred fat partners until I joined NAAFA. Once I heard of FAs (fat admirers—NAAFA's term for people with these preferences), I thought perhaps they were all losers, misfits, or fetishists. While some FAs have fetishes, so do many non-FAs. And as for being misfits, FAs have suffered a lot of persecution themselves. Many relate stories of criticism, pressure, and scorn from family members and friends because of their preferences. Many are still "in the closet" about their preferences, due to such intense social pressure. But many of the FAs I have met are very appealing, healthy people, who are making their own agreements with themselves about what is right for them, and rejoicing in the lushness and abundance of their preferred partners.

I also did not know that people could be fat and healthy, fit, beautiful, sexy, and fulfilled. I thought the propaganda was true, and that fat women could never find husbands or admirers, and could never be healthy or happy. What I learned is that, fat or thin, people who are healthy, fit, sexy, beautiful, and fulfilled do certain things which enable them to maximize these qualities in their lives. The first thing they do is to *assume, or act as if, they are worth having what they seek in their lives*.

FAT AND GORGEOUS

One of the many agreements we have made in late-20th-century America is that fat equals ugly. As we have discussed, you can make a different agreement. Some women who have done so are actresses Mae West, Delta Burke, and Nancy Roberts. Roberts, the sister of actor Tony Roberts, is the daughter of an upwardly mobile, prosperous, show business family. A thin child, she became fat at age six, and started dieting and using diet pills prescribed by a doctor two years later. She could never keep her weight down and, at age 33, after reading *Fat Is a Feminist Issue,* she stopped dieting. She answered an ad for a group of women who wanted to write a play on women and weight, and became part of the Spare Tyre Theatre Company. The company traveled through Great Britain with shows oriented toward weight, and found that people wanted and needed to talk about the impact of the shows. Spare Tyre started and led groups for overeaters. By stopping dieting, Roberts eventually ended her overeating, but her weight remained high. She chose to live her life fully as a fat woman, and eventually wrote her book, *Breaking All the Rules*. Says Roberts:

> We are stereotyped as self-indulgent, lazy, lacking in willpower, and downright ugly. To break through this stereotype, to begin to create positive images of big women must be our goal. The easiest, most direct way of doing this in a society that cares above all about the way we look is through our appearance...So looking good, wearing clothes that we like and feel confident in, is just the beginning. It's the beginning of saying to ourselves and to the world, 'We're OK. We're not going to hide any more. We're going to go out there and grab what the world has to offer. We're entitled to the same choices that smaller women have, not only in respect of our clothes, but ultimately in respect of our lives as well.[4]

Written when fat women had far fewer clothing choices available, *Breaking All the Rules* combines Roberts' personal history with the history of women's shapes; words and pictures from other fat, capable women; exercise, grooming, and wardrobe tips, and recommendations for activism.

As Roberts points out, it takes strength for a fat woman to make a different agreement and define herself as worthy of being beautiful. While many a fat woman has been told she has "such a pretty face," I have found that anybody is beautiful who is lit up from within—in touch with what is important to her, living life fully, being fully herself. And also, we can use makeup, style our hair and, finally, select clothing that expresses our individual style. By being fat and aiming to be as beautiful as we can be, we open up a "fat and beautiful" possibility.

There are more and more books available that include fat women and beauty tips. Remember, we are consumers with buying power. If your hairdresser, or anyone else, disagrees with the possibility of fat and beautiful, take your business elsewhere.

FAT AND FIT

Certain things are common to most attractive people, in addition to their attitude that they are okay. In general, they are physically fit. Being fit does not mean you have to be able to climb mountains or run marathons. It certainly does not mean you must be thin, despite the prejudices of many exercise or fitness "experts." It means that you have the energy to go through your day, even if that entails long hours at the office or carrying a sleeping toddler and the attendant paraphernalia. Fitness requires keeping your body accustomed to some exertion, whether through chores or through other kinds of exercise.

Most fat people of both sexes have been traumatized regarding exercise. They may have been shamed by gym instructors, classmates, siblings, onlookers, parents, or by being unable to find gym clothing in their size. They may have come in last in races and been chosen last for teams. They may have been clumsy and inept, or easily fatigued. As a result of the expectation that one must be slim to be healthy, and the antifat prejudice rife in our culture, many fat people have given up any hope of being able to exercise enjoyably. Many have been given the paradoxical message that they must exercise to lose weight, and that they do not belong among exercisers. Many feel tremendously unsafe around anything smacking of exercise. Understandably. If you have been traumatized and you are a survivor, you are likely to avoid repeating the traumatic experience.

Fortunately, our world is changing for the better. There are more and more exercise options available for larger-sized people. First of all, there is now exercise clothing available in large sizes. Bathing suits can be made to fit any size body. Secondly, there are increasing numbers of exercise videotapes designed for larger bodies. They include yoga, low-impact aerobic dancing, and something called "chair dancing," which provides an aerobic workout and flexibility for people who have difficulty standing through an exercise routine. Finally, there are increasing numbers of exercise classes for heavier people—again, because of sufficient consumer demand.

Have you ever seen a swan walk? Its graceful glide on water becomes a waddle on land. The same animal can look exquisite or silly in its mobility, depending on whether it is in its element or not. A superb element for fat people is water. While fat people may not be built for speed or for gravity-defying motion, we are naturals for water exercise. Water mammals are naturally fat. Fat is buoyant, which gives us a great advantage in the water. Fat is also an insulator, which means that we are less likely to be chilled. It is, finally, nature's way of storing energy. Fat people are perfectly built for long-distance swimming. Even walking in the water provides us wonderful exercise, since the effects of gravity are greatly reduced in the water, while water's resistance strengthens our muscles. NAAFA gatherings often include water exercise classes, and almost always include pool parties. NAAFA water events are so popular because water is a perfect element for fat bodies, and because NAAFA water events are safe from harassing onlookers.

Regarding safety: If you want to find a water exercise class or swimming pool to do laps in, you are more likely to find a range of body sizes and shapes in a YMCA-type setting than in a pricey health club. Also, avoid swimming near adolescent boys, since they tend to be most outspokenly critical of fat people. Swim while they are in school, or in the mornings when they are still asleep. Finally, NAAFA events organizers always seek swimming pools which have steps, not just small ladders. If you are inquiring about a pool, ask also about the steps if it is important to you.

I feel blissful in the water! I feel free and move easily, and since I learned how to breathe correctly, I can swim long distances without tiring. My favorite vacations include water.

Fat people also tend to be sturdy and strong. Look at Sumo wrestlers. It takes strength to haul around whatever poundage we carry. Sports which require strength are good for fat people. Bowling is a good sport, or the shot put, or a tug of war. There have been a lot of very big, strong, heavy football players, such as William "Refrigerator" Perry.

Many fat people are extremely graceful, as was Jackie Gleason. Ballroom and other types of dancing are not just for thin people. You should see NAAFA dances!

Some tips about exercise: You are an individual. Your particular body has abilities and limitations which may differ from others' bodies. The authority on what your body needs is your body. If it hurts you to move your body in a certain way, stop moving it in that way. Pain is a signal that you must heed, to avoid injuring yourself. Several years ago, some numbskull came up with the slogan, "No pain, no gain." Ignore that idiocy. On the other hand, if it feels good, do it, but not to excess. It is useful to find a variety of ways to move your body, so that you can exercise different muscle groups. It is also useful to combine aerobic activity (which keeps your heart and lungs in good shape) with strength-building and flexibility activities. I love yoga for flexibility and for calming my whole self. Several people have told me that, through yoga, they first learned to accept and appreciate their bodies.

It is a good idea to check with your doctor before starting exercising, especially if you have been a couch potato for a while. Also, since fat people are moving more weight than thin people, they do not have to move as quickly to get aerobic benefits. In other words, you do not have to kick your heels up to the ceiling and trot nimbly around the floor to get your heart beating in your aerobic range. Your aerobic range is generally one where you might breathe a bit harder, sweat a little, but still be able to carry on a conversation.

You do not need to wear a particular uniform in order to be legitimately exercising. Wear whatever is comfortable and allows you to move freely. Exercise does not only occur in 45-60-minute segments, three to five times a week. It happens any time you move yourself. You can pick up bits of exercise in the natural course of your day. Carrying groceries or a child, climbing stairs, shopping at a mall are all forms of exercise. So are cleaning house, raking leaves, making love, walking from your car, or trying on clothes. You can exaggerate your ordinary movements in order to add stretching. You can park a little farther away from your destination. You can put away your remote controls and walk to change TV or radio stations.

A tip for those who want to exercise to help themselves get down to their natural size: it appears that doing fairly mild, gravity-bearing exercise (e.g., walking) for longer than 30 minutes at a stretch is more effective in using up fat than are higher-intensity workouts for shorter periods of time. If you want to be as trim as you naturally can, and you can choose either two short stretches of exercise or one longer one, the longer one will support you better in trimming down. The two short sessions may help you keep your energy high all day. Take your choice. You may want as much variety in your exercise sessions as you do in your food.

A great resource for you to look into is *Great Shape: The First Fitness Guide for Large Women,* by Debby Burgard and Pat Lyons.[5] Lyons and Burgard have an attitude that is similar to mine about exercise: it should be as delicious as possible. While Lyons found it delicious to compete in the Bay to Breakers race, many fat people do not find running delicious. But many love walking. Recognize that fitness is available to you, as it is to anyone else, and do whatever activities you most enjoy in the process of becoming/being fit.

I know of nothing better than physical activity to relieve many of the psychological/emotional symptoms people have. I recommend exercise to nearly everyone I work with. Exercise helps people sleep more restfully, have more energy and stamina, digest food and eliminate waste better. It reduces blood pressure (you don't need to exercise at great length for this to happen, either) and elevates mood, reduces anxiety and pain, improves your ratios of "good" (HDL) to "bad" (LDL) cholesterol, and improves circulation.

FROM THE NECK DOWN

Bodies are meant to move, and feel much better when they do so. And they reward you tremendously for tender, loving care. Look at what abuses you have subjected them to—perhaps only because you were trying to make yours thinner—and notice that they continue to endure, anyway. Endurance is only one facet of a body's abilities. What others can you discover? What are some of the most delicious aspects of having the body you have?

You may have difficulty identifying delicious aspects of your body. Many fat people (as well as some intellectuals) do not feel much in touch with any part of themselves below their necks. They feel that below their necks is just a ponderous, ugly source of misery. Hearing that they "have such a pretty face" reinforces this division, and for many fat people is the most stinging insult they recall. If you were told, verbally and through people's nonverbal responses, that your body was faulty, it would make sense to want to disown it. Also, since dieting requires one to ignore one's body signals, it is useful to disconnect from body sensations if one wants to be a good dieter. But your body is what you need in order to live your life, so you might as well start to accept it. If it goes away, you go away.

There are many ways to connect with your whole body. A simple way, and one that is good for your mental health as well, is to breathe deeply, and then imagine fresh air traveling all through your body, all the way to your fingertips and toes. After you inhale, hold your breath for a few seconds, and then exhale for a few seconds. You can count to four slowly for each of these three steps. If you just breathe deeply, feel the clean air going all the way through your body, and then imagine fatigue and anything else unwanted (e.g., toxins, carbon dioxide, problems) going out with each breath, you will feel revitalized. Likewise, if you just breathe in, hold, and breathe out to counts of four (or three or whatever is most fitting for you), you will feel refreshed—and you will also be doing a form of meditation.

A powerful way to connect with your body is to stand in front of a full-length mirror and look at your whole body. Many people find this very difficult at first, since they are accustomed to avoiding any sight of their "unshapely" bodies. Remember to breathe. When you are brave enough to face the mirror, you can inch downward from your face. Or you can start with another part of your body that you accept—perhaps your hands. Just notice what there is to notice, including whatever comments your peanut gallery makes. (Then thank it for sharing.) You may notice that your waist curves differently from your hips, or where on your body you have hair, or what colors you can find in your skin. You can also focus first on a part of your body that has served you well—perhaps your strong shoulders or legs. You can start with one minute in front of the mirror, and work up to 10 or more. Keep breathing. Notice how you look when you are breathing. Aim for the day when you can look at your whole body, from every angle, and appreciate its lush curves and your uniqueness. It is definitely possible! You do not have to know *how* you will get to the point when you can look at your body and cherish it; just stand in front of the mirror and aim for cherishing yourself. You will get there in whatever time you need.

A delicious way to connect with your body is via massage. Experiments have shown that babies thrive if they are held and cuddled, and Baby, you are never too old to thrive from friendly touch. Massage is a wonderful way to give your body friendly touching, and there are massage therapists who can appreciate and work with all sizes and shapes of bodies. Ask your friends, a women's center, a YM-YWCA—or any fat-friendly practitioner you know—for a referral to a good massage therapist. NAAFA is compiling a list of fat-friendly health care providers, including masseuses. You can be a smart consumer, and interview massage therapists on the phone first to check their opinions about or experience with working with fat people. You can also exchange massages with a friend, or trade something you can do for someone else's massaging you. Note: there are all different types of massage. Swedish massage, reflexology (foot massage), and Tragerwork tend to be gentle. Shiatsu, myofascial release, and acupressure may be more intense, but can be effective in releasing unwanted conditions. When you interview a potential masseuse, discuss what results you want. Different masseuses have different specialties. You can also get into the sensuous habit of spreading moisturizing lotion all over your body after you bathe, which gives your body friendly touching as well as soft, supple skin.

Sex, dancing, and other forms of movement are all ways which enable us to connect with our whole bodies. Choose the most delicious ways for yourself.

FAT AND HEALTHY

People who are healthy are not necessarily thin. However, they are at an appropriate weight for their own bodies, whether or not that weight agrees with anybody's height-weight charts. They eat healthfully (generally unprocessed foods including many fruits and vegetables), drink enough (nonalcoholic) fluids, get enough sleep and rest, move their bodies enough to maintain fitness, and get preventive medical care. In other words, they see their doctors long before a condition develops which doubles them over in pain.

While it is a myth that fat people are not healthy, a number of fat people *are* unhealthy. A major contributor to this is prejudice. The stress of being the target of ceaseless hostility and blame negatively affects anyone. While people belonging to other minorities are usually safe from bigotry in their own homes, many fat people do not even have this sanctuary available. Their relatives monitor what they eat, criticize them for being outsize, consider them nutty because they are fat—even if they are the offspring of fat relatives! I believe that many cases of high blood pressure—whether in fat people or in black people—are the result of bigotry's effects on the outcast. Many years ago, medical anthropologist Dr. Margaret MacKenzie found that the blood pressure of women in Western Samoa, where being 200 pounds was perfectly acceptable, was normal.

Since doctors and nurses are products of an antifat culture, they share our national "weight problem," the prejudice mentioned earlier against fat people. Both scientific research and medical treatment have been affected by this bias. The studies of weight and health have not accounted for the impact of bigotry on fat people's health; likewise, they have not studied fat *non*dieters. Innumerable fat people eventually stop going to their doctors because they do not want a weight-loss lecture. Ben Franklin told us that "an ounce of prevention is worth a pound of cure." When people stop getting preventive medical care, many conditions which could be easily treated become major health problems. If the medical community—whose ethic includes above all, doing no harm—realized how harmful their antifat bigotry was, and treated fat people as well as they treat thinner people, more fat people would get good medical care and be healthy.

Finally, our bodies respond to our thoughts. Disliking or hating our own bodies, blaming ourselves for being "too fat," and feeling guilty about our hungers do not improve our health and are detrimental to our physical wellbeing, and our psyches. Likewise, eating and exercising with the attitude that we have to atone for our eating or weight badness, such as by starving ourselves or frantically exercising, is not nurturing ourselves; it is reinforcing that our bodies are bad the way they are. While, like Nancy, you may think a good kick in the pants is good for you, it probably is not.

SUPPORT CAN BE BEAUTIFUL

You are worth being supported in your life. Whether or not you use a support buddy to help you end overeating (see Chapter V), you can probably use as much support as you can get. People who have support in their lives are healthier than those without it. Many fat people and FAs join NAAFA to get the kind of special support that is available from people who have been through the same thing. There has been an explosion of self-help groups throughout the country, led by people who have sought support from others in their situation. There are self-help groups for single, married, widowed, and divorced people; for people coping with specific illnesses, physical or mental; for people coping with various forms of addictive behavior; for parents, grandparents, and for "adult children" of various kinds of parents; for newcomers to an area, and so on. Chances are, if you want support for a specific issue, you can find or create a self-help group for yourself. Many self-help groups are free of charge or very low-cost. You will find listings in the Appendix for the American Self-Help Clearinghouse and the National Self-Help Clearinghouse.

I have been in a support group for the past 13 years. All of us consider it an invaluable resource for ourselves. Our group has supported us through marriages and divorces, relationships, illnesses, deaths, career changes, educational advances, home and business changes, family concerns, financial concerns, and lots of celebrations. We meet about once a month for dinner and talk, and may or may not talk and socialize with each other between meetings. We know we have a resource specifically for support, and each of us has leaned heavily on the group when we have needed to.

You may have a supportive family; if so, you are blessed. When I married an Italian, I found out what tremendous support is available from a strong, willing family. But many of us have moved away from our families (probably one reason why self-help groups are now so popular), while others do not get support from their families—even some Italian ones—for various reasons. While you cannot choose your relatives, you can choose your friends. You might as well choose friends who support you, value you, cheer you up and on. You deserve to have supportive friends in your life.

You also deserve not to have detractors in your life. Detractors are those who take too many opportunities to criticize you, whether for your weight or eating, or for any other reason. Or, even if they do not criticize you, they sap your energy. Unfortunately, most of us have to deal with detractors at some time, whether at home or at work. If you cannot avoid a detractor in your life, you can balance her by filling the rest of your life with supporters. If at all possible, limit your exposure to detractors. You can assert yourself and let them know what they can or cannot say or do to you. You can limit the amount of time you are with them. You can leave them, if necessary. While every relationship has ups and downs, if you have done everything you can or are willing to do to have the relationship support you and it still does not, cut your losses, move on, and find support elsewhere. You are worth being supported, loved, and appreciated. If you get those gifts, you will thrive. This book would never have been written if Iris had not repeatedly told me that I had something important to share with others, and if Joe had not given me space, time, and the benefit of his computer expertise. We can achieve plenty by ourselves, but much more with support. One kind of weight loss that I highly recommend is to clear out the people in your life who do not support you.

Those who love, appreciate, and support you deserve the same treatment from you. People who can be good friends, have good friends. What characteristics would you want, if you could choose anyone to be your friends? Make sure you offer quality to your friends. Keep your agreements, and value your friends and yourself, and you will attract people of quality. The only part of your body whose size counts is your heart.

WORTHWHILE WORK

If you were a worthy person, what would your time be worth? Would you make any changes in how you spend your time? How much of your time would be devoted to weight and eating concerns? While some people take on their weight and eating management like a job, is that how you would want to spend the time of your life? Would you be doing the same work, or not? If you knew you only had six months to live, would you spend your time any differently? Would you still do the same work?

If you would be spending your time pretty much as you are now, chances are you are in the right work for yourself. However, if you would be doing something very different, or working someplace very different, change is in order. First of all, if you are not satisfied with your work life, you may be overeating. Second, all we really have while we are alive is the time we are here. The best way to use it, for our bodies and our souls, is to be spending as much time on deliciousness as possible.

It has taken me a long time of listening to wise people, who have said things like, "Don't worry; be happy," before I was convinced that being happy was really acceptable, and would not turn me into a frivolous, useless burden to mankind.

When you do work that is delicious to you, you are likely to do it well. When you do things well, everyone benefits. People tend to be pleased with a job well done, by themselves or anyone else. In business, satisfied customers tend to return for more. Enough satisfied customers means prosperity for you and your work. It does not matter what the work is that you love; it matters that you love it and do it the best you can.

If you absolutely cannot get into work that you love—because you must keep your job now—you can still get maximum benefits by doing the very best you can at it and finding out how to best enjoy what you have to do.

If you would like to spend your work time doing what you love, but you don't have a glimmer of what that might be, you can definitely get where you want. First, it is enormously useful to know what you do *not* want or like to do. I do not want to do anything involving coal mines, driving for a living, politics and law, or serious conformity. It took me a lot of jobs and a lot of soul searching, when I only seemed to discover things that were not right for me, before I realized that I wanted to work with people. Then it took a lot more trial and error, identity crises, and career changes before I homed in on doing psychotherapy, teaching, and writing.

If you are interested in spending your time doing work worthy of you, some excellent resources are *Wishcraft* by Barbara Sher, *Do What You Love, the Money Will Follow* by Marsha Sinetar, and *Zen and the Art of Making a Living*, by Laurence Boldt.

THE TIME OF YOUR LIFE

During the time of your life, you are worth having the time of your life! You are worth having as much fun as you possibly can. If you play with fun the same way you play with deliciousness, you will probably discover that fun does not look just like the time when you are on vacation or otherwise off from work. Remember, better is better. A friend of mine, who is changing her career and reentering graduate school in a few months, thought that it would be fun to just have some time to do nothing. Within two weeks she wanted to climb the walls!

Just as with food and deliciousness, a delicious life includes variety, balance, and timeliness. Fun varies according to what else is in your life. My friends who have careers and small children cannot imagine more fun than a good night's sleep. When Joe was sick, I could not even imagine fun, only absence of pain rather than intense pain. If you cannot imagine what fun would be like, start with absence of pain, and allow for the possibility that someday a whole other dimension of experience, far better than you can now imagine, can open up. Then give yourself as much tender, loving care as you can, and keep on keeping on. Accept that the best you can do is enough.

I have had the great good fortune to be able to determine largely how I spend the time of my life. I have been able to create my life to be authentic to me. The peanut gallery is quiet most of the time. Using deliciousness as an operating principle, I have found that it is not delicious for me to work constantly; nor is it delicious to be idle too much. I find a lot of solitude delicious, but only when it is balanced by rich contact with dear ones, clients and students, and sprinklings of crowds and the kind of stimulation New York City brings.

If you could have a truly delicious life, worthy of a worthwhile person, what would yours be?

GIVING YOURS, GETTING YOURS

I have found over the years that, when people's basic needs are met, they tend to get interested in making a contribution to others. Even some people on the edges of existence will give their last crust of bread to help someone else. We are a social species, and interdependent. Being able to do something for someone else fills us up in ways that no food, no matter how delicious, possibly could. Twelve-step programs incorporate helping others into their steps—in fact, carrying their message to others who are still suffering is the twelfth step.

There are as many ways to make a contribution as there are individuals on the planet. By being as fully yourself as you can be, by doing whatever you do as fully and responsibly as you can, you will make a contribution to the world. By freeing up all the time and energy you had invested in struggling about weight and food, you will have more than you can imagine, and you can use it to enrich your life and the world.

One way you can enrich our world is to support the size acceptance movement. NAAFA is a leader in this movement, and its message applies to people of all sizes. As the saying goes, a waist is a terrible thing to mind—whatever size the waist happens to be. If you were no longer minding your waist, you would be setting an example for other waist-minders, of a life which is about more important things. You would no longer have to associate thinness or deprivation with goodness, and fatness or fulfillment with badness. You would no longer have to spend your money on people, programs, or products which try to insert morality or worthiness into body size. You can, and should, vote with your pocketbook.

No longer living your life as if you had a weight problem could mean that you would take the courageous step of leaving your house. It could mean daring to wear bright clothing, or actually eating in public. It could be deciding that you will do the research necessary to find a physician who sees you as a whole person rather than as a fat-and-therefore-sick body. It could involve writing to your local movie theater and asking for fat-friendly seating (required under the Americans with Disabilities Act). Or, more personally, telling your intolerant relatives that they can no longer hassle you about your weight and their problem with it. Or deciding that you will never again condemn yourself about your weight.

You could also exercise your rights as a citizen. You could offer your guidance and support, via letters, phone calls, or office visits, to your representatives in state and federal government. You could request that they include weight as a category to be protected against discrimination, just as race, religion, sex, national origin, and beliefs are presently.

WORTH YOUR WEIGHT

What if you were worth your weight in gold or diamonds? If you could live the rest of your life, starting this minute, as if you were enormously valuable, how would you live differently? There is no time to lose in any other way of living, except as an extraordinarily worthy person. That is who you are. Yes, even you.

Enjoy!

1. Harris, Thomas, MD. *I'm OK—You're OK*. New York and Evanston: Harper & Row, Publishers, 1969, pp. 25-26.
2. *People* magazine, 1/11/93.
3. Louderback, Lew. "More people should be FAT," in *The Saturday Evening Post*, 11/4/67, pp. 10-11.
4. Roberts, Nancy. *Breaking all the Rules*. New York: Viking Books, 1986, p. 90. ©1985, 1986 by Nancy Roberts. Used by permission of Viking Penguin, a division of Penguin Books USA Inc.
5. Lyons, Pat, and Burgard, Debby. *Great Shape: The First Fitness Guide for Large Women*. Palo Alto: Bull Publishing, 1990.

APPENDIX

RESOURCES

Reading Material:

Letting go of dieting; normalizing eating:

Berg, Miriam. *The ABC's of Dieting: Twenty-six Ways to Lose Weight Temporarily and Damage Your Health Permanently.* Willendorf Press, 1990.

Garrison, Terry Nicholetti and Levitsky, David. *Fed Up! A Woman's Guide to Freedom from the Diet/Weight Prison.* Carroll & Graf Publishers, Inc., 1993.

Hirschmann, Jane and Munter, Carol. *Overcoming Overeating.* Addison-Wesley, 1988. *When Women Stop Hating Their Bodies.* Ballantine Books, 1995.

Kano, Susan. *Making Peace with Food.* Harper & Row, 1989.

Omichinski, Linda. *You Count, Calories Don't.* Tamos Books, Inc., 1993.

Roth, Geneen. *Feeding the Hungry Heart.* Signet, 1982. *Breaking*

Free from Compulsive Eating. Bobbs-Merrill, 1984. *Why Weight?* New American Library, 1989.*When Food Is Love*. Dutton, 1991.

Schwartz, Bob. *Diets Don't Work*. Breakthru, 1982. *Diets Still Don't Work*. Breakthru, 1990.

Video:

Hayes, Dayle. Body Trust. c/o 1-800/321-9499.

For children:

Hirschmann, Jane and Zaphiropolous, Lela. *Are You Hungry?* New American Library, 1985. Reissued as *Solving Your Child's Eating Problem*.

Satter, Ellyn. *How To Get your Kid To Eat...But Not Too Much*. Bull Publishing, 1987. (Highly recommended.)

Medical, Scientific:

Atrens, Dale. *Don't Diet*. Morrow, 1988.

Bennett, William and Gurin, Joel. *The Dieter's Dilemma*. Basic Books,1982.

Berg, Frances. *Health Risks of Weight Loss*. Obesity & Health, 1993.

Ciliska, Donna. *Beyond Dieting*. Brunner/Mazel, 1990.

Ernsberger, Paul and Haskew, Paul. "Rethinking Obesity," *Journal of Obesity and Weight Regulation,* Summer, 1987.

Polivy, Janet and Herman, C. Peter. *Breaking the Diet Habit*. Basic Books, 1983.

Schroeder, Charles Roy. *Fat Is Not a Four-Letter Word*. Chronimed, 1992.

Feminist:

Chernin, Kim. *The Obsession: Reflections on the Tyranny of Slenderness*. Harper & Row. 1981.

Fallon, Patricia, Katzman, Melanie, and Wooley, Susan. *Feminist Perspectives on Eating Disorders*. Guilford, 1994.

Rothblum, Esther and Brown, Laura. *Overcoming Fear of Fat*. Harrington Park Press, 1989.

Schoenfelder, Lisa and Wieser, Barb, Eds. *Shadow on a Tightrope: Writings by Women on Fat Oppression*. Spinsters/Auntie Lute, 1983.

Wolf, Naomi. *The Beauty Myth*. Anchor Books, 1991.

Image:

Marano, Hara Estroff. *Style Is Not a Size*. Bantam, 1991.

Notkin, Debbie and Edison, Laurie Toby. *Women En Large*. Books In Focus, 1994.

Olds, Ruthanne. *Big & Beautiful*. Acropolis, 1982.

Roberts, Nancy. *Breaking All the Rules*. Viking, 1985.

Shaw, Carole. *Come Out, Come Out, Wherever You Are!* ARR, 1982.

Physical and mental health:

Erdman, Cheri. *Nothing To Lose: A Guide to Sane Living in a Larger Body*. Harper San Francisco, 1995.

Freedman, Rita. *Bodylove: Learning to Like Our Looks and Ourselves*. Harper & Row, 1988.

Hutchinson, Marcia. *Transforming Body Image*. The Crossing Press, 1985.

Johnson, Carol. *Self-Esteem Comes in All Sizes*. Doubleday, 1995.

Lyons, Pat and Burgard, Debby. *Great Shape: the First Fitness Guide for Large Women*. Bull Publishing, 1990.

NAAFA, Inc. *Size Acceptance & Self-Acceptance*. NAAFA, Inc., 1995.

Ornstein, Robert and Sobel, David. *Healthy Pleasures*. Addison-Wesley, 1989.

Rose, Laura. *Life Isn't Weighed on the Bathroom Scales*. WRS Publishing, 1994.

Seligman, Martin. *What You Can Change & What You Can't*. Knopf, 1994.

Summer, Nancy. *Ample Hygiene for Ample People*. Willendorf Press, 1993.

For Children:

Carlson, Nancy. *I Like Me!* Puffin Books. (for preschoolers)

Ikeda, Joanne and Naworski, Priscilla. *Am I Fat? Helping Young Children Accept Differences in Body Size*. ETR Associates, 1992.

Jasper, Karin. *Are You Too Fat, Ginny?* Is Five Press.

History, Sociology:

Beller, Anne Scott. *Fat & Thin: A Natural History of Obesity.* Farrar Straus Giroux, 1977.

Goodman, W. Charisse. *The Invisible Woman: Confronting Weight Prejudice in America*. Gürze Books, 1995.

Schwartz, Hillel. *Never Satisfied: A Cultural History of Diets, Fantasies, & Fat*. Anchor Books, 1986.

Seid, Roberta Pollack. *Never Too Thin: Why Women Are at War with Their Bodies*. Prentice Hall Press, 1989.

Sobal, Jeffery and Maurer, Donna, eds. *Food and Nutrition as Social Problems*. Aldine de Gruyter, 1995.

Personal Stories, Humor, Poetry:

Bailey, June. *Fat Is Where It's At*. HFS Publishing, 1981.

Buono, Victor. *It Could Be Verse*. Nash Publishing, 1972.

Gossett, Harry. *Fat Chance*. Independent Hill Press, 1986.

Higgs, Liz Curtis. *One Size Fits All...And Other Fables*. Thomas Nelson Publishers, 1993.

Mayer, Ken. *Real Women Don't Diet!* Bartleby Press, 1993.

Reed, Kit. *Fat*. Bobbs-Merrill, 1974.

Stinson, Susan. *Belly Songs: In Celebration of Fat Women*. Orogeny Press, 1993.

Wiley, Carol, Ed. *Journeys to Self-Acceptance: Fat Women Speak*. The Crossing Press, 1994.

Magazines:

BBW (Big Beautiful Woman). LFP, Inc. , 9171 Wilshire Boulvard,

Suite 300, Beverly Hills, CA 90210, tel.1-800/707 5592.

Dimensions (Where Big Is Beautiful). P.O. Box 640, Folsom, CA 95763-0640.

Fat!So? (for people who don't apologize for their size). P.O. Box 423464, San Francisco, CA 94142.

Healthy Weight Journal (Research, News and Commentary Across the Weight Spectrum). 402 South 14th Street, Hettinger, ND 58639, tel. 701/567-2646.

Radiance (the magazine for large women). P.O. Box 30246, Oakland, CA 94604, tel. 510/482-0680.

Rump Parliament (Working To Change The Way Society Treats Fat People). P.O. Box 181716, Dallas, TX 75218.

Other Useful Publications:

The Ample Shopper., a quarterly consumer-oriented newsletter with a focus on goods and services for larger-sized people. Published by Amplestuff, P.O. Box 116, Bearsville, NY 12409, tel. 914/679-3316.

Ample Information, the publication of Ample Opportunity. Ample Opportunity promotes health & wellbeing for fat women and advocates size acceptance. P.O. Box 40621, Portland, OR, tel. 503/245-1524.

On a Positive Note, the publication of Largely Positive, Inc., P.O. Box 17223, Glendale, WI 53217, tel. 414/454-6500.

Royal Resources, a directory of products, clothes, groups, etc., for larger people. P.O. Box 41, Camas Valley, OR 97416, tel. 503/445-2330.

Support Groups:

Abundia, c/o Sally Strosahl, P.O. Box 252, Downers Grove, IL 60515, tel. 630/897-9796.

AHELP (the Association for the Health Enrichment of Large People), Joe McVoy, Ph.D., Director. This group is mostly for professionals in health, mental health, nutrition, and fitness who work with fat people. Post Office Drawer C, Radford, VA 24143, tel. 540/731-1778.

American Self-Help Clearinghouse, St. Clare's Riverside Medical Center, Denville, NJ 07834, tel. 201/625-7101.

Ample Opportunity, see *Ample Information*, above. Portland, OR, area.

Diet/Weight Liberation, c/o Terry Nicholetti Garrison, Annabel Taylor Hall, Cornell University, Ithaca, NY 14853.

Heavy, Healthy, & Happy, c/o Donna Pittman, Family Therapy Center, 340 N. Sam Houston Parkway East, #267, Houston, TX 77060, tel. 713/591-1721.

Largely Positive, see *On a Positive Note,* above. Milwaukee, WI, area.

NAAFA, the National Association to Advance Fat Acceptance, P.O. Box 188620, Sacramento, CA 95818, tel. 916/558-6880 or 1-800/442-1214. Local NAAFA groups across the United States and in Canada; some groups may have formed in Western Europe by the time you read this.

National Self-Help Clearinghouse, 25 West 43rd Street, Room 620, New York, NY 10036, tel. 212/642-2944.

Overcoming Overeating, 315 West 86th Street, Suite 17B, New York, NY 10024, tel. 212/875-0442. Centers also in Massachusetts, Chicago, Houston.

Weight Release Services, c/o Dr. Barbara Altman Bruno. Westchester County, NY, tel. 914/747-1525.

International Size Acceptance Groups:

England: Diet Breakers, Barford St. Michael, Banbury, Oxon, OX15 OUA;

Fat Women's Group, c/o London Women's Centre, Wesley House, 4 Wild Court, London WC2B 5AU; tel. 071-281-7819.

France: ADEPF (Association for the Defense and Rights of Fat People); Allegro Fortissimo (Paris).

Holland: Society of Size, P.O. Box 216, 5500 AE Veldhoven, The Netherlands.

Germany: Contact Barbara Bahr, Carlo-Mierendorff Str. 2la, 34132 Kassel.

Russia: Moscow Overweight People's Club, Robin Bobin, P/B 63, 123100, Moscow.

Spain: (In process. Contact Carmen Banuelos c/o NAAFA in Sacramento, CA).

Argentina: ALCO, c/o Alberto Cormillot, MD, c/o NAAFA.

New Zealand:

Auckland: Size Acceptance Network (SANe) and other groups.

Christchurch: Beyond Dieting; other groups in Wellington (c/o Tania Coombs).

Australia: Women at Large, c/o Kathy Sandow, 12 Chancery Lane, Hawthorndene, SA 5051.

Canada:

Portage la Prairie: HUGS, c/o Linda Omichinski, Box 102A, RR#3, Portage la Prairie, MB R1N 3A3, tel. 204/428-3432.

Ontario: Beyond Dieting, c/o Dr. Donna Ciliska, McMaster University; Stop Dieting, Inc., 37 Parkwood Ave., Toronto, tel. 416/968-3942.

Clothing:

Myles Ahead, 6658 NW 57th St., Tamarac, FL 33321, tel. 305/724-0500.

Most department stores now sell plus-size clothing.
QVC cable shopping channel

Underwear: Jockey, Fruit of the Loom; Goddess bras
Vermont Country Store (tel. 1-800/362-2400)

Exercise clothing: Danskin
Arnott Mason Corp (tel. 703/503-2916): riding clothes for women
Hanes Her Way

Bathing Suits: Big Stitches By Jan. 2423 Douglas Street, San Pablo, CA 94806, tel. 510/237-3978.

Bridal gowns: David's Bridal (national chain)
Eden (tel. 818/441-8715)

Menswear:

King Size, P.O. Box 9115, Hingham, MA 02043 (tel. 1-800/846-1600, 617/871-4100)
JCPenney, Sears
Big Clothes for Big Men c/o Freda's Secrets, P.O. Box 2765, Philadelphia, PA 19118.

Children's Clothing:

Big Kids—JCPenney (tel.1-800/222-6161)

Online Resources:

alt.support.big-folks
soc.support.fat-acceptance
big_moms_list-request@butler.hpl.hp.com

Made in the USA
Monee, IL
15 May 2022

Someone To Look Up To

Top Pick Award from Litpick Student Reviews.

By IPPY and Global Ebook Award Winning author.

For all dog-lovers!

Jean Gill has captured the innermost thoughts of this magnificent animal.'

Les Ingham, Pyr International

A dog's life in the south of France. From puppyhood, Sirius the Pyrenean Mountain Dog has been trying to understand his humans and train them with kindness.

How this led to their divorce he has no idea. More misunderstandings take Sirius to Death Row in an animal shelter, as a so-called dangerous dog learning survival tricks from the other inmates. During the twilight barking, he is shocked to hear his brother's voice but the bitter-sweet reunion is short-lived. Doggedly, Sirius keeps the faith.

One day, his human will come.

ACKNOWLEDGEMENTS
Extracts from *How Blue is My Valley* first published in *France Magazine*
Lyrics by Michael Jones courtesy of Sony Music, France

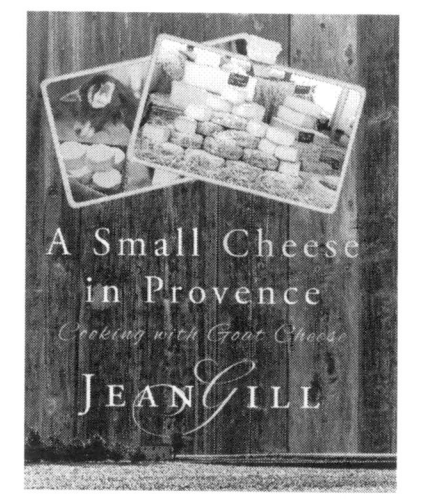

PRAISE FOR 'HOW BLUE IS MY VALLEY'

From award-winning author Jean Gill:
Winner of the Global Ebook Award for Historical Fiction, IPPY and Royal Dragonfly Awards.

'Laugh out loud ... such a picture of the fields of lavender, sunflowers and olive trees that you could almost be there with her.' Stephanie Sheldrake, *Living France Magazine*

'I just laughed and laughed about author Jean Gill's adventures.' Gisela Hausmann, *The Naked No-Fluff book series*

'One of those books that transcends genre; it's as much a travel book as a personal memoir - as is the best travel writing... All in all, a great read.' J.G.Harlond, *The Chosen Man*

HOW BLUE IS MY VALLEY

JEAN GILL

The 13th Sign

ISBN 9782955010150

Cover design by Jessica Bell
Cover images © Jean Gill

Jean Gill's Publications

Novels

Natural Forces - FANTASY

Book 3 The World Beyond the Walls *(The 13th Sign)* 2021
Book 2 Arrows Tipped with Honey *(The 13th Sign)* 2020
Book 1 Queen of the Warrior Bees *(The 13th Sign)* 2019

The Troubadours Quartet - HISTORICAL FICTION

Book 5 Nici's Christmas Tale: A Troubadours Short Story *(The 13th Sign)* 2018
Book 4 Song Hereafter *(The 13th Sign)* 2017
Book 3 Plaint for Provence *(The 13th Sign)* 2015
Book 2 Bladesong *(The 13th Sign)* 2015
Book 1 Song at Dawn *(The 13th Sign)* 2015

Love Heals - SECOND CHANCE LOVE

Book 2 More Than One Kind *(The 13th Sign)* 2016
Book 1 No Bed of Roses *(The 13th Sign)* 2016

Looking for Normal - TEEN FICTION

Book 1 Left Out *(The 13th Sign)* 2017
Book 2 Fortune Kookie *(The 13th Sign)* 2017

Non-fiction

MEMOIR / TRAVEL

How White is My Valley *(The 13th Sign 2021)* ****EXCLUSIVE to Jean Gill's Special Readers Group***

How Blue is my Valley *(The 13th Sign)* 2016

A Small Cheese in Provence *(The 13th Sign)* 2016

WW2 MILITARY MEMOIR

Faithful through Hard Times *(The 13th Sign)* 2018

4.5 Years – war memoir by David Taylor *(The 13th Sign)* 2017

Short Stories and Poetry

One Sixth of a Gill *(The 13th Sign)* 2014

From Bedtime On *(The 13th Sign)* 2018 (2nd edition)

With Double Blade *(The 13th Sign)* 2018 (2nd edition)

Translation (from French)

The Last Love of Edith Piaf – Christie Laume *(Archipel)* 2014

A Pup in Your Life – Michel Hasbrouck 2008

Gentle Dog Training – Michel Hasbrouck *(Souvenir Press)* 2008

For Clare, ma belle fille
who can testify that the contents of this book are the truth,
not the whole truth perhaps
but definitely nothing ***but*** *the truth*

1

FALLING IN LOVE

Every Sunday we feed the toilet or, to be more exact, we make an offering via the toilet to the Good Bacteria which, we hope, inhabit our septic tank. The weekly offering looks remarkably like ready-mix concrete, comes in an unlabelled sachet from a firm unwilling to divulge the ingredients of the magic potion but confident that it will prevent the 'boue' or 'mud' from building up in your 'fosse septique'. Just to be on the safe side, I treat the toilet, and tank, to an occasional yoghurt, which I was advised must be 'live'.

Have you ever scoured the supermarket shelves for live yoghurt, presumably as opposed to the dead variety? Isn't all yoghurt live? I settled on natural and cheap, deciding that the toilet did not deserve an offering of cherry, strawberry or even lemon.

Thanks to the advice of the Welsh farming community I have left behind, I still have a few tricks up my sleeve in case we face the situation of one of those graphic French television advertisements; the scene is a jolly family birthday party outside under the trees, with a ten-year old blowing out the candles on his cake when – horror of horrors – each family member is overcome by the smell of their sadly neglected septic tank and the ten year old vomits on his birthday cake. Needless to say, it is an ad for magic potion and

although we fell about laughing when we first watched it, when we became the proud owners of a septic tank and accompanying house, we quickly stocked up on gray substance.

We didn't wait until we moved to France to find out more about the little practicalities of life from our friends and neighbours. Our ex-home of Carmarthenshire, in the heart of South Wales, is a good place to seek advice on pretty well everything, but septic tanks arouse as much passion as anything else I've asked over the twenty-five years I adopted Wales as home, not worrying too much about whether it had adopted me.

It is essential to have the tank professionally emptied, a process involving a tanker and a presumably nose-dead human, with the reverse set of talents to those which enable the grand noses of France to create new blends of wines and perfumes. To use his - and it's inevitably a man - enormous suction pipe, the skilled workman needs to know where the tank is.

If you've forgotten to find this out when you buy your house in the countryside, then you'll have to look for the clues; over your septic tank, the grass is greener, the smell (if you haven't been following advice) is stronger and if the aforementioned skilled workmen prods the ground, he will be able to detect the outline of the various stages of land inhabited by 'the product'.

If you need to kick off a sluggish tank with a bit of 'oomph', you can't beat a dead chicken, which you should insert directly into the tank as only a total moron would try and cram it down the toilet. The Good Bacteria provided by said dead chicken will get the whole brew stewing again, according to my friendly vet, who also promised me long surgical gloves as a leaving present, so that if I jam the air vent with too much oil from a roasting pan or such, I can stick my arm in, as deep as a cow's birth canal, and unjam the system.

I do not hold it against him that he forgot; I would far rather not have to explain to the neighbours why we keep several packs of long surgical gloves and convince them that this is really not an aspect of standard, or even unusual, English sexual practices.

You're asking yourself how often the septic tank needs to be

emptied? The advice on this is clear. Some people say every two years, some say five, some say ten, some say when it smells and some say never - if you 'look after it'. The advice is clear if you only listen to one person because each one is passionately convinced that he and, once again, it usually is a man, is right but there are always more questions than answers. Why, for instance, do you have to double the dose of magic potion for each week you are away on holiday, as well as for extra people staying with you? Surely if fewer people = happier tank, no people = ecstatic tank? Which brings us back to hedging all bets; to yoghurt (the vegetarian option on dead chicken) and magic potion; to a list of banned substances (bleach, bleach and bleach), and a soakaway outside for washing out paintbrushes and roasting pans. So far, so good.

Just when we've got the hang of all this and are feeling environmentally virtuous, there are vicious rumours that the local commune is complying with new laws and gradually extending its mains sewage so that it might even include us one day. We will then have a maison 'tout à l'égout', a phrase my sister Anne and I, both house hunting, in areas even further apart than we lived in Britain, both mistranslated as 'entirely to your taste' when we read it in brochures of houses for sale. Perhaps we were not so far wrong.

Apart from being toilet-day, the other defining characteristic of Sundays in October seems to be rain. However, even I can accept one rainy day a week, in Autumn, having been promised in every guide book that in Dieulefit we have 300 sunny days a year and that we have a microclimate. I now know that everywhere in France, according to local guidebooks, has 300 sunny days and a microclimate, from the Alps to the Côte d'Azur.

My Welsh friends told me not to take the weather so personally but I can't help it; I have a deep inner conviction that I was not meant to be rained on for months at a time, summer and winter. Perhaps my migrant childhood, including three years in Hong Kong,

following three years in Berlin, left an imprint of places where it doesn't rain all the time.

In a doomed attempt to cheer me up, my Welsh fruit-and-veg man who called each week in his van told me that at least we didn't get that extreme weather like they do in France. It has only just dawned on me that incessant rain *is* extreme weather.

And speaking of dawn … I have suffered many literary raptures about rosy-fingered dawn, and been disappointed at French singer Cabrel's lyrics settling for the old 'rosy dawn' cliché, but now I have seen the light for myself, everything is different. Of course there were occasional wintry mornings in Wales where the shepherd's warning streaked the skies over Christmas card scenes and, as for sunsets, we even had the 'sunset window' in the living room, where the setting sun was framed throughout May every year. That is, if the rising or setting sun could be seen, of course.

And I will probably come to miss living in an elephant's stomach with the usual stew of gray mists all around, but at the moment I feel that I have been starved of light for twenty-five years and I am glutting on it, spinning dizzy with it. You can look at the world through the bottom of a kir, when the cassis will give you blackcurrant-coloured spectacles or you can discard your aperitif and just look, but the effect is the same.

Some of us are born searching for home; if we are lucky, through years of pleasurable - and not so - experiments, we become more sure of ourselves, of the right man, of the right way of life for us and of the place where we belong. As a rational idealist, I don't believe in signs - but of course that doesn't stop me from following them.

When my friend and bridge partner suddenly recited a favourite French poem, of which I thought only I knew the grand opening by heart, it sparked a love affair that has lasted twenty years - so far. No reality checks could reverse my undoing, not the discovery that John had learnt it from a music-hall duo, that he understood not one word of the poem, nor even, most unforgivably, when he lost the translation that I carefully crafted for him (and which he didn't like at all).

It is even possible that South Wales is full of attractive men, any

one of whom would have recited 'El Desdichado' for me but they didn't, and as it was written in the stars (which I also do not believe in any way whatsoever), so it was – right man, sorted.

My restlessness for the right place to be me was a longer home-coming but it has led us both here, to the village of Dieulefit in Drôme Provençale.

Is it in Provence? Dazzling light and blue skies – tick. Olives – tick. Lavender – double tick. Red soil and limestone buffs in woods full of holme oaks – tick. Truffles – tick - black ones of course. In fact, our French guide to the Drôme in autumn states that the best truffles are found in the Drôme, those known as 'Perigord' for 'purely geographical reasons.' The sneer is meant to be heard as far as the Dordogne.

Our French estate agent was very apologetic when he told us about the surprise clause in our house contract; Monsieur Dubois, the owner before the previous owner, had retained the right to drive a small vehicle up our otherwise private drive, so he could water his truffle oaks. I had sniffed the word 'truffles' and was too busy wondering if a pair of Pyrenean Mountain dogs with no known talents could find their hidden potential, and some black gold, to worry about the legal aspects of a neighbour's right of way.

So far, no sign of truffle-hunting genes and you really don't want to know what the dynamic duo do find worth sniffing in the woods, but there is evidence of truffles about, namely good agricultural land laid down to neatly spaced rows of oak trees – and the annual frenzy of truffle markets in November.

What else Provençal? Tomatoes, garlic and wild herbs in the garrigue – oh, yes. The southern accent which makes our daily 'pain' a three-syllable word? Ben oui. Sunflowers – tick- although, like the corn crop, it suffered disastrously from last year's 'canicule', the dogdays of a record-breaking heatwave.

So what is not Provençale? I would be willing to stick my neck out and say that Provence is not noted for fine wine but our local vineyards are the Côtes du Rhône Villages. We are thirty minutes north of the grand reds; Roaix, Sèguret, Rasteau, Gigondas and

Châteauneuf-du-Pape; or, if you prefer, thirty minutes south of the equally celebrated Crozes-Hermitage.

La Drôme does have a growing population of second-home buyers and even foreign settlers like ourselves but there are few Parisians and Brits; the majority are Dutch, Belgians and Germans who have made the Ardèche their part of France and who have explored across the Rhône Valley into la Drôme.

If you draw a line smack across from Dieulefit to Montélimar, that's a rough guide to the imaginary northern boundary where Drôme Provençale turns into the Vallée de la Drôme, Diois territory. These distinctions are vital in a region claiming a Mediterranean south, by culture and weather, not by any connection with the sea. It also claims its north in the Alps. Get it wrong and you'd better swap your olives for edelweiss, and goats for cows, quickly.

What about Dieulefit itself? According to that same unbiased French guide which assessed its truffles as the best in France, Dieulefit is a marvellous village, famous for its pottery, its fine air quality which has led to it being a centre of excellence in the study and cure of respiratory diseases (with enough old people's homes to encourage us to plan for a long future) and for being an intellectual centre surpassed only by Paris and Lyon.

Shall I run that past you again? This village of 3,000 inhabitants, double that in summer with the campsites, hotels, and, yes, the Club Med, is supposed to be where it's at for the intelligentsia. There is historical evidence for the claim; in 1876 only Paris sent more delegates to an international Archaeological Congress.

I would like to think how well we fit in but the truth is that, armed with this knowledge about average local intelligence, I am even more in awe of every workman I meet – apart from anything else, their French is so good. If I am to judge by the notices in the village square, there is a serious basis for the village claim as they can obviously get enough clients to support night classes in Latin and Ancient Greek, with an extra fifteen minutes after class for those particularly interested in grammar.

Can you imagine the class being viable in a comparable Welsh –

or English – village nowadays? In the past, maybe. As recently as thirty years ago, the working men's clubs and the miners' education groups were offering – and being asked for – academic tuition. My ex-miner neighbour in Bancffosfelen could discuss Gerard Manley Hopkins as easily as growing rhubarb; I learnt about both from him.

So far I am too preoccupied with all that is new, and all that is falling down or exploding, to be tempted by the Classical classes. Every day there is a discovery. If you lie on the attic floor and look out of the tiny window designed to keep out heat and flies in summer, and keep in warmth in winter, you will see our best mountain, Mielandre, according to the map, 5,000 feet or 1,450 metres, depending on whether you've converted to new money or not. It is a bare and moody peak which plays the full gamut from snow-cap against azure skies, through misty wreaths to rocky reflections of relentless sun.

The 'hills' we admired through the windows, without lying down, when we first inspected the house, have increasingly earned our respect. The long forested ridge of Grace Dieu has become higher since we trekked up it from Dieulefit, following the limestone path up … and up. Part of one of France's grand footpaths, the Grande Randonneé Number 9, it is almost cobbled underfoot with immense stones, a rock garden created by Titans, which starts to wear on the ankles after an hour's stumbling along.

However strong your boots and ergonometrically designed your walking sticks, with hydraulic bounce, the uneven terrain and variation in pace is tiring and you remember that 3,000 feet is in fact as high as the Brecons, which we called mountains when we lived in Wales. We realise that all of our 'hills' are Welsh 'mountains' and their silhouettes against the night sky or glowing pink in a Provençal dawn are kin to those of Celtic myth, which made you either mad or a poet if you spent a night on their heights.

7

There are many ways of developing madness and poetry; I should have known that when John was talking of death, and looking like it, that he had a cold. Once the penny drops, and I realise that I am unwanted company between four-hourly doses of Lemsip, it seems a good idea to adventure out on my own. My head glowing with autumn, I decide to walk into the village but am tempted to explore first and head in the opposite direction. In Wales, it was normal to reach any given destination by so many different routes that one person could go north, the other south, and both arrive at the same time. The footpaths and lanes surrounding Dieulefit make it perfectly possible to try a dozen different ways to potter off the beaten track but, unlike our Welsh valley, there is definitely one main road and the mountains impose their own discipline on human movements.

If you turn left at Cavet's Picodon crèmerie, a major producer of Dieulefit's a.o.c. goat cheese, you can ford the River Jabron with the promise of 'gué submersible', a flooded crossing, in wetter times, and meander along back lanes to enter Dieulefit near Super-U, the supermarket doorway currently crowded with chrysanthemums.

The bank holiday of Toussaint, All Saints, marks an outburst of floral pompoms, yellow, tawny, maroon, white-tipped ... each perfect plant in its terracotta pot, marred only by the inevitable Halloween posters, with their ghost masks and cartoon shrieks 'OOOOOh'.

The massive pumpkins have disappeared from a local garden where they sat like props for 'Cinderella' from July until now so it seems they might have been real after all, sisters to those brightening the supermarket racks.

Already, I am Frenchified enough to want to touch produce before I buy it; it would be a brave stall-holder in Welsh market who yelled 'Come and try my melons' and yet I don't think twice now about taking morsels of melon, cheese and sausage from an outstretched hand and savouring them as I shop.

My most extravagant impulse buy since we moved has consisted of a mountain cheese that took my fancy (and cost so much that we

expected to own a square of the mountain itself, to add a piece of Alps to the piece of Snowdon I seem to remember that we acquired as National Trust subscribers) Previous peccadilloes were mostly connected with an underwear website – there is something very dangerous about being able to shop while sitting comfortably with a glass or two of wine.

In the village I check the local events board and am intrigued by a talk at the local library with the title 'Je suis aussi un mouton'. Apparently it is to be given by a local historian. Somehow I can't imagine the title translating well in Wales, although I save the idea of 'I am a sheep too' for my future valleys-drugs-sex-unemployment novel, which will have a young male anti-hero and will undoubtedly be a best-seller. It has of course been written but then, what's new?

I call at the newsagent and browse the magazine rack. Although we've met French people who were keen on all things English, especially the language, the Francophilia of Brits is not reciprocal. You won't find magazines in Dieulefit called 'Living in England', and a 'Teach Yourself English' book, if there is one, will have a discreet place on a shelf rather than compete with ever multier-media glossy products which promise to teach you French while you brush your teeth.

There are however just as many magazines on the shelves of the local 'presse' as in any British newsagent's. Like the produce in the markets and supermarkets, the titles vary seasonally, with October a frenzy of 'Make the most of your mushroom-picking', edging 'the Firemen's Monthly' into a less prominent position.

Can you imagine the impact of 'the Firemen's Monthly' in Smiths? Or which shelf it would be on? Make no mistake, firefighters have a sexy image in France too, with more volunteers than there are permanent pompiers, but the stories and photos play up the heroism more than the sex appeal.

In our region, as everywhere in the south, fires are neither rare nor someone else's problem. Keeping our grounds clear of undergrowth is not just common sense, it is a legal responsibility, and when you see how quickly a few brambles can light up, you under-

stand why. 'The Firemen's Monthly' offers a mixture of fire know-how-not, daring rescues and of course, photographs of the daring rescuers. I hover, hoping to glimpse the (other) customers who like pompiers but only tally two local newspapers being bought before I get bored.

As I buy my copy of '100 kitchens', I prepare a sad face for the newsagent himself, who seems to have been bereaved, to judge by the black-edged notice below his counter announcing that he is 'en deuil', 'in mourning'. I read on while he collects my change and remember that I am in a foreign country, where an increase in tobacco taxes can arouse personal fury and the solidarity of a day's strike; this is what the newsagent is 'en deuil' for.

Apparently cigarettes are so expensive in France now that people are even buying them in Germany. Imagine - Germany! I ignore the petition which has already been signed by a dozen good Dieulefitois, protesting the government's interference – as if the Minister's expressed concerns about health had anything to do with it! So the French head all kinds of European leagues for smoking-related diseases? Personal choice!

It is easy to see the contradictions in another culture and I am still amazed at the acceptability of cigarettes – and pets – in French cafes and even restaurants when the World Health Organisation has pronounced the French Health system 'the best in the world' (according to my French information, I admit) and when no-one challenges the reputation of French cuisine.

Although there are increasingly areas which are designated no-smoking, I think it will be a long time before we see workers standing outside their office-blocks, sneaking a drag, in the way that is now commonplace in Wales.

As for the pets, the attractions of spending a night in a hotel room with two Pyreneans and two cats, or eating out with all of my extended furry family, have passed me by so far.

I back out of the newsagent's with apologetic foreign smiles and trace the old road out of town. The lizards want the last trace of summer sun but don't trust its October warmth enough to do more

than poke a head out of a hole. As I walk past a wall, my shadow creates a reflex flicker from nearly every drainage hole, as lizard-heads disappear.

When I was eleven and pestering my parents for pets of every kind from snakes to puppies, my father said I could have a lizard (my latest idea) if I made a grass noose, held it in front of a hole in a wall and lassoed one. He thought this extremely funny and I was old enough to know at least that it was meant to be.

I wish that I could call him up and say I've found a wall where it would work – can I have one if I catch it? – but it is another one of those conversations that cannot happen. Each time you understand a moment of the past in the light of your new, older present – as a parent, even a grandparent – you realise what you have lost when you lost your parents, and why your children cannot share it all with you – yet.

Such reflections suit the cemetery en route, typically walled with family plots for the old names of the village. You sense the familial politics behind Marie being buried here when, according to the plaque, her husband Jacques was buried with his parents, in a different village graveyard. Who do you belong to when you die?

What always surprises me is the old age so many lived to, 18th and 19th century octogenarians. Perhaps there are more of these matriarchs and patriarchs buried in style in their local cemeteries than there are loose-living, die-young migrants? Of course there are the tragic deaths, like the twenty-six year old who was married for 1 year and 7 months, and was buried with the baby she could not give live birth to; the war deaths and the touching tributes from old comrades at arms.

If you want to visit a graveyard to make your spirits soar - and break your heart - go to what must be the most beautiful cemetery in the world, at Saint Christophe aux Oisans.

If you are not driving, you might enjoy the view sheer down mountains as the road twists through the Alps up to a tiny village legendary for its great mountain guides, who led the rich nineteenth century adventurers, particularly from Britain and Switzerland,

enabled them to conquer a peak and, more importantly, to return safely – usually. Giant among these characters is Père Gaspard, who was almost as fascinated by the 11,000ft heights of la Meije as were the foreigners who paid him, and who claimed first conquest of its peak.

The Gaspard family plot is large and there are clearly six or seven other dynasties which flourished in a village so high that supplies often had to reach it by cables in weather too severe for the donkeys. It seems that all the villagers were mountaineers by necessity – not the place to suffer from vertigo, this eyrie, level with the permanent snows of the peaks' dark faces.

The headstones tell of men, including old Father Gaspard himself, wise enough in snow and ice to survive into their eighties, and then be buried with their ice-picks crossed above the lilies at the grave head, silhouetted against the mountains. Other graves tell sadder stories of the young foreigners who earned the right to be buried in St Christophe, the twenty-year olds who didn't make it back down, their ice picks still glinting in the Alpine sun.

2

CONNECTING TO MAINS ALCOHOL

I'm so scarred I could work undercover in a high security prison and when I look in the mirror I realise it could be a men's high security prison, no problem. When was the last time I dressed like a girl?

It must have been Our Night Out when a daughter treated us to our first restaurant meal in Dieulefit, where the menu du terroir, using local produce, sparked the goat cheese project, and where John was so exhausted that it was all he could do to smile and nod.

I suspect the restaurateur and any customers who looked our way thought how kind we women were to take the village idiot on an outing. As I inspect the scars on my arms and the blood on my trousers, I wish I'd left it to the village idiot to weed the rose bed.

This is not as unloving as it sounds. When John can be talked out of the teenager's excuse to avoid weeding ('I wouldn't know which were the weeds') by an unequivocal bed of roses (plants) and grass (weeds), he will finish the job in ten minutes, having removed all trace of weed greenery. However, the concept of removing roots is not one he's willing to accept so I have the choice of quick and easy now and pay later, or do it myself the hard way. Life's like that; you have to choose between underwear which looks good and underwear which feels good – you can't have both.

He has been constructing fences. One of the great attractions of our walled garden was that John would not have to fence it. Having dog-proofed two and a half acres in Wales, with a daughter's help, he was happy to rest on his fencing laurels, until we looked out on our newly planted herb garden to see two Pyreneans playing 'I'm the king of the parsley'. Within a day, the plants were fenced in. Bear in mind that these are dogs capable of turning a heather bed into a war zone, with craters the size of meteor landing-sites – and all in ten minutes. As a puppy, Freyja dug up a six foot high wisteria and dragged it round the house to present it to me, on Mother's Day. She wagged her tail as I shrieked with delight. These are not dogs you mess with

Train them, you say contemptuously? We did the classes and the dog went with us. For abject humiliation you can't beat standing to one side of a large village hall while your dog doesn't come from the other, amidst a dozen smug Belgian shepherds and their owners. It did result in some interesting theories on dominance (our lack of) but we blame hundreds of years' breeding for the independence which is fine in 'Belle and Sebastien' but less attractive when you're on a beach and your dog is high-tailing it off over the horizon.

We take a break and sit on the terrace, drinking too much coffee, and I am amazed to see steam rising from John's head. I have never seen a human compost heap before but he does not seem totally thrilled to be told this.

As if the urgent fencing needed to create a plant zoo were not enough, we felt the sudden urge to try out the caged, three compartments system for composting. Like sister Anne, we have tried the heap, the tumble-turn barrel, the wooden-sided container … unlike Anne we did not have the benefit of Hertfordshire's free plastic composting tepee, which she swore worked so well that she was going to take it to the Pyrenees with her.

Having listened to her advice – perhaps 'listened' is an exaggeration – on the pointlessness of me taking forty boxes of books, and furniture which wasn't worth the removal costs, I was interested in her choices. It's a bit like one of those interview questions; 'If there

was a fire, what would you save and why?' It seems that a Hertfordshire County Council composting tepee comes high up the list.

I have total respect for Anne's gardening knowledge, as I do for sister Ruth's cooking and carpentry and for brother Ian's parachuting, physical courage and adventurous spirit; if only each of us kept to our specialism. And who is the worst? Me of course, Jack of all trades.

The advantage of my interest in everything is clear when I meet the various workmen who keep us up-to-date with the days of the week (If it's Monday, it must be the plumber ...) In our first six weeks living in France we have met nine workmen with different 'métiers' and have arranged to meet a tenth, the chimney sweep.

You don't believe me? Let me see ... there was the plumber, the man who delivered the oil, the boiler serviceman, the fridge (and TV) delivery men, the electrician, the builder – who returned with 'le menuisier' or as I called him 'the staircase-maker' (or according to the dictionary, the 'joiner' – would I have found a 'joiner' in Wales I wonder?), the satellite engineer and the kitchen designer (and cabinet-maker).

It's just as well we bought a house which has been 'fully modernised' (see estate agent's brochure). That's not actually what the electrician said when he looked at the job but as John had already reached the same conclusion and I had blown up the Dyson, I was resigned to a quote which was not poetic at all.

The first plumbing job, however, was unexpected. The bath, which had performed perfectly throughout the two weeks we lived here in the summer, developed a leak and I made my first, painful phone call to ask for a workman to visit.

I was very disappointed in John, who had been working on his French and had been studying the English subtitles to Francis Cabrel's lyrics on DVD. He could quote whole chunks and I thought this would have been the ideal opportunity for 'Il y a plusieurs mètres d'eau dans les rues de ma peine' (literally, 'There are several metres of water in the streets of my pain' – trust me, it sounds better in French) But no, he was happy to leave me with a more prosaic

dialogue, or rather monologue, on an answerphone, which would have been more effective if I'd managed to leave my own phone number correctly (as I found out when I phoned again the next day and the plumber was upset at not having been able to get back to me).

I'll repeat that because I sure as hell didn't believe it; the plumber was upset at not having been able to get back to me. I am only willing to write the next sentences because I no longer live in Britain and will not need the services of a British plumber or electrician again (I hope).

I have lost track of how many plumbers and electricians I phoned in Wales who never even bothered to return the call. I was incensed by a Report from The Basic Skills Agency which said that 9 out of 10 adults could not find a plumber in Yellow Pages; *I* couldn't find a sodding plumber and it was nothing to do with my literacy skills.

Even when I thought I'd found a plumber, he just didn't turn up. Small jobs were worst; if you mentioned a bigger job coming, you were in with a shout of seeing someone. Perhaps this is the true indicator that Dieulefit is not really in Provence, or perhaps Provence has been misrepresented, but I am going to testify, bravely, that every single one of the ten different workmen returned my call promptly, arranged a meeting, made it clear that they were busy but gave rough dates as to when they would give estimates and when they could actually start jobs. Every single workman has kept to those arrangements.

Don't get me wrong – I am immensely grateful for the work on my various houses done by people I respect for their skills. Welsh workmen have been a lesson and an entertainment for me. I will never forget Franz Becker, a German immigrant to the small Welsh village of Pontyberem, who lightened my life by wearing some version of lederhosen as he shifted breeze blocks and swore in German because he'd got carried away and bricked in the space where a window was supposed to go.

It was the usual case of three-jobs-on-the-go and do-the-most-on-time-for-whoever's-nastiest (the same thing happens with

schoolkids doing their homework), and our replacement of windows seemed to be last on his list… nothing out of the ordinary except that I was nine months pregnant and he had promised me that it would be done before the baby came.

He had taken out the old windows when my waters broke; I spent a total of 24 hours in hospital and those windows were all in place when I arrived home with my son. My mother was waiting in York, not even knowing I'd gone into labour and I phoned her half an hour after giving birth to give her the good news. 'The windows are in,' I told her.

'That's great news,' she said.

'And I've had a baby boy.' I think she just shrieked; she had already packed her suitcase and my parents were there within a day to admire the new windows.

By the end of Summer 1984, I knew Franz Becker's shorts better than I knew my own wardrobe, as he and his men were re-plastering the living room walls while I was desperately seeking somewhere private in my own house to breast-feed my baby. Don't talk to me about the need for young mothers to relax in order to breast-feed – a bit of stress never did anyone any harm.

Other key figures in my life for weeks on end were Wayne and the boys. This time I was at home for long periods because I was now working freelance, giving me more time to make the required cups of tea (my mother's genes) and to supervise the work on hand (my father's).

There was the moment when one of 'the Boys' had left his toolbox in the middle of the drive and I neatly scrunched over it as I drove out into town, waving to them as I went. I'm sure I heard one of them muttering, 'Women drivers…'

It was my pond that brought out their best qualities. They had organised a digger to excavate some ground in front of the stables, where they were laying concrete. The digger was brand new, beau-

tiful machinery with a turning circle on the scoop that could have served ice cream.

The four of us, Wayne, his boys and I, stood admiring their mate's new toy and I couldn't help saying, 'I'd love a go in that.' Without a flicker of humour, one of the Boys said, 'You're one of them ambitious women, aren't you,' and I was put in my place.

I asked Wayne if he would scrape our drained bog, while the digger was there anyway, so that we could restore the pond by putting in a plastic liner and a lot of work. Within minutes of me asking, the four of us stood and watched the digger scooping out the pond. I'm good at joining in the bits where we all stand and watch.

One of the Boys, the sixty-five year old, said, 'Your husband could go in there if you do it now.'

We all considered this.

The Boy added, 'Do it for you.'

We considered it some more.

'Thanks,' I said, 'but I'll keep him.'

We thought on.

The other Boy asked, 'Have you got newts?'

As it happened, I did have newts and had even found one swimming in the dogs' outside water bowl (dropped by a heron? pissed as a?) so explained all this enthusiastically.

I was missing the point. 'You can get a grant,' he told me, 'from the council.'

'How do they know you do have newts?'

'They come and have a look.'

'What if the newts aren't there when they look?'

'I can get you some newts for the day.' I turned down this offer even more reluctantly. I love the idea of a jar of newts touring the county to obtain grants but stranger things have happened in Carmarthenshire …

So it's not as if workmen are a novelty, but this time I have to work on my vocabulary before every meeting. In the past I might have managed an ice-breaking 'Hello, how-are-you, nice day' in

Welsh now and again but this is the real thing with people who might not (unthinkable thought) speak English at all.

I look up the words for shelves and woodworm, (wanting one and wanting rid of the other), I need the French for 'excess', as in insurance not partying. I have already enjoyed exploring the French legal system in order to buy a house and consider its ownership.

We love French inheritance law, honest, but the important question is how we can get round it. I need the vocabulary for all of these professional discussions in French. Did you think a 'va et vient' was a sexy line in a seventies pop song? Wrong – it's a two-way lighting switch. You thought an 'interrupteur' was something you told children not to be? Wrong – it's just a light switch.

Our two volume Harrap French/English dictionary is heavy enough to bend a shelf but still has limitations. We are still trying to find out what 'carré rose' actually means but the dictionary translation of 'pink square' seems inadequate to describe a type of film which does indeed seem to have lots of pink, oodles of very naked pink in fact, but not much square.

We consulted Harrap after receiving the electrician's estimate and were curious as to why he would want to put port-holes in the cellar ceilings; he looked up the dictionary with us, unimpressed by its total lack of electrical expertise – a 'hublot' is also a circular ceiling light.

Another word that is now firmly in our vocabulary is 'triage'. I first heard the word when John chatted up the triage nurse at Portsmouth Hospital's Accident and Emergency Unit, as she joined the two ripped sides of a gash in my cheek with medical sellotape.

Heading for a romantic weekend in Normandy, with two hours to wait for a late ferry, I accidentally smashed the car door into my face. It had not been a good week as I was already in shock from a hairdresser's over-enthusiastic attempts to return my hair to its natural colour (whatever that was, prior to golden highlights or 'streaks' as the hairdresser preferred to call them) – she'd dyed it black. Still recovering from hair trauma, I now had a hole in my face.

Luckily the ferry was even later, the nurse was an angel and she

said I could still go on my weekend (complete with painkillers, a bandage and a throbbing black eye). Not even waiting for seven hours for the exceptionally late ferry, surrounded by drunken work parties who had booked a booze cruise, could spoil my weekend.

While I queued for the Ladies' toilets at the docks, the girl beside me, dressed in full warpaint, pelmet and little else giggled at me, 'I can't wait to get pissed, how about you?'

By this time the hair felt very black, the eye was starting to close up, getting pissed was not my life's ambition and we must have looked like 'Before and after – life on the streets.'

Not even an hour throwing up in a restaurant toilet on the Sunday night, while John ate solo, could spoil things. It could have been a delayed reaction to the accident, the scallops on Saturday night, the glacial December temperatures around a Christmas market or all of the above. I was delirious with painkillers, John was my hero and, more crucially, my hotwater bottle, and it was the sort of experience which makes the word 'triage' stick in the mind; it means 'sorting', from the French, the nurse said as she sorted me.

It was with interest then that, in a detailed analysis of types of pedal bin (100 kitchens again) I found that I could have a 'triage' bin, the main disadvantage of which is that the compartments are small. The advantage of course is that you have your recycling 'sorted' (aha!).

My French exists in a parallel universe to the one where real French people speak real French. I communicate but with a series of mistakes which I only recognise much later. As Anne kindly points out, 'That's only the mistakes you know you've made'. Her turn will come.

I have a long history of gaffes, starting well before we moved to France. One gîte-owner was very amused by me telling him that my husband worked as a teacher and 'moi, je traîne des professeurs.' Unfortunately, instead of meaning that I train teachers it suggests that I drag them along, like towing a caravan. He was so tickled by the accuracy of the image that he said I should carry on saying that if anyone asked me what I did for a living.

A French friend staying with us on an exchange and on whom I was practising my French must have been bemused by the local information I provided; I told him that there was a lot of central heating in our valley and I shook my head sadly. There's really not that much difference between chauffage (central heating) and chômage (unemployment) now is there? 'What's a consonant or two between friends' is an approach that is likely to get me into trouble, especially when whole syllables convert of their own volition to completely different words.

I have grown worse rather than better now that we actually live in France. I have asked the post office clerk to give me a recipe for my postage (a 'recette' instead of a 'reçu').

Through poor pronunciation, I asked the plumber to connect our house to mains alcohol ('eau de vie' instead of 'eau de ville'); not such a bad idea and he did say it wouldn't be a problem.

My worst mistake (so far) was undoubtedly when I was sitting in the estate agent's, tired and triumphant, having offered for The House and had the offer accepted, after all the stressful conversations – in both French and English – that house-hunting entails. I knew that I was supposed to show a variety of certificates as evidence for the initial contract and I was clutching The Black Bag which I had prepared back in Wales. Keen to show my knowledge of the French system, I asked the Estate Agent whether he would like to see my swimming certificate.

Surprisingly, he didn't seem to know what to say and John told me afterwards that there had been an interesting expression crossing the poor man's face. I realised that I had said 'natation' instead of 'naissance', corrected myself and the sale progressed but I wish I had the self–possession in these situations to say something like, 'In Wales, we always show our swimming certificates when we buy a house.' I do have one somewhere, proof of floundering a whole 25 yards. I think it's in the box along with other signs of unfulfilled potential; coming 3rd in the junior girls' obstacle race, a pass result at Viola Grade 2, and confirmation of my status as a Schools

Inspector for both Ofsted and Estyn (Wales) – all things of which I am both proud and ashamed.

French lessons are all around me. When I log on to the Internet, I am asked if I would like to send Saint Arnould some flowers? I would not but it is still a novelty to be asked. My homepage also warns me that I mustn't pick mushrooms just after a hard frost; it would be like eating re-frozen mushrooms and would poison me.

I came late to mushrooms, despite a very successful foray into Welsh fields when I was in my twenties. I took carrier bags of button mushrooms into the school staffroom to share with my friends, who all said 'No thanks – you kill yourself if you want.'

On second thoughts, perhaps it wasn't such a successful foray, as I threw most of my treasures away, disappointed with my friends. Now if we'd been in Carmarthen rather than Llanelli, I might have fallen more hippy-side in my friends, who would then have hoped for magic in their mushrooms.

A Carmarthen colleague was called to a hospital bed-side to nurse? bollock? her seventeen year old son who'd fried up some hallucinogenic mushrooms and taken the consequences – luckily very slight and temporary.

No, it wasn't until I was in my forties and walking Normandy footpaths with the new, digital camera that I really discovered mushrooms. We still have two floppy discs with forty photographs of – you've guessed – forty different species – that I was hooked.

The Normandy gîte also offered me a shelf-full of old farming books, one of which gave a remedy for mushroom poisoning; you take three rabbits' livers and two rabbits' brains… (What do you do with the spare brain? Or do you look for one brainless bunny to avoid waste?)

I think the general idea was that the chopped mixture would make you throw up, which might help, but in capital letters the reader was told that even this remedy would be no use against the

real baddies, which take two or three days to kill you but definitely, slowly and disgustingly, kill you. Perhaps my Welsh friends were right and I will, French-style, take my weird finds to the chemist's for checking – a service all French chemists offer.

October's a dangerous month – if the mushrooms don't kill me, then the hunters might – gangs of men at their rendezvous, wearing weatherproof coats, smoking beside their 4x4, while their hounds yelp and tangle leads with excitement. We are not surprised to see one group wearing bright orange hats.

There were forty-six men killed last year in hunting accidents and it is with glee that the newspapers reported the first one this year; he tripped over a branch and shot himself. So far, locally, the versatile pompiers have been called out to deal with a wild boar which, wounded and enraged, charged into the crowd at the Tournon local derby football match, and to rescue a hunting dog which had fallen onto rocks. The boar was shot; the dog was saved. The Patron Saint of Hunting, a Saint Hubert who died in Belgium in 727, must be very busy in the autumn.

We are not yet French enough to pull a shotgun on the hare that lives in Monsieur Dubois' orchard. Sometimes, as we walk the dogs, we find the newly vacant 'form', a neat half-hare shape in the grass like a terrine mold from a posh cookshop. Sometimes we disturb the hare itself and invent the new sport of dog-skiing as we are dragged across the orchard by Pyreneans. We do shoot the hare – with the digital camera, very British.

3

CHRYSANTHEMUMS AND GRAVESTONES

Why is it always in the four days that you're alone, for the first time in a new country, at the start of a major bank holiday, that something which has been working without a problem, packs up?

Despite the local paper's 'Dictum of the Day' 'A la Toussaint, manchons aux bras, gants aux doigts' ('On All Saint's Day, wear long sleeves and gloves') the day has been so hot that it was not until evening that I switched on the oil-fired, recently installed, recently serviced central heating. Nothing happened.

Or rather the Starship control lit up with some green and some red lights, possibly as normal but I really couldn't be sure. I spent a happy hour reading the French instructions and trying to relate a diagram of how a boiler works in general, to the specific red monster in front of me.

I pressed a few switches, thought 'Oh is that what that does,' checked the radiators and the oil supply and got nowhere. I applied masculine technical know-how (swore a lot, stomped around and kicked it) and got nowhere.

I gave in and phoned the service engineer, hoping against hope that the Bank Holiday Weekend had not started. It had. I went back and stood looking at the boiler. The light not so much dawned as

twinkled red, at ankle level, in a recess, indicating a button. So I pushed the button et voilà! We had lift-off. Presumably this was a trip-switch thingy which must have tripped during the 'tempests' the day before (of course – I was alone for two days so what sort of weather do you expect?) and it needed to be re-set. It's a pity that the nice engineer didn't show me that particular button; on the other hand, perhaps he did and I thought he was asking where to plug in his vacuum cleaner.

Today I whittled a toothpick and jammed it in place of a missing spindle in a doorhandle, having nearly locked four very aggrieved pets into their bedroom. When the handle fell off and I could see the spindle disappearing fast through to the other side, I knew exactly what the worst could be.

Ten years ago, John and I took a school trip which ended with one night in a posh Paris hotel, courtesy of the travel company which had cocked up the bookings of our lovely safe holiday cottages near Freyjus. Last-night-of-trip is always a reason for celebration (by the kids) and desperate attempts by the teachers to prevent accidental suicides and incidental pregnancies (mostly of the kids).

As we prepared ourselves for a long night, we received an emergency phone call to our room from one of our colleagues, whose two-year old son had run straight into the bathroom, locked himself in there by mistake and couldn't get out. Hysteria was starting to set in so we pottered along to see what we could do. John called the hotel reception and explained the situation while I decided to play nice cop and try to talk the little bugger out of the bathroom, as if he were on a high-rise ledge and threatening to jump; his mother had by now started on the duty-free whisky she'd bought to take home.

Having watched way too many TV detectives, I asked Maureen for some background info and found out that Superman was the little one's favourite character. I then lay on the floor so my voice would travel under the state-of-the-art stainless steel, handle-less (on the outside), seamless (damn!) unpickable door (and I've done my share of sliding a Barclaycard down the front door so I could get in – my front door, I should say).

'Hi, it's Jean here.' (Establish how calm you are, how normal everything is and who the hell you are anyway). Sobbing carries on in bathroom, mother slurring slightly in background.

'You like Superman don't you Gareth. Well, Gareth, you know what Superman would do?' Sobbing.

'Gareth listen to Jean now,' (teeth starting to grit a bit), 'Superman would look at the door. Can you see the door?' Sobbing moves around a bit, not necessarily anywhere near the door.

'Well there's a little ... (what is there on the bathroom door anyway? These modern things could have anything, chains, bolts, handles, digital press-buttons? What was in our bathroom? Oh yes) metal thingy and it turns – Superman would try to turn that…' You get the idea. Unfortunately Gareth doesn't.

This goes on for some time, an hour according to John, weeks according to me, a lifetime according to the distraught (but mellowing) mother, at which stage Mr-Hotel-Person turns up with an allan key, I get up off the floor as I am clearly in his way, the door is opened, small child and mother hug each other. There is no crisis and Mr-Hotel-Person has gone before we can say, 'What if someone was having a heart attack in there?'

The rest of the night was relatively calm, characterised by some of my sixteen-year old boys treating Paris' most sophisticated diners to a traditional Llanelli last-night by dressing up in drag, with full make-up borrowed from the girls. John's Swansea pupils were bemused (and so were his colleagues), clearly unaware of whatever it is which makes tough working blokes dress up as girls for a really good time (just think of the British armed forces).

It was not the first time I'd done patrol duty in a hotel, wearing a nightie and dressing gown and occasionally telling innocent holidaymakers to keep the noise down and get to their rooms, so the rest of the night was a doddle.

However, this whole experience meant that when I saw a spindle disappearing through a lock, I had visions of the Superman routine again with a bunch of animals to whom I had already announced 'Good morning girls.'

This meant that they were all busting for a pee and ready for breakfast. 'Hang on a minute, I can't open the door,' did not go down well as I rushed off, found some tweezers and rescued the tiny bit of visible spindle before I was doomed to a reprise of Paris, with no man, helpful or otherwise, and, what's worse, no idea of where the allan keys were or exactly what you did with them.

Presumably they would exactly fit that square hole? And turn? I didn't want to find out whether square holes had changed size in however many decades that door had been there). As it was, the pets gave me that disgruntled, 'Can't get the staff' stare as they rushed into the garden, and I went off to whittle toothpicks. Must remember to replace toothpick with metal pin …

While I am home alone, everyone else in the whole of France is celebrating the major Bank Holiday of Toussaint (All Saints) with their families. This is what all those chrysanthemums have been for.

When I call up at Super-U there are queues clutching their last-minute pompoms and, opposite the supermarket, families are spilling out of the cars ranked along the cemetery wall. Three generations, wrapped in scarves against the wind, carry their flowers to dress the graves of their 'proches' for 'the Day of The Dead'.

The police have been putting out warnings on the national news, and on notices pinned to the graveyard gates, against opportunist theft; while people tend the graves, they forget to lock their cars and we are advised to leave nothing of value in our cars, no handbags or jackets, even if we remember to lock the doors.

When did you last see a Sexton on the British news, highlighted for his good work cleaning and polishing the monuments and tombstones ready for today? And it is beautiful in the sunlight, a village graveyard where the living remember their dead with a profusion of flowers. The chrysanthemums catch the colours of the autumn leaves falling in the sunlight amidst the more sombre cypresses.

Not autumn, but Easter is the best time for graveyards in Wales where even the forbidding architecture of chapels is softened by daffodils on the graves and by the green of spring grass, green and

yellow everywhere against the gray of the buildings and, usually, the rain.

Old traditions can be beautiful to the onlooker but a Welsh workmate told me that she would not leave the chore of grave-tending to her children and the local paper tells me that times have changed in la Drôme too; families no longer stay in the same village and cannot always make it back to their parents' graves for Toussaint, and as for the big towns – it seems as if there is a problem of overpopulation amongst the dead, so overcrowded and unkempt are their quarters. I think about my dead and I see that my roses have bloomed yet again, in defiance of November.

November roses will always remind me of my 18th birthday and the special card my mother bought me, with roses on it and Omar Khayyam's words inside:-

'Look to the Rose that blows about us – 'Lo,
Laughing,' she says 'into the world I blow:
At once the silken tassel of my Purse
Tear, and its Treasure on the Garden throw.'

I never planted roses when I was younger, because their beauty was so short-lived and the bushes didn't earn their keep in my garden. I have changed my mind. Beauty, even if only for a day, is still treasure and I have learnt to accept the thorns and the time to scatter petals. I have also grown to love sentimental old Fitzgerald's version of Khayyam:-

'And when Thyself with shining Foot shall pass
Among the Guests Star-scattered on the Grass,
And in thy joyous Errand reach the Spot
Where I made one – turn down an empty Glass!'
Tamam shud
It is completed.

4

GOAT CHEESE WITH A STING

I investigate some mushrooms in our lawn so that I can check them out in my pocket guide, knocking one over to study it better; pure white caps with white gills and neat edges. I idly browse through the guide while I eat my toast and marmalade… that looks similar but it does not sound good… 'like many all white mushrooms, poisonous, in fact deadly… wash hands carefully after even touching it'.

I inspect my hands, the left one a little sticky with marmalade. Merde! Did I turn over the lethal weapon with my left hand (very bad) or right (not so bad, I haven't touched my toast with that one and I don't think I've licked the handle of my coffee cup)?

I wash my hands with all the enthusiasm of Lady Macbeth after a bad night and already I can feel my stomach clenching. John will come home to find me a twisted corpse clawing at the table legs (although if I'm a corpse I'll probably have stopped clawing by that stage). How is he going to get home if I can't meet him at the station? To take my mind off my impending demise, I decide to work on the goat cheese project.

In addition to its air, pottery and IQ level, Dieulefit has its famous goat cheese, le Picodon, so good it is awarded the status of appellation controlée. My knowledge of goats is limited but the emotional

scars are deep. It started well, in the early days of my move to Wales when one of my colleagues who moonlighted (moonlit?) as a farmer, or was it the other way around? gave me a regular supply of fresh goat's milk for a few months. My (other) Welsh friends were horrified at me drinking goat milk – there was obviously no telling what we English people would try when we moved to Wales and played at rural life – but I quite enjoyed the earthiness of it and the words 'direct from the farm' still hold magic for me.

I also ate goat (I think) but the newly ex-graduate friend who revealed what the roast had been, was the sort who also revealed that you'd just eaten hash cake, and I didn't find anything weird, different or exciting on either occasion; the former tasted like pork and the latter like girl guides' fairy buns. However, you do have to bear in mind that I once disgraced myself at a dinner party by commenting, as I turned over a metal thingy with my fork, that I'd got shot in my chicken (it was the first time I'd eaten pheasant and how was I to know that no-one shot chickens?) so I confess to a certain naiveté in my gastronomic education.

Next encounters with a goat were also very positive. An English friend busy pursuing self-sufficiency à la John Seymour, as we did in Wales in the seventies, was babysitting her neighbour's goats and I milked one with moderate success and all kinds of virtuous feelings.

(This was the same friend who needed someone to take in a beehive, for a month. It had to be someone who lived far enough away that the bees wouldn't get confused and waggledance their way back to where their hive was supposed to be. It also had to be someone very gullible as it was May. I spent a month too scared to go to the bottom of my own garden in case they swarmed. How do you know if a beehive's overcrowding anyway? And preferably before the buggers produce a new queen and swarm).

Having all these ill-conceived notions of how sweet goats were and completely ignoring a wealth of western literature in which a goat represents the devil, (if you look at those yellow eyes and square pupils the word 'sweet' is not the first which pops into any sane

woman's head), I volunteered to get a kid for a friend who must have been similarly deluded.

'While you're getting one anyway, can you get me one too?' someone else asked, so I did. I took the estate car that had once been my father's well-polished pride and joy, headed off down the usual Carmarthenshire tracks where the cars trim the hedgerows, did the deal and heaved two squealing, jumping kids into the boot. I tethered them carefully in the garden, thought how sweet they looked and the next time I looked through the window there was only one – and a well-chewed rope. I phoned the friend whose goat had done a bunk and village rumour said it was heading down the hill towards her place. For all I know she's still tearing around Pontyberem, eating plenty of fibre.

This left me with the less-evil one. How did I know which was which? I would have thought it obvious; by a wonderful coincidence, the friend I liked the better was the one whose goat I could still see. Leaving Goatless Friend to find herself a goat, I took great care of the Lesser Evil for the week I was minding her while Better Friend was on holiday.

I discovered that a goat eats everything except the long grass you were hoping it would trim for you; it eats your favourite shrubs, fabric of any kind – especially newly washed – and bricks – at least that's the only way I can account for the disappearing corner on the end of the pigsty.

I had tethered Lesser Evil beside the pigsty so she could shelter from the rain. Surprisingly, goatcoats have no weatherproofing, which is probably what makes kid leather so soft (but you don't want to think about goatskin, do you). I was singing and washing dishes, looking out of the window at the happy little goat, which had jumped onto the pigsty roof. Very cute.

I carried on singing and washing dishes, and glanced out of the window to see a goat in the last stages of death by hanging. Not so cute. She had either fallen or jumped (or even been pushed – the jury's out) and caught the rope around the pigsty gable, suspending

herself by the neck as is the wont of very strange rock stars in search of thrills.

I rushed down the garden path and lifted her heels to relax the noose and let her breathe. As she was still alive and I was alone, and I couldn't hold her and reach the gable, there was only one thing for it – I had to drop her again, with a fairly sickening lurch and a very unpleasant glare from two narrowed yellow eyes. From there on it was straightforward; I had to haul the goat up by the neck to give me enough slack to throw the rope back over the gable.

Lesser Evil was duly lowered, while I kept tight hold of the rope – not even a near-death experience will stop a goat doing a runner, in fact I wouldn't guarantee that it wasn't a set-up – and I tethered her firmly well away from the pigsty or any shelter (bugger the lack of weatherproofing – it was probably a country fiction anyway). She reached Better Friend safely and apparently led a long, placid life – I was just lucky to know her in her salad days.

Despite all of this hard-earned goat expertise, I only discovered goat cheese on holiday in the south of France, where the little Banons from the Vaucluse became a favourite on the cheese-board. They look appealing, these small rounds wrapped in chestnut leaves to keep them moist, or in the many variations where an outer coating of red peppers or spices adds colour and scent to the bland and creamy cheese. They complement so many other tastes; olives, peppers, ham... and they melt in cooking sauces, on pizzas, on pasta.

Goat cheese is a cook's treasure and, having discovered it, I wanted to find some in Wales when we went back home. It shouldn't have been difficult as there are, as I knew, goats in Wales. There is indeed wonderful goat cheese in Wales but finding it is as difficult as finding local apples.

Even at the stall in Carmarthen market that sells a Welsh type of cheddar, with names like St Illtyds, and options of garlic and mustard in the variants, even there the goat's cheese sold was from Somerset. This is a national disgrace and I will never understand why British supermarkets and shops are so reluctant to stock local produce, unless the balance between quality and price has tipped the

wrong way in all retailers. In Wales, it almost seems part of the cultural lack of confidence which says 'If it's from round here, then it can't be any good.'

What food *is* good in Wales? You only have to listen for two minutes to the Italian chef who made Abergavenny's 'The Walnut Tree' an attraction to foodies across Britain, to know the answer. Have you tried sewin straight from the River Cothi, a fisherman's dream of a river that rushes between the good green pastures (all that rain is good for something)? Have you eaten new Pembrokeshire potatoes? Beetroot and rhubarb from a neighbour? Beef from Welsh Black cattle, ordered in advance and direct from the farmer, who is also your milkman and delivers his dairy produce to your door? And Welsh lamb, surely the best in the world?

That's just a few of the mainstream items but in Wales you can easily have the space, and you have the climate, to grow your own – there is nothing like mangetout peas, broccoli and lettuce fresh from your own garden. There are also the wild places, beaches where you can find lavabread (seaweed to you), cliffs where samphire grows, woods full of wild strawberries, hedgerows covered in blackberries and fields full of autumn mushrooms.

If we were French, we would be proud of all of this; we would want to eat it and talk about it – and buy it in our shops. 'He's a farmer' wouldn't mean 'he's some lower class person of diminished brain'.

The farmers, vintners and producers here in France all have their own associations, specialist apprenticeships and a range of agricultural courses. They also express themselves powerfully, usually with several thousand tractors all blocking key motorway arteries or by violent assault against foreign competition; gain enormous subsidies and promote local produce in ways which range from the obvious (through local shops, factory tours and a website) to the downright bizarre (the village boasting the biggest pile of chestnuts in the world).

Our farming specialism here in Dieulefit is goat's cheese so we have an annual fête under the banner 'le Picodon chez lui.' The

Picodon is yet another small round goat's cheese but to gain a.o.c. status as made in the Dieulefitois way, it must be refined and regularly washed in water for a month. People will try to tell you that the Picodon came from the Ardèche (where they allegedly wash them in white wine or eau-de-vie) or from the Vercors but this is of course calumny and you must not believe such terrible lies. The Picodon originated in Dieulefit, 'chez lui' (its home) as the defiant note reads on the banner. Proof? Its oldest mention was dated 1361 at Dieulefit and its name comes from the local dialect 'pico' meaning 'slightly piquant'.

From the moment I saw Cavet's Picodon creamery through my bedroom window, I conceived the goat's cheese project and grew more fired with missionary zeal as I realised the sad lack of books in English about goats' cheese. My Internet research revealed that of the two books I could find, the more interesting was written by an order of American nuns and is now out of print. The time is obviously as ripe as the cheese for the Jean Gill Book of 50 things to do with a Picodon.

I start my research with the goats and even they are different here, apparently living in well-disciplined communes. When we were walking the Pyreneans up in the woods, we knew from the bells that the goat herd was on the move and we reached the lane to see two black and white border collies shepherding the lop-eared bleating source of the noise.

We bonjoured our local goatherd, who probably has a degree in capriculture from Valence University and who sports a beard longer than his lead goat's. (I have never understood why short pointy beards are called goatees – you only have to look at a goat's wispy face decoration to see that it's more like that of a maharishi vowed to hair and saintliness). The herd walks daily and if we are in the garden or walking back from the village, thirty tiny clappers echo across the hills from the woods above us.

My project research continued with the purchase of five blue Picodons at Dieulefit's fête. This was when I discovered that the different coloured cheeses lined up at the stall were the same cheese,

or to be more exact, cheeses made in the same way, but aged for different lengths of time.

Ageing makes the cheese stronger (lucky cheese) and the blue crusted Picodons do have that mouldy tang you would associate with a mild blue cheese like a dolcellatte, while being nowhere near as salty as a roquefort. (I know these are not the words an expert would use but if ordinary people don't talk about it, even using all the wrong words, how are we going to become better eaters? Or buyers?

The French have the best word for it; they talk about 'amateurs de ….', for instance 'amateurs de fromage' meaning what we would call 'experts' – the French word suggests the enthusiasm of non-professionals and I will drink my Côtes du Rhône to that).

Having discovered middle-aged Picodon and started an ongoing conversation with the producer and market stall-holder, I have continued my education on Fridays at Dieulefit's market. This led to me buying a vieux Picodon, which I presented to John at lunchtime with a flourish, telling him that this would have a really strong taste.

I raised the cheese knife and hit solid wood – no, I hadn't missed and hit the cheese board, it was the cheese from which the knife rebounded, blunted.

'Perhaps we won't take a slice off this one,' I suggested, gathering the few shavings that had dropped off the aged Picodon, more in fright at the sight of the knife descending than because they'd actually been cut, and I sprinkled them over my bread.

It was a very definite strongly cheesy taste; 'pico' could indeed be the word if I were a fourteenth century Dieulefitoise. It was not however an elegant way of serving cheese and I couldn't believe I was going about this the right way.

The shavings gave me the idea by reminding me of parmesan (the real thing, that smells of sick and looks like old soap) and so I tried grating it onto savoury pancakes and onto pasta, and voila! it seemed I had some more recipes for my book. I was happily exploring how many things I could do with an old Picodon when I noticed that my face flannel smelt of cheese, my pillows smelt of cheese and unwashed socks smelt less cheesy than anything else in the house.

Either I was losing my nose or I'd overdone the Picodon so I left it alone for a few days ... and discovered olives.

Not just olives of course but how many different varieties there are and what they all taste like. There is an olive stand in Dieulefit market where queues of people stand with their cheque-books out, ready to buy by the carrier-bag; this is the stall you should go to. King of the French table olives is the a.o.c. Nyons tanche, bruised black and mellow, producing the appellation controlée olive oil which is a very expensive treat (and an excuse for another mad village fête after olive-picking in December).

Our current favourite is a green olive in garlic, mild, garlicky and moreish, but we have adventured beyond these. Savouring 'olives in peppers' at lunchtime, I was unable to tell John that they were in fact in chili peppers, until I had downed two glasses of water straight off.

You know that moment when you're young and innocent and you chew on a cool green thingy after eating something a bit too spicy, and someone says, 'Sorry, perhaps I should have told you that the green things are chilies?' It was one of those moments.

We subsequently invented a spectacular French version of chili con carne with the heat provided entirely by twelve olives. Then there were the lemon olives - too lemony. They worked very well in home made foccacia. Last to date have been the black olives in garlic – they were too ... black.

My olive education is in its early stages but two hundred metres to the left (the Picodon Cavet being two hundred metres to the right) is an olive oil producer so I am hopeful that I will become an 'amateur' taught by a member of the appropriate 'confrérie' or 'guild'.

I only wish I could add a garlic expert to my local contacts; they wear some amazing hats in the newspaper photo of the 'confrérie d'ail'. Now that would be a certificate for an ambitious woman like me to aim for in the future – I have after all planted two dozen cloves amongst the rosebeds as a natural insecticide.

While waiting to die of mushroom poisoning, I pot some dried tomatoes, using Carluccio's trick of soaking them first in vinegar to water, 1:4, adding a peeled clove of garlic and then covering them in

olive oil. It's the potting that does it – my new obsession gets the better of me and out come the three old Picodons I have been saving for an experiment which the market seller has told me will not work.

In one of the books I sneak a look at each time we call at the newsagent's, I read the old Provençal suggestion that old Picodons could be turned into delicacies for the cheese board by stacking them in olive oil, separated by a sprig of fresh savoury and with a peeled garlic clove added. My market expert said that the olive oil won't penetrate the hard outer crusts (not to mention the hard inner crust) but if nothing else I will get interestingly-flavoured olive oil.

It's amazing how long four days alone can be when you've grown used to company. I phone Anne; she has reached the Pyrenees but she is so tired that it seems her brain is still in Hemel Hempstead. She tells me that they can see the mountains and I start to hope we might have a conversation. 'Is there snow on the mountains?' I ask.

'I can't tell,' she replies.

I take it slowly. 'Is that because it's misty on the peaks?'

'No,' she says, 'it's in the summer that it's misty.'

'But you can't tell if there's snow on the peaks?' I ask, unkindly.

She panics 'I don't know,' she says and I give up while her husband can be heard prompting in the background, 'There is snow up there.' Perhaps we'll have a sisterly chat another time …

That was the wrong sister to discuss the goat cheese project with so I phone the other one, who is also the mother of my youngest best friend, my five year old niece Ellie. I can't wait for the children to come here and play 'cache-cache' (hide and seek) in the cellars.

Neither apparently can Ruth, who would happily put them both on a train tomorrow and party in their absence. Nine-year-old nephew James seems to approve of me; I am the eccentric aunt of every fantasy book, in whose attic you can drink ginger beer, in whose wardrobes lurk unicorns and satyrs, and in whose conversations appear some very rude words.

Like some obsessive greenie trying to reintroduce an endangered species to the wild, I plan their environment – outdoor chess set, swings, perhaps some fruity ice creams in the freezer – in hopes that

the children will come, so I will be able to tell stories again, to live in a world where the apple with which Snow White was poisoned has accidentally got muddled with the apples from my orchard – is anyone brave enough to taste one of my apples? Or would you like to get your mother to take a bite first?

It is not only the children who fill the house in my imagination; I am a benign grandmother heading the long dining-table set under the trees, laden with the food I have prepared lovingly in my custom-designed kitchen. My student son and his friends are all sleeping in the attic, my four grown-up 'filles' by proxy, who are all 'belles' to me, are in various bedrooms or tents with their partners or friends and even my little belle-petite-fille will be toddling around, the step-grand-daughter who allows me to wear my gray hairs with pride.

Mozart will be playing gently in the background and I will look up, smile and catch my husband's eye. But, even in my fantasy, John is turning an apoplectic purple… my dream is his nightmare. I will have to sneak our people in one or two at a time so he hardly notices. I check the time; I have not died of mushroom poisoning so I will pick my man up from the station and we will think only of each other for a few days.

5

YOUR OWN COUNTRY, WHERE YOU'RE FROM

I am an immigrant and I am British, but that word 'British' is an administrative nationality and has no roots. My parents were deeply Scottish and, as far as they were concerned, so are their children. I know which tartans I am entitled to wear (dozens of them) and am always vaguely disappointed with Hogmanay, but my Scottishness does not run deep – or is too deep for day-to-day.

Apart from a few months aged six, when I went to school in Kirkcaldy and was thumped in the toilets for having an English accent (not the last time this would be a problem), Scotland was the place we went back to for holidays, in between my soldier father's postings abroad.

Until I was fourteen, I had spent a maximum of two years in any one place and postings had sometimes been for as little as six months; based on where I lived, I could consider myself German or Chinese with as much reason as any other nationality.

I discovered early on that it really annoyed my parents if I said I was English so from then on I was English, having been born in Aldershot. My father used to ask, 'If the cat has kittens in the oven does that make them biscuits?' his only contribution to questions of national identity. He was very quick to get British passports for the two of his children who were born in Hanover.

York gave me six years and northern vowels, so there is something north-of-England-ish that I feel comfortable with but it was when I moved to Wales that I really changed from migrant to immigrant – worst of all, English immigrant. There was no doubt in any Welsh mind about my nationality, whatever my own confusions.

Twenty-five years on, Wales is my main country and the goodbyes when we left for France were as good as funeral orations, with the bonus of us getting to hear them. There were prepared speeches from friends on the lines of, 'I want you to know you have always been ...; a handwritten note from the milkman (he of the melt-in-your-mouth beef, who had been our milkman for an astonishing nineteen years); the travelling fruit-and-veg man's good wishes delivered with exceptionally strong boxes for packing (you were right Steve, those were good boxes); the grateful goodbyes from parents of a lad I once taught (grateful because they would no longer have to mow our field, a favour which lasted over a decade) – 'We're sorry you're going – it's all newcomers in the village now,' made me realise I had come a long way in twenty-five years.

Everyone wished us well; many told us their own retirement dreams - a little cottage in the Vale of Glamorgan, where, unlike in the Gwendraeth Valley, the sun always shines – allegedly (I wasn't tempted to change my mind); a villa in Spain for someone else; more than one wanting to return to childhood roots on the Welsh coast in Carmarthenshire or Pembrokeshire. Even the newsagent told me that he dreamed of the States while he worked in Tumble, a typical ex-mining village of terraced houses in a steep ribbon curving grayly up to the Rugby Club.

I stayed dry-eyed through all of this. Closeness is a state of the heart not an accident of geography and I have said goodbyes before; the important ones are only 'au revoirs'. I tried to give my news personally to everyone I could manage; I even told Llanelli's Big Issue seller, whose name is Peter. He shook my hand and wished me luck but this wasn't enough. He unwomanned me completely by giving me a big hug, wishing me all the best and saying 'I'm glad you told me or I would have worried about you.'

He would have worried about *me*. In the past, he has shown me photos of his children and a glimpse into another world. Peter would make a superb concierge for an apartment block; he is unbelievably patient, good with people, conscientious and cheerful in doing a boring job – and he is unemployed.

Twenty-five years ago, Llanelli still offered the steelworks, the tinplate factories and the coalmines – men's jobs. Now the new jobs are jobs in retailing or call centres and even those are mostly in Swansea. The politicians of Wales celebrated when it gained the Objective One grants from the E.E.C., missing the point that it *had* Objective One status – as one of the poorest areas in Europe. I snuffled all the way down Stepney Street after saying goodbye to Peter.

There are of course 'Big Issue' sellers in France – 'les Sans Abris' can be aggressive in their approach to tourists, prowling carparks of large towns on market days, thrusting a magazine into your hand and demanding the money. One of the saddest acronyms in France must be S.D.F. 'Sans Domicile Fixe' hiding the cold, hunger and vulnerability of homelessness in three cold letters.

As in urban Wales, there are those who sleep in doorways and there are beggars, the usual range from genuine hard-luck to easy-way-to-quick-money and it's only if you talk to them that you start to tell the difference. I was particularly impressed by the guy begging outside Super-U with a few cents in his upturned cap – it was a slack day in October so he was reading a novel and smoking, quite relaxed.

Along with a photo of a Montélimar market stallholder, who was also reading a novel on a slack day, it could have been a poster for the 'Get Boys Reading' campaigns popular amongst us literacy experts in Britain.

I am not homeless but I am an outsider, who gave twenty-five years to belonging in Wales and was rewarded with a place in the community of which I am immensely proud. No trip into Llanelli passed without a friendly word, usually from potential muggers and rapists who had starred in my classroom twenty years earlier. Even when I thought I was safely anonymous, I was greeted with 'Oh yes, you're that woman with the big dogs' (It could have been worse). I

have grown used to Welsh ways and if it is indeed a small world, Wales is a very small country, so that when someone starts a conversation by the traditional route of 'You must know Dai Thomas, the engineer, he lives down by you', I can usually respond with the appropriate, 'Is that down by Gwyn Williams' place then?' and we can keep the names rolling for hours.

It was not always so. I had only visited Wales once, to stay for a weekend with my brother at his residential centre in Snowdonia, before I went to live in Carmarthenshire. I was living in Wakefield, working in Leeds and had graduated recently from York University so was free to move anywhere. If the pin had landed differently, it could have been the north of Scotland, Cornwall or anywhere near the sea and with some open spaces. Those were the criteria for the place in which my first husband was going to find promotion and, at twenty-one, I was going to gain a teaching certificate. The promotion turned up in Carmarthen, I was given a place at Swansea University and we were delighted to be given council housing as part of the interview package for the new job. Little did we know.

The first time I saw south Wales was from the train to Swansea. It reminded me of the Yorkshire mining communities, terraces tumbling down hillsides and gray-green hillocks rising behind them, but the difference was the sea, a working sea of half-glimpsed docks and a bay curved around its bed-and-breakfast semis. Having sorted out a place on the teacher training course, I returned to Wakefield for another few months until I was organised to join my husband in the council house, where he had spent a desperately miserable few weeks.

There are council estates in south Wales where neighbours are friends, their houses are immaculate and the views are so good that local councillors fight to live on the estate; this was not not one of them, which is why it was easy to find a house for us. Between May, when I moved into Maesglas, and October when I enrolled as a student, I don't remember a single local person speaking to me outside of their day's work selling me stamps or houses (unless you

count the kids who threw stones at the front door, yelled 'Saes', 'English', and ran away).

The other half of our semi- was occupied by a man with seven children, presumably a widower, who gathered the family around the organ on a Sunday night and led the hymn-singing, loudly. At the time I thought that this was what every Welsh family did on a Sunday night.

Another local character was a goat which moved from garden to garden, whether illegally parked there or grazing with permission, who knows – perhaps that was the true origin of my wild-goat-chase? Certainly I spent longer watching that goat than I did making new friends. It was a lonely time but during the day I had my cats and my books, and in the evenings my husband was home from work. Two of his workmates invited us to their homes; it was the English couple, immigrants like ourselves, who became friends. Coincidence?

I remember seeing graffiti on a bus shelter, 'Rock against racism' and thinking how good it was that the Welsh were aware of the problems suffered by English settlers; I still hadn't realised that hating the English was an accepted national sport. Neither had I realised all the ways in which the English in general – and for historical reasons – had asked for it. But I was twenty-two, rootless and had never even heard of Llanelli (sorry, but I wasn't a rugby fan) before I moved there – it really wasn't my fault.

My integration moved forward a little when I found a Llanelli born-and-bred fellow student who could drive. Having commuted the twenty-odd miles between York and Leeds, then Leeds and Wakefield, without any problems, I couldn't believe that it took me two hours and three different transport systems to travel what was the same distance on a south Wales map. It was to be another three years and several lessons in dependence before I finally learnt to drive.

My first chauffeur, Jeff, taught me the words to 'Mae'n hen flad' and enabled me to enter a pub without getting one of those silences and switches to Welsh. However, he disapproved of me

swearing and refused to buy me a pint, always returning with a half when it was his round. I was homesick for Yorkshire pubs, also full of old men, but ones who would have been playing dominoes and darts with me before I could have said 'Mine's an Old Peculiar.' It looked as if my Camra membership was going to be a waste.

Despite the gloomy predictions of my mother's friends in York, I quickly found a teaching post and my new colleagues were only too willing to teach me Welsh, or rather Llanelli English. I had to stop saying 'here' in that hilarious received-Yorkshire-with-Scottish-undercurrents-sort-of-way; instead I was to say 'by yeeeur'. You have to 'yeeeur' that famous passage from the bible read in a strong south Wales accent to believe it; you know the one – it goes 'Let those that have yeeeurs to yeeeur let them yeeeur.'

I spent many a happy half-hour on 'Dewi' practice, a name which included the Welsh vowel 'ew' which does not exist in English or in any part of my mouth where I could place my tongue and teeth. Among the many mistakes I made was the unforgivable one of travelling to work with a north Walesian and copying some of his accent – trust me, this goes down worse than Yorkshire in south Wales. I once perfected my north Walesian 'Iola' (Yoll- a) only to have the friend in question decide that she had moved to south Wales and she preferred the local Yoe-lah.

There was a time when I thought it odd to hear classroom Shakespeare in strong Gwendraeth Valley; now I even wonder why Shakespeare cocked up the number of syllables in a line of verse. And if I hear a deep male voice with exactly the right Welsh accent like a big cat's purr hypnotising you beneath the words, it reaches parts that only D H Lawrence has described; think Richard Burton or Anthony Hopkins.

But what about Welsh Welsh? By December I had moved out of Maesglas, which still boasts a regular appearance in the magistrates' courts column of 'the Llanelli Star', usually for cases of violent assault or for drugs offences, and my new home was in Bancffosfelen (another half-hour's pronunciation practice for me, and my parents

always pointed to the name on a piece of paper when they came to visit).

This is in the heart of the Welsh-speaking Gwendraeth Valley in Carmarthenshire, the most Welsh-speaking of counties, the one responsible for the casting vote which brought the Welsh Assembly into being.

My neighbours were mostly retired miners and my first contact was a phone call from Dilys-across-the-road to tell me that I ought to wipe the condensation from my window or I would get mould. I didn't wipe the windows and I did get mould but Dilys carried on trying to turn me into a good Welsh housewife.

My second contact was Will-over-the-hedge who was doing things in his garden. I had my own quarter acre of heaven and was raring to go so I asked him what and how and when, and we were friends. My neighbours taught me about the mines, about 'the Durhams' who had settled the village of Carway and never gone back to Durham even when the mines closed, and about the hooks in my kitchen, as in their own, which had been used when the time came for the pigsty-pig to trough in endless autumn.

Their memories led me back through the traditions still carried on, like the brass band playing up our two-mile hill on Boxing Day, to the time in the sepia postcards they brought out in tin boxes to show me. In return, I was the only one light enough to shift the snow from all our attics the year of the hard winter – no-one had laid boards and a heavy foot in the wrong place would have taken a man through the ceiling below.

I learnt enough Welsh to break ice and build bridges but little more. Perhaps more importantly, I learnt that if you speak a minority language, you share your language with a few but you share your perspective with everyone who speaks any minority language, anywhere in the world. To speak English as your first language is to be born into hereditary privilege and many of us abuse this accident of birth every time we open our mouths.

When I was shopping in Llanelli, an old chemist once came up to me and, when I said (in Welsh) that I didn't speak enough Welsh to

carry on in that language, he shook his head and said in English, 'You don't know what you're missing. It's like seeing the world monochrome when you could see it in colour.'

What I saw twenty-five years ago was Welsh dying out in three generations; grandparents were first language Welsh, parents understood it but rarely spoke it (except to their parents and their dog) and the children neither spoke it nor understood it. There were local variations on this and it is all changing again, from political, educational and human pressures.

Nowadays, it is difficult in many jobs to reach a high level unless you speak Welsh; as an immigrant, I accepted this until I realised that my opportunities for Headship were limited by my lack of Welsh and yet I was offered neither the time nor the opportunity to learn the language. As a busy teacher, mother, writer and pet-owner there were limits to what I could cram into my life – and into my husband's, supportive-beyond-the-call-of-duty – so my stop-go attempts to learn Welsh have left me a beginner still. As the majority of those born and bred in Wales do not speak Welsh, they face the same barriers that I have, and there is, understandably, bitterness on all sides of the debate.

Local dialect in Dieulefit has followed the same pattern of three-generation decline without the measures taken in Wales to ensure that the language survives. Monsieur Dubois' father could chat for an hour with his neighbour, totally in Provençale; Monsieur Dubois himself understood most of the conversation but couldn't join in; and his son, who told me the story, has not a word of dialect. Unlike in Wales, there is little co-ordinated action to preserve the language, although it has its supporters, particularly for its literature and history.

My French is better than my Welsh but – or perhaps because - here there is rarely the option of speaking English, which was always a common language in Wales. So, how welcome have I been in Dieulefit? Like Iola, I have changed my name. The Mrs Gill who lived and worked in Wales was 'Gill' as in fish-part. In France, I am Madame Zheel (still spelt G- I-deux-L) and that suits me fine.

My first name is more of a problem. When I was working as an Education Officer for Neath Port Talbot, I was lucky enough to be invited to an Education Conference in Nice, where I quickly discovered that Monsieur Zhion Zheel had been expected. 'Zhion' is not really an option without other aspects of a gender change and I have been 'Jean' too many years to let that go now. French does not contain the sound 'j' as in 'Jean' and the immensely popular Jean Auel has a full French explanation in the fly of her 'Cave Bear' series telling her French readers to say 'Jean', 'd-zh' – as close as French gets to the sound. Prompted by a trendy sales assistant, I have finally settled on 'Jean comme le pantalon' as the American 'blue jean' seems to be known everywhere. If it turns into 'Gin' in a French accent, I can live with that.

What I am still finding tricky is spelling a name which has two of the tricksiest letters for an English speaker – G and J, which are pronounced almost vice versa in French. Simple – all you do is remember that they are vice versa – but then you think, have I already switched them? Do I still need to switch them? What are they in English anyway? What is my name again?

Then there are my alter egos. I'm quite flattered to have 'le Jean's café' as my local bar but I'm less pleased by Jean Gilles being racing correspondent for the local paper – 'Jean Gilles a choisi…' announces this week's tips. If I can manage to stutter out my own name successfully, especially on the telephone, I am doomed if I have to give John's.

There is something very funny to a French listener in Jean being married to John. Once past that hurdle there is the excitement of spelling John Harley Pilborough – enough to make you very glad that your own name is three four-letter words. Still, it provided the French notaire, who carried out our conveyancing, with a Humour Opportunity.

We were all gathered in his office, the estate agent, the sellers, us and the notaire himself, to conduct the formalities of the final signing and handover of the keys. It was a bit like a wedding service with the notaire slowly reading key bits of the contract and us saying

'Oui' now and again, although I did ask a few more questions than when I got married. (Perhaps I should have asked a few more questions then too?)

There was a theatrical pause before John's name then the notaire read, 'Zhon 'Arley Davidson'. Luckily we all laughed – it could easily have been like so many times in my classroom where I Cracked A Joke. I remember once laughing so much at my own joke that my chair fell off the old-fashioned dais on which it was perched. Even then thirty pupils stared at me blankly. In case you wondered what struck me as incredibly funny, it was the way Sohrab and Rustum don't recognise each other and ... No? Perhaps you have to be studying a nineteenth century ballad with a group of fifteen year olds to appreciate the joke.

I think the notaire's office was where our first welcome to Dieulefit took place. We were congratulated and did lots of handshaking, and we were told how wonderful Dieulefit was and how we would be happy here. We then headed off to our new home for the real handover from our Marseillaise sellers (please feel free to hum whenever I say that – John always does). They had a pastis and some bretzels waiting for us and we had the tour of the house that you always wish you had been given in Britain – the one where someone tells you that the key only works if you pull the door just a little to the left and turn the key at the same time; or the exact and individual time at which you should open or close each shutter in order to maximise air and minimise summer heat; or which hosepipe connects to which junction in order to trickle over which bit of garden.

The water system was the real revelation; we had realised that we were using spring water but it had been news to us in the notaire's office that we didn't own the springs – they belonged to who else but Monsieur Dubois, the neighbour with the truffle oaks and right of access via our driveway. All these neighbourly agreements seemed to be working fine and as the relationship allowed us to walk through Monsieur Dubois' orchards into the woods beyond, without any of the maintenance of all this land, there were more pluses than

minuses. However, I was taken aback to find out, after the pastis, that the kitchen was plumbed into Monsieur Dubois' spring water, giving us free water (great?) except when it was freezing underground and there was no water (not so great). As I investigated the house further, I found that the separate W.C. was also on spring water.

This was apparent when all water in the kitchen or to the garden stopped if the toilet was being flushed – and stayed off if the flush stuck. If you've ever played the computer game 'Riven', opening and shutting valves in virtual adventures, you would find our plumbing system very similar.

The handbasin in the WC was also on spring water which meant that the hot tap was connected underneath the sink, inside the little cupboard, to absolutely nothing. Other little quirks, of which every house has its share, included an open fire condemned as 'too smoky – the chimney needs to be taller'.

This I still do not understand. Now I know that the parents of Monsieur Dubois lived here into their eighties with no central heating, I cannot believe that the fire did not function perfectly. Apart from a few woodworm holes there were no other surprises – unless you count the 'remise', an outbuilding which we had missed completely in our viewing of the house.

In the remise, the atelier (workshop) and cellars, Jean-Marie was leaving us all manner of useful things and we said how pleased we were as we inspected the plastic coat, various rusty tins containing even rustier nails, half-used cans of wood varnish, a slightly damaged cane chair and Jean-Marie' fully stocked poison cupboard – allegedly for the garden. I am not sure what we are going to do with a ploughshare and an old scythe – not a sickle but a full, Death the Reaper scythe – nor oak barrels and a rabbit cage but there is a strong feeling that they all live here, did so before us and will do so after us. Some of the left-behinds are definite treasures; a stone garden table with two benches, dozens of terracotta pots – some decorated with a mosaic of varnished fragments – and a pair of fire dogs.

These cast iron bars, for 'guarding' the fire, each have a bust,

sphinx-like, at one end. One is a woman with hair coiled high and a regency neckline to her gown and the other, a man, has a double-breasted collar fastening high on his chest. Napoleon and Josephine were covered in rust, made worse by a sluice and scrub using washing-up liquid. My next idea was to use some car rust remover that I had bought to spruce up our set of boules.

However, the instructions clearly stated that the rusty areas would turn blue – not exactly the effect I wanted and I didn't want to paint something that was to live at the edge of an open fire. Then I considered what I would do if these were rusty, cast iron frying pans and I did it. I smothered them in sunflower oil and baked them for twenty minutes in a moderate oven. They came out gleaming black and a little oil seems to keep them that way. When you think about it, that's more or less how the Royal navy maintains the machinery on their ships, isn't it?

As well as the oddities left here permanently, Monsieur and Madame Manega loaned us basic furniture to make our two weeks camping here in the summer, before the move proper, more comfortable. They not only sold us a house, they were our first welcome here and although they were returning to Marseilles, Madame Manega grew up in Dieulefit and roamed the hills as a girl, so her affection for the valley had drawn her back here.

To keep a foot in both camps, they decided to keep a small 'cabanon' in the nearby village of Poët-Laval and weekend here from their new flat in Marseilles. We were given useful phone numbers of everyone from The Best Vet to The Man Who Vacuums Your Fosse Septique (please let the no maintenance group be right). I was given the full version of Where To Go on a hair-raising drive to France Telecom's office in Montélimar.

Madame Manega is a traditional French driver, the kind who has prompted the Government's multi-million euro campaign to get the French to drive 'comme des anglais'. The flow of instructions along the lines of '...go to the hairdresser's along to the left at the mini-roundabout and ask for Sophie...' she took both hands off the wheel and checked out my hair '... but of course you don't have

your hair done but if you do... and there is a little market at the mini-roundabout, tres sympa... and don't go to the vet in Astuce, mais non...' all this was interrupted by the usual beeping and hand gestures (a new highway code which I understand but can't bring myself to use.

Once, on a narrow road in the Var, John was awarded a particularly eloquent gesture, along the lines of, 'You stupid foreign person don't you know that on a one-track mountain road I have priority and must drive very fast past you while you get off the road, preferably over that precipice' and I was glad not to be the driver.

Madame Manega and I had an interesting French moment as we neared the bottleneck of la Bégude, where a lorry and a caravan had played chicken, neatly fitting both vehicles into a space through which neither of them could now progress. Nor of course could they reverse, as there was a queue behind each of them. In true Asterix fashion, the two drivers were punching each other in the middle of the street while everyone waited for the gendarmerie.

Madame Manega took evasive action, swerved up a side street and, showing off her local knowledge, took us on a detour which added three-quarters of an hour to a twenty minute journey – but we didn't have to stop once. There was one new aspect to traditional French driving; every few minutes Madame Manega would stamp on the brakes with an accompanying 'Merde' and the suggestion that the gendarmerie ought to have better things to do than be out there with speed traps and the uncivilised intent to get at motorists.

Despite – or perhaps because of - the friendly flashes of motorists, warning of gendarme presence, the campaign is definitely having an impact. We have seen the unthinkable – drivers stopping for pedestrians at zebra crossings and even, however rarely, the British driving gesture I love, 'No, after you...' No chance of that with Madame Manega but she did get me to France Telecom, where I delighted a queue of twelve French people by choosing a new telephone from a display of about thirty, while they all waited.

With promises that they would return and take us mushrooming, the Manegas called round to say goodbye, bringing with them the

soppiest German Shepherd in the world, who made it plain that he still lived here.

After they had gone, I mused on my social etiquette. Never mind the fact that I had puzzled them deeply by reminding Jean-Marie to take his mistress with him, referring of course to the 'maitresse', the mattress on the spare bed. Well 'mattress' *ought* to be 'maitresse'. Was it my imagination or did Jean-Marie look shifty for a minute?

No, what was worrying me was more important. 'John, ' I said, 'I think I've kissed people when I shouldn't have.' He gave me one of those looks and replied without interest, 'Recently?'

As he had been doing serious backing off and shaking hands every time I had been throwing myself in to three-kiss my new acquaintance, he was going to be smug, wasn't he. It seems that you should keep to shaking hands until you really get to know someone, unless he's your cousin, nephew, bank manager... I need to study French kissing a bit more. Why do the English call it that anyway when what the French do all the time doesn't even involve contact between mouth and cheek? (I get that wrong too)

This then was the start of our life in Dieulefit. Since then I have been overwhelmed – with locals' patience in listening and responding to my French, with bureaucrats helping me to sort out paperwork over importing car, pets and ourselves, and with the day-to-day smiles and 'Bon journée' in our local shops. In casual conversation, I explain that we have recently moved here and every time the response is the same; 'Vous avez raison', 'You've done the right thing. You'll love it here, it's a wonderful place to live.'

This wholehearted love of your own region is new to me. Yet I have taken visitors on tour in the Gwendraeth Valley and they loved its variety of landscapes; hobbit hills, lush pastures, lanes and hedgerows, and seascapes of all kinds – sand dunes, marshes and wild craggy cliffs. It is just not Welsh to glow with enthusiasm about the place where you live – perhaps it should be.

Who were these welcoming people? Mostly people whose job it was to deal with us. I can hear you saying, so what's so good about that? Think again. What response do you really think that someone whose English is poor is likely to get at the local Welsh – or English – Post Office, or Department of Health or a local solicitor?

Our experience includes the clerk trying to fill in a car registration form with our inadequate help, who phoned the local Nissan garage to get the details we needed and didn't know. Or the nice lady at the mairie, who was amazed that we needed permission from the French Ministry of Agriculture to import more than three pets, suitably concerned for us that we hadn't received this permission, and who organised an 'attestation', a testimony signed by the mayor of Dieulefit to the effect that two dogs and two cats could accompany us to become good Dieulefitois.

The nice lady asked me what sort of dogs we owned and relayed the answer to her workmate typing away in a back room – in very rough translation, our dogs were considered to be big cutie-pies. This 'attestation' was even sent on to our home in Wales because the Mayor had been too busy during the two summer weeks we were here completing the house purchase – you can imagine our surprise when the letter arrived, exactly as promised.

The nice lady was also a big help when we discovered a massive nest of huge waspy thingies in the doorway of the little fuel shed. She told us to phone the fire brigade but we were a little worried at dialling the equivalent of 999, for fire, during the worst regional heatwave since records began, when every night's news told us how overstretched the pompiers were.

We could imagine how chuffed they would be when we phoned up and in stilted French, told them that no, we didn't have a fire, or even know of one, but we had a nest of big wasp-like-thingies in our fuel shed and the nice-lady-at-the-mairie had said to phone.

We delayed phoning and then John had a brainwave. His first reaction to the nest had of course been to rush out of the fuel shed – and into the house for his camera. He had gone back, facing certain death to get a photo of an amazing, intricate structure about eigh-

teen inches deep, honeycombed in a substance that looked as strong as concrete. It had not been there when we first saw the house in April so the thingies had built all of this in three months. It was awesome but it had to go.

We looked up the fire depot on our map of the village and took the laptop computer up there with us. I'm not sure it was what you would call reception but a pompier was hanging around outside, taking a drag, and he was perfectly willing to look at our photos on the computer. 'Frelons' he said. 'Ah oui, frelons,' I agreed and nodded.

Once again we were told that we needed to phone the pompiers for an appointment and that they would sort our frelons out so we returned home to look up 'frelons' in the dictionary. As you've guessed, they were hornets. And big buggers, at that.

It was surprisingly easy as it turned out. The phone number leads to a switch board with so many lines that you are transferred efficiently to one for odd-foreigners-with-strange-thingies-in-sheds and the pompiers call you back to arrange an evening visit (off-peak for fires apparently).

I was understandably excited at the thought of the firemen's visit, motivated further by the calendar left in the kitchen by the Manegas, and the inevitable letdown of the two ordinary men who turned up in an ordinary van was only mitigated by their total professionalism. I especially liked the bit where they came round to the front of the house, where I was keeping well out of their way, and asked me for a bin bag. Presumably they put the whole nest and its population into this bin bag. I wouldn't have done it, not unless I'd been wearing the sort of suit and helmet which would protect me against radioactivity, and these two pompiers had only added gardening gloves to their basic uniform. My heroes.

What's more they were cheerful about their work and told me that they offered a public service, that we would be charged a standard fee for sorting out pests, and that it was 'normal' for them - more professionals who dealt with us in a friendly and helpful way.

Perhaps it is just that being 'English' is acceptable in Dieulefit; some immigrants are more equal than others. When I prepared for

our move by reading whole rainforests of English magazines about moving to France, there was very little awareness that 'one' would in fact be an immigrant.

There is no connection made between the desperate faces behind bars in the huge refugee camps, at Senlis or Lyon, and the Brits who move here, sometimes not even bothering to apply for their residency permits – I mean, Brits can't be considered illegal immigrants, can they?

There has only been one occasion so far in France on which I was reminded of my status. We were signing on with CPAM, the French Health Service, and I asked the clerk whether she wanted my old address on the form or my new one. With a patient smile she replied, 'Your own country, where you're from.' I was hurt. I am the sort of kitten who, if born in an oven, would try very hard to be a biscuit.

6

FLYING PIGS AND CHIMNEY INSPECTION

Today we saw pigs fly. Or rather, we saw wild boar and they were running very fast. John was up a ladder at the time using a lopper, secateurs and a saw, to turn our mulberry trees into amputees like our neighbours'.

We are at the stage of copying everything our neighbours are up to in their gardens, although we still haven't worked out exactly what one vegetable is, a giant-leek-with-palm-tree-top type thingie, that has been carefully encased in cardboard tubes.

Presumably it is part of the region's overwintering behaviour, which gives the impression that we live in a polar region, particularly if you judge by the collection of cut-to-size plastic covers sold in the local garden centres – cut to the size of whole trees and picnic-tables-with-six-chairs, that is.

On a golden November day, there is no sign of the arctic winter, which we are told arrives at the end of December. If we stand still in our walled garden, falling acacia leaves tangle in our hair. As we walk out through the old stone archway into the orchard we brush the seedpods, dangling like huge peapods from the nearly leafless wisteria and we scrunch through mulberry leaves piled high along the drive. Proper crunching walks through autumn leaves are new to me; they used to squelch in Wales.

John is sawing away, muttering something about 'easier with f'n chainsaw... French...chainsaw...' and I am happily deaf, having observed French tree surgeons swinging from plane trees like manic monkeys, clinging perilously to a branch with one hand while chainsawing away at another (branch or hand being equal possibilities). I am content that only our tree will lose limbs while I gather branches and occasionally duck.

In a lull, punctuated by '... bloody big .... chainsaw', I glance across the road and see a flying pig. My instinctive shout, 'John!' makes him turn in his perch just in time to catch the flight of about two dozen wild boar across the field into the woods.

Two minutes later, the inevitable crack of a shotgun suggests why pigs might run so fast. We now have a pretty good idea what it was that dug big holes in the garden and scuffled off when we caught it in the car headlights – at the time we though it might be a badger.

It is a good day for wildlife. Our regulars have all appeared; the green woodpecker which often drills the ground between the rows of espalier apples and pears, so oblivious of us that it carried on pecking the bark of our peach tree while we stood yards away and watched.

Then there is the hare that waits until the last moment before starting from its form. Apart from the excitement of our dogs, the hare has an ongoing game of catch-who-can with a neighbour's Burmese cat, which thinks it owns the orchard. The cat sits, waits and watches; the hare sits, waits and watches.

Then, at some unseen signal, they are off. The hare has sprint start, sprint middle, sprint finish and, as if that isn't enough, dodges well enough to play rugby for France. The cat stops, pretends a total loss of interest, and washes itself disdainfully. It returns to sit underneath a shrub where we have considerately hung a bird feeder.

Although there is a tendency in France to look at something living and suggest which wine would complement it best, there is no shortage of food sold for 'our friends the animals', including wild birds. Our Marseillaise predecessor has left tiny troughs to collect water for the birds and a few little wooden structures which act as

bird feeders. We carefully filled and hung our RSPB recommended feeders, plastic tubes with perches, and waited. And waited. There was no shortage of birds but they took one look at our modern dining tables and complained about the lack of traditional French little wooden houses. Gradually the bolder birds are risking the odd foreign architecture we have introduced and there is now the full range of tits, finches, robins and some with longer tails, garden birds like wagtails. They are not yet as trusting as those in Wales which swooped in gangs before us as if auditioning for the remake of 'Snow White'.

On the September night that we arrived here for good, a barn owl swooped across the road and I saw a chamois poised, a shadow on the verge. At four in the morning, it only took the patches of yellow autumn-flowering crocuses and the familiar stars, the Plough or Sospan as I've come to know it in Wales, and we couldn't have had a better welcome.

Some people have 'three bedrooms', 'large sitting room' or even 'good school nearby' as the must-haves on their shopping list for the estate agent; I wouldn't consider anywhere without the freedom to walk into countryside, straight from the house, or without stars. I don't know how people live without a view of the stars, especially on a winter's night, but I read that eighty percent of England suffers from too much light pollution for stars to be visible; it is the reverse in Wales.

I consider it normal, even desirable, to be woken at three in the morning because there is a particularly good view of Mars (which is closer now than for ten thousand years gone or to come). However, I know better than to share these priorities with estate agents; those who helped us still think I wanted a house with three bedrooms and a large sitting room, but even they know that we really don't care any more about good schools.

Not all the wildlife has been welcome. When we camped here for

two weeks in the summer, I brought only essentials – bedding, cooking utensils, my Swiss army knife and two mousetraps. Let's get something into the open straight away; most houses get rodents at one time or another but, whereas parents in middle England are now, through necessity, almost able to say the word 'headlice' without flinching, no-one owns up to having mice in their attic. I have to protect my friends' identity so cannot name names but I can tell you that a couple who sold their London house for over half a million pounds, regularly put down mouse-traps in that same house.

In case you think I am trying to deflate housing prices in the south-east by rumour-mongering, I also have friends in the north of England who couldn't sleep at night – more from the thought of their little lodgers than because of the delicate pitter-patter of unwanted tiny feet. Even if we're willing to share our planet with our fellow creatures, most of us are unhappy about sharing our house with them and we certainly don't want anyone to know about it.

You can't live with cats without meeting mice – and shrews, and even a baby rabbit. There have been interesting rodent moments, such as my first meeting with my nineteen year old belle-fille, where we were sitting on the edge of easy chairs making polite conversation while I watched a shrew scuttle across the living room like a clockwork toy, disappear under a bookcase and then scoot back again.

Neither of us referred to the entertainment although I suspect our eyes were tracking its progress like a tennis match throughout our non-conversation. One of my cats had presumably brought in its plaything and been distracted. At that time I had seven cats so you can imagine how pleased I was when I was woken nightly by thundering paws across the attic floor – and I don't mean delicate mice patters. Think rat. Think big rat.

After giving a pep talk to the cats (pedigree Birmans, what can you expect?) I bought a kind rat-trap and was given the usual good advice (totally contradictory) as to what to use for bait. One old 'expert' swore by Christmas cake (fine but this was May and I wasn't

making a Christmas cake specially for the rat – would any old home-made fruit cake do? Ambiguous response).

A kind rat-trap is a plastic box into which you tempt your rodent and it then shuts so you can let the little sweetie-pie out in the field. The major disadvantage is that you have to check it twice a day (or you will kill the rat through suffocation or starvation – much worse than a neat guillotine, and a crime for which I will one day have to atone, with regard to a mouse ….) The other major disadvantage is of course that it doesn't work.

The nightly rat parties were driving me crazy. Imagine the worst few weeks ever with a baby crying every night; then imagine that you're not just allowed to, but that it's actually your civic duty to murder the source of your sleepless nights, and you'll understand why I went out and bought a proper rat-trap.

I narrowly avoided another visit to A & E, just missing my fingers when I checked how it worked, and laid the trap. This didn't work either but I know exactly how big that rat was because I found him (why are rats always 'him' to me?) or rather his corpse, lying beside a drainpipe – and the night parties stopped after that. I guess that one of the cats finally earned its keep, or, more likely, the rat had a heart attack at the sight of seven cats, however fluffy. The rat was enough for me and I was glad not to live in Canada, where everything is bigger, and where my uncle had fun and games with a raccoon in his attic.

Post-rat, there were some occasional run-ins with field mice which ran into the attic, into the kind mouse-traps and out into the field, with strict instructions never to darken my doors again. It was therefore with resignation that I visited the cellars with Jean-Marie on our house-warming tour, and heard the exclamation 'Souris!' as a mouse flickered past, heading up. The crucial word is 'up'.

Above the cellars are all the living rooms of the house, including the kitchen. Alone in our new house, the morning after, I quickly realised that these were not chocolate hundreds and thousands underneath the sink, but signs of a regular route to the rubbish bin. Down went the mouse-traps with great success.

The first morning I got up, checked the trap, told John 'Got one!' took the trap to the orchard, gave the usual speech and released the mouse.

The second morning, ditto. The third morning I was less enthusiastic. By the fourth morning it was 'Sodding mouse' and by the fifth I'd reached, 'John, will you do the mouse?'

We carried out this routine six times before we'd got rid of all the mice - or the same one six times until he got bored or eaten by the Burmese, as John insisted. I had vague plans, encouraged by a daughter, to paint it with nail varnish or mark it in some way to settle the debate, but the day was sunny and life was too short, so we will never know.

My sister, Anne, on her parallel house-hunt in the Pyrenees, was also considering the implications of unwanted wildlife. She and her husband talked about their plans to the couple whose holiday cottage they were renting, who took great interest, explaining to them that an area they fancied would be no good because of the 'mice'.

They spoke no English and the word 'mice' did not strike a chord with the Hemel contingent's rusty French so it was time for a mime. The gite-owners gave a wonderful impression of fluttering wings – it clicked straight away.

'Moths,' sister and husband agreed with satisfaction. Everyone was happy and smiling with the pleasure of communication and Monsieur decided to extend his dramatic repertoire. He stood in the doorway and showed how big the 'mice' were, repeating the waving and flapping. Six feet. This was bad news however you looked at it. I mean, who would want to live somewhere frequented by six foot moths?

Alternatively, if it was not moths, what on earth was it? Frustrated again, Monsieur found a book with – wonderful! – a picture of the 'mice'. Yes, there it was, waving in the breeze, six feet high maize, or 'maïs'.

Monsieur explained that it was boring to see nothing but maize fields and, with two crops a year (one for the animals), that was all they would see if they went there. Sister and husband were suitably

grateful to be warned about the mais and went to bed, remembering to skate across the bedroom on dusters specially placed for that purpose to protect the new, varnished floorboards.

It wasn't until October that we suffered our next minor infestation. We had been surprised at the lack of flying insects in the summer, possibly helped by the exceptional dryness of the by now infamous 'canicule' (heatwave) but as soon as temperatures outside dipped slightly, the flies zoomed inside in squadrons. These were not Welsh flies. These flies laid eggs in cat food as it came out of the packet and before it went into the cat. They buzzed in your hair and stamped their dirty feet on your chopping board. Sister Anne explained that I should clean my house with bleach – she seemed to think that what the septic tank didn't know, wouldn't hurt it - I wonder where I've come across that line of thinking before. She has the family weakness of finding solutions for other people's problems and, after research, faxed me a list of ancient remedies for household pests. I printed them out, suspecting I'd need them all at some stage.

By now, we had tried two varieties of sonic deterrent which plug into an electric socket – we only have one reliable electric socket in each room so they didn't last long; two different types of poisonous plastic flowers which adhere to windows – supposedly dangerous to small children but I don't think there's a market for that, and they do bugger-all to the actual flies; three different types of aerosol fly killer – satisfying to use with accompanying 'Take that' but totally ineffective whether used in individual target practice or in overnight treatment of a closed room. Having diminished the air quality of the planet shamefully, we tried Anne's green solutions.

We burned lavender oil, we wiped surfaces down with lavender… even the dogs smelled of lavender. It worked as well as anything else – that is, it didn't. By the time we found some revolting old-fashioned sticky fly-paper, we were down to one fly in each room, so we won't know if that works until next year – if we're lucky enough to have the same visitors back.

Life is too short to worry about flies – when you can worry about the electrics, the walls, the windows, the plumbing and the heating.

In addition to our wonderful modern central heating, we have a wood burner and an open fire. Is this another small sign of winter conditions, I ask myself?

Keen for the comfort of real flames again, we lit the open fire, confident in an expertise gained in the coal valleys of south Wales. The Marsellaise had told us that it didn't draw properly and they thought it needed a higher chimney. We were sceptical and wanted to see for ourselves. Once the fire was lit, we could hardly see at all. They were definitely right about the fire smoking back into the room – it was so bad the flies were dropping like ... well, like flies, so at least there was one side-benefit. Workman number ten? eleven? is required – enter chimney sweep.

Booked two months ago, the chimney sweep finally arrives. At last, a proper Provençal workman, two hours late with a big smile and no hint of apology. He stays a further two hours, spending ten minutes sweeping the wood-burner chimney and two hours discussing the other one – and life. I now know why he was two hours late. I also know that he has eight sisters and that when he retires he wants to sail the Atlantic and so he wants to learn English.

Don't get the wrong idea; every word of the two hours takes place in French, except for a few numbers in English. John comes and goes, unable to keep up with the sociability. The 'ramoneur' is wonderfully patient with my French and when I tell him how much it helps me that everyone is so patient with me, he looks at me as if I'm very stupid. Of course everyone is patient with me.

I say that I hope everyone in England is patient with him when he practises his English. I consider the likelihood. I picture someone trying out very bad English and the patient response he will get. The only place I can picture this is in a Refugee Centre. I am a cynic. I am betraying my countrymen. I hide the terrible secret that when I watched the French TV special on Celine Dion, I wet myself laughing as the beautiful French host referred to the song 'My aaart muzt goo-on.' I do not deserve the patience of French speakers.

Discussion with the 'ramoneur' involves John and me in lying on our backs and looking up a chimney in torchlight, while listening to

a stream of French that includes the words for stove-pipe and flue. As I don't really know what a flue is in English, I ask some very stupid questions.

Monsieur Silvestre is as patient with my ignorance as he is with my French. He insists that there is no mystery about chimneys and that if I do not understand, I must say, so he can explain it better to me. I have worked for twenty years in schools and I am humbled; I have no doubt that this is one of the best teachers I have ever met and that if there were a degree in chimneys, my ramoneur would get me a first in it.

When we don't understand a particular word, we are treated to a mime; Monsieur Silvestre points to his trousers, he pretends to rip them and look sad, then he mimes sewing them up again; this – he shakes his head and his finger – is what he will not do to our chimney because it is not safe and not legal. We get the idea – cowboy repairs are not on the agenda. He will do a proper job or nothing.

This is not the first time we have been told this and although cynics might say that there is more money to be made in a bigger job, that is not the impression I get of our ouvriers' attitude to their work. There is far more work for them than they have time so if they wanted to turn a fast buck, they could easily take on more jobs.

Monsieur Silvestre is not only a chimneysweep; he also fits pipes, inserts and does all the associated work. Although he debunks the mystery of chimneys, he leaves us in no doubt that he is a skilled craftsman as he points to our twelve-inch thick wall and says it would be easy to put a hole in that, giving the air needed to force the smoke up and out.

He draws us diagrams to explain the pipe and the funnel; his eyes light up as he describes a modern insert design with air holes underneath the doors which blast the glass doors clean. When we look dubious and mutter 'cost?' he remains cheerful, says there is always a way, and tells us of a retired engineer who adapted the design principle so he could do it himself. By now I am truly 'fired up' and I ask my usual question, 'How soon can you do it?' I will never learn; last

time I asked, the builder and the joiner teased me with 'Tonight?'. This time, my ramoneur says, 'Doucement, doucement, vous êtes en Provence.' (Slow down, you're in Provence).

I am mortified, not by the gentle reminder, but because it is the sole sentence in the French vocabulary of my five-year old niece. On one holiday in France, Ellie heard 'Doucement' so often that she can reproduce the exact adult-to-impatient-child tone. I have not seen myself in this light. To re-establish myself in the eyes of my ramoneur as a mature, capable grown-up, I offer him a drink… a petit café, a tea, a sirop…

This is something I cannot get the hang of in France. Welsh workmen drink tea non-stop, with ladles of sugar in it. Occasionally an oddball prefers coffee but no Welsh workman has ever looked at me reproachfully, said 'When I've finished the job,' and then asked for water.

This has happened several times now so it seems to be as ingrained as shaking hands on arrival and departure. This apparently slight change of habit has a major consequence for someone whose French is dodgy; your ouvrier settles down for a good chat, usually in your kitchen, while he sips his water, and you have nowhere to hide.

'John' I squeak but he has already vanished. Monsieur Silvestre tells me that there are a few English around here now. 'Mmmm,' I respond non-committally. Perhaps I should tell him that his water's getting warm? 'Did you hear the radio?' he continues.

'Mmmm?'

'There are seventy English people moving into one small village in the Gers. They are all getting so much money for selling their houses in London that they are buying places in France.'

'No,' I say, suitably shocked. I am pleased that my ramoneur realises that I am a person from Wales, who has clearly not become rich, whether by selling a house or in any other way.

We shake our heads at the strange ways of Londoners, Parisians … mad capitalists, all of them. I fail to mention that my sister has just become a Pyrenean, not the big white hairy kind who share my life,

but the mad-Londoner-moving-to-France-kind, possibly one of seventy moving into her village. Smug thought, compensating much for Welsh house prices.

By this time the water torture is dripping to its last drops and Monsieur Silvestre is reading aloud the magnetic words on the huge American fridge-freezer which we bought during the famous heat-wave and which looks as if it landed in the kitchen after a failed attempt on Mars.

Inspired by a metallic surface the size of a small shed, a daughter presented us with a complete set of magnetic French words to motivate us in our grammar practice. Instead I had played around with some lines of vaguely erotic poetry.

This seemed less entertaining when read aloud, slowly, lingeringly, by a chimney sweep prone to asking what the phrases meant. Even he tailed into silence before the last lines as I stuttered that they were not meant literally and that my French wasn't very good. The dregs were finally drained and John re-appeared to shake hands and accept a cheerful invitation to look at inserts with our ramoneur; he would ring us when had found some suitably attractive fires to set into our small chimney-breast.

This was not our first offer of guided shopping. We have already visited a granite factory, taken there by our kitchen designer so we could judge for ourselves whether we wanted to spend more arms and legs than we possess on worktops that could double up as gravestones.

The granite showroom displayed samples of the stone like works of art, each hung separately to catch the light and we discovered quickly that we didn't like blue granite. If you were told the price of blue granite, you wouldn't like it either. The blues and grays are the most expensive, with price further determined by the markings, those cosmic swirls like frozen fire.

Pragmatically, we asked to see only the cheapest and there was no

hint of patronage in response. We were treated to the same enthusiastic discussion of the pros and cons of different blocks of stone, touring the yard to look at the raw hunks... and to touch it.

My sample of granite is a marvel to me. It is 14mm thick, glints even on the raw sides and the polished facet holds all the secrets of time and stonecraft shifting in it shine. How can anyone hold cut stone without feeling awe? How is it got? How is it cut?

When I asked some of these questions I was invited to come and watch the granite being cut; Monsieur Laques, the kitchen designer, would bring me. I am not sure whether these offers are meant to be taken up but I would love to see the cutting tool, heavy enough and yet precise enough – presumably with diamonds – that can turn the bedrock of our world into pretty furniture.

I have always been fascinated by skilled craft and I treasure all those moments when someone has shared a knowledge – and a passion – regardless of how much money I might have available to spend (and it was never much).

These treats have included the lyrical account of the rivers Towy and Cothi, along with some very practical advice given me by the man who sold me my first fishing rod; the engraving skills of Mr Tripp at Tripp's trophies, who created badges for me from schoolchildren's designs; an artist's construction of a rainforest from scraps and knitted strings; and the time I chose a diamond.

There is in Llanelli an old family firm of jewellers with a good Jewish name and when I was sent in there to buy myself a simple, small diamond pendant for an anniversary present, I didn't expect to be treated like a princess.

Lawrence is the diamond expert, so much so that he spends most of the week at Hatton Garden, but he happened to be there and so was summoned by the magic word 'diamond.' When I told him what I wanted, he thought he had 'just the diamond for me' in London and would bring it back for me to see.

A week later, I was shown two diamonds and made my choice, directed to look at the cut, the colour, the light... I could not have been given more attention if I were replacing my crown jewels, and

yet I was not made to feel stupid in my ignorance or let down by my choice. This is the gift of the true craft master; to communicate the knowledge and the passion, a true teacher.

More and more, I realise how badly educated I have been and every French person I meet is only too willing to remedy this. I have not been taught how to store my saucisson? I must hang it and only cut off what I need as I use it.

My stallholder from Haute-Savoie asks if I am from round here; I am, I am proud to declare. In that case he tells me, you must wrap your mountain cheese in a damp tea-towel and it will keep for months. He has already tempted me to his stall with tidbits of saucisson and mountain cheese which shouts of cows and calories and tastes of Heidi recovering all the bloom in her cheeks.

I wonder what he would have told me to do with my cheese if I had said I didn't live here but I daren't ask – he is already giving me more advice. Never, never, never put your saucisson or your cheese in the fridge. I feel guilty. I have treated my produce cruelly. I blame my mother. Why didn't she teach me this – and tell me important things like not to hold an orange pumpkin against a cream jumper when I was peeling it. She could have told me how to preserve kiwifruit rather than my virginity – far more useful.

In late November we catch up on rain, getting five months' annual rainfall in three days. The 24hour satellite weather channel brings non-stop photographs of cars swimming along swollen rivers and the pompiers at work and if we look out the window, we can watch our own personal river flowing down the paved terrace.

The pets are not impressed; they did not leave Wales for this. Villages twenty minutes drive from here are cut off, their drinking water filthy with mud. The photographs of people queuing for bottled water, from the Red Cross, are no longer of Iraq but of the Ardèche. We have a few drips into the attic but I am proud of the house; it has survived red alert extreme weather conditions. As the

floods subside and the rain turns to drizzle, we are restless and what better treat than a food event?

Montélimar offers us a Salon de Gastronomie and we have the excuse that Christmas is coming and so we can indulge (I am Welsh/Scottish/English– I need an excuse to buy expensive food). I am surrounded by over forty hand-picked artisans, experts in a particular food – or drink.

I lose sight of John while I discuss fish soup with the wife of the fisherman; he fishes near Narbonne, she does the cooking and bottling. I don't like fish soup; I taste it. I love fish soup. I had no idea that fish soup should taste like this.

It is the same at every stall. John finds me again and he wants me to try the snail salmi, a sort of pâté. Snail salmi? Yes, with either parsley or roquefort flavouring. Not only do I follow suit and sample the salmi, we buy salmi and the snails themselves, stuffed with parsleyed, garlic butter.

There are tables set out everywhere canteen-style, so we can sit and taste at leisure, discuss properly the merits of the hams, olive oils, wines … It is normal, it is expected that you ask, 'What would you do with that? How would you cook it? What would you serve with it?'

Encouraged by this, we buy dried aubergine strips, lavender vinegar and truffle oil – from one of only four top-award-holder vinegar producers, honoured even in the USA (we are shown the trophy and the news articles). On home ground, I taste local beer, am bemused by the trendy white beers, the 'blonde' and the blanche' which are all lagers to me.

The brewer demurs at my request to taste his Christmas special but then he says, 'You are English - only an English person would be willing to drink beer at that temperature, not chilled'. He has run out of properly chilled Christmas special and at last I am given something like beer, at the correct temperature.

Even the Christmas special is a light beer to me and the brewer laughs at me, inviting me to visit his brewery where I can taste another beer, more like the Irish – my mouth waters at the thought

of Guinness. I am assured we will be welcome. I will take my son around a small French brewery and afterwards we will sit in the sun, drinking dreams in bottles.

I inspect the bottled Picodon in oil, reminded of The Project, and realise I should have cut the cheeses into pieces and that their retrieval from my jars is going to be an entertainment for all the family ... and these ones do not look like old Picodons. Far from being bottled shoeleather these look like young tender morsels. A week to go before I unstopper my gastronomic delights and I don't hold out much hope of them being edible.

Perhaps next year I'll try orange liqueur. I turn my attention back to the potted meat specialist. We buy bottled cassoulet and tins of pâté in strings, regretfully decide against a whole ham, postpone our buying of nougat, Montélimar's finest... enough.

We haul our catch to the car. I chatter all the way, telling John that we can take the oil bottles into the shop and get them refilled, as if this will compensate for the extravagance he does not accuse me of – it is my Calvinist upbringing at work again. Not a Calvinist soul though; if a soul can pig out, mine is going to.

7

KIWIS IN PROVENCE

The hare has retreated from the orchard to the deeper cover of the woods, the finches and tits are fighting over the sunflower seeds spilt from the bird feeders and we have seen two deer racing past our bedroom window.

It is winter and the wild creatures take greater risks, choosing between the hunger and the humans. The wild boar are no longer a glimpse in the distance; the furrows churned in the orchard are signs of our regular night visitors. Determined to see them close up, I sneak out with a torch at bedtime, like Winnie-the-Pooh hunting heffalumps, and on Boxing Day I am rewarded with the most amazing squeaking grunting troughing which evades my torchlight and diminishes to multiple crunchings up near the woods, where I am not brave enough to go.

I have not been able to talk John into these nocturnal boar-hunts but when I have actually caught the digging piggers in action, he joins me in time to confirm that yes, there is something munching out there. Serenaded by pigs, we star-gaze, the clear skies rivalled by the flashing Christmas lights that outline a villa up the hill.

In the morning we inspect the craters, bemused that our visitors charge straight through a whole truffle oak plantation to root around our lawn, which is innocent of even an acorn. We are still

more amazed at having wild boar as neighbours than depressed at the damage they cause; this might not last. Already, when I hear the crack of a shotgun in the woods, I contemplate roast boar.

I have some affinity with clumsy beasts that charge around enthusiastically causing accidental havoc or I would never have chosen Pyreneans as pets. Their latest natural disaster adds realism to my nativity scene. Over the last two years I have collected a few Provençal 'santons', the pottery peasant figures which extend the traditional nativity scene to include the poet Mistral and other set characters.

There is a view that Jesus Christ was actually born in Provence. How widely this view is supported outside Provence I don't know, but you only have to take one look at Joseph, in his striped shirt, hurling his beret in the air as he tells the boys that he's a father, to see he's not a traditional Jew.

We started with the basics – the donkey, the ox, Gabriel (Mary, Joseph and the baby were included with these more important characters) – and we've added walk on peasants. My Christmas present this year included two camels, one allegedly a 'racing' variety (I wonder what I'll get next year? Let me see, how many kings are there again ...) and all was looking homely in the stable when disaster struck.

A Pyrenean earthquake hit the foundations of Provençal Bethlehem, snapped a table leg completely, and caused multiple casualties. Mary, an old peasant lady and a shepherd were decapitated and the stable roof was destroyed. The scene now looks more like modern Bethlehem after a suicide bombing; heads slightly askew after amateur first aid (with the sort of glue 'guaranteed to hold car parts together') and a cracked roof with missing tiles. At least the camels survived intact.

Santon fever hits public places as well as homes and Super-U sports a particularly tacky crèche with peasants of varying sizes and blunt, bashed faces. Dieulefit's main church has a display so spectacular, and so odd, that it makes it into the regional newspaper.

Our santon designer is clearly expected to produce ever more

startling displays each year and so has chosen a Chinese theme. It is certainly different, displaying kimonoed ladies under paper parasols who adore the infant in the stable while clay children fly a well-tensioned kite beside the paddy field, in which each blade is hand-painted green paper. Chinese and Japanese elements mix with the traditional stable scenario, complete with Chinese Mary and Joseph and the message that Christ is everywhere.

The effect is strange. I try to imagine a Provençal Buddha and fail. Or Provençal Ramadan? And yet multi-cultural France is at the forefront of the news. There is even a serious debate in the French woman's magazine, amongst the Christmas recipes and fashions (for the part of the three hour wait at Paris Charles de Gaulles airport that I am not reading about Picodons). The Editorial sets out the case for the recent controversial proposal for a law banning 'ostensible signs of religion in public places'.

The views from the UK are clear, relayed to me by our Christmas visitors. The French are racist nutters, about to persecute non-Christians, particularly Moslems, by preventing them wearing traditional headscarves to work or to school. The picture in France is far more complex.

There is a petition in my magazine, signed by France's female great and good – and France has at least its share of remarkable women – supporting the law, on the grounds that women's rights are denied to those within certain religious sub-groups and that this is symbolised by clothing rules enforced on women. French Muslims are among those who signed the petition and among those who respond to the magazine's questionnaire, supporting the ban. Discussion turns around France's tradition of 'laïcité', which, like Germany's, holds that the state is secular and religious principles are private. Conversely, the UK has laws based on Christian principles and has extended this to include other religious views.

Arguably, the UK discriminates against atheists, starting with its requirement that the Head of State be Head of the Church of England and influencing organisations right down to the legal requirement that all state schools have 'a broadly Christian act of

worship daily.' You ask any atheist Headteacher how she, or he, feels about this requirement – I can tell you from personal experience.

On the other hand, the French political position is untenable to a religious person, for whom her religion is part of her life, not an add-on. It is interesting that at least one version of the Jewish faith attempts to prevent conflict by actually stating that the law of the land shall take precedence over religious observances.

The debate in France has arisen because of the perception that religious differences are increasingly leading to violence. The government's argument is that 'ostensible signs of religion' provoke hostility, so if you get rid of the clothes differences, people will get on better with each other. Theoretically this is all very interesting but which poor buggers are actually going to make a woman take off her headscarf? The police? The Deputy Headteachers? What is the punishment to be?

A declaration of war is always a rallying call to take sides; only the press releases of politicians suggest that it is likely to reduce tension. Knowing I'm not allowed to, would be enough to make me want to wear a headscarf. We immigrants have to stick together.

Visiting season is in full swing. Daughter-turned-kiwi is home for the first time after emigration and is un-phased by home having changed country. We play a gentle one-up-womanship; New Zealand has mountains, blue skies, fresh seasonal produce and empty roads.

One of our days out includes vultures circling the Rocher du Caire, wheeling around the grand cliffs like a squadron of Valkyries. The only winter visitors, in a village closed for the season, we are given a kind coffee in the tiny tourist office. We are stopped by shepherds on a mountain road and watch a herd moving down from the mountains to the low pastures in the old tradition of transhumance.

Amazingly, the herd is led by what must surely be one of the rarest creatures in the world, a working Pyrenean – although I note

the collie weaving constantly from side to side, gathering stragglers, while the Pyrenean looks cheerful and walks at the head. For the record, a very cheerful Pyrenean holds its tail in an arc, known in dog circles (!) as 'doing the wheel'. I am told that New Zealand has the transhumance too, with hundreds of flocks crossing the country roads; there are also miles of unspoilt beaches, penguins and sea-lions. I am defeated.

Then we cook together again, my lovely girl and I, and I realise how stupid I am. Together in Provence, on holiday four years ago, we cooked the best pissaladière ever made and now we peel langoustines for the paella that, with the crèmes that we took turns in caramelising, will be part of this Christmas for both of us. Neither France nor I need to impress but rather just to offer what we are. I am the richer for having a home from home in New Zealand, with unspoilt beaches, penguins and sea-lions, and I see it all in my imagination.

We compare notes on immigration laws; New Zealand is so strictly against the import of foreign bacteria that foodstuffs can be taken back there only in sealed containers and our visitors will clean their walking boots with a tooth-brush to ensure that the boots are allowed back into the country. We also compare notes on house-buying and maintenance, and I am reassured to hear about their woodworm, that wake up annually to fly around the corner of a room on Christmas day and then return to the floorboards for the rest of the year. As daughter and partner, like all kiwis, live in an all-wooden house, they were panic-stricken and called in the New Zealand beetle expert, who was not impressed and told them to call him back if it spread a lot.

They would have been less surprised if they had not had all their furniture from the UK fumigated and vacuum packed into quarantine, to prevent import of English beetles to New Zealand. There was in fact no shortage of wildlife in their new country, beetles included, but they were taken aback when the estate agent told them that there were pink bats in the attic of their home-to-be.

Contemplating the intricacies of bat protection laws, and

wondering how they could catch a bat colony anyway, legally or illegally, they were relieved to discover that the pink bats were a kind of roof insulation. This explained why the estate agent had presented the bats as a plus; they had thought him some kind of over-enthusiastic animal lover.

Inspired by company, we turn a mountain into a friend, walking the full length of Grace Dieu's ridge, with its views across into the Beconne valley. In the Second World War, the maquis were active here and their communications line is now a waymarked path, winding above the lavender to Nyons, at the mouth of the gorge that leads into the Alps.

Nyons marks the beginning of serious olive country but here, further north, lavender rules. We see impossibly steep and curving fields of true lavender, which only grows above a certain height, as well as the hybrid forms planted in the valleys. In winter, the rows are gray hedgehogs, curled up tight against the mistral.

From the slopes of Mielandre, we look down on the lavender and stone cottages of Teyssières, the village where the Sky, weary of work, rested and left traces of his Blue in the rocks as a sign. Sky's Blue certainly sparkles over the valley and keeps us company until the shadows of a deep gorge, St Ferréol-Trente-Pas, so-called because the gorge is only 'trente pas', thirty paces, from one side to the other. As I am not driving, I find this quaint and scenic.

When kiwi-fille is dropped off at Lyon airport, she is caught in a tourist survey and in response to the question, 'Were you satisfied with the service in your hotel', she gives us a glowing report. Our month offering room with full board has brought all the children home-from-home, except for my belle-fille who is now a maman herself and instead she provides us with the dubious pleasure of a one year old in real time over a webcam and microphone.

Conversation is much like Apollo 13 to Space Control, along the lines of 'I can hear you now… I'm losing you…' with the bonus of 'Did you hear her?' (unpleasant drooly sound effects). There is still something to be said for two-dimensional, quiet photographs and we receive those too. It is a pleasure, even at long-distance, to witness

such a blossoming into motherhood – and to know we can pass back the wriggling fruit when it cries or smells.

If I had photos of the last month and flicked them into animation and the illusion that everyone was here at the same time, there would be an extended family eating at my table and telling the stories of their lives. It is not summer, it is December, and we have snow two days before Christmas, which lasts, silvering the fields and footpaths. We are not sitting under the trees but in a dining room with crumbling walls and a desperate attempt at inadequate electric heating. However, one daughter has turned potter and her gift of a 'pichet', a jug for wine or water, sits on the table like a fat blue robin, opening its beak for more, and I have laid the table with the lace cloth we bought in Venice. This is not everything I wanted but it is something, an important something.

First Christmas in France adds to our food education. At last we find out what those mysterious paper-protected vegetables are – why didn't we realise straight away that they are cardoons? Of course, cardoons (and that's the English word)… so what exactly is a cardoon and what do you do with it?

My French Complete Larousse Encyclopaedia of Cookery comes into its own at these moments as it is arranged alphabetically by main ingredient, which makes it virtually impossible to look up recipes and absolutely fantastic if you want to find out what to do with something you've bought by linguistic accident, such as sea urchins – or cardoons.

I also discover that my French gardening book is a useful back-up, telling me how to cook the items I grow in my 'potager'. And so we discover cardoons, a sort of winter celery tasting vaguely of artichoke. Like all the other customers, I leave Super-U looking like a pantomime soldier in Macduff's army, camouflaged by an enormous three-feet high cardoon bundle. This turns into several gratins, popular with the vegetarian contingent.

Less popular is the preparation of the Christmas turkey, which is so unmistakably farm-fresh that it still has head, feet and … bits. Provençal tradition dictates scallops and sea food but we cheerfully

mix old ways with new. According to the media advertising, the one essential is the büche, a Christmas log, and the shops offer büches of chocolate sponge, ice-cream, nougat and every variation of patisserie – 'order now for Christmas!'

Entire Christmas menus can also be ordered in advance and there is a queue at the hypermarket counter for this service. There are promotions on gift-wrapped chocolates and extra plastic children's toys on display but otherwise we notice little difference. Despite the adverts showing Maman, stressed out because she has not yet bought her büche and there are twenty-five coming for dinner, there is none of the British seasonal frenzy. We don't miss the crowds or the traffic jams.

I risk opening my jar of Picodons and it is just as well I do so in solitary secrecy. It is just possible that the wooden doorstops are marginally softer ... I break off a piece... and a little milder... possibly. I absently lick the oil of my fingers, then concentrate, dip a finger in the jar and lick again.

The cheeses might not be a total success but you have heard of olive oil flavoured with basil, with garlic, with herbes de Provence? Flourish of trumpets - I have created Picodon oil. You are ahead of me already, adding your flavoured oil to bread dough, your pasta, your roast potatoes, your omelettte pan... forget truffle oil. The luxury taste of the Gilborough household will be Picodon oil. I sigh and return the jar to the cupboard, to the very back of a shelf, banished from the Christmas table.

I need to do more theoretical Picodon research before I return to the practicalities and a trip to Paris, with a three hour wait at Charles de Gaulle Airport, gives me the ideal opportunity. I discover that the Picodon is not a cheese, it is a war zone.

Unthinkable as it is, not everyone considers Dieulefit to be the centre of Picodon production. More upsetting still, regions outside the Rhône-Ardèche pretend not only that their goat cheeses are

Picodons but even that they produced them first. Although this sacrilege is dismissed by screeds of historical evidence, even my Larousse credits the Dauphiné or the Languedoc with the origin of the Picodon. I am horrified. Things get worse.

The Picodon is illegal in the U.S.A. I remember vaguely some fuss about unpasteurised cheeses and pregnant women but as always, when you know and love an individual against whom there are prejudicial laws, your sense of outrage is suddenly woken. I am outraged. I cannot believe that our unique cheese had to be sneaked onto the 1996 NASA Columbia space mission (by a Drômoise medical specialist) where it proved its nutritional value. I love this French astronaut, who personally made the Picodon the first and only cheese to venture into outer space.

He ranks with the nineteenth century Montélimar politician who made it to the Presidency and whose most important act, from a Dieulefitoise viewpoint, was to ensure that his weekly rations of Dieulefit Picodons reached him in Paris. He must have missed the arrival of the marketday train, nicknamed 'le Picodon' which made seventeen stops on its route delivering coal for the wool and silk factories, bricks for the potteries and Picodons from Dieulefit to Montélimar market, twenty-eight kilometres. Nowadays, two cats blink at the world from the windowsills of the old station, a toy-town house in the middle of a Dieulefit carpark.

The Picodon is not a cheese, it is a flattened round of history, a flavour of home, as to the man who wrote home from the front in the First World War, thanking his wife for the cheeses which she had sent him. The Picodons were 'so good that there is only one left' and the soldier was 'content that Marie is looking after the goats so well and is so sensible and my little Jean too, but I mustn't think of them too much or I will feel terrible.'

It would have been his wife, his mother, or his grandmother, who actually made the Picodon. Goats were 'the cows of the poor' and it was the women who made the goat cheese, handing the recipes down through the family in a purely oral tradition. This is another reason for the Picodon wars.

The upmarketing of the Picodon has led to standardisation in production, to meet the appellation controllée requirements, and now that it is proper work, it is dominated by men and has its own confrérie, a sort of Guild. There seems to be agreement, at least in the Drôme, that the Picodon Dieulefitois is the prince of goat cheese, and that the méthode Dieulefitoise requires more than a month's refinement, being regularly salted and washed.

According to Monsieur Cavet, neighbour and master cheese-maker, there are Dieulefit Picodons.... and the rest is just goat's cheese. From my recent research, I suggest to a worker at Cavet that the Picodons are washed in eau-de-vie and she laughs, shaking her head. 'Water,' she tells me, 'nothing but good plain water, not white wine, not eau-de-vie – and don't believe half the rubbish you read about Picodons.'

Even amongst the experts, the arguments are passionate; different producers have their own techniques for encouraging the final characteristic blue colour, or even changing the colour with wet cloths. Who needs to make up stories when one goat farmer is convinced that not just talking to the goats, but what you say to them, will influence the piquancy of the cheese?

I will keep goats, I will make Picodons à l'ancienne, in the old way... In 1953 the Prefect of the Drôme stated, 'We must do everything we can to prevent the increase of goats, 'l'ennemi de la forêt'.' There has been more battle over the goats than there is now over the cheese. In 1231, the village of Valréas banned goats completely, because they were eating everything green, including the vines and the trees; in 1567, Grenoble banned goats from the vineyards but stopped short of a complete ban because the peasants would starve. In 1725 Languedoc went for a total ban. I contemplate the anti-goat laws; I reflect on the current view that goats are a positive part of conservation because they clear scrub and prevent fires. I remember my own encounters with the devil's spawn, and I settle happily for the goat bells tinkling not too close up in the woods as the herd moves to new pastures.

No-one is interested in the latest information on Picodons. I tell

my family about the confréries and feel a moment's regret. I could have joined the Picodon Confrérie, dressed up in Picodon robes (I know that the Confrérie des Olives wears olive coloured gowns so perhaps Picodon experts wear mouldy cream ones?) and presumably engaged in funny handshakes. But no. It is not to be.

Perhaps I should aim to join SCOFF, which, as you would expect, is an association of cheese-makers, or the Confrérie of the Big Omelettes (honestly, it does exist, and they have just broken the record for the biggest truffle omelette ever made). But again, no.

The most I manage is an attempt to impress with my new found tasting skills and the capacity to rank the cheese's quality according to its after-taste, which, at its best, should have a slight hint of hazelnut and a definite piquancy, and which should definitely not taste metallic or of potatoes .... but then Christmas distracts me once more from the Picodon Project.

Dieulefit holds its 'switching on the lights' ceremony and it is like being back in Llanelli, except for the fireworks and Père Noël being joined by Père Foulard, his spiteful opposite, who plays tricks on naughty children.

Circus entertainment takes over the television screens and the stars of the French pop scene play a goodnatured role in children's musicals and variety shows. We knew of one French singer when we moved to France and we now have a repertoire of a dozen, who drop in on each other's shows in a sociable circuit of duos and trios, epitomized in the annual charity concert tour as 'les Enfoirés' (the Bastards) in aid of the 'restos de coeur', the shelters and food for the homeless.

We are quickly hooked on the melodies and the lyrics, even after we recognise the clichés. No-one has an orgasm in France; everyone 'touches the stars', and love is all very well but you do sometimes wish they'd get out a bit more.

I am, however, impressed by the recognition given to the songwriters, flagged up on album covers, as important as the chanteurs. This is not the case for the musicians and I am Englishly amazed by the abuse of the instrumentalists, who are anonymous and backstage.

I could list twenty rock guitarists who take centre stage whenever they appear, from Clapton to Santana, and not one of them would have done more than smile at the end of the show if they were part of the French scene.

No, if you're French, then you sing or you write – or, if you are especially talented, you do both, but only classical and jazz musicians are fully appreciated. If you are determined to make a noise, you can of course create the interminable techno beat to which there is a strange addiction on French radio.

My choice of French music clears my sitting room of visitors in seconds. I am bitterly disappointed that a voice of broken gravel, which shatters glass when merely saying 'Bonjour' is not more appreciated. How did Garou discover that he could sing? I like to imagine him as a child, volunteering for the school choir, or at breakfast asking someone to pass the milk. I bet his mother told her friends, 'He has a lovely smile but he'll never be a singer,' and everyone laughed.

8

INTERESTING THINGS TO DO IN A BATH

There are hundreds of interesting things you can do in a bath, with or without company. You can stick your toe up the tap and, if it's a mixer, you can set your own reward, betting on whether the first drip will be freezing or scalding.

You can drape a hot wet flannel across your face and breathe through it; in fact a hot wet flannel will make interesting and strange landscapes over most parts of your body. Try shutting your eyes, place flannel randomly, then open your eyes and, looking only at the flannel portrait, decide what might be underneath. A sleeping dormouse? A German helmet? A little bath foam and you can bubble mould your body or sculpt cute animals.

If you find all of that too childish – trust me, for some of us the wet flannel can provide a real moment of Jean-Paul-Sartre existentialist absurdity – but if you're a real thrill-seeker, then try sharing a bath with a clockwork dolphin. The challenge is not to flinch when it goes on a high-powered zig-zag straight for your interesting bits.

You can also play hunt the razor when you've dropped a new blade in a bath opaque with bubbles. You can drink champagne, eat chocolates, read a book and sing very loudly along with your special non-electric bathroom-friendly CD player. You can vary any of the above by drinking the champagne before playing e.g. Hunt the razor.

Then of course there are the variations for two, and the family versions, which include watch-the-baby-turn-blue – or of course red, and very loud.

For all of my past entertainments at bath-time, I never thought I would be washing dishes in my bath, nor checking for splinters – not from the champagne glass but from the hazards of washing up. It's amazing how carefully you check for broken glass when about to sit on it, naked.

Why are we washing up in the bath? Because a kitchen is taking place, slowly, and meanwhile, in addition to intermittent heating and electricity, and a record tally of three white vans and two cars (none of them ours) parked in our drive, we have no kitchen sink.

It's raining men. The pets are conducting a sit-in wherever there is most furniture piled up; they remember this sort of chaos and they're determined that we will only move house again over the combined dead bodies of two Pyreneans and two cats. We feel much the same. John's asked me for the third time what I'm doing about a bin – how the hell should I know? The phone rings and I can't remember where he told me he'd put it.

The garden is full of machinery, tools and workmen …. working. The house is full of workmen's 'trucs', 'things' which include a splendid masonry drill about two feet long, like the horn of a giant unicorn. I tell the young electrician that my husband would love one of those; he tells me it cost three thousand francs. I am suitably impressed, once I have converted to euro, and I run away to blush in private at the stupid things I say – and get away with.

It is like being a young teacher again, understanding the double-entendres too late. I remember the French-speaking French teacher who asked us why her pupils found it funny when she told them that Louis XV had big balls. I would like to say that we, her English-speaking friends and colleagues, were sensitive to the difficulties of speaking a second language and that we delicately, with straight faces, clarified the double meaning. If anyone could have stopped laughing, they might have.

The only time I feel badly done-to in my attempts to communicate is in the local Tourist Office. I want to know if there is a rugby match on in the next fortnight. 'Rugby' is 'rugbi' and 'match' is 'match'; easier than 'valve to bleed a radiator with', no? Definitely no. First the younger, then the elder woman looks at me blankly as I carefully repeat my very simple question.

I am used to the pained and wrinkled expression which crosses French faces, either at my assassination of their mother tongue or to aid them in concentration, I never know which. However, I had really not expected it this time and am lost for other ways of saying 'rugby' and 'match'. The older woman asks me to say it in English. 'Rugby' I say, 'match' I plead. 'Oh,' she says, meaning 'Why didn't you so in the first place?', then she adds, 'rrrrrugbi'.

Now I accept that I should have rolled my rs better (we all get older) but there surely isn't that degree of difference? To add insult to injury, she tells me, 'I thought you said 'marché'. 'Why?' I ask myself – until a great truism about communication finally dawns on me. It was what she expected me to say.

Tourists ask about market days; they do not pop in and ask about rugby matches. It is exactly the same syndrome as makes my husband say 'Yes please' when I am holding a mug, even if what I've actually said is, 'Have you considered the ideal circumference of a drinking container so that you don't bang your nose or spill your drink?'

On second thoughts, perhaps it's not exactly the same syndrome, but prediction and expectation do seem to me to be stronger than sensual experience, until contradicted, in the rugby case by a very frustrated Dieulefitoise English speaker.

Once the euro dropped, my lady couldn't have been more helpful. The rugby boys are trained by the monsieur who owns the wine shop behind the church, but I wouldn't find him in his shop because he would be in the Commerce Bar which is where the team meet up so I would also find notices of meetings up on the board there - and here is his phone number.

I recognise the Commerce Bar because it has a hairy hound lolling outside it in the summer, its tongue dipping in and out of its waterbowl, conveniently placed so the brown beast moves only its head. In winter, the Commerce Dog, is by the bar, like the clients. Strangely the word 'rugbi' is understood instantly in the Commerce but communication is my only success; rugby stops for the Christmas holidays, three weeks in this case. Our local restaurant takes six weeks off and there are shops that close for two months. The winter holidays are infinitely flexible for the self-employed, some of whom have winter work with the snow tourists in the mountains, and some of whom just say, 'What the hell'. No-one seems to worry that customers will not return; everyone feels entitled to holidays and a family life. I cannot imagine Welsh shopkeepers being so confident in their customer base, nor so certain of their summer earnings.

In our experience, when they do work here, they work long hours and work hard – with the compulsory lunch break at mid-day, for at least an hour, usually two. Our plumber drops in frequently with further questions before he starts the job. There is no problem at all answering his questions; we say 'We don't know' to everything.

'Haven't a bloody clue' would be more accurate. Most of the questions start with 'Where…' and include the word 'pipe'. 'Where does the pipe go to take the spring water into the kitchen from the outside sink?' 'Where does the town water come into the house?' The killer is 'Where does the spring water come from?'

I quite like the idea of looking for the source of 'la source' – very Jean de Florette - and, as my John finds himself to be extremely busy painting, this involves me walking around in the orchard with a patient plumber.

You will remember that the spring belongs to Monsieur Dubois, who now lives in Haute Savoie and returns only occasionally to light a bonfire, check his truffle oaks and give me gardening advice. I vaguely remembered him showing me some manholes in the orchard, which supply the hosepipes for watering our garden but

Monsieur Robin shakes his head. This is not the system that goes to the house. We are stuck.

'What about the previous owner? Is he dead or what?' Monsieur Robin doesn't recognise obstacles; whether there's a wall twelve inches thick or a fifty-year old plumbing system crossing underneath an orchard, he looks for solutions. I can do better than 'I don't know' to that one but it involves phoning the builder to contact Monsieur Dubois and by this time Monsieur Robin has also visited another neighbour, who joins us for a second patrol round the orchard, armed with new information. Towards the woods, there is a concrete reservoir about ten feet square and six feet deep, which Monsieur Dubois recently fenced in, presumably to comply with recent laws aimed at reducing the number of small children drowning in ponds and swimming pools – the biggest cause of toddler death in Provence. We've peered in at the small black fish, with trailing fins like tropical goldfish, that seem to come and go as if heron-dropped, but we didn't realise that the manhole cover beside it hides the source of the source.

It is with a triumphant 'Voilà' that Monsieur Robin, aided by Monsieur Girard, lifts the manhole cover to reveal two ancient taps, on which all the water to our house currently depends. Magic formula is applied – WD40 actually (some things don't change) – but there seems to be no chance of turning those taps, encrusted for fifty years. A long pause, then there is an involuntary 'Yes!' 'Ca bouge!' 'Voilà!' from all three of us as Monsieur Robin gives 'one last try' and the miracle happens.

There is now spring water on tap outside, crystal clear and flowing smoothly thanks to a new filter – who said plumbing isn't romantic? Inside, there is mains water. We will no longer lose the water in the kitchen if we flush the toilet or hose the garden – or if the water's frozen underground. In theory, there is now mains water in the kitchen but we don't yet have a kitchen, nor a kitchen sink, let alone water in it.

Monsieur Robin observes the progress of our kitchen – and

indeed our house - with sympathetic interest and a professional eye. He is keen to improve my pronunciation and makes me repeat the 'u' in 'purge', although I am not convinced I will often need to say 'valve for bleeding a radiator' in casual conversation. It was my letter to him, clarifying the various jobs to be done, that really amused him.

OK, so I make things up when I don't know the words. Apparently the French equivalent of 'rail-thingy which heats towels' was not quite the right term but he thought it was cute. He was polite in correcting me when, flustered by my cuteness, I asked him if he wanted a teatowel to light his way upstairs. Now I ask you; why would anyone in any language call a teatowel a 'torchon' if not to confuse me?

There are things about our house that Monsieur Robin does not think cute. About the rickety staircase, which trips him up at least three times whenever he tries it, he mutters 'Quelle horreur'.

When we tell him we don't use the ancient toilet, replacement of which is on his to-do list, he is relieved. He stoops throughout visits to the cellars and the attic, narrowly escaping a headache from the light in the upstairs bedroom. Student son, equally tall and less fortunate in his first encounter with low ceilings, would understand only too well. It's not only tall people who are disadvantaged here; when slim Monsieur Robin squeezes past the new sink and queries the size we've bought, I explain to him that we don't want fat visitors.

So far, Monsieur Robin is our most frequent visitor; the electricians could be more properly described as residents. Like termites, they occupy a room, destroy it and move on, leaving rubble behind them. There are interesting discussions, again in answer to 'where' but this time the keyword is 'prise', power point.

I never thought I would watch a tall, curly-haired electrician bouncing on our bed to show me that the wall lights needed to be higher (presumably in case a tall young Frenchman ever wants to bounce on our bed – and far be it from me to discount the possibility). The systematic destruction of our house has also led to the exciting moment when I could boil a kettle at the same time as

tumble-drying and using the electric oven, without blowing the electrics. The excitement was short-lived as there is no longer a cooker in the kitchen-that-isn't.

Then there are the kitchen fitters, led by Monsieur Speedy, who likes using the odd English word for our benefit and who told us 'I'm speedy' – so we took him at his word (behind his back). There is a culture clash between Monsieur Speedy and me, and it has nothing to do with nationality. I have met his type many times. He doesn't cook, has no time for it, but freely shares his criticism of our kitchen requirements.

Twenty years ago I would have fought with him and brooded over every conversation which I didn't win. Now I am older and wiser, and I am delighted when my dogs drool over his girlfriend even more than he does.

She turns up, knowing that she is visiting a house in trauma, wearing four inch heels, a tight black skirt and full make-up, and she squeals with fear when my dogs greet her. Monsieur Speedy gestures that I should restrain my slobbering dogs and I am suddenly conscious of my paint-splattered jeans, lop-sided fringe (I must pluck up courage and test my French at a hairdresser's) and the distinctive smell which has been following me around for a couple of days – I had put it down to the dogs. Black is a good colour to wear here, I note – shows up the dog hairs a treat as Mademoiselle totters in to kiss the boys hello. I restrict myself to handshakes these days.

I am still awed by the specialism of my workmen but it has its drawbacks. Each person does his own job and I am project manager, a job for which I would never be stupid enough to volunteer in my first language, never mind my poor second. I have endless discussions over who does what first and I walk the job through on the phone and in person, nervous as to what I have forgotten. So far, so good, but I now need the builder to tile one side of the kitchen before the granitier puts his granite on the cupboards.

Monsieur Speedy explains it to me with pencil diagrams drawn on the top of the cupboards themselves. My wall is not straight (sur-

prise, surprise) so the wall edge of the granite will need to be cut in situ after the wall is tiled. On the other hand – a finger is wagged at me – on the opposite side of the kitchen, the granite must be laid first, before the tiling, because the interior walls there are straight? OK? Yes, I've got it. Another set of impossible instructions for me to deliver. Didn't we say we were going to buy a house that didn't need renovating? What went wrong?

At least I will get to see granite being cut after all, and in my own garden. Monsieur Speedy instructs me firmly to look but not touch; all his clients are the same, always in a rush, always wanting to put things in cupboards and use the kitchen before it is ready and 'you have to wait.' I feel like a four-year old who wants to go to the toilet as the finger is wagged again. I have never before been told off for being too keen to use a washing machine.

It is very different for the Pyrenean sister, who will not have to live a nomadic existence in her own home. If her heating or electricity misbehaves she will even have The House Handyman, who has been attached to the domaine for decades and who is called Manuel. House Pyrenees will inevitably now be known as les Tours Fawlty. I am disappointed to discover that Manuel is Portuguese, not Spanish, and that the French name for the series is in fact l'Hôtel de Folles.

My sister will not be sitting in her bedroom while there are electricians in the hall, a plumber in the cellar and kitchen fitters in the once-and-future kitchen. But there again, she won't have the fun of trying out a brand new sunlounger on a freezing cold January day, in an otherwise empty living-room cleared for electrician action. I am also comforted to learn that, although there is indeed mains drainage for les Tours Fawlty, Madame la Previous Owner did not connect the house to it so the Pyreneans do have a septic tank – three in fact.

My sister does not seem suitably respectful towards the Good Bacteria, having been told (yes, more local advice) that bleach in products will cause no problems. I am horrified. Have you ever notice the helpline telephone numbers on cleaning products? I could be the only person who has ever called one – to check whether Cif

(the product formerly known as Jif before continental Europe's problems with 'J' affected marketing) was suitable for septic tanks. But then I only have one septic tank and I do not wish to fill it in six months. I consider the time-scale. I think it as likely that I will have a kitchen, a staircase, four new radiators and a new bathroom in six months as that 'everything will be to her taste' for my sister.

9

CHABLIS, CHARDONNAY AND COLD STONE

When you see someone looking at herself in shop windows, or even in the mirrored panels in the doorways, she is not vain; she is just curious as to what she looks like, after five months of living without any reflective surface bigger than a bathroom cabinet.

The mirror deprivation was deliberate, as part of a doomed attempt to buy on need rather than by convention. After years of living with mirrored wardrobes there is something quite liberating about not knowing what you look like. After all, why do you need to know which clothes go together if you're wearing the same ones you've worn for years? You can always draw conclusions from the expression on someone else's face or from the inflexion in the word 'Fine' which is the best response you get to 'How do I look? but it is very different to face up to the short, frowning woman with stern glasses and a very badly cut fringe, in better shape than feared but dressed like Charlie Chaplin after some slapstick with paint.

The mirror flashes these strangers at us. John says he keeps being attacked by a madman with a knife. The madman doesn't worry me – I've seen him every day for years – it's the baglady he's with that I worry about. As John says, perhaps we ought to reconsider our wardrobe – and I don't think he means the wooden thing with the

mirror now accosting us in our own bedroom. I wonder if it might be easier hiding the mirror but he says we'll get used to it. I suppose we might stop behaving like Amazonian tribespeople confronted with photographs of themselves but at the moment we're still crossing our fingers against witchcraft (what else could have turned us into these odd people?)

Not only do I have an identity crisis but I also have the additional stress of choosing between two men. The plumber gave me clear instructions on how to close off the outside tap when the spring is likely to freeze underground. The builder gives me equally clear instructions, relayed from Monsieur Dubois, who has the authority of this being his patrimonial home, that I must leave the tap running when there is a freeze.

I explain cautiously that the plumber has told me how to shut the system off, I also mention that it would be useful to know where the pipe *is* which takes the spring water to the toilet (plumbing 'where' question number twenty-three) and I have things explained to me very slowly.

Running water does not freeze so if I leave the tap on, the water will not freeze underground at all. Consequently, the water to the toilet will not stop so why would we want to change the system of spring water feeding the toilet. I say, 'D'accord,' which is a very useful thing to say and suggests that I have understood and that I agree while not actually committing me to any promises of action.

I have learnt some even more useful words from the electricians when they accidentally made bits of my ceiling fall down; I already knew 'merde' but 'putain' is a new one and is very very rude. It's interesting the way taboo words in another language merely sound entertaining and the literal translation 'whore' just sounds silly.

In fourteenth century Dieulefit the penalty for blasphemy started at fifty sous for a first offence, jumped to a hundred for the second and the tongue was cut out on the third conviction. Imagine the application of such laws today. On second thoughts, don't.

I think about water and freezing and burst pipes. If I leave the tap running, and the water doesn't freeze (which it shouldn't) then that

will protect the tap and pipes up in the middle of the field as well as the one actually leading to my sink. On the other hand, the plumber taught me all these useful things to do with taps and pipes, and he is … a plumber. There is also some childhood taboo that both John and I feel against leaving a tap running, even though we know that streams and rivers are doing just that.

I wonder whether we should have left the spring water feeding the toilet but there does seem to be something just a little insecure about drawing water from someone else's land, with a flow which varies seasonally… and if we're not allowed to use those springs, we've been told that it's easy to 'forage' and find our own spring. I contemplate this too.

I will make my name as a water dowser; forget Manon des Sources, I will create a bottled water empire 'Dieulefit l'Eau' 'God made the water'. No, it sounds a bit too close to the old office joke about all water in this establishment being passed by the management. Also, I remember my attempts at metal detecting.

I had buried my wedding and engagement rings somewhere in a large vegetable plot while turning it over and, desperate to recover them, I borrowed a metal detector and found not one piece of metal. I wish I could say that the episode taught me not to put my rings in my pocket while gardening but it was not the last time I hunted for lost treasure. I have no reason to believe that I would be any better at water divining than at metal detecting. Anything that requires faith, and the force being with me, is doomed.

So do I choose the builder (and Monsieur Dubois) or the plumber? I turn to my mother's memory for help. What would she have done? What were the feminine management skills I should have learnt from her and didn't? Oh yes, now I remember. She would have said yes to both, then done what she wanted. Or she would have said she wasn't mechanically minded and she would have asked them to do it for her.

I am distracted from the plumbing by the granite arriving. I do get to see granite being cut, by a small man with a huge moustache who is only too pleased to explain his cutting tool to me (Yes, I am

asking those questions again). It is very very expensive, looks like a sanding disc but in sharpest, shiniest metal and it has holes around it to diffuse the noise. I am surprised that there is no need for water but this is a dry cutter, for fine finishing. I watch Jean-Baptiste at work as he joins two granite slabs as worktops and uses his glue gun to mastic them to the cupboards. Monsieur Speedy was quite right and one wall is so wonky that the granite will have to be cut in situ after the tiling is done but Jean-Baptiste gives me his home number and says I must phone him, personally, and he will come out the very next day after I phone. He shows me the sealant I should use twice a year and tells me that if I do stain the granite with, for example cooking oil, the best remedy is to smear the whole surface with cooking oil. Why did my mother not teach me these things? Instead, I come from a household where my father's idea of cleaning the oven was to take a Black and Decker sander to it when my mother was safely out of the house. Now there's an idea …

I have never seen John take such an interest in cleaning products. He is disappointed in the granite; he keeps trying to wipe off the glittery bits, thinking they are breadcrumbs. To me, the granite is cold fire; I see pictures in the pink, brown and gray veins, shimmering as the light changes, and the mica makes me think of dwarves' hordes, in deep caverns. And you can put hot saucepans on it, too. We can't wait to try out the hot saucepans on our range cooker but we have to wait for the tiles to go into place before anything can be connected up.

Meanwhile, in the chaos, I get tea-stains on the new, unused hob. John is not pleased and I find him cleaning the cast iron hotplate. 'John,' I tell him, 'it's a cooker. We're going to cook on it. It's going to get dirty.'

It is no good; this isn't *a* cooker, it's the *new* cooker, and we buy special cleaner for the cast iron hotplate and another special cleaner for its stainless steel façade. The two ovens are respectively 'pyrolitic' and 'catalytic' in their cleaning habits. As long as that means they groom themselves, I don't care for a translation (from the English, that is).

I note that 'Mr Muscles Oven Cleaner' is 'Monsieur Propre' in its French marketing. The English does seem a bit sexier than 'Mr Clean' who sounds like he's one of the least popular Mister Men. I also note that the manual for our wonderful new cooker suggests daily cleaning; don't be ridiculous. As far as I'm concerned, the words 'daily' and cleaning' only co-exist for rich people who get the former to do the latter.

Time slows to the progress of the kitchen and, believe me, that's slow. It turns out that we have chosen tiles which have to be imported from Spain by that universal law which means that 'best' comes from elsewhere, and which meant that my sister waited weeks for her French tiles to reach York.

My habit of finding out what each job involves turns out to be a big mistake with the tiler. I am now very well-informed of how impossible it is to put squares onto a three-dimensional surface. I now appreciate that you start in the middle and work outwards but the middle of what? Much head-shaking.

If you start in the middle of the wall, then the tiling around the sink will finish with a 1cm tiling strip on the far side and that will break when it's cut... shall we have a baguette here? Disappointingly this turns out not to be a break for elevenses but a plastic strip to finish cut tiled edges.

Then there's the sink edging which consists of specially shaped tiles – what could be simpler? Except that the edging drops lower than the hardboard so that the cupboards can't be opened. The tiler pops out to visit the joiner, returns with chipboard and an hour later my sink surface is 1cm higher – perfect - as long as no-one tells the kitchen designer, who has no doubt considered the finer points of ergonomics (for me? for John? for Ms Average-suits-nobody? I always wonder about the ergonomics=one-person-kitchen equation). Surely that's the tiles sorted? No, we have a sink-corner-problem.

We contemplate the two untiled corners and the corner pieces. It's like one of those psychological tests which show that boys have better visual-spatial awareness than girls. I turn the pieces and

compare them with the blanks but the tiler, definitely a boy, is right.

Whichever way up I hold the corners, they each have one straight side and one curved side, where two curved sides are required. They are in fact the wrong pieces. Why the hell couldn't he have said so instead of checking whether I could work this out for myself?

I repeat the test with two ordinary edging pieces. If we can't get corners which fit, we could cut two pieces and make a mitred corner... ? I have done well, I receive nods... exactement. Except that we only have two straight pieces left... I keep up 'And we would need four?' Exactement. So either way, we wait.

I choose a colour for the grout and then I succumb to decision-overload. Too many choices, however trivial, like when I tried to buy donuts at a Tim Hortons in Canada, or a coffee in Starbucks. There are times you just want a coffee and cake for God's sake. Even the cheese counter in the market seems too much; as student son pointed out, you can cope with there being different sorts of cheese but four types of roquefort is going too far. A Headteacher friend used to take a week's holiday from decisions to start the summer break and the words 'You choose' are not always as generous as they seem.

Finally the penny drops. Peter Mayle is a sadist. He has lured thousands of innocent Brits to endless house renovation in the sunshine with the workmen-from-hell and the horror-film flies and the need-to-respect-your-toilet. Thanks to Peter Mayle, those who are not doomed in this way are feeling even worse about not living their dreams and are looking at the rain on the small overcrowded island we used to call home.

There is a certain relief in knowing that you can't win and I return to the job in hand. I take Jean-Baptiste at his word and phone him at home after 8pm to arrange the fitting of the granite against the wonky wall.

Perhaps it is my imagination but his wife sounds a little suspicious when she asks who's phoning. It is Friday evening after all. Even more worrying is the fact that she seems to know who I am

straight away and she relaxes when I give my name and stutter about my kitchen. How funny am I exactly? Ever cheerful, Jean-Baptiste arranges to cut the granite on Monday evening. That might well have happened if John had not exited the bath into a full washing-up bowl, smashed a plastic box and flooded the bathroom at the exact moment Jean-Baptiste arrived.

Torn between rescuing my bathroom and deciding where a cupboard should go, I said 'yes, yes.' Always a mistake. However, Jean-Baptiste had forgotten his glue-gun – did we have one? No, sadly, we did not have one among the interesting objects left in our outbuildings. Now if Jean-Baptiste had wanted a rusty tin of any size, various antique cold chisels or a bee-keeping outfit, there would have been no problem.

When John emerges, very clean, Jean-Baptiste has gone and it seems I have said 'yes yes' to leaving the granite uncut and the cupboard in entirely the wrong position. Tuesday sees the return of Jean-Baptiste but – inevitably - this time without his cutting tool. I grovel. He doesn't give me so much as one of those 'I-hate-bloody-women-who-can't-make-their-minds-up' looks but merely re-re-arranges for Wednesday evening. He gives the granite worktops one last polish before he goes.

I have a bad feeling about Wednesday, D-Day.This should be the day the kitchen becomes somewhere to cook, wash dishes and feel contented. Why should anything go wrong? I have checked again and again with the designer that it is the fitters who will connect the oven, sink, washing machine and finish off fitting drawers.

The fitters turn up on time and from the moment I mention plumbing and electrics, I know this is not going to be a good day. Monsieur Speedy wants to know why I didn't get my plumber to sort out the sink, he does not do electrics and I am piggy-in-the-middle as I relay what I have been told, which only annoys him more as he is le patron, not anyone else.

John goes shopping, a long way away. I listen to the sounds of a very pissed-off workman not singing while he directs plumbing and electrics. He tells me that one power-point does not work. No prob-

lem, I say, that's for the electricians to sort out. Sod's law decrees that they are working away this week but I phone and they promise to be round within two hours.

I pass this information on but it does not lighten the atmosphere. Monsieur Speedy regards my magnificent range cooker with distaste. There is no way he is touching the gas for the hob. I can't say I blame him and I tell him so but point out that I am merely saying what was agreed. He hates me.

At lunchtime I see the vanishing backs of the fitters, no 'bon appètit', no 'à tout à l'heure'. I shrug. Poseurs by name and posers by nature. It is not the first time I have faced an adolescent with a chip on his shoulder.

'Bonjour les chiens' is the first sign of the electricians, exactly as promised, and the dogs welcome them like the long-lost friends they are. They look at the installation of an undercupboard striplight. 'Putain de merde, qu'est-ce qu'ils ont fait ici?' suggests that Monsieur Speedy was quite right to say he shouldn't be doing electric work.

I have forgotten how cheerful they are as they sort problems, then vanish. John switches the oven on and off, and it works. After a month of fast food microwaved or boiled on a camp kitchen, he has been getting cravings for potatoes in potato-shapes and for meat in a big lump. I would quite like fish in fish-shapes rather than cuboids. How – and why - do they do that in frozen meals?

I leave phone messages with the kitchen designer to say that my workmen will sort the cooker out, and with my plumber, to ask him for just that. I check my watch; lunchtime seems long today. I gradually realise that lunchtime is beyond long and they are not coming back. We look around. They have left their ladder and taken with them the undersink bin. We are bemused and I phone the kitchen designer who is not there. Nor would I be. Perhaps he is pinned against a wall?

Unbelievably, the plumber arrives and with his usual patience, works his way through the instructions for changing injectors from natural to propane, adjusts the flames and chats with Jean-Baptiste who is once more thwarted in his attempt to cut granite. He doesn't

seem to mind, accepts a petit cafè and reveals the reason for his equanimity. This is his last job before he returns to Chablis. He has had enough of the attitude in the south, the petty backbiting, the racism. He offers advice on the height of the flames and then helps Monsieur Robin move the monstrous cooker back into place. He polishes the granite worktops as he talks.

'When southerners come north, we welcome them... they bring a little bit of sunshine with them and we appreciate it. All they do when we come down from the north is pass comments behind your back... I hate that. '

I know that Monsieur Robin is from Normandy originally and has no regrets, as he told me when I mentioned that student son missed Wales. 'You'll catch cold up there,' he tells Jean-Baptiste.

'I love the countryside here. I'll be back for holidays... you can't beat the hunting...' and Jean-Baptiste tells us where the best spots are. He pours scorn on the sorts of people who 'massacre' animals – that's not 'le vrai chasse'.

I suggest that it will take me a few years before I head for the hills with my shotgun but I tell them that I used to go fishing and that Wales is fisherperson's heaven. I don't tell them that I once owned a trout lake or rather, I once co-rented a trout lake, to which my friend and I had sole fishing rights, for less than the price of a rugby season ticket.

With a last joke about returning to live with the eskimos, Monsieur Robin leaves, and I find out more from Jean-Baptiste. He warns me that the English are all ros-bifs behind our backs. I consider my time being English in Wales and I think I can live with 'ros-bifs'. I also consider my twenty-five-years-Welshness, including a Welsh accent, and I am not afraid of starting again the process that turns outsider to friend.

Ben oui, Jean-Baptiste will of course still be working with stone in Chablis. He runs his cloth, impregnated with magic solution, over the spotless granite, caressing it one last time. Not stone like this, you understand. Marble is beautiful but the work here is repetitive, basically cutting rectangles.

'And in Chablis...?' I ask, and discover that Jean-Baptiste is a stone mason who will be restoring churches and other historic monuments. How people escape from the boxes we put them in! Why should a craftsman not be an artist? We give Jean-Baptiste a bottle of pastis, a thank-you and an apology, and he promises me a 'piece of stone' when he sculpts one. One of his brothers is a vintner and as we talk, I can taste Chablis, the flavours deepening from the first chilled freshness to the richness of the chardonnay grape. I know that from now on Chablis will always taste to me of cold stone, marbled on my taste buds.

10

THE BADLANDS AND OLIVE OIL CHOCOLATE

There is more to life than a kitchen – or even a house – and so we fill in forms. Our application for a carte grise, to register our car in France and get French plates, has been bounced yet again, or, as the nice lady in the mairie said, 'I told you – they like their paperwork at the préfecture'.

We check the forms together, add some, change some and I explain that we can't send the old carte grise with our dossier because we don't have a carte grise in the U.K system. In fact, as I have explained in a polite letter to the préfecture, the whole point of sending the dossier is in order to *get* a carte grise.

The nice lady understands this perfectly but we both know how little chance there is that this will crack ice at the préfecture. We wish the dossier luck as we send it once more on its way. The only thing which cheers me up is the knowledge that French bureaucracy has dealt a worse hand to le Pen, the should-be-leader of the French National Front.

After a recent near-thing in the run-in for President, where the abstainers nearly left the National Front in national power, le Pen's luck ended this year with him unable to even stand for his own constituency because of – yes – for not filling in the right forms.

After it was too late for him to do anything about it, he was

informed that he did not meet the residency requirements and could not stand. I picture the glee with which a civil service clerk sat on this information. I think of my dealings with the préfecture and go a stage further, imagining the planning that went into downfall by paperwork. My conspiracy theories are outdone by le Pen's rival, who declares that le Pen deliberately messed up his residency forms to gain publicity.

In a country where prosecution for corruption seems to be a fundamental requirement for following high office, I am definitely an innocent abroad. Where are the minor sexual scandals, the marital infidelities, the nepotism that fascinate the British press and destroy their politicians? Hardly worth mentioning, here, not when you have key politicians implicated in fraud on the scale of millions.

There definitely is more to life and we head off to explore the Badlands. They really are referred to as the Badlands, even in French, and only now do I discover what the word actually means. To our children, the Badlands are the wastelands where the baddies hang out in post-nuclear sci-fi films; to me, they're the rocky American deserts where the baddies hang out in cowboy films.

Both generations have missed part of the point. Badlands, so my dictionary informs me, are 'wastes of much eroded soft strata in south Dakota and therefore any similarly eroded region'. Our badlands are iced over, cliffs of shimmering white rock, sheer above green valleys, the domain of trolls and cave bears.

I know that the last time a bear was seen in the Vercors region was in 1938 but that doesn't mean it was the last bear there, does it? When I was a child, my father told me that an uncle of his was hugged to death by a bear in Russia. I was later, more reliably informed that this adventurous Scotsman did indeed go to Russia where he fell for a local lady and never returned to his wife. If he was hugged to death, it wasn't by a bear, but it's always the first story that stays in my mind.

You can understand why a local farmer might worry about what lurks in these mountains. There are some attempts to re-introduce wolves here, to the fury of the farmers who take their sheep and

cows onto the high pastures in the summer. We stay in the valley, watching clouds travel the length of a stone ridge, their enormous shadows flitting like nazgul across the cliffs.

As the sun hits a section, the ice flashes silver, then broods ebony again in the shade. Dazzled, we look down. On the ground, our own tiny shadows cling to our feet. We escort them home.

The wilderness has swept us clean and we feel able to play with the other humans again, finding Nyons in festival mode on an unseasonably hot Sunday. Nyons boasts a Roman bridge built in the fourteenth century (presumably by Provençal Romans who missed the march home); a medieval chapel which leans drunkenly over the village, like a wedding cake with its stone tiers and figure on the top; and black olives of outstanding quality, the famous tanche variety.

Nyons olive oil is one of five to have gained appellation controllée status, the others being further south in the Alpilles, the Alpes de Hautes Provence and Nice, and Nyons a.o.c. sells for four times the price of imported extra virgin.

I only have to cross the road from home to buy local, traditionally produced extra virgin but my neighbour shocked me on my first visit by telling me that he imports the olives themselves from Spain. What's more, he told me, so do all the others round here, even those who tell you differently. Spanish olives are just so much cheaper and it is so expensive to produce the oil in the old ways, who can afford to pay the prices for French olives? It is hard enough for a family business to compete with the good, cheap oil imported from Spain, Italy and Greece. Unless you are Nyonsais, where the a.o.c. label keeps the high price attractive and where the olive groves stretch both sides of the river Eygues, perennial silvery-blue in the sunshine.

On the drive to Nyons, we leave our St Maurice and the Vercors mountains behind to wind along the River Lez, still in lavender country, where the corrugated fields hug every curve in the road or impossible slope. On high bends, we can glimpse to our right the industrial plains of the Rhône, the plumes from Tricastin nuclear power station and, on a clear day, the bluffs of the Ardèche gorges on the far side of the Rhône.

To our left, the hills gradually become orchards, we leave the narrow river valley and the first olive groves flash blue amongst the fruit trees. 'You are now in apricot country' the sign tells us and we know that a little further to the east are the tilleuls, the limes of the Baronnies, where France's biggest herb trade takes place. Just twenty minutes drive from home, we see the giant landmark of the Vaucluse, Mont Ventoux, its bald head unmistakably white, whether with snow or from rock catching the sun.

Just below its highest point is the memorial to Tommy Simpson, the British cyclist who, his body overstretched with drugs, died there on a Tour de France. Passing cyclists contribute to the bizarre collection of tributes left there, which include plastic water bottles, cycle clips, a compass, and of course flowers. We have watched the amateurs struggle up Ventoux, we have seen the professionals challenging the mountain and whenever we drive that way, the first sighting draws one word from both of us, 'Ventoux.' And then we drop down through the groves and orchards into the bustle of Nyons.

The gendarmes on fête duty lean on the barriers that close off the road and they chat. A sunny day, overtime, a little traffic and crowd control ... I'm not surprised they're smiling. The regulation police pullover strikes me as quite flattering ...what is it about sex and uniforms? If I were twenty years younger... and a foot taller ... but navy is not really my colour.

The confrérie of oleaculteurs is here in full green velvet and tricorne hats, also green, joined by some of their Picodon brothers – and, yes, their cloaks are cream (but not mouldy). The centre of the old market square, a cloistered area surrounded by archways and shops on all four sides, has a raised platform for speechmaking, prizegiving and traditional entertainment.

The village loudspeakers broadcast the speeches like diktats from 'The Prisoner'; you *will* hear that our fine tradition of olive-growing has had an exceptional season, despite last year's drought, and you *will* hear who was awarded the prize for the best-behaved olive in show.

I love rural shows; I'm just not very good at being in them. At fifteen, I led a sheep (breed – Derbyshire grit) around the Yorkshire Show ring and then bemused the staff in the Barclays Bank tent by assuming it was a tea-room and ordering coffee and biscuits – they gave us some, too. How was I supposed to know that the trays were supposed to be for clients?

I then had several fallow, sophisticated city years before moving to rural Wales, where my initial signing-on at the Unemployment Office (no Job Centre in those days) required me to spend three days preparing salads for the Three Counties' Show. If you need an expert in lettuce-washing, call me.

I have admired the biggest vegetables in Bancffosfelen, I have breast-fed my baby in the back of the beer tent in Carmarthen, and I have endured endless comparisons of the pea-pod with the elder-flower (wines, that is, and these were the real vins de pays. If smelly socks could have been converted to alcohol, we'd have done it. What is even more embarrassing is that we then saved the best wines for showing and drank the 'not so good'. Can you imagine 'not so good' beetroot wine?).

Then there were my doomed attempts at showing my cats. We were disqualified the first time at the vetting table, for having fleas; my mother was so ashamed that she told her friends that the cat had been 'unwell'.

On the second attempt, we received plenty of helpful advice, such as 'Keep the water dish to the back of the cage in case someone poisons him,' and 'If you cut his whiskers, it will make his face look broader'. We won a rosette but my very stressed cat took to the woods on returning home and it took us two days to coax him down from his tree. We promised him no more shows and we kept our word.

All of this means that I know a good local show when I see one. Nyons' oil producers have turned out in force and they are bouncing. The harvest usually starts at the end of November but the autumn was mild and sunny, the crops continued to grow and the flavours develop, and the harvesting continued late into the season.

This has been a fantastic year for the tanche olive growers. We often passed the harvesters in December, their ladders against the trees, old wicker baskets piled high and now the olive oil nouveau has arrived. I buy a bottle of liquid gold, and am told it can be used straight away but will keep at its best for a year. It should be kept out of the light, in glass or stainless steel, like perfume.

Every olive product you can imagine is on show, for sale and, where edible, for tasting; black and green tapenades, the standard olive pâté; a purer cream of olives; olive oils, straight or flavoured with basil, garlic, peppers or truffle; soap, cleansers and moisturisers based on olive oil; even olive oil chocolate (odd, in being green, but very shiny and hard and ... well, oily).

Then, of course, there are the olives themselves; the tanche, king of the show, medium in size, brownish-black and slightly wrinkled, rather than the glossy raven of Nice or the large Greek olives, and much milder than either; olives in every kind of herb, stuffed, spiced and piqués (a quick method of preparing green olives involving salt and resulting in young, fruity olives, still with bite, rather than soft).

Although the first Sunday in February, the event is a big attraction, and I fight my way through the Sunday tourists to reach the stalls, determined to try and buy. The weekly market is well worth the drive (and well known, as, on a slack news day, the Nyons correspondent for *le Dauphiné* describes every market stall, with the names of the traders and the prices of their produce). Fête days are even better.

The traditional flamenco dancers are clacking castanets on the platform to the Spanish guitars. Traditional? Perhaps the olives here aren't imported from Spain but ... The inevitable cute goat with even cuter kid munch and bleat in the shed that demarcates the children's farm, where small boys chase chickens and small girls stroke rabbits' ears. If only I was accompanied by a small child, I could go into the enclosure, cuddle the chickens and chase the rabbits.

We wear overcoats but the Nyons palm trees stretch up and up into blue, blue skies. By lunchtime, people are stripping to T-shirts and sitting outside in the cafés, a foretaste of spring. Nyons' micro-

climate protects exotic plants in winter and maximises sunshine, quadrupling its population to forty thousand inhabitants in the summer.

I browse amongst the stalls, the Picodons, saucissons, country breads (time bombs that turn into rocks within eight hours), the bottled fruits, jams and savoury spreads, all straight from the producers, but I cannot find any truffles. The olives might have had a good year but it has been dire for truffles.

This should be the peak of the season. Although demand for the black diamonds is highest at Christmas, the cropping is best from January onwards in the coldest months. It is easy, although expensive, to find canned truffles and truffle oil, even in our local Super-U, but fresh truffles stay in the world of the dealers, a certain café in Tricastin on Tuesdays and car boots in Richerenches on Saturday mornings.

I know that the current price is six hundred euro a kilo and I am not expecting to buy one if I do see them. I have given up looking and am enjoying a display of Picodon posters, especially the one based on a fable, so that the fox running off with a cheese carries a Picodon in its mouth, when I spot the real thing, fresh truffles.

The stall carries an odd mix of flowers and fruit, presented in cellophane and ribbons, and at its proud centre are two jars containing eggs and the unmistakable balls of edible horse dung worth six hundred euro a kilo. There must be five truffles in the taller jar. I do a quick calculation - black diamonds indeed.

Someone pushes past me to the stall and all is explained. These are the prizes in the fête raffle, the truffle jars being 1st and 2nd prize. Why the eggs? Because, according to Carluccio, my mushroom expert, truffles have 'an affinity' with eggs and when stored together, they add truffle-flavour to the eggs through the thin shells and hey presto! you have truffle omelette without adding any precious truffle.

I resolve once again to take our truffle hounds around Monsieur Dubois' oak plantation, just in case, but I don't buy a raffle ticket. You never know what tenth prize might be and it was only last week

that John was tempted by a local raffle in which the first prize was a (live) pig and the second a (live) goat.

A stallholder hears my accent and asks me where I'm from. I take the easy option and say I'm 'Anglaise' but this is not enough.

'Anglaise d'où?' he asks. 'D'Etats Unis? D'Ecosse? D'Irlande?'

'From Wales,' I tell him, 'but we live in Dieulefit now'. '

'Ah,' he responds, 'Anglaise Provençale,' and his smile is in acknowledgement not mockery. I like the sound of this and I roll my new identity around my tongue. It dawns on me that 'Anglaise' does not mean English and that my Welsh children don't need to get so incensed at being considered 'Anglais'. Once you realise that it often means 'English speaking', the oddness of being 'English from Wales' is explained.

This does not excuse Welsh rarebit being described on le Pub's menu as a typical dish 'Anglais' and it is difficult to explain the French film title 'l'Anglaise' with a 'young Scotswoman' as heroine, but it does soften the impression that the French only acknowledge England as a country. In the sporting context, les Gallois are treated with great respect by French commentators, and carefully distinct from les Anglais.

Am I an Anglaise Provençale? Perhaps I need to adopt the German habit of creating a monster noun, like 'bustenhalter', 'bosom-holder' for 'bra'. I shall be an Anglaise-Galloise-Provençale-de-provenance-Ecossaise. (I am proud of the 'de provenance'; it is an amazingly long way of saying 'from' which confused me completely when I first saw it on the station announcement board. I thought 'le train de provenance Lille' was at least being manufactured there to deserve such a long word).

I am still having my usual identity crisis. In the 60's 'finding yourself' was a recognised pastime but nowadays the census forms offer us more boxes. We are supposed to think outside the box but always know which ones to tick.

In Galloise mode, I note that Bonnie Tyler is number one in the French charts, co-singing her old hit 'Total Eclipse of the Heart' with French singer Karine. I remember visiting a Swansea valley primary

school and a little one telling me, 'Bonnie Tyler's my auntie you know'. When I say I live in Dieulefit, no-one says, 'Well then you must know Montand the baker, ten years he's lived in that house which used to be a post office...'

I miss the Welsh need to connect people and places, and lived there long enough that there was every chance I would have known Jones or whoever, and if not, I knew to carry it on with 'Now was he related to the Jones who sold out for the wind farm' and the conversation could meander on for hours.

The closest I've got to that here is vicarious; everyone knows Monsieur Dubois, and so everyone knows where I mean if I say I live in his house. When the tiler told me he lived next door, in the house with blue shutters, when he was a little boy, I was already filing it away for a future Welsh-style conversation (You've had the builder in? Nice boy. His parents used to live ... and that was before ...') I also store away the directions given by the tiler to a lost delivery man; he should turn right by the old Cavet cheese factory... I know where the current Cavet is but to know places, as to know people, you need to know where they came from.

I support Wales in the rugby internationals, which I never watched when I lived in Wales. I check the Welsh news online and I know the behind-the-scene politics that makes me delighted to see an ex-Director of Education standing for local government. I am fuming to see the latest embarrassment from the Assembly; international aspirations but brains in their backsides.

A detailed motion as to exactly where in the chamber those backsides should be placed once wasted assembly time until even the Speaker had to express a view (scathing) – not on the proposal but on its very existence.

In short, I am behaving like an exile – not to the extent of joining some ex-patriots' group, and not with any notion of going back – but nevertheless, there is something irradicably Welsh in me. I used to accuse my parents of belonging to a racist group, the St Andrews Society, with its (to me) bizarre membership requirements and I am

wary of 'clubs' with closed membership of any kinds, but I understand better now how they come about at all.

Then I find out about Michael Jones. I have come to recognise some key faces on the French pop scene and noticed that Jean-Jacques Goldman appeared on interviews with his co-singer and co-writer, a tall, lean man with red-tinted glasses. I should perhaps have guessed from the name Michael Jones that this person was not a French native but he shares the lead with Jean-Jacques in singing the anthemic 'Envole-moi', 'Rescue me' and I don't believe there is anyone who listens to modern French music who doesn't know his name, so the penny didn't drop until I heard his bilingual lyrics for *'Je te donne.'* In this song, he offers you a heart bred with rhythm and soul, the heart of a Welsh boy far from home.

Michael Jones was born in Welshpool, like his father, who took part in the Normandy landings and, while winning a war, somehow managed to fall in love with a local girl, marry and then return to Welshpool with his French wife. It is possible that there was a time lapse there but who knows? Michael Jones was born and grew up in Welshpool but on one of his holidays with relatives in Caen, when he was nineteen, he saw an advert for a guitarist who could sing in English to join a French rock band. It was Goldman, arguably the most famous name on the current French music scene, who placed the advert and the musical partnership has lasted thirty years. Michael Jones is a superstar here and an unknown in Wales.

Singing in both French and English, he offers us everything he is, his talent, faults, luckiest moments – and his difference. Yes, that hits home: the Welsh-French boy and his difference.

11

SEEKING JEAN LE BLANC IN THE MAGICAL FOREST OF SAOU

In the mists, through leaf mulch wet with melted snow, I am seeking Jean le Blanc in the magical forest of Saou. Amongst the first violets, wild hellebores are fern silhouettes just about to shake open the pink 'Lent roses' which I once planted by my pond in Wales.

We first saw Saou golden with April, the village nestling against rock before the high cleft which guards the forest. We walked the tourist trails, waymarked by labelled trees, and we opened the wooden flaps to test our French on the quiz questions for children. The river was a mere bubble in which to cool your feet or scoop a thirst-quenching mouthful. A red squirrel crossed John's path but I missed it, sulky at being left out.

A lost world, the forest stretches between stone cliffs on all sides with narrow entries through gorges north and south. Until November 2003 it was in private ownership, although open to the competing interest of hunters, walkers and families day-outing, and the champagne was cracked officially when Saou at last became a Departmental Park, owned by us, les Drômoises. To the hunters, walkers and families day-outing - no change – but the future should be interesting if the neighboring Vercors National

Park is anything to go by. In the February mists I imagine wolf-howls.

It cannot be the same place we visited again in August, to find a full carpark and crowds carrying their picnics to the clearing at the start of the forest. It didn't matter that the ready-made tables were all fully occupied as the later-comers all brought full French picnic paraphernalia. We saw car boots expanding like Dr Who's tardis to provide tables, chairs, hampers, cases of wine and of course full, spotless table linen, including napkins. Lunch, especially outdoors, is a serious matter.

Babies and dogs competed on the grass for crumbs under tables and no-one seemed to mind the overcrowding as long as there was enough shade to go round. Even then, with new arrivals by the boot-load for the best part of two hours, it took only two minutes walking to lose the noise – and the people - amongst the trees.

No-one else is here on this February day and the trees wrap all sounds into quick, muffled silence, our voices too bright and loud for this place. The river, still shallow, is cold enough to kill – and has done so at least once this winter. The footpath follows its stony route, even where the river disappears underground for some ten minutes' walk, whether by natural or artificial intervention we cannot tell. The bare roots of an immense fallen tree block a side path – another reminder of the worlds beneath our feet, below the surface, where water dives deeper than any whale.

It is from the car that I glimpse Jean le Blanc – two of them. I am sure of it, I can see a flash of white on the backs, the distinctive shape of birds of prey, smaller than buzzards. From the moment I read that Jean le Blanc, a short-toed eagle, can be found in the forest, I hoped to spot him.

Somehow the name makes him a personality, a shy woodland inhabitant with whom I want to be on nodding terms. 'Saw Jean le Blanc today,' I want to say. 'How was he?' I'll be asked. 'Doing fine,' I'll reply. I don't tell my visiting Welsh friends why Saou is so popular with Jean le Blanc, the snake-eater, nor do I mention the seven varieties of snakes (three very rare) that are to be found there.

There are some aspects to my sorties into the forest that I keep to myself.

More dangerous than snakes, is the 'ambroisie' of which my local paper has warned me, ranting about recent sightings with a hysteria never reached before, even in accounts of the wolves of the Vercors. I am confused and the dictionary increases my puzzlement. It does mean 'ambrosia' so how exactly is the food of the gods 'an infestation' against which articles 1382 and 1383 of the Civil Code, as well as 220-221 of the Environmental Code, oblige all property-owners to do combat? It turns out that 'ambroisie' is also 'a plant dangerous for your health', 'ragweed' in the States and 'ragwort' in Britain. All I know about ragwort, the leggy weed with yellow flowers, is that it poisons horses, and we automatically destroyed the odd specimen which appeared in our field in Wales. I had no idea of the havoc it causes in the States nor the very real threat it is to the forest of Saou.

I don't notice any of these triffids (a relief - what am I supposed to do if I do see any?) as we follow the 800 metres detour to see 'remarkable trees'. I feel sorry for the unlabelled forest. 'You're all remarkable,' I tell them, remembering a school where class sets were named after trees (and some trees were far more popular to teach than others), but I still crick my neck looking up at the officially remarkable Scots pines, up ... and up. John photographs their swaying tops ... and their bases ... and has no chance whatsoever of getting both in the same shot unless he lies on his back in the mud. He settles for poor photos.

There is something cave-like about a forest dripping in mist and we shake off the damp with a coffee in 'L'oiseau sur sa branche'. Half the tables are laid for lunch and it will doubtless be full but we had no idea how popular the restaurant is when we arrived there last summer, hot and hungry, hoping for a sirop and a sandwich.

Tables spilled across the terrace to the very edge of the village road and as one set of occupants rose, another took their place. The waitresses whisked mats, steaming plates and chilled bottles of red in a quick dance between customers and we had little hopes of 'just a sandwich' but we tried anyway.

The inevitable 'no, we only do lunches,' left us nursing our mint sirops disappointed and hungry, but not hungry enough in the heat to appreciate the plates piled with filo pastry concoctions or casseroles. There was no chance of any shops being open during lunchtime and no cafés within ten miles and we must have looked pathetic enough to touch a maternal chord because back came our waitress with the suggestion that we could have a dessert ... how about apricot tart? Every mouthful of that tart was true ambrosia, sweetened with sunshine.

The chef of 'l'Oiseau sur sa branche' wears what I think of as full whites, despite the fact that his restaurant interior is about the size of my living room, and his credo is engraved in a window; 'Here, we do not acknowledge any hindrance to free speech, to the exchange of ideas, to utopias or to dreams. We do not accept any brakes or restraints to the exercise of free will. The only law is the challenge of debate.' Who needs Paris and the left bank?

I consult the bird book but it is inconclusive. The white bits seem to have been in the wrong place but in the mist, and in flight, who knows ...

At least I know a cormorant when I see one, and they hang out in gangs exactly where you would expect them to, on sandbanks and driftwood in the Montélimar canal, with views of apartment blocks and industrial wasteland. Like urban foxes, cormorants make the most of what they find, and my ex-colleagues in Port Talbot still wave to my talisman, who sits on a lamp-post above the central reservation on the M4, on the slope down from Baglan to the city God would like to forget.

Every day for three years, driving to and from work, I looked for his silhouette, the U-bend neck, wings outstretched like the eagle in a Roman standard as he dried them or hunched in sleep. To see him was to start the day right, like a marital kiss, and to catch him in flight between his lamp-post and the docks, was a moment's magic. He vanished just before I left too – moving on, I wondered? Dead, I was told by jolly workmates, squashed on the motorway.

One of the same jolly workmates phoned me six months later –

not only was my cormorant back but he had company. If ever you drive along the M4, between Baglan and Port Talbot, where the steelworks spouts gray clouds and the clouds spout gray rain, look up. If the water sprite, or one of his friends, is there, he'll shake off the rain, stretch, in his element. He might visit his new statue on Llanelli promenade, approve it and play on the sandspits for the summer, but he'll always go back to the power station and the bare hills opening into the south Wales valleys.

Montélimar's cormorants have rich pickings. The wind tears our eyes, rips our uncovered ears raw, as we count the seconds. We lose count and the diving bird reappears like a magician, impossibly distant, in a different direction from where it first went under. The U-bend of the throat contorts – we have seen eels two-foot long succumbing to a bird's determination, even reappearing - only to go down again as another gulp dooms the wriggling prey – and breakfast is gone.

It is now two weeks since the fitters went for lunch and their ladder is still where they left it. We have, as they say, moved on (which means that when the builder said 'We can knock the wall and stairs down on Thursday' and we replied, 'Fine', the slightly-unfinished-kitchen ceased to be a priority). Besides which, we are busy with more-to-life and preparation for a visit to the doctor to organise a routine prescription.

If John is ill, he considers it too stressful (when he's feeling ill anyway) to go to the doctor's and if he's well, there's no point in going, is there. This interesting logic impacts even more when the language of consultation will be French. I talk him into a visit (when he's not ill of course – I'm not that brave), we agree that doctors all speak a different language anyway and John swots the relevant chapter in his French lessons while I play with the big dictionary. 'Pins and needles' turns out to be 'fourmis', 'ants' and as we learn new

vocabulary, we are disappointed not to have more medical problems – what a waste of all our new words.

Before leaving Wales, we asked our local G.P., or rather the receptionist, for our medical files. There are receptionists and there are rottweilers; this was the latter, who behaved as if we were asking her to break the Official Secrets Act and defect to England.

When the photocopied files arrived, I read them as if they were the latest best-seller, crammed with sex and violence – and they probably are, if you know the stories behind the 'three stitches in forehead' (good one, that – I was dripping blood all over Llanelli's A & E and, as they do, the doctor said, 'Now then, what seems to be the matter?') or the one which starts 'vomiting since 4pm, ate oysters on 28/8…' It is like being a child again, eavesdropping, or reading notes between teachers who mention your name, and I am fascinated by the letters between GP and specialist, referring John because of a frozen shoulder or some such problem.

From specialist to GP, 'Thank you for referring this very pleasant 57 year-old…'.

From GP back to specialist, 'Thank you for seeing this very pleasant 57 year-old…' What if he hadn't been very pleasant?

I check my own file but all I find is the odd space which suggests that something was carefully blanked out of the photocopying. I draw my own conclusions … 'This very **** **** **** of a 47 year old?'

I do not communicate well with doctors. I don't understand this as my Welsh vet became my friend and already I like and trust my vet in France, even if I don't share his enthusiasm about dog interior design. Doctors, on the other hand …

There was the one who suggested I might have got the idea that I had a vaginal infection because there was a lot about it on television at the moment… I changed doctors.

There was the one who always prescribed orange juice, particularly but not only in situations where he wouldn't want to give antibiotics because people use too many of them generally. My difficulties have not just been with male medics, and not just with

doctors. There was the female nurse who gave me instructions on when to take a tablet and when I asked what it would do, said 'You'll find out soon enough' and laughed. I was a very naiive young woman, in hospital, and it was a suppository.

I have given a reading from my first novel in a stroke ward where the nurses were too busy to do more than park a few victims in the day room, my lively, lovely mother among them, and leave me to work out whether four of them were still alive at the end of the reading (they were – they could hold the bookmark I gave each of them).

There have also been angels - a midwife who listened and believed and a G.P who did prescribe penicillin - but not enough of them. The U.K. system seems to work on the principle that if people wait long enough for treatment, enough of them will die to save money and enable the system itself to stagger on.

In fairness, I must confess that I am not a good patient. I feel sorry for the nurse who asked me what my religion was – she was only doing her job, filling in forms – and when I replied, in a very foul mood, 'Indeterminate,' she asked innocently, 'In the what?'

There are few times I come away from consultation anything other than deeply depressed or pathologically steaming. The only time I remember being actually elated was thanks to a Llanelli chiropodist with a Geordie accent, who asked me to bring in my shoes for his consideration.

'All of them?' I asked, the Imelda Markos of Llannon. We settled on me showing him a selection and I spent a happy half-hour selecting my favourite shoes.

I felt my entire shopping habits were justified when I sneaked a look at the letter he wrote referring me to a Sports Podiotrician, 'The lady has excellent shoes.' My husband has grown very tired of the quotation.

Our comedy double act at our new, French doctor's is therefore dogged with bad history, and we shuffle our feet and our brains as we inspect the African wall-hangings or flick through magazines.

The receptionist is a pussy-cat, there is only a five-minute wait

and we make a good start. We hand over the Gill/Pilborough dossier and I wonder what a French doctor will make of my 'very pleasant man'.

He manages to convey his disdain for the British system without actually being rude; he offers a 'more modern' prescription and he can arrange for a consultation with a specialist within three weeks, if desired.

Our notes are exactly that – *our* notes. We get them back to show to whichever medical consultant we choose and our health - or unhealth – is more within our own control than I have felt it to be for years.

I know that the French Health Minister resigned last year because so many older people died, in homes and hospitals, during the exceptional heat; I know that there are problems supporting the current system financially; but, as someone who grew up assuming that the British National Health system was the best in the world, and who has been let down by it, I feel that I and mine will be better cared for here, in Dieulefit.

12

PARSNIPS AND PARTISANS

Spring is dancing around winter, one day flaunting bluebells and primroses in the sunshine, then, the next, stilled by a snowfall. Early one morning at the end of February we see four black-tipped ears in the orchard as two hares play advanced kiss-chase. Apart from this one occasion, we never see more than one hare – do they take turns in teasing us? I look forward to March madness – but perhaps this needs another male? I read of an Australian woman boxed to the ground in her own garden by a kangaroo that bounded out of the neighbouring woods. I think I could take on a hare, even one in a very bad mood.

Vs of birds migrate north and the first summer visitors arrive to replace them, among them a black and white songbird that displays bright yellow when it spreads its wings and wagtails that don't walk like wagtails. For the first time ever my garden will display daffodils for St David's Day, the first few just frilling their petticoats along the garden path. Local lore tells me that, at the beginning of March, gangs of Montiliens (people from Montélimar) head into the countryside to pick wild daffodils. Monsieur Speedy and his kitchen-fitters skipping through the fields with bunches of daffodils? I think not.

It comes as a shock to hear from the kitchen designer – it is now

three weeks since his boys went off to lunch and their ladder is still resting against our wall. It seems that the designer has been very ill, in hospital, is now sorting out our 'little concerns'; we forgive him, agree on what's left to do, part friends – and another three weeks goes by.

Instead of the sunset window of our Welsh home, here we have the sunset wall, the same one which glows pink at dawn, turns evenings golden, shadows and silhouettes sharpened by the spring rain. We are still discovering our own home, which gives us presents daily, some more practical than others. We find five wooden troughs in an outbuilding and paint them into flower-planters. A wooden pole with a round end becomes a tool to tamp down mortar around the legs of the new pergola. I mix the mortar, stirring the giant gray cake mix until it turns into hippopotamus mud.

While we work we can hear the woodpecker drumming and the songbirds' 'carpe diem' insistence is echoed by one neighbour's rotavator, another's tractor. No-one forgets that summer is coming – or what last year's was like, not a cloud nor spot of rain for four months.

We plant our tomatoes with some hope that here they might just ripen and we consult our French gardening book for more adventurous seeds. We are informed not only of planting times and distances, but also which combinations are friendly and which unhelpful, and even which phase of the moon is ideal for each planting.

We have not yet taken on consideration of the moon but I am closer to understanding the tendency when I look out my bedroom window and see the Evening Star or the Dog Star, so bright I wonder if I have ever really seen them before.

There is indeed a new star in the sky, or rather a previously undiscovered planet now officially recognised. If a planet twinkles and no-one sees it, does it exist? Whatever the philosopher's answer, Sedna is now categorised by humans. I look out the window and say 'Sedna' but it sounds to me like office-workers spotting the tea-lady ('S'Edna') and I have forgotten what I once knew, that Sedna is an

Inuit spirit, an earth-goddess, and I feel guilty for my irreverence when someone reminds me. Language trips me up once again with its 'faux-amis', its sound-alike.

My French is improving but television programmes still leave me inventing half the plot and consequently confused by endings which convict the guy I thought was the hero. It's as if my hearing gives up completely at times, the worst being in 'Lord of the Rings' (luckily, as the subtitles revealed, they were speaking Elvish), with 'Shogun' a close second (no subtitles and no distinction between the dubbed French and the original snatches of Japanese).

It is getting harder to think of anything we need from Britain as we find what we need here or substitute the local product. Up to now, visitors have brought everything from videos of our favourite English TV detectives to pasta flour (interesting potential conversation at customs; 'So, you're saying that this white powder is in fact flour… and they don't have flour in France?')

As keen owners of a bread-making machine, we find it more difficult to get a range of specialist flours here than in Wales. My Pyrenean brother-in-law went one stage further and wrote to 'Good Housekeeping' before moving to France to ask where he could buy suitable flours here. He received a very sarcastic reply, on the lines of 'I think you'll find that the French do know how to make rather good bread …'

A few disastrous attempts to use various French flours taught me quickly that they are completely different, seem generally to give more volume for the same weight and anything other than the basic Type 55 sinks your loaf like lead, so British flours are still welcome presents. The oddest nostalgic craving we've suffered has been for parsnips.

We have scoured the markets and supermarkets, which display everything you could imagine from lychees to oak-leaf lettuce, but no parsnips. There was nothing for it but to start from scratch and John duly returned from a weekend in London with a packet of parsnip seeds (and eight gas canisters for my hair curler, also inexplicably non-existent here). Another interesting potential customs

conversation; 'You do realise Mr Pilborough that there are no parsnips in the whole of France because they carry the deadly francophobe virus which springs into life at the first 'oui'.'

I worry about the possibility that I am married to a smuggler of illegal vegetables and I look up 'parsnip' in my French gardening book – a full, reassuring double spread rewards me. It stands to reason that if it's in my Traité Rustica, then they grow it in France. But then why is the region that produces four-fifths of the nation's vegetables bare of parsnips?

It is when I am clearing an area of scrub and hardcore that the garden gives me its most unexpected present. The patch is a wilderness just outside our walled garden, but for all the old bricks and stones, the soil is rich and black, and last autumn a crop of courgettes suddenly ripened amidst the weeds, so this must have once, long ago, been cultivated.

I tug on yet another stone and it gives a bit in my hand. I recognise the greenery just sprouting on its white top and I carefully uproot the conical white root. This could be the only parsnip in the whole of Provence and I am truffle-proud. I tell John that it is a sign and I ignore his reply.

Thursday 11th March hits the whole country, the whole of Europe and further, as a sign of a different kind. No home can shut out the trains bombed in Madrid, the thousand injured, the official tally of one hundred and ninety dead – and how many of these because the emergency services could not cope?

My Pyrenean sister now lives near Basque country, where the sense of outrage runs high over anyone thinking for a minute – let alone the government proclaiming it 'probable' - that Eta carried out the attack. My sister tells me that there is a man who was in New York on September 11th, lost friends there and moved with his family to somewhere safer – Madrid.

I think of the old story where a man sees Death walking along his street. Death is surprised to see him but the man runs… and runs, right around the world, where, the very next day, Death comes for him, saying 'I couldn't believe it when I saw you yesterday because I

knew I was to meet you here, today.' To have escaped, when your friends have not, is hard. To do it twice?

It is the aftershock which shakes me. If the elections had been on the Wednesday, the government would have remained in power… it falls, and the swing in voting has some kind of moral I do not understand. However, I do understand that I might have to carry my suitcase on my lap when I take the train on my way to Paris, that the airport staff will not smile at me when my hairslide makes the metal bleeper go off, that when I travel I am a potential terrorist and will be treated as such. I understand the old lesson of the old story, that nowhere is safe…

but some places are safer than others. Since we moved here, Dieulefit has had what counts locally as a crimewave. It had its first murder for twelve years (no contest for Llanelli's tally), a dispute between neighbours in an apartment block. The excitement of having real news (and being able to drop the detailed account of each stall in Nyons market) sent the local paper into reporting frenzy. Everyone and his cat was interviewed and all agreed that the victim was 'sans histoire'. I can think of no worse epitaph than to be described as a woman 'with no story' and even now I know that 'histoire' was being used in the sense of 'a record', it is a phrase that haunts me. Everyone has a story, including a man who died in accidental violence and whose balcony could be recognised as the only one covered in flowers, his life brightened by all manner of hanging baskets and containers.

I didn't blame us for the murder but I did wonder about my part in the theft. When I visited a local pottery for the third time and tried once more to get someone's attention for service, it was only to eavesdrop on a phone call to the gendarmerie and a panicky reconstruction of how the takings could have disappeared. 'Anyone can look around the showroom,' the Manager told me, 'like you now'. I agreed, having spent the previous two visits wandering around, totally unable to get any service and unwilling to knock on the back door where I could see women hand-painting olives or lavender sprigs onto plates.

'It might have been that 'type' who hung around last week,' was the view of the 'décoratrice'. Neither she nor her boss seemed to consider me as a suspect – in fact they were perfectly happy to share their whole security arrangements with me and we were all saddened by the thought that they might have to lock away their takings box in future.

Despite this downward trend, the shocked reactions locally to petty theft indicate that we are once again living where you can forget to lock up and – usually – get away with it. Local graffiti still proclaims political idealism, 'Liberté pour José Bové' and 'le Pen – danger' rather than the usual town obscenities. A teacher-friend once said he knew he'd made it when he saw his own name up on the wall of the local toilet – perhaps le Pen feels the same.

The French media attitude to crime is familiar to us but the attitude to criminals, or rather to suspects, is completely different from the British. It's not so much a case of 'guilty until proven innocent' as hung, drawn and media quartered long before trial.

Full details of cases appear in the papers, with none of the 'no comments' from the gendarmerie – no, indeed. They provide helpful background information and make it clear who done it – in their opinion.

One such case which aroused strong feelings in the whole département was of an ex-Maquis (Resistance) leader whose garden shed was deliberately burnt down and, in it, three thousand copies of his books about the war days. On his garden fence was painted a black swastika and, as the story unfolded, the sense of community outrage was fully expressed in letters of support and sympathy from everyone, from the Prefect down to the-Monsieur-in-the-Rue.

Until the police tracked down the victim's ex-wife, and her current partner, at which stage the police, the Editor and we, the readers, clearly understood that this was a crime of petty spite. The only decision left for the courts is what sentence to give – everything else has been sorted (the good old 'triage' at work again).

I don't know if the fact that this crime of passion took place between a newly-divorced couple in their eighties is heartening or

depressing; I do know that my oldest friend is eighty-five, my youngest five, and that their passions run deeper and wilder than I would have believed when I was twenty.

If it *had* been a crime sparked by the Maquis past, it would not have been hard to imagine here, where the walkers' grand footpaths along mountain ridges follow the communications routes of the second world war, here between the high Alps and the mountains of the Vercors, where every peak is a natural fortress and where the clear springs were once poisoned weapons. The official version of local history does not duck the enthusiasm with which La Drôme welcomed the compromise with the Germans that enabled it, as part of Vichy France, to maintain the illusion of autonomy.

The girls in a local primary school sang 'Hommage au Maréchal', praising Petain as a hero who had preserved France and it is recorded that, on a fête day, the crowd was chanting 'English murderers', 'Long live Jeanne d'Arc' and 'The English are butchers'. There was no shortage of official support in la Drôme for 'the peace' but public face seems to have been one thing, private action another.

Dieulefit seems to offer its own political, as well as meteorological, microclimate; even during the Revolution, the only death recorded was that of one man who refused to shout 'Vive la République' and had his head cut off'. In lines with the Republic's edict against God, Dieulefit was re-christened Mont-Jabrou – and naturally regained its name when it was safe to do so.

What today is a source of great pride in la Drôme is Dieulefit's ancient reputation as a safe haven, continued in the Second World War by the many individuals who sheltered Jews, dissidents and war fugitives of all kinds.

There are hundreds of stories, especially of Jewish children hidden in the community; Marguerite Soubeyron and Catherine Krafft ('Mamie' and 'Athie') who hid Jewish children in their school in Dieulefit; Suzanne Vallette-Viallard, a Red Cross nurse who hid fugitives in her house - even taking wounded men off a train bound for Germany - then obtained false papers for them and smuggled

them to safety; the Mayor's Secretary in Dieulefit, who specialised in false papers (plus ça change…).

Then there was the Mexican nun, Soeur Thérèse d'Avila, who was trapped in Italy when war was declared and who hid in a convent to escape the internment inevitable for someone from an enemy country. She then headed for France via the mountain pass at Gap and ended up at a hospital in Buis les Baronnies, just south of us, where she became known as 'the Maquis Sister' for her work tending the wounded.

Even the Bishop who published each Vichy statement in the diocesan newsletter opened his doors to everyone persecuted by the Nazi regime. There was also the open defiance shown by the small gesture, raising the Tricolore on your haybarn for a fête day, and the grand, such as the stylish desertion of young lieutenant Narcisse Geyer, who asked his men, the eleventh cuirassiers, to follow him – and the regimental standard – into the mountains; they became the first knot of armed resistance in the département, founding the eleventh 'leatherjackets'.

Increasing in numbers, organisation and contact with London, the Maquis conducted raids and bombed … trains. Does it really only depend on who wins as to who were the good guys when you look back?

So which refugees came to Dieulefit in particular? You might have guessed … it was the intellectuals, especially the dissident writers, musicians and artists, fleeing German-occupied parts of France. The Gestapo labelled Dieulefit 'that nest of Jews and terrorists' and the village put on more concerts and conferences than ever before, thanks to its new stock of glittering names. The composer Barlowe, a refugee himself, said, 'You get more events here than in the big towns.'

The current newsletter to us Dieulefitois residents reinforces the village's self-image; our Mayor tells us that we are a diverse lot and that we must make everyone welcome. There is an apology for the briefness of a report because our local councillors have been 'talking

about rubbish' – more plans for recycling. We are not doing well in the local league of villages and we must do better.

Since we moved here, John and I, the very epitome of cultural diversity, have personally increased Dieulefit's recycling by one thousand per cent (rough estimate based on volume of Gill/Pilborough recycled waste compared with size and weekly fullness of village recycling bins). Like good immigrants, we are perfect citizens, contributing in every way to our community.

I am smug, preparing the roast pork, roast potatoes and ceremonial roast parsnip. I sniff it and the first doubt creeps in; it does not smell anything like a parsnip. It looks like a parsnip, it cooks like a parsnip – I am prepared for disappointment and I am prepared for it to be an oddly shaped turnip.

What I am not prepared for is a mouthful of wormwood-bitter juices, with a worse aftertaste. John leaves his on the plate, as instructed. He thinks that, as it looks so like a cooked parsnip, perhaps it's just an eighteen-year-old reverted-to-the-wild parsnip. It is not, it is a poisonous root of the kind medieval monks used to murder each other with, and I am going to die, horribly poisoned. What sort of sign is this?

13

SLEEPING ROUGH AT CARDIFF AIRPORT

I could be the only person to have ever dossed down overnight at Cardiff Airport. I should have known when the taxi-driver said, 'Ah' in a very ominous way, that reaching the airport at 10pm to check in at 5am was not a good idea but what's the point of buying bucket-cheap flights if you blow the difference on three hours sleep in a hotel? And if you've lain on the floorboards of the overnight ferry from Crete to Piraeus, then surely Cardiff Airport is luxurious? Even if you were twenty-three then and now you're not.

Perhaps it was the invitation to actually stay in student accommodation on my First Visit Back that sparked a sense of adventure. More likely it was the same sort of thoughtlessness which has led me to hospital A & Es now and again. Thank God student son gave me The Bed, although, as I couldn't help getting up early, we came up with a neat arrangement where I went out to explore early morning Bristol and he finished his sleep in The Bed.

When you have moved 'abroad' you are always being asked what you miss – according to a recent poll the top three items on the miss list for Brits if they were to do something so foolish would be 1) roast dinners 2) a curry out 3) fish and chips. Do these people not cook? And what would they be glad to leave behind? Reality TV shows. Believe me, there is no escape from reality television, nor

from les idols pop. I put the big question to Bristol – what can you offer me that I can't get at home in France? It's not the shops – I lose interest quickly; it's not the newspapers – I feel I've had more European and international news from the French media; and it's certainly not my understanding of the language around me (I find Bristolian harder to pick up than provençale French). No, what I treasure are certain moments ...

Unable to find anything resembling breakfast, I leave the students sleeping and hit the streets. At the bottom of Park Street I find a café which spills out onto the pavement and tempts me with bacon sandwiches. Be-suited customers fend off human contact with laptops or a café newspaper, cramming into understair seats or the dark oak corner pews of a traditional English tea-room. This is what we do before work, we city-Brits, and however wicker the chairs outside, this will never be the pavement café outside Dieulefit's le Pub and I love the difference – almost as much as the bacon sandwich, freshly made, layers of meaty morning in granary bread, with a caffeine wake-up.

It's as if we have to pretend that this is practical, our working routine, and hide the sheer sensuous pleasure of this little haven. Not one face shows that the bread is warm, crumbly-fresh nor that every order takes the time of making it and is brought to your table with a smile, and yet these customers come back for more. I know because I am there, solitary and contented, every morning. Does anyone ever tell the cook how wonderful her bacon sandwich is? I do, sounding like a patronising git or a rich American, but I see she is pleased all the same. It is part of my mission in life, to tell someone when something is good, but I suspect it is a vaguely embarrassing trait in Britain. Oh well, since when has that stopped me?

I phone home, confident that nothing much can happen in three days, my first three days away from home in seven months. I am wrong. The first call is entertaining; I have missed the arrival on a truck of a fully constructed staircase, which inevitably stuck in the doorway. After the removal of the shutters and the door, the stairway progressed to approximately the position in which it would

be useful – in fact, indispensable – and was then abandoned, not quite finished. John's French was not quite good enough to know whether the joiner had given a detailed explanation of why and what next but we suspect not.

The second phone call is not entertaining. Apparently there was a visit from five bosses in charge of the ongoing roadworks and we are stuffed. I was expecting this; I knew from the start that someone would build a motorway through our house but I thought they would wait until all the renovation was finished before giving us the bad news. But no, it isn't a motorway.

It is the news that our brand new kitchen sink and brand new washing machine are emptying illegally onto the main road, not into the septic tank at all. Some pretty green dyes were used to demonstrate to John exactly where in the ditch our washing-up water was contributing negatively to the environment.

We need to get the waste round the entire house into the septic tank, probably requiring a pump and the destruction of the entire garden. And we need to add a filtration tank to the septic tank and that will have to be built on Monsieur Dubois' land as there isn't room on ours. It sounds bad but it is always possible that it is 'merde' and 'putain' and solvable rather than us being totally stuffed. We won't know until we've spoken to the plumber. And anything is better than a motorway. And anyway I can't do anything about it in Bristol.

Son and I visit the cathedral, scuffing our brains a bit at having seen better, but then we read between the stones. It is the women who surprise me, so many of them (great and good) named in their own right, from traders to translators, as well as the wives and daughters. Reminders of Bristol's trading, slaving past are everywhere; Jamaica and Barbados are a commonplace of birth and death. One effigy takes my fancy, a knight who will not lie down but must be up and doing, as if he's saying, 'So I'm dead, so what's next?'

Then my culture hunger is fed with a portrait exhibition that challenges us to compare Andy Warhol's Marilyn Monroe with a Rembrandt. We know when we should be impressed but we are not.

It is instead an old-fashioned portrait of three sisters that makes me smile; the artist has captured so well how they are like and not-alike.

Best of all is the beer but I know this vicariously these days. I watch and smell the drinking of beer while assaulted by the aural tricks of the whispering gallery in a Bristol Weatherspoon's, which suddenly plays a conversation in your ear – no sooner have you attached the speech to the beautiful Chinese girl sitting in a circle of twelve than she laughs, leans forward and fades. 'Can they hear me?' I ask, too loud and, for once, am silenced by paranoia.

As we juggle goodbyes with a suitcase at a Bristol bus-stop, I know exactly what I miss the most and it has nothing to do with place.

My return from Bristol to Rhws, involves a bus, a train and a taxi, as the out-of-town setting of Cardiff Airport is not easily accessible at night. Perhaps there is a good reason for this. I like Cardiff Airport – like Goldilocks in the three bears' house, I judge that it is just the right size. You can't get the terminal wrong. You can find your car in the car park – you can even walk from the terminal to the car park.

The Cardiff sniffer dog is a cute golden retriever that reminds you of your grand-puppy in New Zealand. There are bilingual signs and, when I arrived here, just reading the Welsh made me feel queasy at not having a car in the car park, at not having a house in the Gwendraeth Valley and at getting on a bus going the wrong way, to Cardiff Station.

I felt better when two old men talked at each other all the way, capping the bombs in Swansea during the war with the closure of the mines, to the evident amusement of a Dutch lady, fresh from my plane and probably ticking her 'real Welsh' list with each topic.

I was waiting for them to harmonise on 'Bread of Heaven' but that seemed to be all they missed out. The 'excellent transport links from the airport' consist of one bus which picks up market-shoppers all the way through the rural Vale of Glamorgan before trundling into the central station forty minutes later. You can travel the twenty miles from Charles de Gaulle Airport to central Paris more quickly.

On the other hand, you could also spend your entire life lost on

free shuttle buses going around the airport complex at Charles de Gaulle; or die of a heart attack lugging your suitcase towards exit signs that turn out to be barricaded off and as you're on the third floor anyway what you need is a lift; or be so bemused by the shopping arcades that you think you'll go just a bit further before you buy some water and it's too late – you've gone through the gate and there are no shops left. Rhws Airport tells it to you straight; 'No food after this' says the sign on the closed café.

'Who won the football?' I pass the time with the taxi-driver en route.

'Wales,' is the reply, in a middle eastern accent, and I smile at the back of the driver's neck. Only this side of the border would that be the answer, the right answer on two counts.

'Good. Do you know how England did?' I ask.

'Drew I think,' is the dismissive response. I carry this little bit of Welshness with me into the deserted airport. I find that there is a good reason for there being no public transport to the airport at night; it is because the airport closes down.

The doors might stay open but the only people there between 11pm and 4am are security guards who walk around, shining torches into dark corners, and, on this one occasion, there is also a middle-aged woman curled up on two seats in one such dark corner with a red woolen scarf for a pillow. The security guards pretend she is invisible and she pretends it is the most normal thing in the world to try and get a few hours sleep, alone amongst chairs upturned on tables.

I find it very difficult to choose somewhere to sleep, spoilt for choice amongst the entire departure lounge, bar and café seating – at least those not turned upside down on top of tables or each other. I expected to be with other adventurous overnighters curled up on their rucksacks and I have planned to loop one bag through my suitcase and to hide my handbag under my red scarf just in case there is an attempt at theft while I am asleep.

I take these precautions but I have to say that I think they are a bit unnecessary. My first choice of bed is a very comfortable double

padded bench in a well-lit area; somehow I feel safer there. It is well-lit because the only facilities available all night in Cardiff Airport are the slot machines, which play snippets of inane pop lyrics at random but frequent intervals. After ten bursts of 'At the car wash' in as many minutes I would confess, if asked, to having murdered the Queen, and I move to a dark corner of the bar. The hell with theft, mugging or rape – I can now only hear the canned music, which allows me to drift in and out of sleep for whole minutes at a time.

I survive Rhws and Charles de Gaulle, and sleep on the train to Valence, despite a free-for-all over luggage storage. Because of the latest terrorist threats, the baggage compartments are all closed and as we all got on at an airport, the competition for putting large cases into small overhead racks is fierce and muscle-wrenching. I don't play. I wait till the war is over then politely ask someone opposite if I can put my case in the empty seat beside her. This is not popular but, with the proviso that I will move it if someone gets on at the next stop, it is accepted.

The train is a French T.G.V., Train à Grande Vitesse, fast and efficient with few stops, and I get my sleep, sharing a few words with an amazingly polite young Frenchman, who even asks me if I mind if he eats his sandwiches. He lives in Paris and is spending a few months in Valence apprenticed to a journal, to learn the trade.

The French seem to have a very well-organised system of 'stages', vocational placements which provide in-depth experience of the chosen job. My companion was given advice about living out in the wilds and he shows me the outdoor clothing he has brought – padded anorak, wooly hat, gloves…

The atmosphere has certainly turned chilly at home. John is stressed out and I must do something straight away about the illegal sink, the illegal septic tank, the unfinished staircase… I explain that Cardiff Airport is really not a good place to sleep and at 2pm I am unconscious as soon as my head touches the pillow.

Within a day after my anguished (but restrained) phone calls, the plumbers arrive (it is serious enough to need two plumbers' brains) and find 'une solution' (our favourite word) which only means

moving the oil tank temporarily, drilling through the concrete under the base of the new staircase and completing the hole for the waste pipe by drilling through from the oilshed. No problem.

The septic tank? That can wait. The plumbers go and an hour later a joiner arrives and announces 'I've come to finish your staircase' and he does, working until nearly nine o'clock on a Friday night and smiling when he finishes. We smile too, having delayed our evening meal until the joiner goes, and we are starving. We eat, we don't think about drilling through concrete and we start to relax.

John has recorded my favourite TV detectives while I was away and tells me there is one I must watch. Wary, I am presented with the detective, the 'flic', trying to win attention from his wife by swotting up on … Gerard de Nerval. He quotes That Poem and I see one of our moments broadcast to the whole world on popular French television.

'No,' I say, wondering if I've written a French detective episode and it's escaped from the manuscripts moldering in my desk drawers, or whether there is some kind of French Jean Gill live-alike.

'Never did trust their relationship,' says my husband.

Kiwi-fille empathises by phone about Bristol and sympathises about drainage.

'We have mushrooms in the cellar', I tell her.

'No', she says, appalled. I put her right. We finally found mushroom spawn, after searching the Internet (which offered many interesting but unwanted hallucinogenics) and even pleading with visitors from the UK to find some for us. It was only a matter of waiting for the correct season and then our local garden centre offered a full range from champignons de Paris (button) to shiitake. As a major attraction of the house in the first place was that the wine cellar offered the ideal environment to grow mushrooms, we would have felt cheated if we hadn't found this precious box of mould. Into the cellar it goes, to be sprayed with water daily (but not soaked) and we have three weeks to wait for the 'white filaments'.

I am delegated to tend the mushrooms as we have had too many gardening disappointments recently for John to want another one. I

was impatient to get tomatoes growing, moved them outside too quickly and they now look like cooked spinach. I am now in charge of planting more tomatoes. We found what we thought was a cold frame (and now know was used to make honey), put carefully nourished seedlings outside under its glass top, forgot to remove the top on a sunny day and fried the contents. I am now in charge of planting more basil too.

On the other hand, I have taken one critical comment too many on my accuracy (lack of) with paint. I have no idea how green gloss paint appeared a foot above the shutters I was painting, on the bathroom sink and nail brush, and on my stomach. And yes, I was being very very careful. I hate gloss paint and John is now in charge of painting the rest of the shutters.

14

TOULOUSE RUGBYMEN BEAT THE SCARLETS

'No, we don't get the rugby.' The barman at le Pub shrugs and returns to his other customers. This is a disaster; we had planned to watch the Quarter Final of the Heineken Cup on le Pub's television, complete with French atmosphere. All of this by special request of my rugby-fan friend who still cannot believe she is in Dieulefit to see me while the Scarlets are playing Toulouse at Llanelli's home ground, Stradey Park.

Her mobile phone is hot as she texts the ground to 'check everyone has got there all right'. Whether she means her mother or the team is unclear but her need to be there sends static around the sitting-room where we are trying to create a suitable atmosphere – or at least not to add to the tension.

'It doesn't feel right without singing.' is the next complaint as she stands up and sits down yet again. I offer a rendition of 'Penblwydd hapus y ti' (Happy Birthday to you) as it is the only Welsh song I know all the way through, but this is rejected with one glare.

When I was a Headteacher, I learned the whole of 'Mae'n hen flad' for those occasions when I was facing a hall-full for concerts, prize-givings or even St David's Day, but I am back to singing the first two lines, a few mutters, and then an enthusiastic 'Gwlad, gwlad'

(because we're all glad to be Welsh and singing what is, viewed objectively, the best national anthem of them all).

I nearly offer the unofficial Welsh anthem but I know that neither John nor my other visiting friend will join in a rollicking version of 'Delilah' and I get the feeling I'm making myself unpopular with Scarlet friend.

If you have ever been in a Welsh pub when someone has started off 'Delilah' you will appreciate how contagious it is but why a song about adultery and murder should be so close to Welsh hearts is a mystery. The Welsh Assembly Member for Llanelli even attempted to have the song banned as 'inappropriate' which embedded it even further in the local psyche. If only I knew the whole of 'Sospan Fach', the 'little saucepan' song which is Llanelli's own, I might redeem myself.

I was better off in the hotel restaurant at Charles de Gaulle; when 'Belle', a popular love song, came on the loudspeakers, I was one of those singing along. Waiters, customers queuing to pay their bills and busy travellers were all mouthing romantic snippets as they went about their business – all those who spoke French, that is.

I sit very quiet in the rugby lounge, the only one who doesn't know the rules; John was once a player and horse-whispering friend has rugby in the bone although she no longer goes to matches. She whispers in my non-equine ear what is about to happen and it does. At half time, mobile-to-mobile enables Scarlet friend to hear the atmosphere and share the angst. Things are not going well. I am dislocated by the mobile. Among the sounds of Stradey will be my son, shouting himself hoarse, so far away, so close.

The Scarlets attack, the room explodes, we can't see the screen as Scarlet friend tries to enter the TV and run for the line and John's foot twitches as he joins in but our efforts are not rewarded. The defence holds – they are all built like tanks – and Llanelli fights its way to a loss. I am ashamed. I am a bad host and I have allowed my friends' team to lose while they are guests in my house. If I were Japanese I would unsheathe the sabre and die honourably but I'm not, so I get some more wine. I have been cheerfully

drinking and nibbling throughout but Scarlet friend has not risked distraction.

I am no stranger to supporting – or losing – but football (the kind with the round ball) is my sport of choice. France is close to heaven for an Arsenal supporter (by marriage, fickle woman that I am). The commentators support the team with unashamed bias and they can even pronounce most of the team's names correctly, apart from the English ones). The days of hearing from Manager 'Arson' Wenger or 'Robert' Pires are long gone and I am amazed to hear how articulate and fluent are Arsène and Rrrrobair in interview – in French.

Of course I knew that English was their second language but I never really took in how much someone's personality is disguised by his level in a second language, even when this is competent. In my own second language, I can now give a passable match commentary, including frequent emotional outbursts, much laughter and occasional comments on the oddity of British behaviour.

One match was played in Portsmouth in the pouring rain and much of the commentary was along the lines of 'Typically English weather…look at those supporters – they don't even have hats on! But what can you expect – they are English'.

Neither have we left Beckham behind, or rather Bay-kam. Real Madrid often appears on the screen and Beckham is as much a focus for commentary as Zidane. Off-pitch Beckham stories are a wonderful opportunity for the French press to both report the story and mock the British press – always an open goal.

Our local paper gleefully reported that 'that typical British paper' *the News of the World* was reporting the supposed French view of Beckham's alleged infidelity as being an 'admirable' quality. In one swoop, *le Dauphiné* managed to titillate us with some Beckham gossip and give us French a wonderful feeling of superiority over these British with their stupid stereotypes.

Perhaps Dieulefit's lack of top class rugby is not such a bad thing, given Llanelli's result. It is certainly good to be a very long way from Biarritz and all wounds heal in time … with some retail therapy involving soap, flavoured oils and nougat. We are starting to estab-

lish our own tourist route, which includes one of Montélimar's many nougat producers.

I know that Montélimar is The Place for nougat, and that top quality nougat has to meet standards for the ratio of pistachios to honey, but as far as I'm concerned the crucial word is 'tendre'. Nougat which is not 'tendre' should be used for road repairs and certainly leads to dental ones. In contrast, 'tendre' melts in the mouth, evokes Montélimar's Moorish past and makes a moreish present.

In the seventies, when the main holiday route, the N7, ran through the centre of Montélimar and blocked solid for hours on end, the nougatiers would run out to the cars, take the orders, and deliver the nougat to the frustrated families whose cars had moved fifty metres – if they were lucky. When the autoroute was built, Montélimar became somewhere you whizz past on your way south and there was a trade crisis. Advertising campaigns, and marketing ploys such as tourist promotion exhibitions in Amsterdam, have brought back the visitors and Montélimar makes the most of its proximity to the Ardèche.

More than that, despite its Drômoise status, Montélimar only seems to acknowledges the Ardèche as a neighbour and there is not a trace of Drôme provençale publicity in the Tourist Information Office. The intellectual, pottery and good air centre of Dieulefit might as well not exist for all you can find out about it in Montélimar. I scent bad blood and my instincts are confirmed by the Dieulefit column of le Dauphiné.

Montélimar is holding a pottery fête and the Dieulefitois committee members have demanded of our Mayor how the usurper has got away with this travesty. Our Mayor is embarrassed and wriggles but admits that there was no consultation and that none of the potters invited are from Dieulefit. Double horror.

To add insult to injury, our wise Committee decided to preserve the quality of our Pottery Fête, and public interest in it, and so we are only having a biennial celebration. Montélimar's Pottery Fête just down the road in the year Dieulefit has none, is a 'bitter pill to swal-

low' and it is clear from the article that all good Dieulefitois will boycott this declaration of war. We dutifully avoid Montélimar for two days, wondering if perhaps next year will see the Dieulefit Nougat Festival?

The orchard turns impressionist painting and for the first time we truly experience a 'carpet' of flowers. Instead of a parasol and a small child, it is with a large dog that I float between the trees, wearing combats rather than a crinoline. First the grass shimmers blue with wild grape hyacinths, then a week later the yellows of celandines, dandelions and delicate frothy unknowns take over, to mix another week later with white stars. Strange stalks sprout and, on the principle that if there's only one, it must be an orchid, I identify orchids with equal certainty and error. I finally hit gold, or rather pink, when the brown speckled balls at intervals amongst open-mouthed sprays convince me that I have found a bee orchid.

The real things are buzzing around first the white pear blossom and pink peach, then the white apple. The wisteria, which I now know for sure to be over a hundred years old, is a canopy of scented purple cones and you stand underneath it at your peril, auditioning for 'Attack of the Killer Bees'. The zooming shadows make you itch and swat instinctively but if you look up, you freeze; the biggest blackest buzziest bees you have ever seen are harvesting the wisteria. You don't need to be warned that they are dangerous; 'Bees and wasps – they sting you and - ' shrug - 'that's all . These ...' we look up at 633 Squadron overhead, 'these are dangerous.' I look up the French word I have been given for 'these' – it translates as 'bumble bees'. Let me tell you now, there is absolutely nothing in common between cute yellow-and-black fuzzy fatball insects that star in children's picture books, and these monsters.

I am proud of all the careful pruning I did over the winter and when Monsieur Dubois comes to tend his orchard, I show him my handiwork. He brings over his secateurs and lopper, and reduces my vines to firewood.

When he is happy that I have understood what needs to be done, he repeats this process with the kiwi fruit. We patrol the garden and

I get full pruning instructions but I have missed the time for the roses, which should have been laid low in autumn and pruned again in February. I did prune them, I start to explain but I know the answer – I have to cut more off, hack them to bits in fact.

We inspect the olive tree and I am told that I can only cut it back when the moon is young. This I do not understand; my very scientific, very practical French gardening book is also full of instructions as to which phases of the moon are appropriate for which gardening operations and it all strikes me as superstitious gobbledygook.

I remember a neighbour in Bancffosfelen, a science teacher, finally succumbing to folklore as he waged war against moles in his garden, so that he laid his beer traps according to the tides. Did it work? As far as I remember it was no less effective than his other 'solutions' – and no more; the moles moved on before he found the final solution.

It is nerve-wracking, like going on interview, to show someone around his own family home, currently being destroyed by the electricians, the plumber et al but it is also fascinating to accumulate the stories, of the house – still known locally as 'maison Dubois' - of its people and of the village.

My tales of French bureaucracy are nothing. I hear of planning permission rejected for a villa in the orchard – but granted for a retirement home 'down in the river' where the old people have to sit 'with their feet actually in the water'; after accepting for twenty-five years the annual payment for two plots with planning permission, when actual building rights were requested, the mairie turned the request down because there the area was 'thirty square metres of land short of what was necessary'.

On another occasion, Monsieur Dubois found that, since his last visit, a water reservoir had appeared – on his land. No notice, never mind consultation. And as for us telling him that our council visitation had suggested that we find a safer exit from our property than our driveway onto the main road; he had applied to access his own property, at his own expense, from an existing lane – refused.

Our neighbour had asked to move his private drive further onto

his own property so his exit view would not be obscured by a house – refused. Safety? They don't know the meaning of the word, they certainly don't know what they want and as long as they make more paperwork they're happy. 'Usually, we can arrange things between ourselves'.

Not that it is any better in the Alps, Monsieur Dubois' main home nowadays, where his attempt to set up a petrol station led to a Paris tribunal. I learn that service stations in the mountains have to be equipped to fuel rescue planes and helicopters, with the special fuel and safety regulations this necessitates. A neighbour's appeal against the planned business led to requests for more and more detail, engineers' reports and feasibility studies; 'You are asked for twelve things and you always have eleven of them'.

We must have done something right as Monsieur Dubois brings his wife to meet us. She peoples the house with the loved ghosts of her in-laws, who saw no need for central heating until in their eighties – and even then were found at Christmas by their son 'not cold enough' to switch the heating on; a couple who made wine and verveine liqueur in the days when there were indeed truffles to be found under the oaks; who produced honey from the beehives still up in the woods behind our house; who kept a donkey in the workshop, and a goat in the cellar; who remembered stories of the days when silkworms lived in our mulberry trees; and whose melons were the sweetest ever tasted (unlike their wine, which according to their grandson, was undrinkable).

I already know about the two dogs buried in my garden, one a much-loved fourteen-year-old, going blind and deaf, who strayed onto the main road, probably tracking a badger scent. It's not a bad way to go, a dream of the chase and then – oblivion. I am comfortable with ghosts and graves – it wouldn't be a home without them - and I feel they are comfortable with me.

I think about badgers, never having managed to catch sight of one living, but often told of where they'd been. In Crwbin there was supposed to be 'the nine o'clock badger' crossing the road punctually each night, but I never saw him. Then there was the pub tale of one

local man's kind-heartedness; he'd run over a badger on a back lane so he tried to reverse over it to make sure he'd killed it. When he looked in his rear-view mirror, the badger had gone. 'Bloody tough, badgers,' was the moral of this tale. One of our walk leaflets tells me that the nature-lover will see 'evidence' of badgers, among that of other wildlife, and I regret my missing education once more. What does badger shit look like? And what's the posh name for it?

Over a coffee I do not ask Monsieur Dubois about badger shit but I do tell him that John would like a chopping block and he charges off across the road to where the council workers have entertained us by setting up a contra-flow, parking a digger and attempting to reach kiwi-fille via drainage channels.

It does at least mean we still see workmen, even while those who should be in our house – yes, they have succumbed to their Peter-Mayle image – are missing, presumed working away. The council workmen seem cheerful enough when asked to donate a tree trunk to our deprived household from the debris they have stacked across the road.

'Does your husband have a chainsaw' causes a moment's embarrassment. We all know that my answer means that he is not a Real Man.

The moment passes and Monsieur Dubois says he will bring his round. All goes to plan. A tree trunk appears outside our shed, followed the next day by an efficient Monsieur Dubois with chainsaw. The chopping block is cut to exactly the right size (no protective clothing anywhere in sight, not even goggles, and I tell myself that Real Men here regularly shoot their friends in the woods while out hunting) but all goes well until John casually puts the smaller block onto the bigger block – and traps his finger. He exits for a plaster and Monsieur Dubois produces his laptop computer for the help we offered in using the new toy.

Two hours later I am very pleased with our step forward in social integration. John has given Excel tuition, I have set myself up as the Word expert and we have learned more about cycling. As enthusiasts

of the Tour de France, I include in my limited social chat the fact that it is coming this way in July.

I am telling this to someone who has, on several occasions, been part of the 'cadre', the police escort for *le Dauphiné* Tour, which he considers to be better than The more famous Tour; less money equals more sport. It is apparently very difficult accompanying a tour as a motorbike cop because you have to go faster than whizzing cycles to stay ahead downhill without heading off a cliff on the bends, and you have to go slower than wobbly-moto-slow uphill, just ahead of the cyclists. I believe him. I am confused by the Alpine connection and John is quicker than I am to realise that *le Dauphiné* is the newspaper sponsor, not the region, and that *le Dauphiné* tour is a huge event.

After Monsieur Dubois has left, I am still congratulating myself on us being such pleasant well-integrated Dieulefitois when I remember John's poorly finger. I take him to the first aid cupboard and only then do I see that it is horribly mashed, cut, bruised and he is certainly going to lose the nail. I realise what a Real Man is; it is someone who spends two hours trying hard to understand and speak French and to solve computer problems with a beginner, while he is thinking 'Ow, ow, ow' or words to that effect.

15

OVER-SEXED FOREIGN BEES

The first cuckoo of spring has an 'aaaaw' effect; twenty 'cuckoos' later and it has all the charm of the Carwash song on a Cardiff airport slot-machine. Perhaps I'm a little edgy from having faced the xxxxxs on the calendar which tell me that vast quantities of family will arrive in three weeks - and it is as many months since we last saw the electricians.

Patience is not one of my virtues. In one job interview a perceptive governor asked me, 'Would you say you were a patient person?' and I snapped back 'Yes', mentally adding, 'Or I wouldn't be answering questions from a stupid old git like you.' He read my eyes - I didn't get the job. I consider the words 'Wait and see' to be a form of mental torture so, all in all, I am close to sainthood in response to French workmen. Half the house is without electricity so we're worse off than when we moved in; agreed, it was lethally dangerous, but I've reached the stage where I'd rather risk death by switching on dodgy lights than by tripping over a cat in the dark. Was there really a time when the workmen turned up at all, never mind on the due day?

Monsieur Dubois recommends locking their tools in the cellar at the end of each day they are working here but first I have to get them back at all. I make phone calls, expanding my dramatic range from

long-suffering, to pathetically inadequate and tearful, to 'explosive' (this apparently works for Monsieur Dubois).

'This is not a second home!' is my favourite phrase. I quite like 'explosive' – this could be my new, French personality, and thanks to the workmen, I do have some of the necessary vocabulary.

Not all the new birds are as irritating as the cuckoo. A field nearby sprouts long-legged egrets, dozens of them, stalking the green rows like old-fashioned teachers on corridor patrol. Perhaps, like our recent visitors, they left Llanelli's wetlands for a break in the sun. We don't see a single egret anywhere else, despite a false alarm over a row of plastic-bag-scarecrows, glinting white in the sunshine, and we wonder if we dreamt them, a mirage of waterless herons.

We pass that way again and yes, the egret field is real, so we add it to our mental map, along with the precise spot on the main road where we are likely to see a hobby hovering overhead, unmistakably hawk despite its swallow-shape.

We also add the curve of the narrow footpath along the gorge where one Sunday morning we met a solitary rider, dancing his white Arab past us, smiling 'Bonne journée' at us beneath his gaucho hat, and strolling on, in and out of the shadows above the ravine. We know where to stop on the road to Eyzahut, and look up at the wind-eroded cliffs to see the 'Trou de Furet', a hole full of sky, and we know where, a few steps later, the rock's eye winks shut and there is no sign of the 'Trou'.

Landmarks of our short history here blend with landmarks of long history, like the ancient Knights' village of Poët-Laval, which catches the sun impossibly even when you would swear there is not one ray. John's scientific explanation is that a past Master of the Order of St John sold his soul to the devil for eternal sunshine.

This is as rational a hypothesis as we manage and we do see a few who would sell their souls to the devil for some sunshine – or at least sell their children to the campsite 'animateurs', or funleaders - as the tourists start to arrive in their campervans and are frustrated by the unseasonal grayness. Our hairdresser is philosophical; bad weather means more customers.

There are now dozens of bee orchids and I am disappointed with modern British sex education which tells you how to roll a condom onto a plastic penis, and nothing whatsoever about the birds, bees and flowers. This means that I don't know if what I read is true, and whether Mediterranean bees will try to mate with bee orchids whereas British bees will not. You can imagine it, can't you, the British bee bumbling along, zinging to itself as it checks out a sexy fake-bee-on-a-flower; 'Sex toy huh? We Brits don't do that sort of thing' and onward it? he? she? flies. Whereas your Mediterranean bee now, high on sun and flowers, enjoys what's on offer and doesn't look too closely. Do you have a better theory?

Despite frequent dog-walks among the bee orchids, we don't see one amorous Mediterranean bee; instead we see approximately twenty thousand in their annual reproductive ritual. I scramble down from the woods, attached to a Pyrenean, and spot a shimmering black cloud hanging from a branch a dozen yards away.

It is shaped like a rugby ball but bigger, about two feet, and it is not far from the old beehives. I know that at least two of these are active and I suddenly register what I am seeing. It is strange how you can suddenly perceive more detail once you have identified what it is that you are looking at and I now see individual bees around the edges of the dense community ball. Dogs in tow, we take no risks, but head off in the opposite direction. It is only later that I want to go back to investigate.

Although I explain to him that bees are at their most docile in a swarm, gorged on honey and contented in the company of their old queen, John disappoints me by refusing to dress up in the antique beekeeping outfit (still in the garage).

I was hoping to get one of those photos, 'Man with bee-beard' but I suspect I would have been lucky to snap 'Man running away very fast.' By the time we go back without dogs and with camera, the swarm has moved on, so presumably the scouts returned and gave the all clear to move into the new home. In the old hive, the newborn virgin queens are fighting to the death until the sole survivor can get on with the job – breeding.

It is of course That Time Of Year and there are new inhabitants in the old nest in our porch. Our back entrance has an old stone porch like a mini-version of the gateway to Cawdor Castle, even down to the wooden shutter-window through which Macbeth's porter could inspect visitors, and it is in an ancient niche near the roof that we see a flicker of movement.

The birds are brownish-black, finch-shaped with orange-red beneath their tails, and they chirrup with irritation when they return from foraging to find that we are feeding our pets between the birds and their nest. One will hover in the doorway, using tail feathers as a fan to stall its flight, then retreat to the wisteria until feeding time is over. There is no sign of the goldfinches, called 'chardonneray' because they eat the 'chardons', thistles, a species that includes the 'cardons', those winter vegetables that puzzled us so much.

In place of the goldfinches, the swifts and house martins are moving in. Everywhere there are birds carrying twigs and even the ladybirds seem to turn up in pairs, so it is not a huge surprise when we hear that another grandchild is on the way. We just hope that we can make our nest a little less of a death-trap before the children come.

After a gray, wet Welsh-style spring, we suddenly find the garden drying out and the hose system is tested. John cannot understand why all his neatly laid new hosepipes, with regular holes to water 'goutte à goutte', drop by drop, are not watering at all. He picks an ant out of one hole. Then another... then another... ah. The ants are using the pierced hosepipes as undercover highways and blocking every single drip outlet. As John contemplates his blocked system, he sees more ants carefully collecting the grass seed I sprinkled yesterday. They amass it into a pile, leaving not one seed on the area I was trying to patch.

Two mushrooms have grown so far and, although I spray water daily on the spawn, and I know the wine cellar offers the perfect environment, there are only a few white threads visible. Undaunted, I try shiitake mushrooms, carefully germinating the granules in a wardrobe, then choosing an airy, shady place to grow my sheets of

mouldy cardboard into gourmet produce. Unfortunately, John chooses the same place to dump the pasta maker and several bottles of tonic – on top of the shiitakes-to-be. How was he supposed to know that wasn't rubbish?

Lessons in patience are everywhere, for both of us. I green-gloss-paint some more shutters. I know what I said but I'm only going to paint the ones overhanging the septic tank so how much care does that need? More, apparently. John summons me and he opens the bathroom window to show me a screwdriver glossed to the shutter, swinging out with it. I wondered where that had got to.

The good news is that the plumber has re-routed the sink so that it no longer empties onto the main road but into the septic tank. The bad news is that no-one can work out where the toilet empties.

The very bad news is that the septic tank is cracked and needs replacing, soon. We deal with one disaster at a time while the electricians work happily (it's not their 'putain' nor, more literally, 'merde'). We phone Monsieur Dubois, who knows exactly where the toilet drains and who calls round to show the plumber – and us.

Do you remember that the green dye sent down the toilet didn't come out on the road, so we thought we were OK? Then the plumber found out that it didn't come out into the septic tank, so we weren't OK. Well guess what. The toilet emptied all its green dye into its very own centuries-old septic tank underneath the workshop floor – and if that tank fills up, then an equally old pipe carries the gunge under the house and out onto - you guessed – the main road, a bit further along than the sink pipe.

Three plumbers get excited as they lift the old hatch in the workshop. One calls me to come and have a look, knowing I will appreciate the finer aspects of workmanship. 'Beautifully constructed' the plumbers agree, as two of them are upside-down, shining torches into the green waters of our newly-discovered septic tank. One hundred? two hundred? years old, big and clean, solid stone – and no use to us whatsoever.

So, if I've got this right, we need a new septic tank, plus a filtration tank, all meeting the new national regulations, and then we need

the toilet re-plumbed to empty into the new septic tank. John has glazed over; the plumber is already organising the hole through the wall from the toilet to the outside world and a quote from a septic-tank-installer. Our builder calls round to see if we can find a solution that does not require using our neighbour's land, and walks the problems through with me. We stand by the condemned septic tank; the builder, a man of few words, pronounces that it's 'foutue'. My dictionary translates this as 'buggered', or ruder, which I had kind of worked out. It's a pity someone didn't mention this a year ago. I email a friend; in deep shit – don't mention the septic tank.

There is progress; I keep turning on the lights, unable to believe that if I press this switch – here – then that thing on the ceiling lights up – in all the rooms of the house. Not only that but there are actual lights, after months of living in torture chambers with bare bulbs swinging from cables. I have discovered that in 1888 Dieulefit was (along with Valrèas) the very first town in France to have electric lights, powered by the hydro-electric station at Beconne. So who put in the electric lights before electricians were invented?

The locksmiths, of course. In Dieulefit these were the Sestiers, who installed sixteen public lamps and ninety-nine private ones, and presumably can be considered the first electricians. I try to imagine there being electricity available somewhere but no electricians - not an entirely new experience. On the other hand, the electricians seem to have done better historically than the builders; the Dieulefit fortifications planned in 1345 were finished in 1425.

It might not be to create fortifications this time but the village centre has even more cranes and diggers than the road outside our house, as the council removes and replaces all the old mains water pipes. Perhaps we didn't choose the right place after all - we definitely didn't choose the right time. Dieulefit's Council considers this the ideal opportunity to create new road surfaces and pavements so a trip to the bank becomes just that, an ankle-breaking scramble through hard-core, tugging down the helpful red-and-white ribbon when you trip. We get cheerful newsletters thanking us citizens for putting up with the chaos in the interests of a new and better Dieule-

fit; the spirit of the Revolution is alive and well but not necessarily in my house.

We were good Llanelli citizens for three Christmases when the pedestrianised town centre was a building site, once because the previous new surface had completely and unevenly sunk. I mutter and scuff stones, only marginally cheered up by seeing that Jean's law of wet concrete remains universal. A man, a child and a dog are approaching their own front door and to reach it they will have to cross a wooden plank erected over the wet concrete pavement. Two red-and-white ribbons flutter as trick hand-rails, asking to be grabbed so they can collapse and ensure that a trip becomes a fall.

But Jean's law has yet to be confirmed . For a moment, it looks as if I will be disappointed as the dog sits on command, before the gangplank. Then 'Viens!' ('Come') and woops! there she goes, one foot straight over the edge into the wet concrete.

There is a real sense of history about being there at the precise moment that the inevitable pawprint is fixed as a Dieulefit landmark. There is a pub in York unimaginatively called 'The Roman Bath', because built on one, and in the good old days you could look through a glass circle cut in the floor of the lounge and see the old paving of the baths. It took me a while but I spotted it; an ancient Roman dog-print.

When I get home, I find that the council workers have dug a trench from across the road to a spot under my sitting room window. I smile at the nice men in hard hats, who have a good view of our furniture from their swivel seats in their red and yellow dinky toys.

Then a nice man in a hard hat calls to tell me that they can't find the mains water pipe to our house. We cannot help. Then he finds the pipe. Loudly. I think that was when one lot of 'Merde' and 'Putain' could be heard. He comes back to tell me that they have broken the pipe but that they will make a temporary replacement and fix it permanently tomorrow.

Why does the word 'demain' not reassure me? He is now very very nice and when he comes back again to help us stop the tap

spurting brown fluid, he is upset when I aim the hose into the flower bed. 'Your beautiful flowers,' he says, pained, and takes the hose away from me, pointing it over the less delicate lawn, 'It would be a pity to spoil them'.

I negotiate the roadworks to get in vital supplies and make contact with the outside world. I buy *le Dauphiné* at the supermarket and know when I am queuing at Fleur's checkout exactly what will happen. Sure enough, despite eight people waiting behind me, Fleur stops totalling in order to read the paper, at her own pace.

'What are you doing?' asks the man behind me in the queue and, as the French are less prone to sarcasm than the Welsh, Fleur looks up innocently and tells him, 'I'm reading the paper.'

Everyone in the queue has a 'Well there we are then, all explained' expression but Fleur is feeling sociable so she expands, 'I always read the headlines of the first paper that comes through – it saves me buying one,' and then she returns to finish the verdict on the burglars tried at Valence. Perhaps it is the breathtaking honesty that leaves us all speechless – it is after all my paper – but I just think it's entertaining and the queue waits patiently.

Eventually I read my own, slight crumpled newspaper, and I note that nuclear protestors are more unhappy than usual and that we are going to have even bigger nuclear reactors just down the Rhône from us.

Did I forget to mention another less attractive aspect of our beautiful home? We live within thirty miles of France's nuclear powerhouse, our valley being described in my Almanach as 'the most nuclearised in the world'. For good measure, the reactors are apparently built along a fault line with a high likelihood of earthquakes, and, as if that wasn't enough, the reactors had to close down occasionally during last year's heatwave and there is concern that the exceptional heat might have caused cracking.

How much consolation is it that Dieulefit has only a moderate threat of earthquakes, which requires only standard earthquake measures in all building regulations. What exactly are standard earthquake measures? Are they affected by council workers

destroying your cellar and plumbers destroying the rest of the house? Did I ever ask to be shaken to my foundations? if I did, it was most definitely only metaphorical, and only a wild whim. I was younger then. I have changed my mind.

I can do nothing about disasters, domestic or international. Instead I am Cleopatra floating along the Nile with beautiful slaves fanning enormous palm fronds, roses underfoot and in the air; I am me, fanned by tiers of acacia branches, through which the blue blue sky offers summer. I am definitely lounging but I call it research – two interesting facts about Dieulefit for every two hours drifting along the sky amongst the roses. A hint of fading lilac and a back note of wild thyme adds complexity to enough roses to drug Mark Antony. Blowsy vermilion peonies flaunt yellow stamens amongst old-fashioned roses all shades of red.

John's favourite has a darkness shadowing its crimson petals but then his loyalty wavers as yellow spikes open, and then tiny pompoms cluster on the new pergola … they grow like weeds and blossom like in a fairy tale. Roses inside the wall and poppies outside, usually scattered through verges, waste and arable land but suddenly torching a complete field with blazing red. We toast the early summer with Côtes du Rhône rosé.

16

EXAMINING GRAVEL AND LIVE-HEADING ROSES

We pick up pieces of gravel, consider each one carefully then place them on a piece of wood near where we sit. There are gray edges to some chippings and rose glints in others. We don't put them in our mouths, although we think about it. Instead we weigh one chip at a time, closing a hand around it, feeling its exact graveliness.

Not even a Chinese philosopher can meditate endlessly on gravel so we get the ball next. After a spell of bending it like Beckham, dribbling around two hot Pyreneans who have seen it all before, we take position at opposite ends of a plastic sunlounger, tilted to optimal ball-slide angle.

We make the ball roll down the green smoothness and discover basic laws of physics as the ball uses human energy to go back up to the top. Lots of human energy.

We are bored with the laws of physics so we go live-heading roses. This is a lot more fun than dead-heading but then destruction usually is. I try to pick roses already on their way out, and I do have sympathies for the pro-euthanasia groups, but there is a definite wince factor as the velvety petals are shredded and rain on the lawn.

We have already sung and acted out 'The Grand Old Duke of York'; now it is Khayyam's turn.

> 'Look to the Rose that blows about us – 'Lo,
> Laughing,' she says 'into the world I blow:
> At once the silken tassel of my Purse
> Tear, and its Treasure on the Garden throw.'

This new little rose has certainly blown into the world laughing and she expects me to join in.

By this time, perhaps ten minutes has gone by. I am babysitting for my belle-petite-fille of eighteen months and I am exhausted. You forget, don't you. Her father and pregnant mother are climbing Mielandre. Given the choice of climbing a mountain or entertaining a toddler, John got his boots out.

Thank God for Auntie-fille who allows me to abandon grand-motherhood for pizza-making. Home on the range. What with the baby and the cooking, we enter other time zones. Baby-time crams a year into twenty-four hours, with action slots of five minutes each and quiet spells of ten minutes if you're lucky and hours of desperate recovery when it's asleep.

Breadmaking slows the pace, takes the time it takes. Now there's a real meditation for a philosopher – watching dough rise. Another favourite is making a risotto. It's not only the stock that's absorbed as I stir and watch the swirl of rice and liquid.

It has the same effect on me as fishing; you start off impatient, wondering why you're wasting precious time, you check your watch and only three minutes have gone. Then, as you watch the ripples and your hands cast (or stir) while your brain floats, your friend nudges you and tells you five hours have gone by. You don't believe her but you feel lighter somehow, as if you've cast at least some of your troubles into the water.

Auntie-fille passes the parcel and we play indoor games. Sitting on the window-sill is the best place to see every kind of mechanical digger known to toyshops, most of them a disappointing

cream but some actually are the bright yellow of a two-year old's dreams.

We already know that the grabber looks threatening as it swings too close to the house wall, lurches drunkenly down and excavates more rubble than a small girl could sift in a lifetime but it is the roller which rumbles like thunder on approach, rings the ceramic lampshades like tram-bells as it heaves by the house and passes like a minor earthquake only to repeat the process in the opposite direction.

From the windowsill we can smile right into the digger cab and wave to the men in hard hats, our best French friends, who wave back with the enthusiasm due to a blue-eyed blonde – her, not me. Belle-petite-fille is the sort of baby who is approached by a strange man in Super-U, who asks Belle-grand-mère 'Which shelf did you get that one from?' and who is rewarded with baby smiles – from her not me. She could do cute for Wales; I couldn't.

After several baby days and four hours twenty three minutes grown-up time, intrepid-fille returns, having climbed her mountain. Like most mothers, she is relieved and disappointed that petite-fille is still in one piece; relieved because she worries when they are apart, disappointed because she half-wants to be irreplaceable, even for a few hours.

I remember this temporary madness, along with the guilty mother's knowledge (and is there any other kind of mother?) that the baby was actually in your care, not with the mother-substitute at all, when it fell down the stairs/ate half a clothes peg/was clawed by a tortured cat.

I am pleased with myself because, in addition to none of the above having happened, I didn't let petite-fille sleep. I remember how it felt when someone told me how good the baby had been, 'slept all morning', and I knew we were in for a long afternoon and night. I am also pleased with myself because I kept to the food rules which come attached by their parents to all modern babies.

This, I am in no position to mock. Feeding time at the Gilborough zoo is a delicate operation. One Pyrenean has a tendency

towards stomach ulcers and our move to France meant that a Kidwelly vet's brand of chicken-and-rice petfood had to be replaced with risky foreign stuff (my dogs have the gourmet habits of our grandmothers). We settled on 'special dog food for giant dogs with sensitive stomachs' for main meals and biscuits 'guaranteed to give pleasure' for breakfasts. I am deeply tempted by the biscuits.

For the cats, we chose dried cat food that had pictures of beautiful Birmans on the front. One sister asked, 'Do you feel the marketing influenced you just a little?' but the way I see it, if sex sells everything to humans from cars to deodorants, then why shouldn't my toothless, smelly pets imagine they're ten years younger when they look at the show-winning pictures and eat their biscuits?

One month into the new French regime, Sensitive Dog stopped eating. I tried all the usual tricks, including the pills packed in my 'emergency starter kit' by my Welsh vet, and we went two steps forward, three steps back. I told myself that it was only her stomach that was sensitive, that she wasn't pining for Wales, but one morning she looked miserably undeniably in-need-of-vet ill.

As it was John's birthday, his treat for the day was our first trip to the French vet. When he saw my expression and realised that I was coming out of the surgery without the dog, he thought that it was going to be a very bad birthday but actually that was going to depend on the vet, the dog and a bit of luck. I had been completely misled by her past history and Sensitive Dog had in fact developed a womb infection and needed an emergency hysterectomy to save her life. Our new vet phoned us personally at lunchtime to tell us the operation had been a success; at tea-time to tell us that the patient was recovering (at which stage we remembered the old joke, 'the operation was a success but...)

Next morning we were told that things were going well... but. The 'but' was predictable... but she couldn't come home until she'd eaten something – and she wouldn't eat anything. Well of course she wouldn't. She's a Sensitive Dog, in Dog Prison, where they don't even speak proper human. It took them three days to coax her to eat something (or to give up and lie about it) and for us to organise a

triumphant homecoming. When I called at the surgery to collect her, thinking how little moving country had changed the excellent quality of vet care, the vet himself popped out to see me.

'Wait here', he instructed, and disappeared behind the counter into the back room, only to reappear with a kidney dish full of wobbly yukky gunge. Beaming, he asked, 'Do you want to see what I removed?' I didn't have to think long to decline the offer, much to his disappointment. Some things are very different here.

The Other Half of the Pack had been subdued and seemed very pleased at the returnee. There was much tail-wagging and mutual greeting until Well Dog took one huge sniff and inhaled 'Vet'. She couldn't be seen for dust and avoided contact – and contagion – for days, leaving Sensitive Dog to muse on the unfairness of life and contemplate her dissolving stitches.

Since then, we have had several phases of 'Will I, won't I eat' and the current solution involves puffa rice, chicken stock (home-made of course) and one tempting piece of charcuterie – times two of course because, although we are One Pack, we will also kill each other if there's better food in not-my-bowl.

I imagine the reactions to be much the same during feeding time at the crocodile park although I have not yet observed this. It happens on Tuesday and Sunday afternoons and apparently crocodiles only eat twice a week so if you fall in with them on any other day, they won't eat you.

I am lucky enough to see the crocodiles when I am being Auntie Jean, so I am allowed to be an under-10, staring at the water until a log blinks prehistoric mildewed eyes, or at a pile of fifteen monsters, surely dead, until a forearm stirs and a curiously human hand flexes. Handbags, I tell them, and shoes, but they answer me with their perfectly adapted bodies, their lack of non-human predators and above all their totally silent movement.

Being Auntie Jean is differently tiring from being Grandma. We dress up as Provençal beekeepers (so those hats and the white overall from the garage were useful after all) and we visit the yellow box

hive in the woods. It is active and end-of-day busy as the workers return with their treasure.

We look at the empty nest in the stone porch where two families of black redstart have hatched since the spring. We pick pears and magic them into jam (I can prove it is today's jam because it has today's date on it). I do the disappearing act, using the magic of an old house's architecture and am flattered that my sister thinks, even if for only a minute, that I might have climbed up the chimney or out of the window.

We walk around the garden and eat some of the flowers (like small print, I warn that this is not to be tried at home or without an irresponsible adult). We eat the blue borage flowers and the orange nasturtiums, and casually give Mum the nasturtium seeds, laughing when her tongue zings with heat. It is allowed to laugh a little at other people when you are under ten, but not for long, and not if it makes them cry. Mum does not cry, not even when she tries the disappearing act, gets stuck in a wardrobe and discovered. Instead she laughs, we all laugh, and the house hoards the laughter for echoes after they have gone.

We go to a jazz concert from a seven-piece band in the old Knights' village of Poët-Laval and the hall swings with summer, the old songs reaching a new generation. Under-10 is not too young to play the clarinet; not too young to say that if you hear the same things played on the same instruments by different people they will still never be the same; not too young to be treated seriously as a fellow musician by the jazz clarinetist who gives his autograph along with technical advice on mouthpieces. He is German, I am Scottish-English from Wales, and we talk in French; his music spoke to us all, in a hall-full of tourist languages.

And if nine is not too young, seventy ? eighty? is not too old for the presenter who, encouraged by the audience, replaces the pianist at the end of the second and final set, and plays the jazz he loves. Throughout the concert, his mouth has made little moue shapes along with the rhythms, he has followed the flights of improvisation with a smile and the tilt of his head, and now his hands are where

they wanted to be, chasing the keys into the past, outside time and back into the moment of enthusiastic applause.

To be nine and full of curiosity. Or to be six, before the word 'real' has power to destroy the corner where the toys discuss their numeracy work. My niece and nephew charge about, and fade, and charge about and fade, while the grown-ups take turns to play and – more often – fade completely. The rhythms of parenting soar bright and brassy as each player contributes, miss the odd note as someone extemporises and the others miss the clues, and cross-over in a mixture of the familiar and the individual. We reinvent the old tunes as best we can.

I have learnt about myself through my visitors, and not all of it is welcome knowledge. I am older than I thought, very set in my ways. I get up too early in the morning, go to bed too early at night, and like food at set times in between. I prefer spontaneity to be planned so that I can organise the cooking. I feel vaguely demeaned by hanging out visitors' underwear.

I must put the record straight here; no-one asked me to hang out their underwear but when washing was left in the machine and the visitors were out holidaying… I have been taken back to old, old resentments about gender and roles that I thought I had left behind years ago. How can I blame my male visitors, for assuming that women do washing, when that's what happens? How can I blame my women visitors when they thank me for helping them? I get very different reactions when I say, sometimes truthfully, that John hung it out. Then, there is a sense of guilt at making the poor man do such a thing (or shock at me making the poor man do such a thing). It has been interesting, the underwear test, a sort of touchstone of gender roles, but I am me and from now on I will be grandma, mother, auntie, friend and host without being pushed into stereotyped behaviour I never adopted in the past.

I decided long ago that domestic chores are an irritating game of chicken, won always by the person with the highest tolerance of dirt and untidiness. Unfortunately, this is not usually me. From curiosity, I once left a cat furball lying where it had been puked, on the

worktop in the utility room. It wasn't that the two adults with whom I shared a house were unwilling to clean it up; they didn't even notice it. By the time you can think of nothing but furball, you have four options; go insane, leave forever, clean it up yourself or ask someone else to do so. If you choose number four, however politely, you are a domestic tyrant and, whatever is said, the person you've asked is wondering why the hell you didn't clean it up yourself and why you make such a fuss over such simple things. Sometimes, life is full of furballs.

17

LAVENDER AND THE BLUES

Happiness is an utterly selfish emotion. How can you be happy when someone close to you, isn't? How can you be happy in the face of war, starvation, poverty... And yet. How does your misery change others' lives for the better? Who is helped by your depression? Isn't it from some kind of secure self that you can reach out a helping hand?

I am surrounded, and sometimes overwhelmed, by others' blues. I know about survivor guilt and it is not only those who have been through genocide and war who feel this. It is also the burden of those who know that, in the face of logic, they retain an underlying sense of happiness, or, at worst, the belief that it is possible to be happy.

I escape the indoor blues into the outdoor ones. The lavender is in bloom. Sprig by sprig and field by corrugated field, the valleys turn lavender blue. The hybrid 'lavandin' alongside the road is first to bloom, one field actually planted in curves to follow the bending road. On impossibly steep slopes, high into the mountains, true lavender, 'lavande', is later.

We argue about 'blue'. Why, when the colour is actually lavender, a shade of purple, do both English and French refer to 'bleu lavande', 'lavender blue'. I wonder what the Welsh is, knowing that the colour 'glas' can be the blue of the sky or the green of the fields, something I

have only ever understood as a consequence of the Welsh weather. Whatever our disagreements about colour, there is no mistaking the scent, delicate over the fields and summer markets or blasting the car as we drive past a distillery. When we are lazing in the garden, a sudden whiff of lavender follows in the wake of every metal-gridded trailer, stacked high with blue? lavender?-flecked bales en route for la Roche St Secret or Nyons.

There, at the distilleries, you can watch men streaming with sweat as they stoke the fires from old bales and steam the essence out of new ones. Steam distillation, John murmured lovingly, the chemist at heart, when he first saw the process, and however often I ask him to explain it to me, it retains for me the magic of microwaves; I just have to believe what I do not understand.

My unscientific methods cause clashes in the kitchen, where I use actual, variable spoons to measure ingredients and where John has a gamut of precision tools – jugs, cups, stainless steel 'spoon' measures – and he frequently uses four during one process. I prefer him to be my sous-chef but he has quickly become le chef du confiture as we make enough jam to fill a table at a WI fête.

Why does preserving fruit have such a staid reputation in the UK? What is more sensual than picking ripe fruit, sneaking some bites and dribbles along the way, boiling it in a cauldron (yes, that's what Macbeth's witches were really up to), watching the sugar dissolve and the light reflected from the suddenly polished surface, which then bubbles and froths to the magical point of setting. Or rather not-so-magical point of 'syrup', disguised as dessert topping and milk shakes but always recognized by the chefs as failed jam.

Inspired by Delia, I once made Seville marmalade, doubling the quantities in my enthusiasm. There was a painfully loud moment when, copying the television performance exactly, I squeezed the muslin bag of pips and pith into the boiling liquid from which I had just removed it – Delia, why didn't you tell me to let it cool first?

Nursing my raw red right hand, I followed instructions less trustingly and quickly spotted that the pan was going to boil over (perhaps those double quantities weren't such a good idea) and almost

prevented sticky stuff hitting patches of tiled floor. I think it was a week before my trainers lost that squeak that they get from walking in marmalade and even then it was still possible to moonwalk if you found the right spot in the kitchen. Undaunted, I produced two batches, one set like rock and the other like honey. Not what you would call an unqualified success.

Given my past record, I was apprehensive about jam-making with the added complication of French ingredients – unidentified types of pear or peach, I could cope with, but my dictionary let me down again over types of sugar. We passed a happy hour reading the backs of sugar packets and discovered magic sugar. The ingredients assure us that it is suitable for vegetarians – so no gelatine – that it contains various plant extracts, none of which I recognise, and that it makes perfect jam in seven minutes from any chopped fruit, boiled up. There has been no looking back.

When we sample jars at the Dieulefit annual Picodon and local foods market, I can look the stallholder in the eye and ask, jam-maker to jam-maker, what she does with her vanilla pod, knowing that, with a little help from magic sugar, we can try it out at home.

Jam sorted, we expand into chutney but are stumped once more by cultural difference. There is no such thing as 'pickling spice' for sale although we can get coriander seeds, juniper berries, dried chillies, bay leaves - you name the spice and it's there, by the hundred grammes on a market stall.

Neither can I work out what 'malt vinegar' is, and when I return to the confiture stall and ask the professional, she tells me that she varies her vinegar with the ingredients – cider vinegar with apple chutney, white wine vinegar with apricot ... I trawl my collection of cookery books for a recipe for pickling spice and find not one, not in the 'how to make perfect preserves' nor in 'everything about herbs and spices'.

I have to thank the hundreds of Americans who post their recipes online for the variations they offer me and I now know what mace is used for – I always wondered. I also learn a little respect for British cuisine. My Cookery Larousse explains to me that 'chutney' (there is

no French word) is a 'condiment anglais' of Indian origin which is ideal with cold meats.

I am doubly proud of my British ancestors, who showed the twin strengths of their native gastronomy; enjoying foreign food (once you can get them to try it that is) and tweaking the recipes with home-grown ingredients and cooking techniques. It might be debatable whether Britain, or its various component countries, has a cuisine at all, but what they do have are fusion experts, their motto 'Steal and substitute.'

What did we learn about food at school? I am the product of the grammar school system, or rather two systems. My first secondary school (after six primary schools) was a mixed grammar school with a fast lane for one class selected on their high results in English and Maths. This top class then studied three languages and no practical subjects. The very word 'practical' carried a sneer.

Being in the top group suited me fine except that my marks were going down the toilet as I had discovered boys and fighting. It came as a shock to move at fourteen to an all girls grammar school in York, where needlework and cookery lessons were part of making me a well-educated woman. The needlework I survived, having already sewed from necessity as the only way of getting clothes which were not bought from M&S and always too big for me (bought for my growth and worn out by the time I grew). My experience did not make me popular however and my report card was scarred with C for Needlework and complaints of 'dumb insolence' (if you don't say it, how can they blame you for it?) from the moment I was caught machine-sewing a pinned seam. I was convicted of gross arrogance for not having tacked it and still enjoy feelings of wild rebellion when I race down metres of pinned curtain material.

Cookery lessons replaced German; hours of entertainment spitting 'ss' and 'ch' sounds, were exchanged for torture. Not since I'd failed to make a paper windmill when I was five had I suffered such public humiliation for my clumsiness. Anything using a brain and talk, I was fine; anything involving my hands and common sense, I was lost.

The teacher gave up after one lesson, decided I was 'too far behind' and set me the task of making a sponge cake every single lesson until the end of the year, when 'options' saved me. I suppose that my peers did at least take home some edible product each week and, if they weren't put off cooking for life, they might have learnt some basic processes – the girls, that is. Boys (in our mirror school) did woodwork and technical drawing. All I learnt was that I couldn't cook.

What I did at home didn't count as cooking and reinforced my self-image as a bumbler but, as the only daughter at home of cooking age, I had to take on some responsibilities on the rare occasions when my mother was not home to prepare a meal. My father dreaded this but never enough to take over, which I now know he was perfectly capable of doing. He was unhappy at finding that his packed lunch contained raw carrots and honey sandwiches (well that's what I liked in mine at the time). He was even more unhappy when he told me that he didn't like garlic in his omelette and, after I told him that I hadn't added any garlic, he found out that the eggs had been bad.

At fourteen, I never questioned my responsibilities, not even when I tried to iron sheets by spreading them across four chairs and sliding a bit at a time across the ironing board. No-one else questioned my duty either, rather they made it clear I wasn't very good at being mother, especially when I risked my own life or theirs by my ignorance, as when I washed the electric toaster.

The 'food technology' teachers I have worked with have told me they miss the cooking, the chance to give basic life skills, particularly to youngsters whose parents have none. I ask the daughters, individually, about their education in cuisine and I make a strange discovery. The pupils of one comprehensive school in a small Welsh town can all be recognised by a sort of masonic code, retained from their Food Technology lessons – and that is all they seem to remember. Ex-Penyrheol students can all chant the washing-up song; 'Glass, silver, cutlery, china, tins and pans, wooden boards...'

For total authenticity, it should be sing-song, with 'cutlery'

pronounced 'cutelry'. It is reassuring to know that our dirty dishes are being washed up in the correct order but I am still wondering about the silverware obviously owned by many Gorseinon families.

Forget abstractions; I discover figs and Jamie Oliver's 'sexiest salad recipe'. I steal the idea and substitute goat's cheese for mozarella ... I must get my 'fifty ways with goat's cheese' into print. The infrastructure is in place – I'm sorry, once a school inspector always unable to speak English. What I mean is that my Picodon-making neighbours recognise me now and might not send me off with a flea in my ear if I offer them the once-in-a-lifetime- opportunity to sell my Picodon recipes at their crèmerie.

A Cavet worker tells me she thought of us suffering the road-works so close to our house. Yes, we thought of us too. I ask about my wooden doorstops, still 'softening' in olive oil, eight months later. Yes, she says, people really do eat them, just as they are. She personally doesn't even like the stronger, Dieulefitois Picodons, she likes the milder ones and the fresh 'fermiers'.

I gather from her expression that it is a bit like going for a hotter vindaloo, somewhat macho, to go for the strongest Picodon. I think I might get back in touch with my feminine side and admit that I really don't like the aroma of smelly socks, the texture of bark and the bitter taste of my ancient Picodons. I wonder what bread would taste like with some Picodon shavings added...

Having stocked up on the Picodons I do like, I then head in the opposite direction to my olive oil neighbour so that I can fill my empty stainless steel 'bidon', an oil container, with Dieulefit extra virgin.

It takes ten minutes of shouting 'Il y a quelqu'un?' before a brown mongrel appears with a man much older than the producer I met last time. When I introduce myself, very loudly as he is hard of hearing, does this traditional resident, probably born and bred here, think 'Oh my God another bloody foreigner who can hardly speak French.'? If he does, there is no sign of it. His smile and his handshake are warm as he says, 'Voisine' as if this makes all the difference in the world and it is as his neighbour that he introduces me to the

grand-daughter, who has been left in charge of sales while her parents are out.

She takes as little interest in me, my sister and olive oil as is possible and tries to hide her knowledge of English. I would have been exactly the same at her age. I buy my five litres, cold pressed (this I am told is no guarantee of quality), traditionally produced (ditto), extra virgin (those are the words that matter – as well as knowing the smile of the man you bought it from).

Every kitchen should have olive oil on tap – and every cellar its 'en vrac', a plastic barrel of wine filled from a petrol pump, direct from the cave. You will even get professional labels so that if you choose to bottle it, rather than enjoy a quick five litres, your friends will read that this Côtes du Rhône was 'bottled by the buyer'. It is the foodstuff of poetry (with a little stealing and substitution);

'A loaf of bread (dipped in good olive oil), a glass of wine, a Picodon and thou...'

It is tough but I actually say no to the plumber, Tuesday is not convenient for him to install the second toilet. We are going to watch the Tour de France. He is indulgent and tells us to take umbrellas. It is indeed gray on the Monday evening and twenty drops of rain fall, if that. We have now had three months without rain, rivaling last year's drought but not as unbearably hot. The cloud cover on the Tuesday morning means that we will not fry as we wait.

We have chosen our spot beforehand, avoiding the village of la Bégude (too many people), deciding against the open countryside (dodgy parking, no shade, no chance of getting away afterwards) and we are in a tiny village called Charols, where we can have a leisurely coffee before the fun starts. Two weeks ago, I passed the time of day with a waiter in la Bégude. 'You'll be busy here when the Tour passes?' He shrugged, indifferent. 'They'll go past' he gestured at the street, 'and that's it over'. Undeterred, I am looking forward to it.

I was slow to appreciate le Tour, unable to see why my husband

spent so many television hours watching men on bikes, when you couldn't even tell whether the ones you were watching were at the front or trailing two days behind everyone else.

My first moment of revelation was on a school exchange visit, when I crossed the road from the Dali Museum in Figueras, went into a tourist shop and saw a glass case proudly displaying Indurain's yellow jersey, signed by the great man himself. My nine year old son explained its significance to me and there was something magical about the way we found it. Then, after I'd holidayed in more parts of France, watching the Tour was like flicking through a photo album, Col du Galibier in the Alps, the road through the Pyrenees into Andorra, Mont Ventoux – yes, been there, seen the yellow Tshirt. Finally came the stage of dreaming about house-buying, the stage when I grew very irritated that the television cameras moved on so quickly from that stone mas of character set in its own grounds that I spotted behind the peloton as they speeded through the Vaucluse.

We live fifteen minutes from this year's route and the crucial stage is between Valréas and the Vercors, the first time for seven years that le Tour has crossed la Drôme so it seems only polite to go along, to cheer and wave. We are among the last to drive along the actual Tour route and I feel uncomfortably like the Queen, accompanied by police motos and cars, crowds already lining up behind the barriers in the villages or setting up their deckchairs by cars parked on every drive opening or field verge.

Charols is just as we hoped it would be and after our coffee, we take up position, sitting on a stone wall overhung by trees. The café staff have hung a banner across the road 'Richard, Chef du Jour' and there is no question as to which rider we French support. Despite being over thirty, Richard Virenque is once again wearing the spotty king-of-the mountains Tshirt and giving disarmingly modest interviews. The people of France pay homage to their idols in traditional ways; Virenque was presented with a Saler cow by the Mayor of Saint-Flour, on behalf of the Upra Association of breeders.

Stuff of legends, Lance Armstrong is a strong bet for the final yellow, but he is just too good, too unbeatable and too … American

to capture the French public in the same way. He speaks some French in interview, he is upset about drug allegations, and he does try very hard to be human. More convincing as a human is Tyler Hamilton, upset because his golden retriever, Tugboat, has just been put to sleep. I realise how young these cyclists are when I am told that Tyler was nine when he had Tugboat as a puppy.

On our left is a French woman in her forties, who has in her charge three children and a young woman of about twenty, with Down's Syndrome. The four of them are instructed to sit on the wall and 'ne bougez pas', not to move, as Madame darts about in front of them, warming up for the 'caravane'. All four giggle, wriggling with anticipation. On our right is a family, parents and two older children. The boy, probably thirteen or so, looks bored, with the studied disinterest of the adolescent.

An hour before the cyclists are due, preceded by more gendarmes, the first cars of the 'caravane' arrive. These are company cars, dressed up like village carnival floats, blaring music and honking as they pass at speed. They are apparently staffed by fluffy coffee beans or elves, who throw freebies to us, the crowd. Madame risks life and limb as she dives for free comics, plastic whistles and paper fans, supported by her four gigglers, who are accumulating little piles of treasure. 'Ne bougez pas' she warns them as she gives a 6.0 athletic performance and smiles at us when we pass over the junk which has landed on us.

However old you are, there is something satisfying about catching free gifts; for me, it is a throwback to my sixties childhood when we ripped cereal boxes apart for the 3D paper specs hidden at the bottom. There is also something of life's unfairness about the freebies not coming your way. Madame is a professional at attracting attention, waving and smiling, her gang of four clinching the handful thrown from each car as it whizzes past. Some of the goodies reach us, probably by misjudgement of the throw, but I note that John is wearing a lanyard with a team logo.

Not much goes further on, to the teenage boy who has half-heart-

edly held out a hand, then retreated further into his shoulders when nothing comes his way. He knew it wouldn't, it never does.

Then something flies towards him and he catches it. His shoulders lift a bit, he puts it in his pocket, feigning nonchalance, and stands a little nearer the road. More comes his way, he starts to swagger, and by the end of the hour's procession of mad fancy dress and even madder customised vehicles, the boy is rivaling Madame, waving, shouting and beaming.

The mood is contagious; it seems possible that I giggled when a fake fireman hosed us down from his passing van, but no-one will ever be able to prove it. I buy the Tour souvenir pack of a cap, a yellow Tshirt, a cuddly bear wearing the King of the Mountains spotty 'maillot' and an inflatable yellow bag. Of course, I am only thinking of my niece and nephew when I indulge but, even if I weren't, I would have asked to swop the 'extra large' Tshirt they gave me. I muse on this. They took one look at me and grabbed 'extra large' out of the boot.

After the caravane is another wait. We know from the free newspaper (one of our first catches), from checking online beforehand, and from the local papers, the time the racers are expected. We have been given two options, to the minute, according to the precisely calculated likely speed. John has warned me that we are too close to the start of the race (about fifteen minutes before they reach us) for the cyclists to have separated out. Also, we are on the flat, which guarantees that there will be a mob going past. We see a flicker coming along the road, then whizz, whizz and – just as the waiter from la Bégude predicted – they are gone.

Two hours' wait, months of anticipation, for 30 seconds' excitement. I dismiss the sexist analogies that come to mind (but John seems to think they're funny). So what did we see? We compare notes to pool anything to add to our experience.

We definitely saw the teams, groups of riders wearing the team colours; John saw the US Postale team, with Lance Armstrong presumably in there somewhere. He also saw the yellow jersey,

currently worn by a very popular young Frenchman. I am disappointed – I didn't.

I think I might, perhaps, have seen the spotty jersey of Richard Virenque, among the front riders, but it is only when I see le Tour on television that night that I am convinced that I was right. I was expecting the spots to be all over like on the teddy bear's Tshirt but they're not. There are pink stripes up both sides and the spots are more like a dalmation's than like measles. Why did no-one tell me this? Never mind, I'll know next time.

18

DON'T WORRY, ONLY THE FEMALES KILL

It is true, however hard to believe; I am wishing for rain. I am a changed person after four months without the wet stuff (unless you count a few drops which didn't even change the colour of the paving stones).

There are hosepipe restrictions but we can ignore them because we have the spring water, true wealth. The daily watering ritual starts as soon as the sun can be trusted to have called it a day and we are proud of our flowers and crops, nurtured through the drought. Monsieur Dubois takes one look, shakes his head and says we are not watering enough.

'How much water do you think an apple tree needs each day?' he asks. I am not good with quantities. Neither am I any good with the French for quantities. I have recently ordered a fifty-litre 'pichet' of wine in a restaurant and my smiling waitress brought me the usual small jug – 'centilitres' is not a word that trips off my tongue. Then there was the purchase of a babyseat when petite-fille came to stay. I was asked 'How old is the baby?' and four people queuing to be served laughed out aloud at my answer, along with the salesman and my husband, who helpfully corrected my 'eighteen years' to 'eighteen months'. It's because you don't say the 'years' bit in English at all, I tried telling John afterwards, that it's a habit in French to add 'ans'

automatically. No quarter was given - or is that twenty five centilitres. It could be worse; I could be called Connor, like a daughter's Irish aquaintance. It is tricky introducing yourself to French people when your name means 'F'ing Idiot' in their language.

To be on the safe side, I mumbled something inaudible in reply to Monsieur Dubois, who told me, 'Fifty litres a day' (so my wine-ordering habit would have worked), 'Fifty litres a day… and they are like people'.

I look at my apple trees, impeccably pruned on their espalier wires, fruit swelling. What sort of people are they? Cattle rustlers strung up? Pregnant women at the clinic? Jolly rosy-cheeked farmers and their wives, straight out of 'Old Macdonald'?

Apparently this is not the point. 'Just like people. To be healthy they need their water every day, a bit at a time, not all in one go…' Tell that to the provençal skies which gloom and gather, then deposit their treasure in the neighbouring valley, whatever the weather forecast says. We play out the scene in 'Jean de Florette' where the townie shakes his fist at departing thunderclouds which have passed by his garden yet again.

We use all our old standard guaranteed rain starters. We hang out the washing, John waters the garden, we walk the dogs… nothing works. The air steams with humidity, our shirts run with sweat, we snap at each other as we wait for the storm that doesn't come. It is like going through labour without giving birth. We are exhausted by two complete days of nearly-about-to-rain-honestly-perhaps-well, maybe not. Then the sun comes out again and we get on with our rainless lives.

It is August so all roadworks are suspended while the council workers holiday. I just beat the down-tools and managed to sweet-talk two men with a digger into taking a scoop out of our drive, so that the car doesn't crunch the tow-bar on the turn. Before the wonderful new road, there was no problem, and I am assured that it will be made good …. some time in September. It is not just the council workers who take August off. Even my optician is shutting up shop and I won't be able to get my new varifocals until he comes

back, by which time I will have thought of a way to raise the required cash – the cost of a new laptop.

If you live in Dieulefit, where do you go for your holidays? The Alps, I am told, or Brittany, or the Pyrenees. Exploring France is a matter of local pride but cheap flights and package holidays are attracting more clients. A market-stallholder is just back from Thailand and my optician is off to ... Ireland. When he heard I was from Wales, he sniggered, then apologised. I asked him to explain, He said, 'No, I shouldn't say,' I said, 'Go on,' and eventually, he did. He had just watched a film about a mountain in Wales, no, he corrected himself, about *the* mountain in Wales. Did I know how high it was? I did. He laughed, 'And they are proud of it.' I told him that if he only had one mountain, he'd be proud of it too.

When I walked out of his shop, I could see the encircling mountains, the ridge of Dieu Grace, the St Maurice range, Mielandre ... all of them around a thousand metres or more and considered nothing by the locals, who live within an hour of the Alps. I ask about Ireland to distract myself from the pain of the estimate, barely eased by having a pair of prescription sunglasses thrown in – for that price I should be getting a cute guide dog thrown in.

My optician is looking forward to the countryside, the culture, the people, the unspoilt beaches, the swimming... The swimming? Ireland is a lot like Wales, I tell him, gently, and it might not be as hot nor as sunny, as it is here. I don't tell him that I remember the swimming all too well ... every time I opened my back door.

It finally rains, with cymbals and drums that send Sensitive Dog into a frenzy. She has almost got over her fear of men in yellow jackets, thanks to the daily immersion therapy provided by Dieulefit council; she's no longer scared of ambulances and fire-engines as she now sings along - the particular note in French sirens has taught her to howl for the first time in her life; she has not had a recurrence of the blue-balloon-in-the-sky trauma; fire risks have led to a fireworks ban so we are spared that bout of hysteria; but the natural bangs in the sky turn a dog, supposedly of the only breed capable of taking on a wolf, into a hyperventilating, shaking, whining Mummy's girl.

I'm not surprised that increasing numbers of wolves are worrying sheep in the Vercors, if Pyreneans have anything to do with stopping them. I suspect the Pyreneans are worried too and if you've seen a worried Pyrenean, you'll know it's not a pretty sight. It seems to consist mostly of something heavy and panting racing round the room and trying to jump on furniture. Why the floor should seem a more dangerous place, I haven't worked out yet.

Still, whatever the costs in dog, and consequently people, trauma, it is raining proper rain. I enjoy the freshness of the air and we even leave windows open, seeking out the spray. We listen to the orchestral performance on the house instruments, the clay tiled roof, the metal shutters, gutters and drainpipes Then I remember that I don't like rain and sulk at the lack of light. The dogs won't go outside and their tails droop; the cats have to be carried over the wet paving to get their food. Everything is back to normal.

After-rain is dirty. This is not soft Welsh water; it is loaded with minerals that leave streaks and scum on every surface, on the garden chairs and the windows. The supermarkets sell a hundred anti-calcium products to add to your wash-load, your kettle, your show-erhead. The mobile toolshops sell as just as many gadgets – magnetic circles to clamp around your pipes to ionise the water and convert the calcium into harmless deposits – or some such pseudoscience.

The gadgets are about as effective as the flykillers and I have to take much the same measures – regular, tedious, old-fashioned removal. I discover how effective vinegar is on limescale, and I add descaling the kettle to my Sunday jobs. In twenty five years in Wales, I only once realised that water could leave dirty tracks, and that was when we had a freak wind blowing from the Sahara that deposited sandy streaks across cars and windows. Soap always lathered, bubble bath left baths clean, irons and kettles never furred. Now, I de-scum the bath and the tiles, and although I quite like the extra shine on my hair, I know exactly where it comes from and I call it 'minerals'. It sounds nicer than scum.

It is unfortunately not vinegar that scents the bathroom but, unmistakably, the new fosse septique. The plumber suggests that I

use a lot of Scotch as a temporary measure; he will even get the Scotch for me from his van. My parents warned me that the bottle was never an answer, even temporarily, even good Scotch, but I am tempted. The plumber reappears with a roll of bright orange sticky tape. It seems that the smells from a very active septic tank are feeding back somehow through the bath and to see us through the visiting season we need to seal the overflow and a gap in the tiles with Scotch, and to leave the plug in and some water in the bath all the time. Why, we ask our septic tank expert, has this only happened after our brand new tank has been installed. He doesn't catch my eye as he answers. Because, he says, the old one was foutue. Ah. I try not to think about where the gunge used to go.

You assumed from their absence that the electricians had finished? No chance. We are not at all surprised that there is no question of them working in August and we will welcome them back in September if they arrive as promised. It is no longer a question of basic living requirements, so we are more relaxed.

The key moment was when André sang the fuse box into being. Always one to sing and talk to himself while working, he created a folk opera around the triumphant climax of connecting dozens of wires into the new fusebox. Working my own kind of magic in the kitchen, I couldn't believe what I was hearing, as each wire had its own little melody and, with a verbal accompaniment of 'Voici le micro-onde,' the cable for the microwave was sung into place.

Every time I switch on a light, I know it is part of the circuit of home, made safe by this wizard of the wires who has given us the key to the magical cupboard, in his own handwriting. When the storm crackles, André's surge-protector trips the whole system and the house blinks into darkness in deference to the elements, then dances light again, clicking and whirring as the gadgets wake up.

The rain brings out even more insects, which reach their summer peak, or rather pique, and 'pique' they do, snacking on my arms and legs. I read a helpful leaflet from the local chemist, telling me what is mostly likely to kill me in the summer and what to do to prevent this. My brother-in-law looks at the pictures and is

convinced that he held a deadly millipede in his hand while in the Lot.

I am reassured that our big black 'bourdons', the not-bumble-bees (whatever the dictionary says), are 'inoffensive' and 'only sting on rare occasions' – which is just as well, given that they are 24 to 28 millimetres, with 'massive bodies'. This I know already.

I am glad I am not swimming in the sea, facing lethal jelly fish, Portuguese men o' war and sandflies, nasty little stripy mosquitoes with black eyes. These pass on 'highly dangerous' diseases, but it's actually only the females that draw blood, so as long as you only mix with the boys, you're all right.

I pat myself on the back when I see 'ticks' among the 'highly dangerous' because I can use the old nail varnish remover/alcohol trick to get rid of those little buggers. I become more thoughtful at the information that between 10,000 and 28,000 people die in France each year from a disease passed on by a tick (again, only the female).

As cause of death to those allergic to the venom, bees and wasps are right up there with the ticks, scorpions and vipers. Whether you're allergic or not, a hornet sting is no fun, and I note that wearing perfume winds up the 'hyménoptères', the winged stingers, especially in autumn. My medicine cabinet is sadly lacking in specific anti-venoms but what I do have is exactly the pump kit recommended in the leaflet. I have irritated everyone who has been out walking with me over the last five years by complaining that none of them have been bitten by a poisonous creature to allow me to test out my Antivenin kit. Some sensitive souls even got so jittery that I wasn't allowed to mention it.

This pocket-sized essential has a suction pump and different sized attachments (big for viper, small for wasp) to enable you to suck out the poison efficiently. I have investigated the kit and how it works, in the privacy of my own home, but it's really not the same as applying it in the field to a very grateful human being. Thanks to my leaflet, I now know that a viper will bite without injecting venom in 90 per cent of cases, so I won't worry if, when someone's bitten, I

can't get any poison up into my syringe. I suppose it's just possible that I'll be the one who's bitten but that's not nearly as satisfying a scenario to imagine, so I don't.

Pyrenean sister has had two weeks of rain, of which we achieved two days. I don't think she believes me. The Pope is visiting her, or near enough, for the Fête of the Assumption and I decide to honour the religious festival in true French/Welsh fashion. If there's a special day in France, there's a cake for it and you don't have to be religious to make a ritual of the appropriate food. There is the 'galette des Rois' for Epiphany, with a gold paper crown on it, sold for two months after the day the three kings must have reached Baby Jesus, even allowing for leaves on the camel trail. Like an old-fashioned Christmas pudding, the galette contains some trinket related to the nativity.

As well as the usual Easter eggs, there are special appetizers for religious highlights in between, melting confections to celebrate Jesus resisting temptation, and other seasonal treats, anomalous to the outsider. My favourite indulgence (shouldn't that be a cake too?) is a 'jesuit', choux pastry with patisserie cream filling, closely followed by a 'religieuse', a nun, and a 'sacristan'. I wonder how the advertising campaigns in English, emphasising the 'sinfulness' of 'naughty but nice' cream cakes (did Salman Rushdie really coin that one?) would go down here. 'Feeling wicked – try a nun,' doesn't quite work.

With outdoor temperature at 32°C in the shade, I cook comfort food, baking Welsh cakes on the griddle, the way my Scottish aunt made drop scones. It's not only the cakes that bake in the heat but it is worth it as they magically disappear from the wire rack, without time to cool. The day eases to a lazy close and we head for bed – to re-emerge an hour later. The ban on fireworks has apparently been lifted and Dieulefit celebrates the fête with no consideration for Sensitive Dog, who is no longer destroying her bedroom door but has not yet stopped trying to jump on the couch, a quivering wreck. I had hoped we were past the sleepless nights stage, but no. Here we go again.

19

THE VILLAGE WHERE NO-ONE IS A STRANGER

Sunflowers have self-seeded along the banks of the Jabron where six weeks ago amorous frogs were revving up like Harley Davidsons. The yellow-headed stragglers are small, pale relatives of the cultivated sun-slaves that fill fields with their huge golden faces. I am wary of their obedience and I only tolerate the wild accidents in my garden – I will not plant these aliens. I remember too well a nineteenth century poem by Dora Greenstreet, portraying the woman as a sunflower and the sun, her lover;

> 'His eye is like a clear
> Keen flame that searches through me;
> I must droop
> Upon my stalk, I cannot reach his sphere;
> To mine he cannot stoop.'

I might be 5' 1' but he can damn well stoop, I tell the sunflowers, and there will be no drooping stalks around my garden so cut it out now. I do not think you can love someone unless there is a 'you' to do the loving.

Madame Dubois is also thinking about love. When she and her husband visited her mother-in-law in a retirement home, an old lady

talked to Monsieur Dubois, thinking him her dead husband. She stroked his cheek, looked into his eyes and said, 'Que tu es beau… tu étais toujours beau.'

'We don't say this to our husbands today,' Madame Dubois laughs and finishes lightly but her hand rests on her husband's arm and her eyes tell a different story. 'You look so good … you always looked so good…'

It is a year since we watched Mars at its ten thousand year closest; it is also the best two nights in the year for watching the Perseids, a meteor shower which seems to come from the constellation Perseus (although of course, despite its name, it doesn't. They don't make life easy, these astronomers).

The night is clear and so, armed with binoculars and telescope, we choose a window and wait. I am getting better at waiting and I lose myself in stars, my focus blurring until they all seem to dance around the sky.

The moving light of an aeroplane tricks me into a 'There's one … no it isn't' but after about twenty minutes, they start, one white squib flashing across the sky. 'Is that one?' we ask, not trusting our eyes any more, binoculars and telescope abandoned, useless in tracking a moving object.

The second confirms our sighting, then a third … and a fourth, some more dramatic than others, a quiet firework display on a universal scale. I wish upon our shooting stars, a wish for someone else, so that it will be protected from the caveats imposed by the gods on dreams come true. John does not wish. Where did it come from, this fear we both have of letting even the air hear our hopes? We watch ten or so of the four hundred meteors in the shower and are contented.

The next night is cloudy and the night after makes the firework display, the meteors and the previous storms seem mere rehearsals. It is not just sunset wall that turns pink when the lightning strikes, but the whole landscape, up into the hills where the eerie outline of the fork shimmers a few seconds before night falls again, too early in the evening.

The storm plays overhead and we watch it instead of television, the house electricity having flashed a few times in empathy then submitted to total power loss. All the electric lighting in the valley now comes in jagged strikes, no time to count after the thunder that shakes the house like the road roller used to do. Bursts of heavy rain add to the percussion, and Sensitive Dog contributes some of the higher notes as we switch viewpoints. I have never seen an electric storm with forked lightning in all directions, west, east, south – the house has no window looking north – but what amazes me most is the pink light that flashes on and off.

With the sudden change of mountain weather, there is a mist hugging the road, completely masking the hills, adding drifts of pink ground cloud when the flashes come. Just as suddenly, the mist lifts and once more white sears the sky above the St Maurice, Mielandre and Mont Rachas. The rage turns to rumbling, the house wakes up with all the clicks and beeps of electric gadgets starting up and we realise that two hours has gone by.

We are safe, dry and warm but what about others? The pompiers will have been out in their storm, ensuring that any lightning fires are out, helped in their work by the rain, but it turns out that it is the rain itself that does the worst damage.

We find out later that the River Ardèche rose so much in three hours that over a thousand campers were evacuated and spent the night in village halls and a young life was lost. It is not however images of the Ardèche which flood our television screen but Cornwall, then Perthshire, with warnings for our own south Wales. York sister tells me of floods there again, ominous in summer with winter rains still to come, and the elements remind us of the respect due to them and of our own fragility.

Our house is safe in flood and storm; it is fire that scares me, the forest fires of the Midi, sparked by tinder dry scrub and spread like the wildfire it is. I have a plan of course, for the moment when I smell smoke and see a wall of flames advancing from the woods, taking the truffle oaks en route to our orchard and my newly established lavender hedge.

We will go into the wine cellar and hide until the fire has gone. The basic idea seems quite sensible; the cellar is underground, there are solid stone walls, and the fire will sweep across overhead but there are some details that make me unhappy. How will we know when the fire has gone, and not get burnt to death popping our heads up to have a look, impatient as I am? How will we manage with two dogs and two cats in a confined space for an unspecified time (don't even think about a litter tray)?

And what if the fire comes down into the cellar and reaches the wooden door of the wine cellar? This is not how I want to go. I would rather go, running around outside screaming, 'Fire fire don't panic' and pretending I'm Jeanne d'Arc. John says we don't live in a forest and he has no interest in discussing the cellar as a fire refuge. But then he wasn't the one summoned by two council workers who appeared at our gate and told me there had been a fire on our land.

Disbelieving, I followed them to the corner of, not our but Monsieur Dubois' field, where the charred earth and acrid smell told their own story. The council workers had been driving past when they saw flames so they stopped, jumped out of the van and put out the fire with the sand still piled there by the roadworkers. 'What started it?' I asked.

A shrug. 'Who knows? A cigarette thrown out of a passing car probably.'

Stupidly, I say, 'It's not my land, it's a neighbour's.' We look from the fire across the hundred yards to my house. The men say nothing. 'I know,' I say, ashamed, 'It's all the same to the fire. What should I do?'

'I think we've put it out but check it in half an hour, an hour…'

'And if the fire starts again?' I can feel the panic rising. There is no longer grass in the field, just occasional spikes of almost dead herbs and flowers, waiting like matches for the spark.

The shrug. 'Call the pompiers. There is nothing you can do.'

I wonder whether to call Monsieur Dubois, in his other home in Haute Savoie, to let him know that there was this near-terrible thing, a fire on his land, but the council workers' words echo. There is

nothing he can do either. He has been a good citizen, he has meticulously cleared all the undergrowth, mowed around the truffle oaks with his sit-on, stacked dead wood away from the trees and saved it for the autumn bonfires – he can do nothing to protect us from a stray fag-end. It is just another of those 'what-ifs'.

Not that I'm against contacting the pompiers. It is the season for pompier heroics and it seems that every other person is a volunteer, if not a full-time hero. If the age restriction is relaxed much further, I might yet join the uniformed elite. The job is not just fires and floods (as if that were not enough), nor even, British style, cats up trees and small boys stuck in railings; road accidents, fallen climbers, lost cavers, wild animal sightings – whatever the emergency, the pompiers are expected to get there and deal with it.

As in Britain, there is a feeling that the risks are not reflected in pay and pensions, nor insurance for the vast army of volunteers without whom the summer fatalities would be even worse. Perhaps they would take me on for the little things... not too much climbing and carrying people.

Oddly, my height (lack of) affected my career choices more when I was sixteen than it would today; in those days I was barred from all of the uniformed forces and from being an air hostess. I have never really understood why an air hostess had to be tall; I'd have thought it an advantage on a plane to be little. On the other hand, in those days, air hostesses were chosen on the same sort of criteria as Miss World, so perhaps there were other factors excluding me from a job I only fancied because I was barred from it.

No, fire person is a far more interesting prospect, especially since a visit to the Gorges du Verdon, where a pompier speedboat left our little pedalo spinning in its wake. Opening the throttle full, her long blonde hair flying in the wind, Mademoiselle Pompier was making the most of her authority, carving up the tourists as she sped to an emergency – or to a picnic with her Pompier partner, in a far cove. It gives a whole new meaning to the word 'siren'. I picture her leaning against her motorbike in her jackboots and I wish I were younger.

Can you have a pompier speedboat, a motorbike *and* a cute fire-engine or do you have to choose?

The rain stops me worrying too much about fire. I know that this year is not like last year here; although as dry, it is cooler, we – and the farmers – have been able to sustain our gardens and crops. Already, I can join in some of the 'remember when?' and 'That was the year…'

My neighbour and her dog Mimi stop to talk. Usually I am be-Pyreneaned and Mimi, traumatised by a previous experience with a German Shepherd, has to be kept away well beyond talking distance. Madame takes the opportunity to ask how we have settled in and I say, truthfully, that it feels as if we've lived here for years, that everyone makes us feel welcome, helps us when we stumble with the language. 'Mais c'est normal,' she tells me, clearly wondering if there really is a place on earth where the locals don't try their best to welcome strangers. There are indeed such places.

It is the little changes that we notice. The families whose houses back onto the Jabron have put out their summer ladders so the children can paddle in the river, the pebble labyrinths have been built across the flow but this year's stone monsters are different. Someone had a remote control boat for his fête day and the vessel shoots across the mini pool inside its ring of pebbles while the boy's mother half-watches, half dozes, sitting on the bank.

We drive around Montélimar, half-noting the usual statues at each roundabout – the massive bull has gone, replaced with a rearing horse. Apparently someone made the Council an offer they couldn't refuse, so they sold the bull, bought the horse and pocketed the profits – sorry, I mean they used the profits to benefit the people of Montélimar.

I don't miss the bull but I would be sorry to lose my own favourite. It is in the centre of a particularly difficult roundabout, usually characterised by beeping horns and cars cutting in from wrong lane. Right in the middle of this chaos is a stone kiwi wearing ice-skates. Head down, concentrating on the imaginary ice, with its

long nose profiled against the grass, it always makes me smile. Is that why it's there?

A new roundabout has appeared amongst all the roadworks near our house and I wonder what will be the centrepiece there. Floral? Sculpture? The ancient plane tree, well over a hundred years old, has been preserved and the whole roundabout planned to leave it shading a side road that was once the main route into Dieulefit. Beside the plane tree, a warehouse wall still demands liberty for José Bové although I know for sure that he is now as free as any of us; I have seen him on the television news, attacking a field of maize, fighting against genetically modified crops (which do not usually fight back).

There is so much I haven't done, not just the Picodon project but the stories I haven't found out, including the 1920s Dieulefit artists; Edmeé Delebeque, known as 'le corbeau', the raven, because she always wore a black cape and who always put cypresses into her landscapes whether they were there in reality or not; Willy Eisenchitz, who said that the discovery of Provence was the most important, most liberating in his life.

There are the teachers, not just those responsible for smuggling Jewish children to safety, but also those who ran 'l'école de plein air', 'the school in fresh air', for youngsters aged 3 to 13 with problems – whether pulmonary or behavioural.

I feel kinship with the sixteenth century curate, Jean Morel, who had 'no brakes on his mouth'. Who were the key figures in the old silk trade, running the factory in Dieulefit (now the hospital)? No doubt they were Protestants, as in the Cevennes. Why do silk and Protestant go together, or Quakers (the Rowntrees and the Cadburys) and chocolate?

Who was Yet Rhoosenthal, whose grave, in the village cemetery at nearby Poët-Laval, is adorned with an ironwork eagle and a tribute from the British Airforce Escaping Society? What part was played in the Second World War by this man with a Jewish name, who lived until 1972? How wonderful that when he did die, someone official

cared. Who is 'l'Anglais' who donated the old altarscreen in the cathedral at Die and why did he do it?

It's not just what *I* haven't done that occupies my thoughts. Will the chimney sweep ever come back? I suspect that the electricians will, but when exactly? And will the filtration tank to complete my fosse septique be co-ordinated with the making good of the drive promise by the council roadworkers? Will someone buy Club Med and will it become noisier?

This is a good place to live - and to grow old. We have seen the old people sitting outside their houses, on benches in the village square or outside the churches, and there seem to be a lot of them. This augurs well for longevity – unless of course these 'old people' are all in their thirties, prematurely aged by the sun and their house renovation. We have some plans before we stop and just sit. We have Mielandre and Mont Rachas to climb and we are going to Strasbourg in December, to see Cabrel in concert and to rediscover Christmas in France's most famous seasonal market.

The story never ends; the writer just chooses when to stop telling it. If it is to be Literature then you have to stop at a moment considered sad, horrific or violent – preferably all three with bonus marks for irony, which makes it eligible for the 'black comedy' tag. I choose to stop here, now, with a spider absailing down the washing, fine silver threads of dew? sap? dripping onto me occasionally from the acacias, the sound of my husband mowing lawns drowning the cicadas. A lizard scuds across the stone path and disappears behind a potted geranium. I am nobody, adrift in sunshine and mountains. Is this Provence? Who cares ... Dieu le fit... the village where 'Nul n'est étranger', 'no-one is a stranger'.

Aquéu païs Diòu faguèt e l'amarés coumo lou paradis

This is a land created by God and you will love it as if it were Paradise.

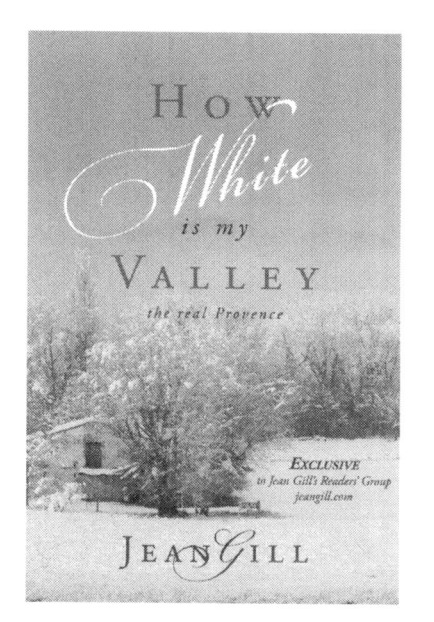

ABOUT THE AUTHOR

I'm a Welsh writer and photographer living in the south of France with two scruffy dogs, a beehive named 'Endeavour', a Nikon D750 and a man. I taught English in Wales for many years and my claim to fame is that I was the first woman to be a secondary headteacher in Carmarthenshire. I'm mother or stepmother to five children so life has been pretty hectic.

I've published all kinds of books, both with traditional publishers and self-published. You'll find everything under my name from prize-winning poetry and novels, military history, translated books on dog training, to a cookery book on goat cheese. My work with top dog-trainer Michel Hasbrouck has taken me deep into the world of dogs with problems, and inspired one of my novels. With Scottish parents, an English birthplace and French residence, I can usually support the winning team on most sporting occasions.

www.jeangill.com